LIBERATION AND DEMOCRATIZATION

Social Movements, Protest, and Contention

Series Editor Bert Klandermans, Free University, Amsterdam

Associate Editors Sidney Tarrow, Cornell University
Verta A. Taylor, The Ohio State University
Ron R. Aminzade, University of Minnesota

Volume 11   Mona N. Younis, *Liberation and Democratization: The South African and Palestinian National Movements*

Volume 10   Marco Giugni, Doug McAdam, and Charles Tilly, editors, *How Social Movements Matter*

Volume 9   Cynthia L. Irvin, *Militant Nationalism: Between Movement and Party in Ireland and the Basque Country*

Volume 8   Raka Ray, *Fields of Protest: Women's Movements in India*

Volume 7   Michael P. Hanagan, Leslie Page Moch, and Wayne te Brake, editors, *Challenging Authority: The Historical Study of Contentious Politics*

Volume 6   Donatella della Porta and Herbert Reiter, editors, *Policing Protest: The Control of Mass Demonstrations in Western Democracies*

Volume 5   Hanspeter Kriesi, Ruud Koopmans, Jan Willem Duyvendak, and Marco G. Giugni, *New Social Movements in Western Europe: A Comparative Analysis*

Volume 4   Hank Johnston and Bert Klandermans, editors, *Social Movements and Culture*

Volume 3   J. Craig Jenkins and Bert Klandermans, editors, *The Politics of Social Protest: Comparative Perspectives on States and Social Movements*

Volume 2   John Foran, editor, *A Century of Revolution: Social Movements in Iran*

Volume 1   Andrew Szasz, *EcoPopulism: Toxic Waste and the Movement for Environmental Justice*

LIBERATION AND DEMOCRATIZATION

The South African and Palestinian National Movements

Mona N. Younis

Social Movements, Protest, and Contention
Volume 11

 University of Minnesota Press
Minneapolis • London

Published by the University of Minnesota Press
111 Third Avenue South, Suite 290
Minneapolis, MN 55401-2520
http://www.upress.umn.edu

Library of Congress Cataloging-in-Publication Data

Younis, Mona.
    Liberation and democratization : the South African and Palestinian national movements / Mona N. Younis.
        p.   cm. — (Social movements, protest, and contention ; v. 11)
    Includes bibliographical references and index.
    ISBN 0-8166-3299-5 (hc : acid-free paper) — ISBN 0-8166-3300-2 (pb : acid-free paper)
        1. Blacks—South Africa—Politics and government—20th century.
    2. National liberation movements—South Africa—History.
    3. Palestinian Arabs—Politics and government—20th century.
    4. National liberation movements—Palestine—History.   5. Arab-Israeli conflict.   6. African National Congress—History.   7. Munaòòamat al-Taòrår al-Filasòånåyah—History.   I. Title.   II. Series.
    DT1758.Y68 2000
    956.95'3044—dc21   99-054991

Printed in the United States of America on acid-free paper

The University of Minnesota is an equal-opportunity educator and employer.

11 10 09 08 07 06 05 04 03 02 01 00   10 9 8 7 6 5 4 3 2 1

To all who insist on the necessity and power of caring,
especially my parents, Najla and Ahmad.

"I don't understand this comparison between us and South Africa. What is similar here and there is that both they and we must prevent others from taking us over. Anyone who says that the blacks are oppressed in South Africa is a liar. The blacks there want to gain control of the white minority just like the Arabs here want to gain control over us. And we, too, like the white minority in South Africa, must act to prevent them from taking us over. I was in a gold mine there and I saw what excellent conditions the black workers have. So there is separate elevators for whites and blacks, so what? That's the way they like it."

—Raphael Eitan, Minister of Agriculture and the Environment, chief of staff of the Israeli army during the 1982 invasion of Lebanon, speaking in a guest lecture at the School of Law, Tel Aviv University, 24 December 1987, quoted in Yediot Ahranot, 25 December 1987

Contents

Acknowledgments   xi

List of Abbreviations   xiii

1. The South African and Palestinian National Liberation
   Movements in Comparative Perspective   1

2. Liberating the Nation: Social Movements, Democratization,
   and Class Formation   22

3. Merging Elites as Nation and Movement Formation,
   1910s to 1940s   36

4. Middle-Class Hegemony and the Containment of Class,
   1940s to 1970s   75

5. Merging Class and Nation in the Expansion of Popular
   Struggles, 1970s to 1990s   121

Conclusion   172

Notes   183

Works Cited   225

List of Interviews   243

Index   247

Acknowledgments

Innumerable people contributed to the realization of this project. A little bit of each one of them can be found in the pages of this book, most obviously those who made history, those who recorded it, and those who retold it to a graduate student seeking to demonstrate competence in a field and answer questions she personally sought. Less directly discernible, but in no way less significant, are the contributions of many others whose assistance, support, and encouragement made this project possible. I am grateful to many people but to no one more than Michael Burawoy, my dissertation supervisor, and gifted diviner of the intellectual best in his students. Michael's own intellectual rigor and courage, wholehearted dedication to students, and tenacious commitment to social justice continue to inspire me.

I would also like to thank the members of my dissertation committee, Peter Evans, Kim Voss, Franz Schurmann, and Kiren Chaudhry, who were consistently supportive and accessible. Their advice, largely heeded at the beginning of the journey, made the end attainable.

In the course of field research, I accumulated additional debt to many wonderful people. For their invaluable assistance and gracious hospitality during my two stays in South Africa I thank Glenn Adler, Owen Crankshaw, Jeremy Cronin, Ran Greenstein, Vannessa Kruger, Jeff Mkabela, Sue Rabkin, Gay Seidman, Ari Sitas, Eddie Webster, Thokozani Xaba, Joanne Yawitch, and the late Andrew Mapheto. Similarly, research on the Palestinian case required the generous assistance of many old friends and some new ones in Jordan, Lebanon, Syria, Palestine, and the United States, especially Suad Amiry, Taysir Aruri, Joel Beinin, Beshara Doumani, Said Abdul-Hadi, Raif

Hijab, Nayef Jarrad, Majida al-Masri, Salem Nahaas, Ibrahim Qub'a, Sukeina Salameh, Gershon Shafir, Daoud al-Talhami, and Salim Tamari. While my South African hosts had to contend with the exploratory questions of a relative novice, my hosts in the Middle East encountered the critical questions of a relative old timer. Which was more taxing I can only speculate, as they were equally magnanimous in their support of my desire to learn.

My deep appreciation goes to the many ANC and PLO leaders and activists, unionists and community organizers, and their supporters and critics, who so generously gave of their time for interviews. Although listed impersonally in the bibliography, I am very personally appreciative of their readiness to converse with a student about matters of central importance to their lives. Their voices, laments, and insights helped bring this project to life.

The patient assistance of tens of librarians and archivists facilitated the otherwise daunting task of navigating archives. For work on South Africa, I would like to express my thanks to the staff of the ANC Library at Shell House; Hoover Institution; Howard Pim Library, University of Fort Hare; South Africa History Archive; library of the University of Witwatersrand; and the Mayibuye Centre, University of the Western Cape. In the Middle East, my thanks go to the staff of the following libraries and institutions: Birzeit University Liaison Office (Amman); Institute for Palestine Studies (Beirut); Joint Jordanian-Palestinian Committee (Amman); Jerusalem Center for Development Studies (Amman); Palestine National Council (Amman and Damascus); and Shoman Institute (Amman).

I gratefully acknowledge the following sources of funding for making the research in South Africa and the Middle East, and the writing thereafter, possible: American Association of University Women Fellowship; Institute on Global Conflict and Cooperation Research Fellowship, University of California, San Diego; Mellon Grant, Center for Middle Eastern Studies, University of California, Berkeley; Rocca Family Scholarship, Center for African Studies, University of California, Berkeley; and Sociology Department Work-Study Research Fellowship, University of California, Berkeley.

Many friends in and out of graduate school know how very much I valued their support during this period of my life. Here, I will confine my heartfelt thanks to Richard Anstiss and Diane Binson, whose wonderful support facilitated the two most difficult junctures of the journey: the beginning and the end.

Abbreviations

South African Case

AAC	All-African Convention
AMWU	African Mine Workers Union
ANC	African National Congress
APO	African People's Organisation
AZAPO	Azanian People's Organisation
BAWU	Black Allied Workers Union
BC	Black Consciousness
BCM	Black Consciousness Movement
CNETU	Council of Non-European Trade Unions
CONTRALESA	Congress of Traditional Leaders of South Africa
COSATU	Congress of South African Trade Unions
CPC	Coloured People's Congress
CPSA	Communist Party of South Africa
DBSA	Development Bank of South Africa
FOSATU	Federation of South African Trade Unions
FRELIMO	Front for the Liberation of Mozambique
ICU	Industrial and Commercial Workers Union
IDAF	International Defence and Aid Fund
IIE	Institute for Industrial Education

ILO	International Labour Organisation
MK	Umkhonto we Sizwe
NAFCOC	National African Federated Chambers of Commerce
NEC	National Executive Committee
NEUM	Non-European Unity Movement
NLC	National Land Committee
NP	National Party
NRC	Natives Representative Council
NUMSA	National Union of Metalworkers of South Africa
NUSAS	National Union of South African Students
OAU	Organisation of African Unity
PAC	Pan Africanist Congress
RSA	Republic of South Africa
SACOD	South African Congress of Democrats
SACP	South African Communist Party
SACTU	South African Congress of Trade Unions
SAIC	South African Indian Congress
SAIRR	South African Institute of Race Relations
SALB	South African Labour Bulletin
SANNC	South African Native National Congress
SASO	South African Students Organisation
SPP	Surplus People Project
UDF	United Democratic Front
UP	United Party
WIP	Work in Progress
YL	Youth League
ZAPU	Zimbabwe African People's Union

Palestinian Case

AHC	Arab Higher Committee
ANM	Arab Nationalist Movement
CBS	Central Bureau of Statistics
CPI	Communist Party of Israel
DFLP	Democratic Front for the Liberation of Palestine
EC	Executive Committee
FATULS	Federation of Arab Trade Unions and Labor Societies
GFTU	General Federation of Trade Unions
GUPS	General Union of Palestinian Students
IDF	Israeli Defense Forces
JCP	Jordanian Communist Party
JPJC	Jordanian-Palestinian Joint Committee
LNM	Lebanese National Movement
MCA	Muslim-Christian Associations
NGC	National Guidance Committee
NLL	National Liberation League
PAWS	Palestinian Arab Workers' Society
PCP	Palestine Communist Party (pre-1948)
PCP	Palestinian Communist Party (1980s)
PFLP	Popular Front for the Liberation of Palestine
PLA	Palestine Liberation Army
PLO	Palestinian Liberation Organization
PNA	Palestinian National Authority
PNC	Palestinian National Council
PNF	Palestinian National Front
UAR	United Arab Republic
UNCTAD	United Nations Conference on Trade and Development
UNLU	Unified National Leadership of the Uprising
UNRWA	United Nations Relief and Works Agency

1

The South African and Palestinian National Liberation Movements in Comparative Perspective

The 1990s witnessed two of the oldest national liberation movements governing after nearly a century of organized resistance: the liberation movement in South Africa led by the African National Congress (ANC) and the Palestinian liberation movement led by the Palestinian Liberation Organization (PLO). The preceding decade was decisive: In the 1980s, mass uprisings shifted the momentum of what had been exile-based liberation movements back into South Africa and Palestine, carrying both the ANC and the PLO into negotiations with their opponents. With these massive uprisings both movements had achieved more than at any time in the decades since their emergence in the 1910s. In 1990, the South African government reversed the nearly 40-year ban on the ANC, signaling its readiness to negotiate with movement leaders. In 1991, Israeli negotiators met with PLO-approved Palestinian representatives from the occupied territories, and began negotiating directly with the PLO in secret parallel meetings the following year.

Although the uprisings strengthened both movements' positions vis-à-vis their opponents, the national movement in South Africa has proven more successful than the Palestinian national movement. In 1994, black South Africans achieved their goal of a nonracial, democratic state in a unitary South Africa. In contrast, the PLO-led movement has not only failed to achieve the original goal of a nonsectarian, democratic state in all of Palestine, but even the less ambitious goal of such a state in the West Bank and Gaza Strip remains elusive. In 1993, Palestinians achieved partial self-rule in the form of a Palestinian National Authority over an as yet undetermined entity and elected their first legislative council in 1996. While awaiting final status negotiations, the Declaration of Principles, signed by Israel and the PLO in 1993, entails no provision for a future Palestinian state. A Palestinian state may, however, yet emerge. If so, every indication points to a state bereft of sovereignty—an "independent national state" of the South African bantustan variety, which the ANC and the national liberation movement had rejected for the people of South Africa.

Prevailing explanations for the differential success of the South African and Palestinian national liberation movements point to demography, international support, and state strength as explanatory factors. Israel's advantage is contrasted with South Africa under white rule to explain both the relative failure of the PLO-led Palestinian national movement and the success of the ANC-led movement in South Africa. I argue that these explanations are inadequate because they do not sufficiently consider the extent to which the factors they identify are themselves functions of the success/failure of the movements they claim to explain. It is necessary to capture how successful resistance by blacks contributed to the whites' inability to alter their minority status in South Africa, to international sanctions, and to the state yielding to movement demands. Likewise, it is necessary to recognize the extent to which Palestinians' lack of success contributed to Israel's demographic advantage, its international support, and its ability to withstand the national liberation movement's challenge. This indicates that social movements themselves, including unsuccessful ones, are more significant than prevailing explanations suggest. Yet, such movements are the product of the very conditions they seek to alter and cannot be more than those conditions allow. An approach that captures both is required.

The current political arrangements in South Africa and Palestine are the outcome of nearly a century of efforts by the indigenous populations to eliminate settler-colonial domination in their homelands. Both movements developed over three phases of resistance, each of which is distinguished by a particular configuration of class forces, leadership, and that leadership's relationship to the movement's mass base. In this development, which entails the progressive democratization of both movements over time, lies the explanation for both movements' greater success in their latest phase of resistance. The particular character of settler colonialism, however, and whether it was inclusionary or exclusionary of indigenous labor, was decisive: inclusion/ exclusion contributed to the existence of particular social forces and not others and permitted certain forms of resistance and not others, with implications for the movements' dissimilar effectiveness, despite the remarkable parallels in their development over time. This divergence, I suggest, explains the greater relative success of the movement in South Africa as compared to the Palestinian national movement.

Indeed, two indigenous populations waged liberation struggles against settler-colonial states; one was successful in achieving its declared objective, the other was not. An explanation for this difference in outcomes is sought from a comparative historical examination of the two movements, beginning with their rise in the 1910s to the threshold of negotiations with their opponents in the 1990s. More specifically, through a class analysis of the South African and Palestinian national movements over three parallel phases of resistance and under divergent conditions of inclusion/exclusion, I propose to explain: (1) the greater success of both movements in their latest phase of resistance; and (2) the greater relative success of the movement in South Africa.

Defining Success

Defining success is no easy matter as many "successful" movements themselves reveal. Is, for example, the Vietnamese victory over American forces a success given that Vietnam has yet to recover from the devastation wrought upon the country by those forces? What do the current strife and atrocities in Algeria reveal about the success of the Algerian liberation movement that has ruled since gaining the country's independence in 1962? Would the establishment of a democratic South Africa represent a success if the majority of its population continued to be exploited for the benefit of a few? The difficulty is compounded when success is assessed over time. While I do not claim to have resolved this matter, I propose two measures to evaluate movement success: (1) the movement's outcome relative to its declared objective; and (2) the movement's gains relative to those of its opponents.

As noted, blacks in South Africa have achieved their goal of a nonracial democracy, first articulated in 1943 as a demand for "the full participation of the African in the Government of South Africa."[1] It is fair and necessary to ask, however, what democracy has brought or is likely to bring to the majority of South Africa's black population. The exercise of electoral rights by blacks carried the ANC to power but has yet to deliver economic relief to the mass of the dispossessed. For many blacks, this is an indictment of the national liberation movement. But the ANC promise of majority rule embodying civil rights and liberties that distinguish it from both its predecessor's rule, as well as from that exercised elsewhere on the continent, may be said to have been achieved. Moreover, various segments of the population that were asked to delay their sector-specific demands for the benefit of the "national interest" during the "national democratic" struggle may now press ahead within the political space they themselves unlocked. It may be debated what exactly is realizable within that space—particularly with regard to the economy—nevertheless, new possibilities do exist. Examining the development of these groups' capacities as they evolved over the history of the national movement reveals a greater potential in South Africa than in Palestine to protect political democracy and expand sector-specific gains. Potential, however, must be realized.

In contrast, as noted, Palestinians have achieved neither a unitary, democratic state in all of Palestine, nor a democratic state in the West Bank and Gaza Strip, despite an international consensus, which includes the United States and Western Europe, regarding the illegality of Israel's occupation of the territories. This is not to say that a Palestinian state may not still be realized. Any entity, however, that is engendered by the current Israeli-PLO agreements will remain dominated by Israel. Furthermore, Israeli leaders are adamant about retaining annexed East Jerusalem and surrounding territories, which comprise 28 percent of Palestinian land occupied in 1967, and additional sections of the West Bank and Gaza Strip are to be permanently absorbed, thereby eroding further the 24 percent of Palestine that Palestinians declared an acceptable alternative to a state encompassing their entire homeland. Israeli settlements within these areas are also to remain, a number of which continue to be expanded. Not only will Israel's domination persist through control over security, foreign relations, immigration, and the territories' water resources, but the Economic Annexes to the Oslo Agreements lock the Palestinian entity's economic development firmly into Israel's. Most telling is the fact that PLO rule has been achieved with a promise to quell by force opposition to the Israeli-PLO accords; something that does not bode well for Palestinian democracy.[2] Historically, the limited capacity of the Palestinian labor movement, and subordinate classes in general, to act on their class-specific interests renders these segments much less capable than their counterparts in South Africa of protecting and expanding political democracy—let alone realizing their sector-specific goals.

At this point we might ask whether the differential success of these movements is attributable merely to differences in the movements' goals. It may be that the liberation project in South Africa was somehow easier to achieve than that attempted by Palestinians: Blacks struggled for political inclusion in a unitary state of South Africa, while since 1974 Palestinians have sought a separate state independent of Israel. How it came to be so is one aspect of the larger question of differential success I hope to answer. I suggest, however, that the goal itself is not a determinant of movement success or failure in these two cases. The political transformations blacks sought in South

Africa—the reintegration of the "black homelands" and "white South Africa"; the replacement of racially based, four-tiered administrative structures by a single, nonracial structure; the integration of cities and townships; the reorganization of government bodies including its coercive apparatuses—are tantamount to the establishment of an entirely new political entity. Indeed, transforming state apparatuses that had been designed to divide, separate, and render unequal on the basis of race into those that are intended to unify, reconcile, and equalize racial groupings involves nothing short of the creation of a new state—at least in political terms. Thus, although the liberation of South Africa did not involve the carving out of a new entity, in all other respects the South African state for which blacks have struggled should bear little resemblance to the one that existed and therefore constitutes the establishment of a new state. Moreover, it may well be argued that a separate Palestinian state was easier to achieve given the provision for such a state in the 1947 UN resolution that produced the state of Israel, as well as the international consensus that recognized the legitimacy of Palestinian demands for an end to Israeli rule over the territories occupied in 1967.

Comparing the national liberation movements' gains to those of their opponents under the new political arrangements we find, once again, greater ANC success. The white minority government of South Africa is no more, the scrapping of apartheid legislation has eliminated white entitlement based on race, and the territorial integrity of the country has been restored, thereby ending legally sanctioned white privilege and domination in a territorially divided South Africa. Whites, however, have retained control over the country's economic power, rendering doubtful the actual extent of tangible black gains that will be possible in the "new" South Africa. Indeed, the economic policies that have been embraced safeguard the position of what is overwhelmingly white capital. Although individual blacks are gaining entrance to economic domains previously the sole preserve of whites, they form a new privileged minority while the prospects for the majority remain grim. Increasingly, supporters of the national liberation movement cite this as evidence of the movement's failure. But rather than a condemnation of the movement's claim to success, I suggest that it is an indictment of the national liberation movement goal of a nonracial democratic state that retains existing economic relations intact. How that came to be so is addressed in the present study.

In the Palestinian case there is no question as to which of the opponents has the advantage in the Israeli-Palestinian agreements. Palestinians have effectively relinquished their claim to historical Palestine within its 1948 borders, Israel has been relieved of the UN-endorsed demand to repatriate and/or compensate Palestinian refugees, and Israel's relations with Arab states have begun to be normalized. In return, Palestinians are gaining self-rule dispensed piecemeal in a small portion of their homeland. Thus, while the South African movement has replaced minority rule with a government that is thus far politically responsive to its constituency, Palestinians have neither secured freedom from Israeli domination, nor, indeed, certainty of democratic rule under their own leaders.

A final note is warranted. If success were measured by the goals of these movements' opponents—the South African and Israeli states—then even the PLO-led national movement would have to be considered a success. The PLO did in fact succeed in forging a Palestinian national movement out of a dispossessed and geographically fragmented refugee population, thereby thwarting Israeli leaders' solution for the "refugee problem" that required the assimilation of new generations of Palestinians born outside the homeland into the Arab region. Moreover, any territorial compromise with Israel is a success given the Zionist movement's goal of *Eretz Yisrael* intended to encompass all of Palestine, and Israeli pressures aimed at inducing Palestinian emigration from the West Bank and Gaza Strip.[3] These accomplishments notwithstanding, what Palestinians have achieved remains a far cry from what the PLO promised its followers to accomplish. The question is how this is to be explained.

South Africa and Israel Compared

No comprehensive comparisons exist of the two national liberation movements under examination. Most work on South Africa and Israel has concentrated on the extensive political, economic, military, and nuclear cooperation between the two states, particularly since the 1970s.[4] Minimizing the extent and implications of such cooperation,[5] Israel's uncritical supporters have insisted that relations between the two states in no way suggest uniformity beyond their roles as bastions of Western civilization restraining "Soviet expansionism" and non-Western "barbarism" in their respective regions.[6] Israel's critics have suggested that the similarities between the two states, including their origins as settler states, explain their comparable global alignments and extensive cooperation.[7] Indeed, most comparisons tend to be long on lists of similarities, which are presented as indictments of Israel, and differences, which are invoked in its defense. Only a few scholarly investigations have sought to determine the full extent or nature of these states' similarities and differences (Greenberg, 1980; Moore, 1989; Will, 1990; Greenstein, 1995). These, however, are studies of the dominant groups, state formation, and/or the states and not of the movements that have challenged them. Because states are shaped not only by the forces that construct them but also by the forces that challenge them, an equally comprehensive comparison of the two liberation movements is required.

The following is a review of prevailing and possible explanations for the differential success of the two movements under examination. These have been gleaned from explicit or implicit references within comparative work on South Africa and Israel and treatments of the two movements in the media, as well as alternative explanations. With regard to the latter, I am indebted to invaluable discussions held in South Africa, the Middle East, and the United States.

Explaining Differential Success

Explanations of movement success or failure are generally of two sorts: those that emphasize structural factors that facilitate or impede movement success, and those that focus on agency or organizational attributes—strengths and weaknesses—of the movements themselves. Broadly speaking, the former focus on the environment within which movements operate, and the latter on what they have to work with within that environment. Typically, studies of social movements privilege one or the other, even while endeavoring in earnest to bridge them.

As noted, structural explanations for the differential success of the two movements under examination point to demography, international support, and state strength. The disadvantage of whites in South Africa is posited as an explanation for the ANC's success; similarly, the PLO's lack of success is attributed to the advantage enjoyed by Israel in these respects. Competing with structural analyses are those that attribute success and failure to the movements themselves. In such a framework, the ANC's superior leadership, resources, and/or strategies and tactics are credited for the greater success of the South African liberation movement as compared to its Palestinian counterpart. Both approaches are reviewed and critiqued.

Demography and the Force of Numbers

Virtually every comparison of South Africa and Israel alludes to the implications of their demographic differences: Africans are the undisputed majority in South Africa while Palestinians are a minority in Palestine.[8] The implication is treated as self-evident: majorities ultimately have the capacity to determine outcomes. Indeed, the subtext is that whites, who accounted for no more than 14 percent of a population of 36.6 million in 1989, could not have hoped to dominate a majority population forever.[9] Regardless of how long it may take, the implicit, if not explicit, conclusion is that it was inevitable that the liberation movement by the black majority should have succeeded; once the movement took off, it was merely a matter of time. In contrast, the argument goes, Palestinians who constitute a minority of 40 percent in the total historical area of Palestine—Israel, West Bank, and Gaza Strip combined—had very little hope of succeeding.[10] What is more, Palestinians under Israeli rule do not even constitute a majority of Palestinians: in post–June 1967, Palestinians in Israel, the West Bank, and Gaza Strip accounted for 49.6 percent of all Palestinians—by 1987 their percentage had been reduced to 39.8.[11]

The implications of demography are manifold. While ANC leaders and activists were exiled, the popular base of the South African national liberation movement remained in its homeland. Because blacks remained the majority in South Africa they enjoyed the potential for becoming a formidable force from within. Once activated, the argument suggests, the advantage of numbers within their home territory ensured the movement's success. In contrast, the Palestinian national movement, rooted in the refugee population exiled from the homeland, could not hope to present such an internal challenge to the Israeli state.

There are a number of problems with "matter of time" demographic arguments, not the least of which is that they are of limited comfort to those enduring oppression in the present. In addition, however, demographic explanations treat as given what needs to be explained. Namely, how did Palestinians become a minority in their homeland when, in 1900, Jews constituted less than 10 percent of the population, and in 1947, on the eve of the establishment of the state of Israel, less than one-third.[12] Even if a demographic explanation were to be considered useful in explaining the lack of success of the Palestinian national movement today, it does not explain its failure in the pre-1948 period when Muslims and Christians constituted the overwhelming majority of the country's population. What is needed is an explanation of how Palestinians became a minority in Palestine; how European Jewish settlers succeeded in overtaking the indigenous population, while South African whites failed in doing so. The answer cannot be found in demography.

Another problem with demographic explanations is that they treat numbers as uncontentious facts that can be abstracted from their social or political contexts. Social classifications, however, are constructed by economic, political, and social forces. Their very definitions are the products of struggles between those with the power to define and the less powerful being defined. Thus, former Prime Minister of Israel, Golda Meir, was able to insist, "It was not as though there was a Palestinian People in Palestine considering itself as a Palestinian People and we came and threw them out and took their country away from them. They did not exist."[13] Similarly, all Jews are treated as de jure Israelis who enjoy a permanent "right of return to the land of Israel."[14] Thus, the Israeli state has decreed that Jews, irrespective of their citizenship, are the legitimate claimants to historical Palestine, and deny this right to its indigenous inhabitants. Of course the concept of "indigenous" itself must be addressed. The Zionist claim over Palestine rests on the assertion that Jews, regardless of citizenship, are indigenous to the territory. The claim put forth by the Zionist movement is not merely that non-Palestinian Jews have a right to the territory that is equal to the right of the native inhabitants who remained, rather the claim asserted is a superior one. This contention would be comparable to African Americans demanding the right not only to return but to colonize and/or displace the inhabitants of a territory in Africa based on their claim to indigenous origin. Therefore, when addressing issues of demography, the question becomes: who counts? The fact that relevant Palestinians are confined to those residing in the occupied territories—thereby excluding nearly 3 million Palestinians in exile—while no such restriction is placed on considerations of the relevant Jewish population, is not a fact given by demographic reality. Moreover, that Palestinians expelled from their homes less than 50 years ago should be denied a right of residence in the country while Jews irrespective of citizenship are granted the "right to return" to *Eretz Yisrael* based on a Biblical claim is certainly not a self-evident truth. Indeed, it is conceivable that under different conditions the population of Israel, the West Bank, and Gaza Strip could identify itself as Arabs and Europeans rather than as Jews and Palestinians. Including in the former the majority of Israel's Jewish citizens, who are immigrants from Arab countries and their descendants, would produce an entirely different demographic reality. Demographic explanations tend to obscure such possibilities from consideration. In short, the categories and definitions being used as the basis of determining who counts in a demographic explanation of the success of the South African and failure of the Palestinian resistance movements are just as much open to question as the problems they claim to explain.

A more sophisticated version of a demographic explanation stresses the structural implications of carrying out liberation struggles from exile. Palestinian refugees, scattered throughout the region, rendered the Palestinian movement vulnerable to manipulation by their Arab host countries to a greater extent than that experienced by the South African movement in the region of southern Africa.[15] Indeed, at a number of points in its history the PLO became embroiled in enormously costly inter-Arab conflicts, thereby distracting the movement from its main objective. If, however, exile were the determining factor, there would be no accounting for the fact that the 1987 uprising known as the *intifada* erupted at a time when the proportion of the Palestinian population inside Palestine was at its lowest.[16] In any case, given the ability of a minority community in South Africa to suppress the majority population for centuries, it is clear that numbers alone are not sufficient to account for movement success or failure. Indeed, the experience in South Africa indicates that specific conditions and developments were required for the advantage of numbers to translate into a means capable of producing change. This, it may be presumed, applies to both large and small populations; both majorities and minorities.

International Support and Freedom to Maneuver

Another explanation for the differential success of the South African and Palestinian national liberation movements emphasizes the different international standing of the two movements and the states they challenged. Such an explanation suggests that greater Western support for both the ANC and Israel was responsible for their eventual triumph over their opponents.

Both South Africa and Israel functioned as vital regional surrogates for Western interests during the Cold War. However, Israel's proximity to the former Soviet Union, as well as to the oil-rich Arab states, rendered it a more valuable strategic asset than South Africa,[17] and Israel was rewarded with enormous American financial, military, and political support. In U.S. aid alone, Israel annually receives $3 billion, which is the equivalent of $4,000 for every Israeli citizen; by conservative estimates U.S. aid totaled $59.5 billion between 1951 and 1990.[18] In comparison, the services rendered by the white minority government in South Africa, although substantial, were less considerable. Therefore, South Africa did not enjoy comparable American political patronage, let alone financial support.

Nor was Western support for the ANC and Israel confined to governments. Active and influential advocates within various Western capitals, particularly in the United States, where both South African blacks and Israelis have vocal and active ethnic counterparts, proved extremely effective in generating pressures on governments and businesses on behalf of the ANC and Israel. In the case of South Africa, such pressures resulted in sanctions and divestment, which have been credited with generating divisions within the South African ruling elite, ultimately leading to the momentous reforms and the dismantling of apartheid. Comparable action against Israel was thwarted by Israel's supporters in the United States. Thus, the argument suggests, because white South Africans and Palestinians lacked comparable groups of supporters, they lacked the potential to influence Western government policies and business interests in their favor.[19] Supporters of the ANC and Israel successfully mobilized well beyond their ethnic counterparts. Zionism, as an "ideology of liberation" of the Jewish people, it is argued, attained legitimacy that apartheid as an "overtly" racist ideology could not. This is reinforced by the association of the state of Israel with the survivors of the Holocaust and Palestinians with terrorism. In short, while Western actions constrained the minority regime in South Africa, Western support permitted Israel freedom to maneuver. In the absence of pressures on Israel from abroad comparable to those credited with bringing about the end of apartheid, the argument suggests that the Palestinian national movement was bound to fail.

U.S. support has been, without question, vital to the state of Israel. American political support has enabled Israel to defy international laws with impunity; military assistance has ensured Israel's military superiority over Arab armies; and aid has enabled Israeli citizens to live at a higher standard of living than their economy could possibly have afforded them, thereby blunting the impact of the diversion of resources to the conquest, colonization, and retention of Palestinian territories. In correcting any misconception regarding the Clinton Administration's pursuit of an "evenhanded" policy towards Israel and the Palestinians, Assistant Secretary of State for Near Eastern Affairs, Martin Indyk declared, "'Evenhandedness' is not in our lexicon. We have a very special relationship with Israel."[20] But again, this approach treats as given what needs to be explained. U.S. support, which is based on assessments of geostrategic interests, is not immutable. Indeed, had the Palestinian liberation movement been more successful in its quest to liberate Palestine—in the process emboldening other movements in the region—American policy makers no doubt would have been forced to become attentive to Palestinian demands. It is certainly no coincidence that the U.S. government expressed readiness to dialogue with the PLO in December 1988, that is after the *intifada* was well under way and on the eve of an *intifada* in Jordan in April 1989, which forced King Hussein to hold the first parliamentary elections in decades. Likewise, the failure of Israel to contain the Palestinian movement would have forced the United States to look elsewhere in the region for a more capable surrogate, thereby rendering Israel a less likely beneficiary of American assistance. Indeed, the United States was moved to apply pressure on the minority regime in South Africa only after the anti-apartheid movement inside the country had become a serious threat to "business as usual" and the liberation movement itself showed signs of success.[21] Prior to the uprisings that engulfed South Africa in the 1980s, the United States, Britain, and France regularly exercised their veto in the UN Security Council on behalf of South Africa.[22] Thus, just as Western action to isolate the minority regime in South Africa came only after successes were registered by the South African liberation movement, so too the lack of success by Palestinians contributed to the enormous Western support for Israel.

Indeed, while the presence of mobilized supporters in Western capitals was undoubtedly beneficial for both the ANC and Israel, it is inconceivable that African Americans and their allies, who have had mixed success in shaping domestic policies, have the power to determine U.S. foreign policy. Likewise, for all its success in influencing election outcomes across the country, federal budget allocations, and media coverage of the Middle East, the pro-Israel lobby falsely equates a coincidence of interests with independent power. Any divergence from the seemingly perfect congruence between U.S. and Israeli government interests will reveal the limits of the lobby's power. Some suggest, however, that given Arab oil, markets, and proximity to the former Soviet Union, had the United States acted merely on its regional economic and political interests, it would more likely have supported the Arabs in the conflict with Israel. Moreover, owing to their immense investments in the United States and Europe, Arab oil-producing states enjoy considerably more potential clout than Israel. Yet, with the exception of the 1973 oil embargo, a consistent or concerted attempt by these states to use their economic power to pressure the United States toward a more evenhanded policy in the Middle East has been mitigated by the economic interests that bind them; shocks to the Western economy would reverberate throughout the Arabian peninsula. Additionally, as the Gulf War dramatically revealed, the oil-rich states themselves depend on American protection to ensure the longevity of their patently undemocratic regimes. Thus, secure in the knowledge that the Arab kingdoms and sultanates would not align themselves with the Soviet Union, the United States could support Israel without risking its relations with Arab oil producers.

Yet the more favorable view of Zionism compared to apartheid that is propagated in Western discourse must be explained. Zionist and apartheid texts share striking similarities with regard to the societies their proponents envision for themselves and their relationship to the subordinated "other."[23] Therefore, the more approving view of Zionism in the West cannot be treated as self-evident. Indeed, supporters of Israel present Zionism as an ideology of liberation of the Jewish people, but for Palestinians, Zionism, as it has been practiced and as they have experienced it, has been precisely apartheid. In 1975, the majority of the worlds' nations agreed when they passed a UN resolution that censured Zionism as "a form of racism and racial discrimination" because it granted Jews privileges based solely on ethnicity. By the late 1980s, 117 countries accorded the PLO formal recognition, nearly twice the number of countries that formally recognized Israel.[24]

A related point is the different standing of the two liberation organizations themselves. It should be recalled that as late as 1986, the ANC was classified as a terrorist organization by the U.S. government.[25] Moreover, leading members of the Israeli government, including two former prime ministers, were once wanted by the British mandatory government in Palestine on charges of terrorism.[26] Although the examination that follows addresses this, definitions of "terrorism" are a function of who is doing the defining and that itself is associated with success.[27] Indeed, between 1965 and 1988, thirty times more Palestinian civilian deaths were caused by Israeli violence than Israeli civilian deaths caused by Palestinian and PLO violence.[28] Further, the ANC was removed from the American list of terrorist organizations without the organization changing either its tactics or its program. More important, however, such arguments erroneously imply that either a direct relationship exists between public opinion and a government's foreign policy or that foreign policies are formulated on the basis of such moral considerations.

In short, like demographic explanations, explanations that focus on international relations to explain the dissimilar outcomes of the South African and Palestinian liberation movements are not adequate. This is because they do not sufficiently address how movement success or failure itself shapes assessments of national interests and foreign policies. Indeed, they take as the point of departure the balance of forces as they exist without sufficiently considering its antecedents. Thus, they credit external support for the dismantlement of apartheid rather than the South African liberation movement's successful resistance, which, among other things, wrested that support. Conversely, they emphasize the ways in which Western support has afforded Israel's success, thereby treating Israel's worthiness as given, without giving sufficient attention to how the Palestinians' lack of success made this possible.

State Strength and Successful Suppression

Yet another explanation for the differential success of the two movements may lie in differences in the strength of the two states and their ability to combat the liberation movements. Whether in terms of competence or capacity the question becomes: is the Israeli state stronger than the South African state?

Prior to the emergence of the *intifada,* Israel had been credited with containing Palestinian resistance with "minimal" brutality. Its ability to do so was attributed to Israel's cost-effective approach to control, measured in terms of resources, personnel, and world opinion,[29] which, it was contended, contrasted markedly with the apartheid state's reliance on overt coercion. Israel's success was also attributed to its relatively just treatment of Palestinians: Palestinians within Israel's 1948 borders obtained Israeli citizenship and were accorded equal rights under the law, while Africans were disenfranchised and later even dispossessed of South African citizenship. —

Political incorporation is one of the most effective means of neutralizing a political challenge. The granting of citizenship to Palestinians inside the 1948 boundaries was, indeed, astute. This, however, was less a reflection of Israeli leaders' adroitness and more a reflection of Palestinians' weakness. The political incorporation of Palestinians posed no threat to the existence of the Jewish state: on the eve of the *intifada,* Palestinians composed 18 percent of Israel's population and less than 13 percent of Palestinians worldwide.[30] The astuteness of Israeli policy makers does appear, however, in the distinction between "citizens" and "nationals," which effectively denies even Palestinian citizens of Israel a broad range of rights and benefits reserved for Jews.[31] Thus, by granting parastatal agencies control over a variety of social and economic functions—including land ownership in the state of Israel—which they discharge solely for the benefit of Jews, Israel is shielded from charges of discrimination when non-Jews are excluded from those benefits.[32] Similarly, having granted control over matters of "personal status" to the religious authorities, and lacking provisions for civil marriage, the Israeli state effectively deters intermarriage between Jews and non-Jews without legislating prohibitions.[33] Thus, the Israeli state has achieved ends comparable to apartheid without drawing similar condemnation. That is, until 1967 when Israel began to rule territories with a majority Palestinian population.

Like their counterparts in South Africa, Palestinians in the West Bank and Gaza Strip who fell under Israeli rule in 1967 remained politically excluded and disenfranchised. The *intifada* rendered supporters of Israel hard pressed to explain how the "benign occupiers" came to behave in the Palestinian refugee camps of Jabalya and Bulata as the apartheid government had behaved in the black townships of Sharpeville and Soweto. Rather than recognizing fundamental similarities between the two states, Israel's reluctant critics have tended to blame the right-wing Likud government for this "aberration," ignoring both the history of repression in the occupied territories and the fact that a Labor Party Defense Minister, Yitzhak Rabin, in the Likud-led government oversaw the execution of the very policies that embarrassed Israel's supporters abroad.[34] When confronted with similar popular uprisings, Israel and South Africa responded similarly. Differences that did exist between the two states' strategies of control were too insignificant to explain differences in outcomes.[35]

Measuring state strength in terms of autonomy from competing internal interests we find the South African state at a marked advantage. The salient divisions within the dominant group in South Africa have been confined to fractions of capital, capital and labor, and Afrikaans and English speakers. Moreover, since coming to power in 1948, the National Party governed South Africa without interruption, and enjoyed at least a two-thirds majority in Parliament in the last seven of the nine elections prior to 1994.[36] In contrast, Israeli society is plagued by numerous manifest and latent cleavages between fractions of capital, capital and labor, *ashkenazim* (Jews of western origin) and *sephardim* or *mizrachim* (Jews of eastern origin), religious and secular Jews, and early and recent immigrants. Israel's political system has enabled a variety of social forces to influence and constrain government policies and actions to an extent that far surpasses their numbers. Moreover, the 1977 election of a Likud government in Israel broke the Labor Party's political dominance, which had been in force since the establishment of the state in 1948.[37] Even in 1984, when the Israeli electorate returned the Labor Party to government, Labor's slim margin of victory prevented it from forming a coalition independent of its rival.[38] The Unity Government, which rotated leadership between Labor and Likud, reflected the lack of consensus that pervades Israeli politics. Thus, state strength in terms of autonomy from competing internal forces favor South Africa and as such cannot explain the differential success of the two resistance movements.

Finally, the South African state's resources far surpass that of Israel. South Africa enjoys a wealth of natural resources as well as advanced industrial development that have permitted the country a considerable amount of self-sufficiency. Except for the substantial aid obtained from the United States, the Israeli state can be considered relatively resource poor compared to South Africa. Moreover, the latter's domination of the economies in the region of southern Africa provided South Africa with considerable power over its neighbors; power that Israel, unable to break the Arab economic boycott, lacked.

In short, measured in terms of strategies of control, autonomy, and resources, state strength as an explanatory factor does not necessarily predict greater Israeli success as compared to South Africa. The explanation for the South African liberation movement's success, and lack thereof by the Palestinian movement, must be sought elsewhere.

Movement Strength and Resistance

A movement's success or failure may well be its own doing. Thus, another explanation for the differential success of the South African and Palestinian liberation movements may be found in differences between the ANC and PLO in terms of leadership, resources, and/or strategies and tactics. Although the present study explores these in detail, it remains useful to identify some of the most commonly held perceptions regarding differences between the two movements.

One view that is particularly prevalent among movement observers is that ANC leaders were both more capable and more democratic than PLO leaders, thereby ensuring their movement's effectiveness. Palestinians themselves widely share this view.[39] Differences in discipline, approach, and styles are captured well by contrasting Nelson Mandela's oft-stated "We in the African National Congress," or the self-effacing Oliver Tambo, to Yasser Arafat's "I ruled Beirut." Movements, however, confront constraints and respond to opportunities that are not of their making. Moreover, movement leaders are democratic to the extent that their supporters both demand it and have the means of enforcing it. How the mass base was capable of asserting this—to the extent that it did—in the case of the ANC-led movement, while failing to do so in the Palestinian case, becomes the question.

In terms of resources as conventionally defined, Palestinians were at a distinct advantage in comparison to blacks in South Africa. Financially one of the best-endowed liberation movements in history, the Palestinian national movement also boasts a highly educated population,[40] as well as an economic base in the West Bank and Gaza Strip, which is more developed than what remained of the indigenous economy in South Africa. Additionally, Palestinians, who are overwhelmingly Arab and majority Muslim,[41] have had the advantage of an ethnically more homogeneous society as compared to blacks—Africans, Indians, and those of "mixed race" classified as "coloreds"—in South Africa.[42] Indeed, Africans alone comprise nine distinct language groups and well over a hundred religions and sects.

The strategies and tactics of the ANC and PLO have come under particular scrutiny. The ANC's early tradition of nonviolence has been contrasted with PLO terrorism.[43] In 1960 the ANC abandoned its reliance on nonviolent, passive resistance and turned to armed struggle. It did so, however, while retaining a policy against attacks on "soft targets"—that is, civilians. In contrast, with the exception of the Palestinian Communist Party, no PLO member organization ever adhered explicitly to such a prohibition. Terrorism—the indiscriminate assault on civilians with the aim of inducing leaders to yield concessions—is a tactic of the weak. More notably, failing by other means, terrorism is used to demonstrate to supporters that something is being done on their behalf. This applies equally to the state terrorism carried out by South Africa and Israel, which, as noted, in Israel's case had caused thirty times as many Palestinian civilian deaths as PLO violence was responsible for among Israeli civilians.[44] Although such acts were by no means the rule in Palestinian resistance[45] and, for reasons explored in chapter 4, were carried out for the most part in the early period of the consolidation phase of the national movement, an explanation for this divergence in movement policy and its implications is proposed. It should be emphasized, however, that the difference cannot explain either ANC success or PLO failure.

Indeed, half a century of passive resistance by the ANC between 1912 and 1960 failed to achieve even the organization's limited demands. Likewise, Palestinian passivity, appeals to the UN, and decades of "nonexistence" achieved nothing. Palestinians only secured international attention to their plight with the launching of hijackings twenty years after their dispossession. The price of that attention has been fervently debated within Palestinian organizations; nevertheless, they point out, such actions affirmed that Palestinians could no longer be ignored.[46] Arguments suggesting that Palestinian independence could have been secured through nonviolent methods were not supported by evidence, which included the Zionist movement's own success in establishing Israel, as well as the ANC's failure in its early phase. More important, however, strategies and tactics are adopted from existing, rather than hypothetical, choices. In contexts of settler-colonial struggles these are delimited by inclusion and exclusion.

First, the resort to terrorism is weighed against the alternative of inactivity. As will be shown, the inclusion of Africans in the South African settler economy rendered the settler project potentially vulnerable in multiple ways. From armed peasant revolts in earlier centuries to workers' strikes and township uprisings in the twentieth century, inclusion rendered a number of forms of resistance possible from the onset of white colonization in 1652. In contrast, Palestinians' exclusion until 1967 buffered their opponents. Viewed in the absence of alternative means of political action—revolts, strikes, boycotts, and the like—terrorism became a means of penetrating the barriers erected by their opponents. It also became a means of countering international neglect as organizations sought to use courts and trials as a forum for the Palestinian cause.[47] But terrorism is an admission of powerlessness and is used to counter popular demoralization. Indeed, while the Palestinian organization that launched the first airplane hijacking in 1968 gained substantial Palestinian support and members as a result,[48] the organization that hijacked the Achille Lauro in 1985 did not.[49] Having wrested international recognition, established institutions and structures, and developed programs of action, the Palestinian movement had moved well beyond such tactics in terms of strength.

A second and more fundamental consideration is the relationship with opponents that is projected for the future. After nearly 350 years of resistance in one form or another to the white colonial presence in South Africa, the economic inclusion of Africans made their resignation to the whites' presence and a unitary solution possible. Both were reinforced by the coerced dependence of Africans on the white-dominated economy as well as the fact that Africans remained the majority in the country. Acts of terrorism directed at whites could only undermine efforts to gain support for a unitary vision among whites. In contrast, Palestinians launched their armed struggle when the reality of dispossession was less than 20 years old. Moreover, as will be shown, Palestinians' goal of a future state mirrored Israel's as no form of dependence had developed between them, at least prior to 1967. The lack of the need to seek Jewish support for a unitary vision reduced the need to consider the implications of Israeli civilian casualties. Indeed, for some organizations early attacks on civilians were intended to discourage Jewish immigration thereby stemming the colonization drive Africans had failed to check in South Africa.[50]

Third, the economic inclusion of Africans in South Africa eventually forced white progressives and democrats to become attentive to African national demands. Palestinian exclusion reduced pressures on Jews to do the same. White ANC leaders were important in formulating and/or reinforcing policies and tactics that excluded terrorism against whites. Furthermore, over the course of the national movement, while the ANC could point to scores of white militants who devoted their lives to the liberation movement, the PLO could point to very few Jews who had done so for the Palestinian movement. While the majority of both whites and Jews were committed to exclusionary states in South Africa and Israel, as will be shown, the economic inclusion of Africans in South Africa permitted an inclusionary vision that had the potential of gaining support from significant sections of whites in South Africa; Palestinian exclusion obviated this possibility in Israel.

In short, inclusion created conditions that favored an ANC policy against civilian casualties while exclusion rendered such a consideration unnecessary to most member organizations of the PLO. For enough Africans, inclusion was conducive to a unitary vision of a future South Africa and presented alternative possibilities for action, both of which were reinforced by the presence of whites in the movement. Paradoxically, Israeli-imposed exclusion permitted Palestinians the realistic possibility of seeking a future exclusive of Jews while simultaneously closing off virtually all avenues of resistance until the occupation of the remainder of Palestine in 1967. The internal challenge to both—a separate future and disregard for Israeli civilian casualties—was not reinforced by the participation of Jews in the Palestinian movement.

To conclude, explanations that attribute to movements determinant power are inadequate. Movements' choices regarding leaders, resources, and strategies and tactics are structurally constrained and to a large extent circumscribed. The adoption of armed struggle by both movements, the ANC's embrace of nonracialism, and Palestinians' adherence to Palestinian nationalism, among other things, were choices made from among a limited array of possibilities. How well movement leaders and organizations maneuver and make use of what is possible is another matter. Both the possibilities that were available and the choices that were made are explored in the present study.

Explaining Comparable Success

Thus far I have said very little about the first objective of the present study: to explain the greater relative success of both movements in their latest phase of resistance. There are two dimensions to this question: (1) the similarity in form and ensuing effectiveness of the massive uprisings in the 1980s; and (2) the similarity in timing of the negotiations that followed in the 1990s. Each is addressed briefly.

A historical comparison of the two national movements uncovers parallels in the class nature of the movements' leadership and relationship to the movements' mass bases over three phases of resistance. As noted, both movements have attained their greatest success in the latest phase: The ANC and PLO now witness the emergence of protracted uprisings in both South Africa and the West Bank and Gaza Strip, which present the liberation organizations with the long-anticipated opportunity to pressure their opponents on the internal front. But this is only one in a series of parallels that characterize the development of these national liberation movements. Because no comparative historical studies have been conducted that trace the development of these movements over the course of the century, no attempts at explaining this exist. This study presents an explanation that is derived from a class analysis of the movements as they evolved since their emergence in the 1910s to negotiations in the 1990s.

As for the parallel timing in the commencement of negotiations, a number of explanations have been forwarded. The decline of the Soviet Union, a significant ally of both national movements, compelled movement leaders to seek a speedy resolution to the conflict. Conversely, uncontested American hegemony reduced the significance of both South Africa and Israel for the United States, thereby inducing both states to negotiate with their opponents. Essentially, space and interest in "old conflicts" was diminishing in the "new world order." Although important, these explanations remain incomplete because they are confined to explaining contemporary parallels. The present study proposes to account for the similarity in the shifts and their timing over the course of the century from one phase of resistance to another toward their resolution.

An Alternative Approach

The preceding examination identified the ways in which prevailing explanations fall short in accounting for the success or failure of the movements under examination. The inadequacy of demography, international support, and state strength as explanations is only somewhat mitigated by the inclusion of an examination of the role of the movements themselves. Having said that, we now return to these factors for a new look.

Taken together, there is no question that demography, international forces, and opponents' strength are relevant to understanding the fate of the two national liberation movements under examination. As the preceding examination demonstrated, however, their contribution is neither straightforward nor determinate. It is in the process of struggle between movements and the states they challenge that demographics include or exclude; international forces reward or punish; and states withstand or falter. Their contribution to the success or failure of movements is mediated through the movements' own successes and failures. Therefore, an alternative explanation for the differential success of the South African and Palestinian national liberation movements is required, and one that avoids both the structuralism and voluntarism of the prevailing explanations. Unable to untangle structure and agency, our point of departure becomes the process and product of their interplay over time.

By examining process and product in each of three phases of resistance in South Africa and Palestine we find striking similarities despite their separation by geography and culture. As will be shown, similarities in the process of liberation are due to the movements having shared the dynamics of the same global context and internal movement development. Differences in the product, however, are equally notable and may be attributed to the fact that global and internal dynamics play out on a field of struggle where opponents meet in particular ways circumscribed by inclusion/exclusion. The process and product are thus mediated by the indigenous populations' inclusion or exclusion in the settler projects—that is, by class. These are inextricably bound: In both South Africa and Palestine, the current political orders took shape in the very process of national liberation that produced them.

2
Liberating the Nation: Social Movements, Democratization, and Class Formation

A national liberation movement's ability to realize its objective and the objective itself are forged simultaneously over time. The "democracy" that successful movements ultimately deliver to their followers is constituted during the process of national liberation. As such, two literatures guide this investigation: social movements and democratization. Both are examined and their contribution to the study of national liberation movements identified. From there I present a synthesis that places class at the center of attempts to understand both the process and the product of movements of national liberation.

National Liberation Movements as Social Movements of Democratization

Broadly conceived, social movements are collective efforts to achieve political objectives through extra-institutional means.[1] National liberation movements are social movements in amplified form: the disaffected (those compelled to act) are virtually entire "nations," using not merely extra-institutional means but anti-institutional action for a political objective that is nothing short of the elimination of the existing state. The convergence of multiple movements of workers, peasants, women, students, professionals, and others produces this collective action on a grand scale. The clarity of the collective grievance renders the convergence of disparate class forces possible, generally over several generations: freedom from domination by a population that sets itself apart on the basis of national identification. Conquest in the name of one nation stimulates an unprecedented convergence of classes within the other. As a result, movements of nations that seek their liberation are distinctively multiclass social movements.

In contexts of settler colonialism specifically, liberation is sought from an externally imposed national group that comes to be "indigenized" and thus competes with the native population in its identification with and claim to the land. Dispossessed, displaced, and excluded from the structures of power, indigenous populations generally resist. By endeavoring to expand access to political power and the territory's resources—whether in a single unified state with their opponents or in a separate state exclusive of their opponents—movements of national liberation become democratization projects that seek to achieve for their followers what their opponents claim for themselves and deny those they dominate. In order to succeed, such movements must become projects of democratization in yet another respect: by mobilizing the broadest array of social forces within the dominated population, thereby producing unprecedented levels of popular political participation. Relationships between leaders and followers, sector-specific and national interests, and, most important, competing class interests are played out within this mobilization. There are implications here for both the successful execution of the liberation project as well as for the postliberation political order. Indeed, democratization of the new political order is a function of democratization of the often very old and lengthy process of liberation that produces it.

Democratization: Classes without Process

A substantial literature has formed around attempts to identify the prerequisites of democratic political arrangements, most of which take as their point of departure the relationship between capitalist development and democracy. While diverging with regard to the precise nature of the relationship and the significance of the outcome, "modernizationists" and classical Marxists alike have attributed causality to the class agency of the bourgeoisie to explain the historical association between capitalism and democracy—at least in its particular form, pejoratively labeled by Marxists as "bourgeois democracy." A wealth of comparative work has since been conducted to identify the class agency involved in securing democratic political arrangements.

Moore contributed one of the earliest comparative investigations to demonstrate the variability of political outcomes associated with class agency. Democratic political systems (the product of bourgeois revolutions) required the elimination of the landed elite, which had resisted the commercialization of agriculture; the transformation of peasants into producers for the market; and a bourgeoisie.[2] By eliminating, transforming, and/or creating classes, economic development renders particular political outcomes possible. Class agents, however, produce political outcomes only in alliance with each other. Alliances, in turn, depend on the political autonomy that classes enjoy from both each other and the state. Although painstakingly tracing the origins of classes, Moore does not show how classes develop the capacity to act on their interests and advance desired political arrangements—he overlooks class formation. Furthermore, while distinguishing different political outcomes, and even different forms of capitalist development, Moore does not distinguish different democracies. Adhering to a procedural definition of democracy, Moore misses the point that democracy itself is variable.[3]

O'Donnell and Schmitter investigated both historical and contemporary transitions from authoritarian rule to democracy. They concluded that before such transitions could occur, the bourgeoisie must first be convinced that authoritarian rule has become "dispensable," either because it has already secured the prerequisites for capital accumulation or because it has failed to do so.[4] Actual transitions to democracy, however, require the popular sectors; the bourgeoisie cannot do it alone.[5] The popular classes, however, are confined to roles as instruments of the elite or obstacles endangering the democratization project through their impatience and radicalism.[6] As such, the authors suggest that the best hope for democracy is "pacts" between elites even though this "deliberately distorts" the very essence of "citizen equality."[7]

While upholding the strictest of democratic procedures,[8] O'Donnell and Schmitter counsel that inaugural election results "cannot be too accurate or representative of the actual distribution of voter preferences."[9] Democratic in form but not in content, democracy in this sense means results that do not alienate the military by a determined effort to bring them to justice, where the bourgeoisie is not dispossessed, and where the left does "not win by an overwhelming majority."[10] Indeed, the authors caution, a democratically elected government dominated by the left is undesirable given that hostile foreign powers will seek to subvert it; a disgruntled indigenous bourgeoisie could wreak havoc on the economy with dreaded capital flight; and/or the military, feeling threatened, could find itself needing to take back control.[11] The asymmetry is intriguing: election outcomes should not punish the military and bourgeoisie and should not reward the popular classes. This reveals one of the functions of "democracy": to deprive the working classes of their only real source of power—the ability to disrupt.

The authors would deny this. Pacts, they argue, are intended to preempt any inclination on the part of all consequential actors to disrupt by ensuring them all a "place in the game."[12] But even though pacts may secure such a commitment on the part of all actors, the powers of these actors are not equal: the working classes' only power is precisely its ability to disrupt, while this is not the case with either the military or the bourgeoisie. Why would working classes agree to such a "democracy?" The conditions under which working classes accept such terms or press for alternative ones is not addressed by O'Donnell and Schmitter because of their elite-centered understanding of political change.

Moore considers the origins of classes and class alliances in advancing particular political arrangements but remains vague regarding the process by which they accomplish this. O'Donnell and Schmitter treat classes as given and focus on how elites act to determine political outcomes. In this process, subordinate classes are either tools to be wielded by the elite or obstacles to democratization. Rueschemeyer, Stephens, and Stephens upend the focus, viewing subordinate classes, rather than dominant classes, as the motor force driving the expansion of political space and democratization.

Rueschemeyer, Stephens, and Stephens note that working classes have propelled transitions to democracy, not the bourgeoisie. Although the bourgeoisie has championed the expansion of political participation beyond the nobility to secure their own inclusion, they have "rarely fought to include others";[13] this has been accomplished by subordinate classes. But their contribution to democratization is by no means straightforward. Although pressure from below forces dominant classes to expand access to political structures, that pressure cannot be "too strong" or it risks a more concerted determination to exclude. Democratization is a function of both the "relative class power" of the working class and the perception of threat by the dominant classes:[14] Workers must be strong enough to be taken seriously, but not so strong that they are too much of a threat.

A strong, highly organized working class is only possible where capitalist development has created the conditions for one. The interests of the working class, however, are socially constructed; working-class organizations have displayed a variety of forms, political inclinations, and commitments.[15] Indeed, dominant classes were slow to learn but eventually did so: labor is not always a revolutionary threat and is even less likely to be so when integrated into the political system.[16] An organized working class, however, is a necessary but insufficient factor in democratization; workers need allies.[17] The search for allies takes the working class to the middle class,[18] whereupon the "density of autonomous organizations" that empower the subordinate classes as a "shield protecting these classes against the hegemonic influence of dominant classes" becomes critical.[19]

Missing from the analysis by Rueschemeyer, Stephens, and Stephens is the process by which the working class is able to establish the all-important autonomous organizations and mobilize to resist the hegemony of dominant classes. Indeed, they do not distinguish cases in which the working class realizes its own democracy from those in which it adopts the dominant class(es)' definition of democracy that it then delivers through pressures only it as the working class can apply. The existence of classes and class capacities is merely given; their actions are the focus of investigation. The process by which autonomous organizations are constructed requires a social movements theory. Lacking such a theory, the authors are unable to show how working classes mobilize and organize to forward their own vision of democracy, as opposed to merely delivering some version acceptable to the dominant classes. Because Rueschemeyer, Stephens, and Stephens stick to a procedural definition of democracy, they, like the previous authors, do not explore this distinction.[20]

Procedural definitions of democracy are unenlightening as they say nothing about actual practice, access, or benefits. The meaning of democracy itself must be problematized. Indeed, classes vary not only in terms of their interests in democratization but also in the democracy they seek or fear. Even as classes come to agree on particular rules and procedures, they have different interests in what their use is intended to accomplish. Are democratic procedures intended to equalize access to political resources, or do they merely involve the abandonment of the subordinate classes' only substantial political resource: their ability to disrupt? What does access to political resources mean in the absence of the democratization of economic resources? Is it to be used to achieve social transformation or to channel popular pressures away from such objectives? Is there potential for altering economic relations or does the political system insulate economic power from challenge? How democracy is ultimately defined and practiced at any one point in time is the outcome of struggles between classes to extend, expand, and alter its content in their favor. The very meaning of democracy is continuously cast and recast through such struggles. Thus, the question becomes "whose" or "what" democracy is to prevail. This, in turn, requires a theory of social movements that captures the process whereby classes organize, mobilize, and lead while also forging and rendering hegemonic their conceptions of democracy.

Social Movements: Process without Classes

In the 1970s, extra-institutional, collective attempts to influence or alter the policies and institutions of the state became a legitimate and worthy object of study. Sociologists now problematized collective action: activity that did not conform to patient and orderly reliance on the operation of formal political channels to achieve political ends. They also rejected definitions that confined "the political" to the activities and institutions of the state. What people were doing when they organized, mobilized resources, resisted laws, took to the streets, and the like was indeed political. A branch of sociology emerged that took as its object of study movements that were conducting "politics by other means." Social movement theorists have since contributed a plethora of anatomical studies of the phenomenon of collective action by investigating organization, leadership, ideology, strategies and tactics, and alliances, among other things.

For much of the 1970s, the dominant approach in the study of social movements was Resource Mobilization Theory (RMT). RMT theorists concurred that an improvement in access to and control of resources promoted the likelihood that aggrieved groups would launch a challenge and succeed, but they could not agree on precisely what resources were consequential. Distinctions have been made between material and nonmaterial resources, consumable and nonconsumable resources, among others, encompassing such a wide array of assets that virtually anything could be considered a resource.[21] Underlying the diverse definitions is a shared, if often only implicit, assumption that the powerless in society are so because they are resource poor, which, in turn, prevents them from overcoming their powerlessness.[22] But this vicious cycle depiction was contradicted by cases of resource-poor groups that had succeeded in achieving their political objectives.[23] Rather than continuing to expand an already ambiguous and unwieldy concept, a number of theorists took the study of social movements in a new direction, one that rejected the necessary association of resource poverty with powerlessness. The point of departure for the new Political Process approaches is how social movements are embedded within political power relations.

Piven and Cloward, McAdam, and others contend that, with the exception of the most deprived groups, subordinate groups possess power derived from their ability to disrupt. For Piven and Cloward, disruption involves "the withdrawal of a crucial contribution on which others depend," which is "a natural resource for exerting power over others."[24] McAdam elaborates that while lacking "positive inducements" such as money, votes, influence, and the like, subordinate groups can realize political objectives through the exercise of "negative inducements" whereby the "cessation of the offending tactic becomes a sufficient inducement to grant concessions."[25] This latent power or leverage, which is a critical resource for otherwise resource-poor groups, is a function of the group's location within the system. Piven and Cloward explain that producing classes can exercise leverage through the functions they perform while the "lower classes" are often "so isolated from significant institutional participation that the only "contribution" they can withhold is that of quiescence in civil life: they can riot."[26] Insurgents' power is thus a function of their place within the system that they seek to alter. As such, the focus becomes the relationship between the aggrieved groups and the structures of power they target for change.

Moving away from "the more resources the better," Political Process approaches shifted the focus to the latent power of aggrieved groups and the opportunities for action afforded them within existing political power arrangements. Opportunities for action are neither constant nor confined to resource-rich groups. Even resource-poor communities may make use of what Tarrow calls political opportunity structures: "consistent—but not necessarily formal or permanent—dimensions of the political environment that provide incentives for people to undertake collective action by affecting their expectations for success or failure."[27] With structures of political power as context, Political Process theorists have made insightful advances into the study of social movement agency in its various dimensions of organization, leadership, tactics, and, of course, resources.

Indeed, Political Process theorists' attempts to address the limits inherent to RMT as an explanatory framework suggest an important distinction between resources as assets and resources as relations. By viewing resources as appropriable by the clever or through deals with elites—by definition resource rich—RMT theorists effectively treated resources as assets. Indeed, RMT's conception of resources renders the focus on elites in the study of social movements almost inevitable: the powerlessness of aggrieved groups is due to their resource poverty; in order to redress their powerlessness they require resources; to obtain resources they must turn to those who possess them; as a result, resource "donors" become the focus of attention.[28] Having identified successful challengers who lacked access to conventional forms of resources, Political Process theorists recognized the latent power or leverage inherent to structural relationships and have begun to privilege relational resources. Thus, the Political Process critique of RMT hints to an important distinction between different types of resources—assets and leverage. These are class specific: classes are differentially endowed with each.

While recognizing how social movements are embedded in political power relations is an important development, Political Process approaches have too often ignored the economic embeddedness of movements. In their focus on movement organizations and protest groups as agents, social movement theorists often lose sight of the social forces from which these agents emerge. As social forces are constituted and reconstituted over time, so too are the movements to which they give rise. Without contextualizing movements in class relations they cannot explain the dynamics of movement changes over time except as exogenous political or economic pressures that influence movement decisions and actions, rather than altering not merely the conditions under which movements must operate, but the very social forces that constitute movements; forces that then bring to bear different class resources to a movement.

Indeed, although recontextualizing social movements within political power relations is a definite advance, see-sawing or stimulus-response conceptions of state-social movement interactions persist. Rather than a collision of two fixed or unchanging forces, at each moment there is a unity; a particular combination of state and social movements, environments and actors, structures and agents. Understood in this way, the state comprises not only the forces included within its formal bodies, but also the forces it excludes and that challenge the state; those excluded define the system through the ideological justifications and structural provisions required to preserve their exclusion.[29] Similarly, economic structures are more than those included or the employed; the excluded or the unemployed are integral to an understanding of the economic system. In other words, structure and agency cannot be defined apart. Each "contains" the other. Of course, structures "contain" agents of collective action in two senses: structures give rise to agents, which they then also restrain. When agents become capable of launching a challenge because of those restraints, they are well on their way to altering the structures. Thus, states and social movements are constituted and reconstituted together, not separately, over time.

Given the class specificity of resources, the origin of social forces in particular economies and structures, and the necessary unity between structure and agency, the following suggests an approach that places class and class relations at the center of an investigation into movements that seek to alter political and economic systems.

Class Formation and the Political Process of Democratization

Different configurations and alliances of classes produce different political outcomes, democracy being one. Democratization theorists tell us this even though they do not go far enough in distinguishing between different democracies. A class's power to forward particular political arrangements, including democracy, requires the mobilization of resources and supporters under its hegemony. That process has been the object of investigation by social movement theorists even though they have generally neglected class agency. Indeed, if much of the democratization literature is concerned with class but fails to show how classes become political actors, the social movement literature jettisons class once the organizations and movements identified as important political actors appear. Class, however, is central to both the process and the product of national liberation movements.

Classes are differentially endowed with conventional resources such as economic assets (i.e., material resources of various kinds), human assets (i.e., skills, education), organizational assets (i.e., associations of particular kinds), as well as structural power or leverage. Assets and the relational resource of leverage differ. First, acquisition of assets does not require a relationship with one's adversaries. Indeed, linkages with opponents are detrimental to asset accumulation, as dominant groups actively obstruct the accumulation of all types of assets by those they dominate. In contrast, leverage, a relational resource, requires a relationship with the aggrieved group's opponents as it is derived precisely from its location within the opponent's system. Second, assets can be transformed into power, but, in contrast to leverage, that power is indirect in two senses: (1) assets must be converted (e.g., into weapons, organization, mass mobilization); and (2) classes that wield assets require the mobilization of other classes in order to transform such resources into a source of power (e.g., armed fighters, organized members, striking workers). Thus, assets must be converted into a source of power, and even then it is an indirect source as it relies on the mobilization of others.

Given the economic imperative underlying national domination,[30] the most critical resource of all is the latent power of leverage derived from the dependence of the opponents on an indispensable economic function performed by the indigenous population. Structurally, indigenous classes are not uniformly in a position to induce concessions through disruption. Leverage is the preserve of some indigenous classes but not others. It is the latent power of the "economically exploited" classes as opposed to the "economically oppressed."[31]

Wright makes an important distinction between exploitative and non-exploitative economic oppression. Economic oppression exists when: (a) "[t]he material welfare of one group of people is causally related to the material deprivations of another"; and (b) that causal relation "involves coercively enforced exclusion from access to productive resources."[32] In contexts of settler colonialism, although all classes within the dominated national group may be economically oppressed, they are not all economically exploited. To classify as economic exploitation an additional condition must be satisfied: "In exploitation, *the material well-being of exploiters causally depends upon their ability to appropriate the fruits of labor of the exploited.*"[33] This relationship between exploiters and exploited entails a "dependency" that "gives the exploited a certain form of power, since human beings always retain at least some minimal control over their own expenditure of effort."[34] Repression or coercion alone are generally not successful in achieving the level of activity sought, thus some level of consent is required involving "constraint" on the part of the exploiter, which "constitutes a basis of power for the exploited."[35]

As a result of settler-colonial dispossession, dominated populations can be said to be, with few exceptions, economically oppressed across classes. However, not all indigenous classes are economically exploited by their oppressors.[36] But all classes may resist. Given the economic imperative underlying national domination, the system is most vulnerable in the realm of production. It is there also that the latent power of the exploited class(es) is to be found, where "the exploiter *needs* the exploited since the exploiter depends upon the effort of the exploited."[37] But an exploitative relationship presupposes that indigenous labor is integrated into the settler project. This raises an important distinction between inclusionary and exclusionary settler projects: inclusionary systems incorporate indigenous labor, exclusionary systems do not. Although all settler projects have combined inclusion and exclusion, dominant tendencies and dynamics are generally readily identifiable.

Under inclusionary settler projects, settler capitalism eliminates, undermines, transforms, and/or produces particular classes in the indigenous society; exclusionary settler projects render the indigenous society free from the impact and implications of settler capitalism. In the absence of the transformative effects of settler capitalism, social forces within the indigenous society may be preserved. Therefore, depending on whether it is inclusionary or exclusionary, settler-colonial projects preserve, undermine, transform, and/ or create classes within the indigenous society—classes that are differentially endowed with resources. Inclusionary settler projects obstruct the accumulation of assets while unavoidably allowing leverage as a potential form of power; exclusionary settler projects cannot obstruct the accumulation of assets and entail no leverage for the excluded indigenous people. Each permits certain forms of resistance and not others. The significance of class, however, is not confined to resources in resistance.

Different classes have different inherent capacities and means at their disposal to bring to a national struggle. Organization, leadership, tactics, and strategies, among other aspects of collective action, are significantly class specific. The same movement under the leadership of the traditional elite, the middle class, or working class will display significant differences in form and content. Indeed, resistance, liberation, state-building, and democratization projects vary markedly depending on which class or alliance of classes has succeeded in asserting its hegemony over the movement.

Class is implicated directly in yet another way: classes' autonomy from or dependence on each other determines whether they are free or constrained to act within political movements in decisive ways. As multi-class movements, national liberation movements are based on a "class truce" that may have been carefully constructed or forcibly imposed. Whichever it is depends on a class's autonomy from or dependence on other classes, which in turn determines the extent to which social forces are free to make use of their class-specific resources in collective action. National liberation movements have generally been led by middle classes. Whether they are constrained by elites or powerful working classes makes for very different movements under their leadership. When the traditional elite wields critical resources upon which other classes depend, it will be able to retain a considerable measure of control over the national movement. When these resources are eliminated or undermined, or when elite leaders fail to achieve the movement's goals, middle-class contenders may find it possible to appropriate leadership. At some point, workers may forge a working-class challenge to the middle-class leaders. Working classes, however, which are dependent on indigenous dominant classes, can be expected to act very differently than those free of such dependence. Indeed, elites and middle classes seek to transform their assets—authority and organization, respectively—into power through the mobilization of the popular sectors under their hegemony. A dependent working class may well be used in this way; an autonomous working class is unlikely to permit it and instead will seek to assert its own agenda within the national movement.

Of course, once formed, classes and class capacities do not remain fixed. Indeed, neither settler projects nor indigenous movements of liberation remain unchanged over time. Economic development shapes and reshapes settler and indigenous classes and class interests. Workers, for example, in early, extractive settler economies are very different from workers in later, industrialized economies. Whether economic development is occurring under conditions of inclusion or exclusion entails different implications for the resistance potentials of classes within national liberation movements.

Moreover, indigenous classes vie continuously for influence, if not hegemony, within the national movement. Shifts in leadership occur when the leading class is undermined, thereby improving contenders' chances. State repression, popular disaffection with a failing leadership, and/or the elimination of critical resources may all contribute to openings that permit shifts in leadership to occur. Accompanying each shift is a reassessment of movement objectives, strategies, tactics, and more, reflecting the relative strength of the classes within the alliance. These differences prove to be critical for both the long and arduous process of national liberation as well as its outcome.

Finally, the case of national liberation movements raises yet another insight regarding the relationship between political and economic arrangements. Operating under conditions of political exclusion, the relevant "environment" or context for the study of movements must, by necessity, be more than the prevailing political power arrangements, particularly when the countervailing power of groups that are fully excluded from the formal structures of political relations—citizenship, franchise, and representation—is to be assessed. Comparing national liberation movements that are politically excluded, and yet operate under conditions of either economic inclusion or economic exclusion, illuminates what political inclusion is often deliberately intended to obfuscate—the relationship between political and economic power.

The South African and Palestinian Movements Compared

As noted, the objective of this study is twofold: (1) to explain the greater success of the South African and Palestinian national movements in the 1980s as compared to any time since their emergence early in the century; and (2) to explain the greater relative success of the South African movement as compared to the Palestinian movement. The first objective requires a review of the history of each movement, from its inception in the 1910s to the eve of negotiations in the 1990s. The second objective necessitates a comparison of the two movements. The following is a summary of my main arguments and findings, derived from the comparative history of the two movements and examined in the three chapters that follow.

The historical examination of the two movements reveals notable parallels in their development. As chapter 3 demonstrates, elites dominated both movements in their formative phase (1910s to mid-1940s). In the movement consolidation phase that follows (late 1940s to early 1970s), a radicalized middle class asserts its leadership, the focus of chapter 4. Finally, chapter 5 addresses the movement expansion phase (mid-1970s to 1980s) that is launched by the popular classes, which, while embracing the leadership of the liberation organizations in exile, assert their distinctive contribution, thereby rendering the movements' challenges to their opponents more effective. Thus, as one leadership failed to achieve the movement's goals, another asserted itself, in the process bringing to bear new class resources, introducing new relationships between leaders and followers, and, eventually, delivering to the movements greater success. This success may be attributed, therefore, to the democratization of the process of liberation that accompanies the shift in leadership and participation from one constellation of class forces to another.

Democratization, a process with a history and variable ends, may be said to be occurring when the political participation of subordinate classes appears and expands, ultimately creating autonomous formations that eclipse dependence first on elite and then on middle-class leaders to define and direct political action. Working-class autonomy renders the political participation of subordinate classes more effective while also reducing the possibility that their postliberation economic interests (i.e., the economic interests of the majority) are sacrificed in the name of an amorphous nationalism that serves the dominant classes. Thus, democratization is defined by the expansion of direct political participation (rather than mere representation) of the working class, of which one indicator is its ability to assert its economic interests in the cross-class political alliance that is forged. While I argue that this shift toward the expansion of popular political participation explains the greater relative success of both movements in the 1980s as compared to any time in the past, the greater success of the movement in South Africa remains to be explained. To do this I turn to a comparison of the two movements.

The comparison reveals crucial dissimilarities in terms of the underlying balance of class forces, the resources they wield, and their resistance potentials, which ultimately account for the differential success of these two movements in their latest phase, despite their similarities. These, in turn, are a function of the extent and character of the integration of the indigenous and settler economies and the preservation, dissolution, and/or creation of class forces within the indigenous economy over time.

Indeed, early struggles between capital and labor were resolved differently within the white–South African and Jewish-Israeli settler populations. Under the slogan of "Hebrew labor only," Jewish workers succeeded in enforcing the exclusion of Palestinian labor from Jewish-owned enterprises early in the century.[38] In contrast, despite tremendous struggles, white workers succeeded only in securing limitations on white employers' use of black labor—in the form of "color bars"—but never its complete exclusion.[39] The inclusion of black labor meant that it would remain integral to the evolution of the settler project in South Africa; the exclusion of Palestinian labor meant that it would not, and Israel would evolve largely independent of it. As the examination reveals, these differences produced divergent constraints as well as divergent opportunities and potentials for resistance by the national movements that subsequently emerged.

In South Africa, inclusion would contribute to the dissolution of the indigenous resource base and social relations, dependence on the settler-dominated economy as a matter of survival, and the creation of a strong black working class with leverage derived from whites' dependence on their labor. In Palestine, exclusion resulted in the preservation of the indigenous resource base and social relations in the remnants of Palestine free from Israeli control, limited, though growing (after 1967) dependence on the settler-dominated economy, and the emergence of a weak working class with limited or no leverage in the settler-dominated economy. As the following examination reveals, the resulting differences in class forces, resources, and resistance potentials, and the liberation organizations' utilization of these, contributed to the differential success of the national movements, despite their parallel development. The examination further shows how these differences account for the divergent "democracies" the two movements ultimately delivered to the people of South Africa and Palestine.

3

Merging Elites as Nation and Movement Formation, 1910s to 1940s

British moves to secure their interests on the African continent and in the Middle East presented Africans and Arabs with fundamentally new political realities early in the century. In 1910, Britain, without regard for the indigenous African population's concerns or aspirations, turned political control over to the whites in what would become South Africa. In 1917, the British occupied Palestine, reneged on their promise of independence to the Arabs, and later secured a League of Nations mandate for their rule. Multiple, fragmented territories with no history of unity were merged to form the Union of South Africa, while Palestine was cleaved from a larger, centuries-old, Muslim entity. Africans were to be subsumed into an entity dominated by the more powerful British colonies and Afrikaner republics. Palestinians' links to the territories that made up the once powerful Ottoman Empire were to be dissolved.

Britain's duplicity took both indigenous elites by surprise. Earlier, African and Arab leaders had turned to the preeminent imperial power for support in achieving their freedom from Afrikaner and Ottoman Turkish domination, respectively. In South Africa, there had been a history of conflict between Britain and the nationalist settlers dating back to the arrival of the British in the Cape (1806), the Afrikaners' flight known as the Great Trek (1835), and the discovery of diamonds (1867) and gold (1886) in Afrikaner-controlled territory, subsequently seized by the British. The Anglo-Boer War (1899–1902) was additional evidence of British readiness to challenge Afrikanerdom. Thus, the indigenous elite—both traditional rural leaders and their urban counterparts who had emerged from British missionary schools—came to place their trust in Britain. In Palestine, too, the indigenous elite believed British promises of independence that would end four hundred years of Ottoman rule in exchange for Arab cooperation in defeating the Turks in the First World War. Not only would independence not be realized, but Zionist settlers would obtain British support for the establishment of a Jewish "national home" in Palestine. In both cases a time would come when the imperial power would entrust its regional interests to European settlers whom they had challenged at one point and assisted at another in their colonization of African and Arab territories.

In each case, the indigenous elites would initiate attempts to present their people's case to the new rulers. They were compelled to act by the threats the nationalist settlers and colluding colonial states posed to their interests, as well as by pressure from those who bore the brunt of colonial domination. Having already been subjugated in the nineteenth century Wars of Dispossession when traditional African armed resistance was effectively eliminated[1] and Africans were stripped of most of their territories, the urban African elite now endeavored to retain the limited social and political inclusion they enjoyed under British rule. Palestinians were yet to experience their "wars of dispossession." Their society intact, the Palestinian elite kept its sights on independence. Through the espousal of amorphous notions of African and Arab unity, both elites would attempt to assert their leadership and forge a following that transcended communal divisions. In both cases, the organizations they founded would bring members of the elites together and rely on traditional social organization to reach the mass base. Their leadership would be continuously challenged, but the elites would retain dominance of their respective national movements for three decades.

Elites, Authority, and Restraint

Communities under assault turn to their established leaders. Social organization that sustains a community under ordinary circumstances is expected to enable the community to overcome exceptional external threats such as colonialism. Thus, existing social relations and authority come to form the basis of organized resistance with leaders drawn from a community's elite. The power and authority of leaders are derived from their command over resources, which are generally inherited. Control over decisions regarding land allocation—the community's primary productive asset—forms the material basis of their authority. Elaborate reciprocal relations and interdependencies ensure both communal survival and loyalty to leaders. Whether tribal elders or feudal lords, leaders are expected to protect the community from internal disintegration by ensuring all access to subsistence and from external threat by mobilizing forces to repel invaders. As long as they do so successfully, they can count on continued recognition of their authority.

Because of their technological disadvantage, indigenous populations have been no match for colonial invaders bent on conquest. Their forces defeated, indigenous elites find themselves subordinated to an external power. New arrangements are imposed by the new rulers. When they have a service to perform, indigenous elites are propped up, even while the economic foundations of their authority begin to erode. That service, to the extent that it exists, is invariably social control over the mass of the conquered population. This is at least the case with inclusionary forms of settler colonialism where the cooperation of indigenous labor is demanded. Where it is not, the elite is as superfluous as the remainder of the indigenous population, and may be eliminated or expelled along with them. Indigenous elites obtain a role in the new arrangements as long as they are capable of delivering control over their communities.

Having already been defeated, members of the elite who are given a stake in the new order are likely to seize it. They tend to be cautious and non-confrontational, ever aware of their dependence on the sufferance of those who now rule. With the settlers' territorial ambitions threatening the mainstay of the indigenous elite's power and authority (land), they are vulnerable. Their lack of leverage within the settler group augments their vulnerability; their only relevance to the new rulers is indirect, and that is in securing their community's cooperation. Failing to do so, the rulers may dispense with them altogether and institute more direct means of control. Indeed, the indigenous elites' only power is the authority they wield over their followers. This power is precarious as elites must reconcile their roles as agents of control in the service of the new rulers and leaders of their people's quest for freedom from that rule.

The ability to secure their people's cooperation is the power exercised by elite leaders. Restraining, rather than promoting, mass resistance becomes the hallmark of traditional elite leadership as mass mobilization and resistance run counter to their interests. Having failed to prevent the community's fall to the invaders, elites are aware that, once mobilized, their followers may target them. However, failing to demonstrate their ability to lead and make gains for their followers, they are likely to lose their claim to leadership in their community, a loss that would eliminate their relevance to the new rulers as well. The tenuousness of their position is accentuated by the gradual disintegration of the basis of their authority, which rests in their control over land upon which the community depends for its survival. Passivity would mean certain loss of leadership. Thus, under the threat of mass pressure, they

adopt more militant positions than they would otherwise take merely to in-
sure that they remain the acknowledged leaders. Again, however, having
been defeated militarily, traditional elites vacillate: they will do the minimum to provoke the new rulers and the minimum to incite their followers.
Nevertheless, when popular pressure has been sufficient, elites have led
organized resistance. Although the traditional elite's power vis-à-vis the ruling powers is derived from their promise to restrain their followers, this says
nothing about their actual ability to deliver. Their interests incline them toward restraint, but they may be forced to lead a movement not of their making. Organizational efforts are invariably stamped with specific features.
Authority rooted in agrarian social relations forged over generations is patriarchal, paternalistic, and certainly not democratic, although generally consultative. Embedded in traditional social relations, organization along territorial, tribal, or sectarian lines is fragmented and hampers the effectiveness
of resistance. Indeed, through strategies of divide and rule, colonial invaders
actively seek to transform such differences into powerful divisions. And yet,
colonialism introduces the possibility for new bases of collective action to
emerge out of the shared condition of exploitation and/or oppression. But
elite leaders operate in the old world and are not equipped to lead in the
new. In the old world, elaborate relations of dependence bind the community together and to the elite. Unable to break free of such dependence, and
lacking an alternative collective context within which to organize, the mass
of the population may continue to follow their ineffectual leaders. Combined, these elements impede successful resistance to settler-colonial domination by national movements under the leadership of the elite. Indeed, lacking leverage within the settler population, and eager to demonstrate their
usefulness to the new rulers, elite leaders come to act as levers that control
their followers' resistance.

South Africa, 1912 to 1948

In 1910, the Union of South Africa was formed, combining the former British colonies of the Cape and Natal, the Afrikaner republics of the Transvaal
and Orange Free State, and what remained of the indigenous African kingdoms that had successfully resisted conquest.[2] Struggles ensued over which
set of policies were to prevail in the Union: British Cape liberalism or
Afrikaner racial exclusivity. In actuality, it was a question of which economic
interests were to prevail: those of largely British mining capital or Afrikaner
agricultural capital, each with its distinct labor requirements and political alliances to consider. Africans were given no voice in the state's deliberations
concerning either of these or the future of the country. In the first two years

of the Union, a series of laws was issued that served to consolidate white power, leaving no doubt as to a minimum accord between English- and Afrikaans-speaking whites at the expense of Africans and soon thereafter of the Indian and colored populations.[3]

The eventual social and political exclusion of Africans would begin with segregation, which was experienced variably by class. For the majority of rural African producers, segregation would mean confinement to the negligible remnants of African holdings that constituted the rural "reserves." By preserving peasant producers and the reciprocal ties that bound them to their migrant kin who labored in the mines and on white farms, segregation was a means of subsidizing the capitalist sector of the South African economy.[4] Such ties permitted the economic inclusion of African workers to be expanded while keeping their labor "cheap." The fate of the native population in this period, however, was cast and recast as alliances of white classes and class fractions fought over the precise terms of inclusion of African labor. For the African middle class, segregation entailed the reversal of the incorporation they had enjoyed under British rule and hoped to extend to the other provinces of the Union. In order to achieve an accord with Afrikaans speakers, however, even liberal, English-speaking whites were now prepared to endorse the application of segregation to the African middle class as they sought to consolidate their hold on the country. The tensions and contradictions between the ongoing social and political exclusion of middle-class Africans and the increasing economic inclusion of African workers eventually becomes apparent. In the meantime, African unity would be counterpoised to white unity, and to a lesser extent an African nationalism to Afrikaner nationalism.

African Unity and Middle-Class Exclusion

On the eve of the Union's establishment, members of the urban African elite initiated the formation of a political organization to present African concerns to the new government. Although numerous attempts to organize Africans politically preceded the establishment of the ANC in 1912,[5] the ANC was to prove the most enduring even while its eventual eminence could not have been predicted during this phase of the national movement.[6]

The ANC emerged on the scene as a small group of African intelligentsia—teachers, clergymen, lawyers, and other educated Africans—as well as traditional tribal leaders. The keynote address delivered by Pixley ka I. Seme welcomed "chiefs of royal blood and gentlemen of our race" to the inaugural conference where no workers or trade unionists were to be found among the organization's founders.[7] In a move aimed at reaching the mass of

Africans who remained in the rural reserves, eight paramount chiefs were named as Honorary Presidents in the Upper House of the organization.[8] The Lower House, an elected National Executive Committee (NEC), was composed of four ministers, three lawyers, an editor, a building contractor, and two teachers.[9]

The educated urban elite's inclusion of tribal chiefs reflected a recognition on their part of both the tenuousness of their links to the majority of the African population (who remained rural residents directly under the authority and influence of tribal leaders) and their need for financial resources for organization building.[10] The influence of tribal leaders extended to the urban workers who retained strong ties to the reserves, where their families continued to reside. As such, middle-class ANC leaders had no choice but to include tribal leaders. For their part, tribal leaders supported the efforts of the African middle class because of their interest in the land question—the basis of the chieftaincy that was once again under threat.[11] While articulating support for the chieftaincy and traditional social relations, the educated urban elite had little in common with either the traditional elite or the African populace in or out of the reserves beyond its own ethnic origins and extended family ties. Members of this class aspired to integration into white-dominated society.[12]

The coming together of members of the African elite was a significant expression of race consciousness. It marked the first enduring attempt to organize as "Africans" across tribal divisions and represented a notable departure from earlier expressions of class consciousness in which middle-class Africans vigorously emphasized their affinity to their white counterparts and conversely their dissimilarity to the mass of the African population.[13] Writing in 1905, one African intellectual exemplified this earlier perspective well:

> If the white people and the King were to desert us now . . . there is a great section of us who have approximated to . . . the white man's way of living . . . and there is a large number of us who have not advanced at all. . . . I am afraid that those who have remained in their former state would kill us all, particularly civilised natives, because we have bought land, they do not approve of the ownership of lands. They know too that whenever there has been a war against Natives like ourselves, we have always been with the government.[14]

The persistent government assault on African rights, such as they were, prompted the African elite to organize as Africans. Members of the missionary-educated African elite nevertheless enjoyed privileges denied the majority of Africans, which they were eager to protect and averse to risking: a qualified franchise for those in the Cape, exemption from pass and curfew laws instituted to control African mobility, and rights to property and business ownership in some cities.[15] This ambivalence would hamper the African elite's efforts to organize an effective pressure group. Indeed, the racial dimension of the assault on African rights would carry the elite closer to the popular sectors of the African population, but the elite's social distance from the majority of Africans, and its persistent desire to prove its worth to educated whites, would prevent it from succeeding in reaching the majority of the population for much of this phase of the movement.

The paramount goal as it was spelled out in the inaugural conference of the ANC was the formation of a "national union for the purpose of creating national unity and defending our rights and privileges."[16] Writing in 1911, Seme, the first treasurer-general of the ANC, identified the main obstacle to such a "Native Union":

> The demon of racialism, the aberrations of the Xhosa-Fingo feud, the animosity that exists between the Zulus and the Tsongaas, between the Basutos and every other Native must be buried and forgotten; it has shed among us sufficient blood! We are one people. These divisions, these jealousies, are the cause of all our woes and of all our backwardness and ignorance today.[17]

Tribal divisions were blamed for Africans' weakness and their defeats in the Wars of Dispossession. Forging a national union that transcended tribal divisions, creating a national unity where it had not existed before, were the means through which the organization would seek to defend African rights. Rather than as a challenge to whites, African unity was pursued as a means of achieving an equal partnership with them. Indeed, the African elite believed firmly in the realizability of integration into white-dominated society and, therefore, remained committed to constitutionality; they sought rights within the existing system rather than its elimination. As such, the ANC strove "to become the medium of expression of representative opinion and to formulate a standard policy on Native Affairs for the benefit and guidance of the Union Government and Parliament."[18] Cape province "liberalism" with its qualified African franchise was pronounced as the ideal that they hoped to extend to the other three provinces of the Union.

Upon its formation, the ANC was faced with the Natives Land Act of 1913, which established that Africans were to be confined to the reserves that constituted a mere 7.3 percent of the country's land area. Territorial segregation was a direct assault on the small but prosperous class of African landowner-producers who had managed to buy back some of the land from which they had been dispossessed and who now competed with white, mostly Afrikaner, farmers outside the reserves.[19] It was also a means of inducing peasants to seek employment outside the territories.[20] The limited and inadequate land area reserved for Africans, however, threatened to undermine the basis of the chieftaincy.

The ANC campaigned vigorously against the act and succeeded in attracting supporters across the country. Appeals were directed to the government, and ANC representatives were dispatched to London where they received a "cold reception" by the British government.[21] The ANC's conciliatory and moderate approach was demonstrated repeatedly. With the outbreak of the First World War, the organization as "a patriotic demonstration, decided to hang up native grievances against the South African Parliament till a better time and to tender the authorities every assistance."[22] Deputations to London resumed once again in 1919 for a third time and, once again, in vain.[23] The government was clearly intent on preventing the extension of the Cape's liberal policies to the other provinces, and the British were content to allow this.

Despite seemingly inexhaustible patience, ANC faith in both white liberals and government channels for consultation began to give way to disillusionment and frustration. Moreover, the Hertzog electoral victory in 1924 and installation of the Pact government[24] signaled an intensification of discrimination. The color bar was extended to industry through the Color Bar Act of 1926, and the "civilised labor" policy, which set differential criteria for wages based on race, further reinforced white workers' advantage in a strategy intended to preempt the emergence of a unified working class.[25] In 1925, in keeping with electoral promises, Hertzog proposed the elimination of the African franchise. The Hertzog Bills were debated and reformulated for years and then passed by parliament in 1935. Lacking direct participation in these debates, Africans pinned their hopes on the liberal white members of Parliament who preached patience only to abandon them yet again by supporting Hertzog's Bills.[26] The Representation of Natives Bill eliminated the African franchise in the Cape, and the Native Trust and Land Bill of 1935, which, although expanding (at least on paper) the land area for Africans to 13.7 percent, reasserted the commitment to territorial exclusion.[27] As a form of compensation for the removal of Africans from the common roll in 1936, the government established the Natives Representative Council (NRC), yet another channel for consultation without direct representation.[28]

These and other significant entrenchments of discriminatory policies and political exclusion highlighted the ANC's inability to influence events in favor of Africans. Some authors point to the ANC's organizational weakness between 1924 and 1939 to explain this.[29] Just as important, however, was the weakness of the ANC's links to the mass of the population because it remained an organization of the African elite over this period. Indeed, due to the organization's preoccupation with internal struggles to purge communists,[30] the ANC had virtually nothing to do with attempts to organize African workers who were responsible for major strike activity in the 1930s.[31] In any case, ever intent on demonstrating their capacity for restraint to the country's rulers, ANC leaders shunned workers' more militant activity that threatened their preferred strategy of gradualism.

Recognizing their weakness, however, ANC leaders sought an alternative framework to respond to the Hertzog Bills. In December 1935, a conference of all-black organizations was convened and resulted in the establishment of the All-African Convention (AAC). This was not the first time cooperation was attempted with other groups. In the 1920s, radical members of the colored African People's Organisation (APO) joined the ANC and other African organizations. In 1927, leaders of the ANC and APO participated jointly in a unity conference of "non-Europeans" and formed the Non-European Unity Movement (NEUM). Colored membership in the ANC, however, small as it was, would be reversed by the more nationalist ANC leaders who headed the organization in the 1930s.[32]

Cooperation with Indian organizations was even slower to develop. While Indian delegates participated in the various non-European conferences, the conservative business elements that led the South African Indian Congress (SAIC) (1920) were generally opposed to working with other national groups.[33] By and large, Indians and coloreds were reluctant to risk their relatively advantaged positions by joining forces with Africans; they could, instead, turn for support to the nationalist movement in India and Afrikaner paternalism, respectively.[34] The conservative elements that dominated the two communities reinforced the preference to rely on such assets. Even the Communist Party of South Africa (CPSA), formed in 1921, came to join forces with Africans only circuitously. Nevertheless, by 1925 the leadership of the CPSA was multiracial, and CPSA members were found in the leadership of the ANC and the SAIC. They were viewed with suspicion, however, particularly by the more nationalist leaders who dominated the various organizations. These elements would succeed in expelling communists from the ANC leadership in the 1930s.

The AAC was to function as an umbrella organization with the ANC as only one member organization.[35] The membership traversed a wide array of political organizations and ideologies and included labor union leaders, communists, and students, as well as members of government advisory boards, church leaders, and prominent individuals.[36] Despite common rejection of the Hertzog Bills, the AAC was a fragile combination of reformists who insisted that "a half loaf" was "better than none" with regard to the Cape vote and those who argued that defense of the Cape vote was an empty goal given that it was confined to Africans voting for white candidates.[37] Finding the AAC too radical, the ANC withdrew its membership one year later.[38] One reason was that the ANC permitted its members to serve on the NRC, something the AAC rejected.[39] Ten years later, the ANC would reverse its policy on participation, determining that it was indeed useless.[40] In the meantime, however, the more radical AAC failed to either develop a mass following or eclipse the ANC.[41]

With the outbreak of the Second World War, the ANC once again expressed its support for Britain and the government, although less vigorously than it had in the previous war.[42] Interpreting the Smuts government's suppression of a pro-Nazi Afrikaner rebellion as a sign of liberalization, African leaders were only to be disappointed yet again with the 1943 elections.[43] The ANC, under President-General Alfred Xuma, would respond with the "African Claims" (1943), which, among other things, called for "the extension to all adults, regardless of race, of the right to vote and be elected to parliament, provincial councils and other representative institutions."[44] Accompanying the radical demands was the restructuring of the organization. Traditional chiefs were removed, the organization was centralized, and democratic principles of organization were instituted.[45] Without abandoning efforts to involve the chiefs, the organization would now strive to build organizational structures directly in the rural areas to reach the populace.[46]

The end of the war also witnessed greater cooperation between the various forces opposed to the minority government. In 1946, radicalized by legislation aimed at containing or prohibiting land ownership by Indians in Natal,[47] a more militant leadership emerged within the reformist, middle-class-led SAIC that called for joint action with Africans.[48] In March of the following year, the ANC and SAIC signed the Xuma-Dadoo-Naicker Pact to coordinate their efforts toward achieving a full franchise.[49] Similarly, colored leaders were radicalized by the government's decision to establish a Coloured Affairs Department in 1943, which they considered to be analogous to the Native Affairs Department, that portended eventual disenfranchisement and greater segregation for coloreds.[50] While seeking closer cooperation with Africans, however, colored leaders chose to concentrate their efforts on the more radical NEUM, thereby detaching themselves from the mainstream of the national movement.[51] In short, recognizing signs of their eventual exclusion, middle-class Indians and coloreds began to consider alternatives to patience and reliance on their patrons.

Paralleling these developments was the emergence of new, young, militant, nationalist leaders inside the ranks of the ANC, who were entirely disillusioned with the organization's tactics that had yielded nothing of substance. In 1943, they established the Youth League of the ANC. These young leaders would introduce more militant politics to the ANC, reinforced by the example of 75,000 African miners who, in 1946, launched the largest strike in the country's history.[52]

Black Labor and Inclusion

The South African economy underwent substantial change during this period as the contribution of manufacturing to the national income came to exceed agriculture in 1930 and mining in 1943.[53] During the war years, laws controlling the influx of Africans into the urban areas were temporarily relaxed and the number of Africans employed in industry mushroomed as employers resorted to using African workers to fill openings in the newly expanding industrial sector and those left by whites recruited for the war effort in Europe.[54] Now, substantial numbers of African workers entered industrial employment as an alternative to laboring in the mines or on white-owned farms. The ratio of the number Africans employed in mining compared to the number in manufacturing, construction, and electricity combined narrowed dramatically and rapidly: 316:87 in 1932; 348:187 in 1939; 328:321 in 1946.[55] In 1934, approximately the same number of white and African workers were employed in the manufacturing sector. By the Second World War, however, this sector doubled in size and Africans made up two-thirds of the labor force.[56] This trend continued steadily as an acute decline in the productive capacity of the reserves, coupled with increased taxation, compelled rural Africans to seek employment inside the cities.[57] By 1946, nearly one out of four Africans resided in urban areas—a fully proletarianized workforce in contrast to the migrant mine and farm workers who retained ties to the reserves.[58]

Mining capital had introduced the migrant labor system to ensure adequate labor supplies for the massive diamond and gold extraction in the late nineteenth century.[59] Various mechanisms were instituted, including taxation, land laws, and service contracts, that would compel Africans to leave their homes and families in the rural territories to labor for most of the year in the mines. Reciprocal relations characteristic of the traditional economy ensured migrant workers' access to subsistence for themselves and their families, thereby relieving capital of this portion of wages—the basis of the system of cheap labor that was so profitable. But the very dynamics of labor extraction would begin to undermine the productive capacity of the reserves: a growing population on a fixed and inadequate land area, the inevitable intensification of cultivation, and the persistent drain of the territories' most able and productive men would combine to erode the viability of the very rural economies that kept labor cheap in South Africa. Already by the 1930s reports noted with some alarm the deterioration of conditions in the reserves.[60]

The expanding industrial economy required a larger workforce than white workers could provide, and a more stable and more skilled labor force than could be supplied by African migrant workers. A permanently urbanized, fully proletarianized segment of African workers was in the making that was deprived of the possibility of drawing from the underdeveloped reserve economy to cover subsistence requirements. This new workforce would be more readily organizable with a greater potential for militance as a result.

Large-scale trade union organization among blacks had already begun in the 1920s.[61] Two organizations were particularly prominent in the organization of workers: the Industrial and Commercial Workers Union (ICU) (1919) and the CPSA. The ICU began by organizing Cape Town dock workers in 1919. Successful strike action by two thousand dockworkers brought a doubling of their wages and the rapid growth of the union followed.[62] More a "mass movement of the dispossessed" than a union,[63] the ICU's membership included teachers, domestic workers, rural farmworkers, and small traders.[64] At the height of its success in the mid-1920s, it was the largest existing black organization with a purported membership of 100,000.[65] ICU leaders, however, remained cautious and did not condone illegal strikes, and those who did strike without the Union's approval could not count on its support.[66] Nevertheless, for a number of years ICU activity surpassed that of the ANC.[67]

Economic recession in the 1920s, combined with concessions made to white workers following the 1922 Rand Revolt, led to massive waves of demonstrations and strike actions. The ANC took no part in these, remaining firm in the direction of constitutionality.[68] Indeed, despite an overlap in membership between the ANC and ICU, the ANC had very little to do with the latter's attempts to organize African workers, and did not, by and large, support ICU strike activity.[69] By 1930, the ICU had all but disappeared as a combined result of repression, internal purges of communists (which deprived the union of some of its ablest organizers), undemocratic practices, inefficiency, and alleged corruption.[70] The still limited development of industry and of a black industrial working class also made transforming the union into an industrial union difficult.[71] Out of the ICU, however, emerged a number of individuals, particularly communists, who went on to organize new unions.[72]

The CPSA began as an organization of white socialists, mostly immigrant workers. The Party's nonracialism did not hold up well when tested during the Rand Revolt the following year. The CPSA was stigmatized among blacks by its support for white mine workers on the Rand who had struck under the slogan of "Workers of the World, Fight and Unite for a White South Africa."[73] In their own defense, communists insisted that they supported striking mine workers in their struggle against mine owners and not the color bar, which the workers endeavored to protect.[74] In any case, Party leaders argued, rather than improving the conditions of African workers, the elimination of the color bar would have served only the interests of mine owners by reducing the position of white workers to that of Africans.[75] Although raising the position of black workers to that of white workers was a preferred goal, it was not deemed feasible at that time.[76] Thus, support for the striking white workers was necessary, they contended, even if the inferior position of black workers was temporarily preserved in the process. Communists seemed to be unaware that striking white workers were motivated as much by racial as by class interests, thus exposing the CPSA to accusations of betraying black workers,[77] something the Party would not easily overcome. However, one of the lessons the CPSA learned from the defeat of the strikers in 1922 was the need to organize African workers.

The CPSA's recognition of the need to organize African workers was rather opportunistic, prompted by employers' ability to use African workers to undermine the position of white workers—the presumed vanguard of the working class[78]—thereby subverting the paramount struggle against capitalism.[79] Following years of dissension over policy, the Party ultimately committed itself to the struggle for the political emancipation of Africans and adopted a nonpaternalistic relationship with African workers.[80]

In 1924, at the behest of the Communist International (Comintern), the CPSA implemented a policy of "Africanization" of the Party. Four years later, the Party's leadership included Africans who now made up approximately 1,600 of the 1,750 members.[81] Also in that year, the CPSA's initial unsuccessful attempts to promote working-class solidarity across race gave way to a policy to advance the African struggle for liberation. In 1930, the Party spelled out its program for a Native Republic, calling for the achievement of majority rule—the first such call ever in South Africa[82]—as a necessary step toward the attainment of a "workers' and peasants' republic."[83] The program also committed the Party to developing an alliance with the national movement,[84] a major departure from the earlier critique of African nationalism and its "bourgeois organization," the ANC. The new approach to the national movement reflected both the Comintern's policy shift toward anticolonial national movements and the influence of African communists, a number of whom were or would become ANC leaders. The CPSA spent the early 1930s in self-destructive purges as it was being "bolshevized," reemerging in the middle of the decade to adopt a "popular front" strategy against fascism.[85] During the war, the Party actively promoted nonracial unions through the Council of Non-European Trade Unions (CNETU) (1941), which by 1945 had succeeded in enrolling 158,000 members in 119 unions nationally, representing approximately 40 percent of African workers in commerce and manufacturing.[86]

Despite the depression, the migrant character of most African workers, and legislation circumscribing union organization, a trade union movement among African workers had emerged in the 1930s.[87] The growth and urbanization of the African working class during the Second World War positioned African workers to respond in defense of their interests when at the war's end white workers and employers sought a return to the status quo ante.[88] Workers thereafter became increasingly more militant as evidenced by the strike that shut down the Transvaal's gold mines in 1946. Debates abound regarding the extent to which the CNETU-affiliated African Mine Workers Union (AMWU)—the union that called for the strike—could be credited with the rebellion.[89] Moreover, the ease with which the state was able to suppress the AMWU indicates that the union's organizational foundations were still extremely weak.[90] Nevertheless, the strike remained a powerful indication of possibilities. Indeed, although harshly repressed, one outcome of the 1946 strike was the Industrial Council (Natives) Bill of 1947, which allowed for limited recognition of African trade unions as the state and industrialists sought to check African workers' emerging militance.[91]

The relative success of the striking mine workers would reverberate throughout the country. The younger generation of African leaders were particularly impressed by the potential the strike revealed for action, reinforced further by the government's and employers' concession of limited recognition for African unions.[92] Moreover, the radicalizing impact of the government's segregation policies that were beginning to be imposed on other "non-white" groupings stimulated new and more earnest efforts toward cooperation across race.

The state's response to these developments would come in the 1948 election results that would bring the National Party (NP) to power and with it "apartheid." Apartheid would be the NP's solution for the evident failure of the segregation form of inclusion, the diminishing benefits from the reserve system, and the increasing militance of black workers.[93] Secure in the ability to control labor, the new government would clamp shut the limited space wrested by African mine workers in 1946. The failure of the African national movement was glaring. The new system of African inclusion/exclusion—apartheid—would delimit the terrain and terms of struggle for most of the remainder of the century.

Explaining Failure

The resolute consolidation of white control over the newly formed Union of South Africa prompted an African response. To the apparent unity of whites, the African elite would counterpoise African unity; something that traditional bases could not accomplish given their inherent fragmentation along tribal and linguistic lines. Through the ANC, the African elite would promote an amorphous African nationalism that emphasized the shared experience of dispossession and oppression at the hands of whites.

But the experience of oppression was not uniform across African classes: the lives of urban, middle-class Africans bore little resemblance to those of rural or urban workers. As members of a missionary-educated elite, middle-class Africans enjoyed advantages that distinguished them from the mass of the African population. Such advantages reinforced their belief in the realizability of social and political integration into white-dominated society, something that must have seemed as remote to African workers and peasants as becoming mine workers would have seemed to the urbane and well-traveled middle class.[94] Indeed, among the middle-class African leaders were those who continued to speak down to the populace about unity while remaining "upward"-looking in their aspirations, emphasizing their similarity to their white counterparts as the basis of their hope for better treatment.

Yet for much of this phase of the national movement both the African middle class and the mass of migrant workers remained dependent on the chieftaincy for essential resources. The dissolution of traditional social relations and identification among workers and the emergence of new bases were gradual and uneven, and both processes remained incomplete; the traditional elite continued to wield authority. Moreover, although capitalist penetration promoted both processes, elements within the state would eventually recognize the need to intervene to prevent the dissolution of the traditional economy and social relations. Of course, Africans themselves endeavored to do the same. In other words, the state and capital as well as the indigenous population shared an interest in the preservation of the rural economies, albeit for different ends.

For Africans, traditional social relations presented a means of securing both their survival and freedom from the settlers; for capital and the state, they were a mechanism for extracting surplus value from labor and social control. However, interests in the preservation of traditional social relations were not uniform within the indigenous population. Chiefs were concerned with protecting the power and authority they derived from their control over land allocation decisions within communal production relations; peasants and migrant workers needed to preserve access to subsistence that communal relations ensured; the middle class required the chiefs' political and material support both in their careers and in their political endeavors. But the rapid disintegration of the reserve economies threatened each one of these interests. With the reserves' capacity to subsidize migrant workers' wages diminishing, workers began to find it necessary to remit earnings to their beleaguered families back home. Pressures to secure their needs within the developed sector of the South African economy fueled the militance of urban African workers.

Organized efforts to respond to these mounting pressures multiplied as organizations based on class, race, and/or ethnicity proliferated, with goals ranging from nominal reforms to socialism. However, there was limited cooperation and coordination between the numerous organizations that emerged in this phase, even though individual memberships, including those of leaders, traversed the various organizations—ANC, ICU, CPSA, SAIC, APO, and others. And while the state's assault on "non-Europeans" stimulated greater cooperation between the three groups, mutual suspicion abounded, fueled by government policies that perpetuated competition over what little remained after white demands had been satisfied.

Most notable was the limited cooperation between the political and trade union organizations of the day. The ANC showed little interest in the organization of workers as workers. Even preparations for the 1946 strike were not taken seriously by the national ANC leadership.[95] However, those who were organizing outside the ANC—ICU, CPSA, workers, women, urban residents—when successful, made only sector-specific, community-specific, or issue-specific gains that did not translate into national gains. That is, although there were many mass-based efforts, these did not translate into a coherent and cohesive national challenge. The one organization that presented itself as a national political organization—the ANC—remained intent on proving to the whites that Africans could be trusted. Moreover,

African workers were still too weak to form a political force; the majority remained mine workers and laborers on white farms where labor organizers
confronted problems of access.[96] Their migrant character also meant that
they continued to identify with and depend on traditional social relations in
the reserves, although both were rapidly giving way.

African leaders during this phase of the national movement protested in
ways that did not transgress the very constitution that excluded them, con-
fining their activities to moral appeals and petitions to the rulers, delegations
to London in quest of British justice, and protest demonstrations. Even in
the late 1940s, and despite evidence of new tactics and alliances, the leadership of the African political movement remained extremely cautious.
Reformist and ever determined to demonstrate loyalty to the government, it
did not turn seriously to organize the populace. Even Xuma, who, during his
tenure as president-general (1940–49) initiated important reforms that expanded the organization's membership, was no proponent of mass participation.[97] A number of explanations have been forwarded to account for this
and for the elite's commitment to evolutionary change more generally.

Some authors point to the African elite's adherence to Christianity and
the ideals of western liberalism that they imbibed through their missionary
education, reinforced in many cases by study abroad, to explain their faith in
moral persuasion as the route to reform.[98] Believing it was merely a matter
of time and education before whites would put into practice the very ideals
they preached, the African elite preached patience. Magubane, too, points to
the influence of the westernizing ideology upon these early leaders, but sees
it as the outcome of a systematic attempt by the British in the previous century to create an African elite "as a medium of control and communication"
over the oppressed.[99] Their ideological conservatism was consistent with the
class role they performed. However, Magubane argues that once they recognized their contradictory position within the structure erected by the whites,
and the limits imposed on their advancement, it was natural for them to resist as they had the most to gain from change. Gerhart focuses on the
African elite's objective lack of power, viewing these early leaders as "realists"
who recognized the implications of the profound technological and organizational disadvantage of Africans compared to whites. As such, they saw no
alternative but to wait for change from above, hoping that whites' self-interest
would ultimately allow them to recognize what was obvious to these leaders,
that both blacks and whites had a common interest in their mutual progress
and that the continued progress of whites depended on that of blacks.[100] In
defense of these early leaders, ANC historian Meli suggests that reliance on
deputations and appeals was due to its consistency with "traditional African

political custom"; belief in the possibility of obtaining concessions from the British who were themselves in conflict with the Afrikaners; a lack of more direct means of challenging the white government given the weakness of the African working class; and "betrayal" by white union leaders and workers and their lack of sensitivity to the national oppression of Africans, which rendered Africans leery of slogans regarding the "class struggle."[101] Mbeki reminds us that Africans turned to such forms of struggle after they had "failed . . . on the field of battle" in the previous century.[102] Viewed against that background, Mbeki suggests that early ANC leaders had very little room to maneuver.

Indeed, the African elite had to maneuver within the reality of dispossession and relative powerlessness resulting from their military defeats to whites over the span of centuries. Their real powerlessness, however, was due to the lack of leverage they exercised within the system of white domination. The sole function of the traditional African elite was social control, and for the educated elite it was to act as a moderating influence in African politics. Recognizing their resource weakness, they endeavored to compensate with the pressure of numbers that the African majority could provide. But mass mobilization was alien to the elite leaders, and their persistent vacillation hampered their ability to mount an effective challenge. Furthermore, emerging from a period of relative inclusion under the British, integration into the system erected by whites must have seemed attainable, so they were wary of more radical and disruptive tactics that would alienate whites. Their problem was in misreading the class interests behind white domination, a misreading that was consistent with their preferred vision of evolutionary change and practiced tactics of appeals and deputations. But their repeated appeals to the British reflected the elite's additional misreading of the relationship between British imperialism and the settler-colonial project, attributing conflicts to ideological differences over color rather than to competition between capitals—foreign and national—over the benefits to be derived from the subordination and exploitation of the African majority.[103]

In short, although there was tremendous regional variation,[104] by and large the strategy and tactics of early ANC leaders remained within the bounds of constitutionality and to no avail. This did not mean, however, that Africans waited passively for the national movement to advance and include them. In fact, a new African militance was beginning to appear from two sources: African workers flexing newfound leverage and a new generation of educated Africans disillusioned with the early ANC leaders' patience and tactics. These two segments would discover each other in the phase of resistance to follow.

Palestine, 1918 to 1948

In December 1917, having defeated the Ottomans, a triumphant British army marched into Jerusalem where they were greeted as liberators. The residents of Palestine did not suspect Britain of intending to replace the Ottomans as the new rulers. Their naïveté was due in part to British promises of independence as spelled out in a series of correspondences between the Sharif of Mecca, Hussein Ibn Ali, and the British High Commissioner in Cairo, Henry McMahon, from 1915 to 1916. Having fulfilled their pledge of a revolt against Turkish rule, Arabs expected independence to be granted.[105] They were unaware of the secret Sykes-Picot Agreement (1916) concluded between Britain, France, and Russia that divided the region among them, with Palestine to be administered internationally.[106] One year later, the British issued the Balfour Declaration, which rendered independence even more remote as it committed Britain to establishing a Jewish "national home" in Palestine.[107] This was the beginning of a series of contradictory promises and prevarications by the British, creating a quandary from which they would become all too eager to extricate themselves three decades later.

In the aftermath of the war, Arabs debated the merits of several independent states versus a single unified Arab state.[108] Their plans would be preempted by British and French designs on the region, but the preservation of Palestine's "Arab-ness" ('uruba) would remain at the center of their demands throughout this period. Borders erected by the colonial governments separated communities and relatives from each other, producers and traders from their markets, and landowners from their land, thus straining or dissolving linkages that had been forged over nearly four centuries of Ottoman rule and 1,300 years of Muslim rule. Palestine was severed from a larger entity to be delivered piecemeal to European settlers useful to British imperial interests. Under British rule, the colonial government of Palestine would assist the Zionist movement to establish a foothold in the country from which it would eventually realize its objective of a Jewish state. Episodes of fierce Arab resistance would force the British to waver in their backing of Zionist colonization of Palestine, but only temporarily, as they would reaffirm their support once Arab resistance waned.

Judaism was native to Palestine, where Jews retained communities even after Roman conquest. In the late 19th century, pogroms in Central Europe and Russia would spur the first modern waves of Jewish immigration to Palestine. Destitute and fleeing repression, the religious idealists set about establishing agricultural colonies with the assistance of Western European Jewish capitalists. Simultaneously, anti-Semitism in Europe was stimulating the formation of a political movement of Jewish nationalists that would proclaim Palestine as the Jewish homeland at its founding convention in Basle in 1897. The economically and politically beleaguered Ottoman state would accede to European and Zionist demands for Jewish immigration to Palestine. However, even by 1914, Jews made up less than 9 percent of the population.[109] With British backing, immigration was stepped up to unprecedented levels.

At this time, Zionist colonization and conquest was not military; instead, it assumed the form of the highest relative rates of immigration and capital transfers in the world.[110] The interests of certain segments of Jewish capital abroad and those of Labor Zionism met in the establishment of self-sufficient Jewish colonies that excluded the native inhabitants of the country. Jewish capital made the purchase of land and establishment of industries possible, while Jewish labor "conquered work" by securing the exclusion of Arab workers from Jewish-owned enterprises, dominating employment in the state sector, and actively boycotting Arab produce. Indeed, Palestinian exclusion in Zionist ideology was complete: the indigenous population simply did not exist as Palestine was "a land without a people" waiting for "a people without a land."[111] And the British colluded in this exclusion when they issued the Balfour Declaration without regard for the native inhabitants referred to as "non-Jews" at a time when they constituted over 90 percent of the population. Jewish colonization, financed from abroad, implemented by immigrant settlers, and "under the shadow of the British gun"[112] would stimulate a Palestinian Arab nationalist response.

Arab Unity and the Preservation of Palestine

In February 1919, delegates to an All-Palestine Conference pledged support for Amir Faisal's four-month-old Arab government in Damascus. The conferees called for the integration of Palestine into an independent Syria, and elected delegates to represent them at the First Arab Congress held in Damascus that spring.[113] In July 1920, however, the French ousted Faisal, thereby aborting unity plans. The young Palestinian nationalists who supported a single Arab state now had no choice but to cooperate with the older traditional leaders who preferred an independent Palestine and cooperation with the British.[114] Together, the Arab politicians of Palestine were now forced to look inward to deal with a British presence that was remaining longer than imagined and a steady stream of Jewish immigrants that was altering the demographic composition of the country.

The first Palestine-specific national political bodies to form were the

Muslim-Christian Associations (MCA) in 1918. Although widespread, membership in the MCA was confined to the elite of both communities and did not constitute mass-based formations.[115] As their name suggested, they were devoted to unity across the sectarian divide.[116] The disproportionate representation of Christians among professionals, and the notable success of those in commerce who, as Christians, enjoyed favored relations with Europe, disturbed Muslims with similar aspirations.[117] Strains characterizing relations between the two communities, however, would be mitigated by their shared opposition to the British and Zionists;[118] the largely Muslim peasants and landowners feared Zionist colonization of the land while the predominantly Christian merchants feared competition from Jews with access to foreign capital.[119] Moreover, stressing continuously the secular nature of Arab nationalism in the making, Christians were represented at least in proportion to their numbers on delegations abroad and to the Arab Congresses, the core of which were the MCA.[120]

In 1920, the Third Arab Congress elected an Arab Executive headed by Musa Kazim al-Husseini. Presenting itself as the representative of "all the classes and creeds of the Arab people of Palestine," its members were drawn from the landed *(iqta'iyin)* and religious *(ashraf)* elite of "notable" *(a'yan)* families who dominated the social and political life of Arabs under the Ottomans.[121] Most prominent of the notable families were the Jerusalem-based Husseinis and Nashashibis. Their substantial landholdings[122] and command of strategic religious posts and institutions, combined with appointments in the mandate government, enabled the elite to preserve its dominance under the mandate.[123] The elite, however, was not a cohesive class and it suffered tremendous interfamilial and regional rivalries. Such rivalries extended from the cities and towns to the remotest villages where local families and clans were divided in their support of one or the other of the urban-based notable families—the source of patronage protection. Through alliances with local village clans and control of religious institutions, the landed notables also influenced villagers who were neither tenants nor agricultural laborers in their service.[124] So pervasive was the system of patronage alliances that even Christian families were allied with one or the other of the dominant families.[125]

The British authorities made full use of the Husseini-Nashashibi rivalry, deftly manipulating their enmity. The Nashashibis were the more willing allies of the British. The wealthier of the two clans, their family members were among the more successful entrepreneurs and citrus exporters to England.[126] Both families, however, demonstrated a willingness to cooperate with the British to undermine their rivals. In 1920, the British authorities removed

the politically vocal Musa Kazim al-Husseini as mayor of Jerusalem and replaced him with the more moderate Raghib al-Nashashibi. The tables would
turn the following year when British officials arranged the appointment of
Haj Amin al-Husseini as Mufti of Jerusalem, even though he had failed to
qualify in the elections that the Nashashibi-backed candidate had won.[127] In
the same year, al-Husseini was appointed president of the Supreme Muslim
Council, thereby investing him with substantial power through control over
the Islamic endowments, courts, and other institutions, including employment within these.[128] In short, both families demonstrated their readiness to
circumvent democratic processes when expedient, and the British authorities actively facilitated this. Nevertheless, when confronted with an external
threat, the elite proved quite capable of containing familial divisions and rivalries, revealing that they did, in fact, recognize common interests.[129]

The early Arab leaders of Palestine seemed certain that the British
would ultimately look favorably on their demand for independence given
that it was consistent with repeated British pledges and statements during
the war and Britain's pronouncements regarding self-determination.[130] As
products of late Ottoman modernizing and foreign, mostly missionary,
schools, the notable leaders believed that it was only a matter of time before
the British government would apply the liberal ideals it preached and fulfill
the promise of independence.[131] Indeed, they considered themselves the
most loyal of allies, expressing alarm to the British government regarding
Jewish immigrants who were not only intent on "spreading Bolshevik principles" in the area and fighting the "wealthy,"[132] but intent on combating the
British government as well.[133] These early leaders were so certain of British
promises that many interpreted the Balfour Declaration as a mere expression
of sympathy for the Jewish people, stressing that the text's inclusion of the
proviso "it being clearly understood that nothing shall be done which may
prejudice the civil and religious rights of existing non-Jewish communities
in Palestine" precluded Zionist objectives of colonization and dispossession
of the native inhabitants.[134] They would thus rely on petitions and delegations to London.

The first Palestinian delegation to London in 1921 presented the Third
Arab Congress's demands: the establishment of a national government and
parliament to be elected by the Muslim, Christian, and Jewish population
residing in Palestine prior to the First World War; the abrogation of the
Jewish national home concept; the cessation of Jewish immigration until
the newly formed national government could decide on immigration policy; the application of Ottoman law and repeal of British regulations; and
the preservation of ties between Palestine and its Arab neighbors.[135] The

British rejected the demands. Britain was to obtain the League of Nations mandate over Palestine the following year, and an Arab government was far from what they had in mind for Palestine. British offers of a representative assembly in 1921, a consultative body in the constitution of the Mandate in 1922, and a representative council in 1923, all met with Arab rejection.[136] By requiring Arab recognition of the mandate, enshrining the Balfour Declaration in the Constitution, and/or granting the British and Jews absolute majorities, it was impossible for Palestinian leaders to accept the various proposals without risking popular rejection of their leadership.[137] Later in the decade, Palestinians would accept a council on condition that recognition of the mandate was not required, but this time the Zionists would reject the idea.

While Palestinian delegations persisted in their quest for justice in London and other European capitals, Palestine was rapidly undergoing change. Under the mandate government's sponsorship, immigration expanded the percentage of the Jewish population in Palestine dramatically—13 percent in 1922; 18 percent in 1931; and 29 percent in 1936.[138] With each wave of immigrants new land was purchased by Zionist organizations with conspicuously substantial purchases in 1921, 1925, 1929, and 1934–35.[139] Of the land acquired up to 1936, 52.6 percent had been purchased from large absentee landowners, 24.6 percent from large resident landowners, 13.4 percent from the government, churches, or foreign companies, and 9.4 percent from small holding cultivators.[140] In the process, and contrary to customary rights, resident peasants were evicted with the transfer of title. Dispossessed peasants who thronged to the cities where prospects for employment were dismal responded with violence, most notably in 1921, 1929, 1933, and 1936—years of substantial Jewish land purchases and/or immigration.[141]

Arab leaders were averse to the use of violence and generally apprehensive about peasant-led actions, both because of the threat these posed to the elite's relations with the government and for its potential to be directed at them.[142] On the second day of the rioting in August 1929, leading figures issued an appeal to the participants:

> We call upon you O Arabs in the interest of the country, which you place above all other considerations, to strive sincerely to quell the riot, avoid bloodshed and save life. We request you all to return to quiet and peace, to endeavor to assist in the restoration of order and turn a deaf ear to . . . unfounded reports and rumors. Be confident that we are making every possible effort to realize your demands and national aspirations by peaceful methods.[143]

Arab leaders would be commended repeatedly by the British authorities for their cooperation in seeking to quell disturbances throughout this period.[144] Compelled by the events of 1929, once again, Arab leaders sent a delegation to London to demand a halt to Jewish immigration, to secure the inalienability of the land, and the establishment of a "democratic Government in which all inhabitants will participate in proportion to numbers."[145] The British response was once again negative. Arab leaders' disillusionment, however, was alleviated somewhat by an international commission investigating the events of 1929,[146] the Hope-Simpson commission inquiring into conditions confronting the peasantry,[147] and the British government white paper of October 1930 on land shortage in Palestine,[148] each of which acknowledged the damaging effects of the prevailing immigration and land transfer policies.[149] However, Arab leaders' hopes would be dashed once again by the revelation of a secret agreement concluded between the British Prime Minister James Ramsey MacDonald and the Zionist leader Chaim Weizmann, which involved the scrapping of major parts of the white paper.[150] MacDonald's "black letter"—as Arabs came to identify the agreement—to Weizmann was more lenient on Jewish immigration and conceded the right to Jewish exclusivity in Jewish-owned enterprises. This latest in a string of breaches would lead a new generation of Arab politicians to abandon confidence in the British and eventually in the Arab Executive's moderate leadership as well.[151]

Popular pressures were mounting on the traditional leaders who continued to preach moderation while conditions worsened. Paralleling the politically moderate MCA were organizations led by a younger generation of figures disillusioned with the traditional leaders' reliance on petitions, delegations, conferences, and peaceful marches, and who began to advocate extralegal tactics.[152] As the 1920s passed and failed to secure either a British withdrawal or the cessation of Jewish immigration, advocacy of such tactics became more widespread among the new middle-class political figures who emerged from the expanding class of professionals, teachers, and employees in the mandate administration, and businessmen who thrived from commerce and trade in the coastal cities.[153] In the 1930s, middle-class nationalists initiated the formation of a number of new political parties. Yet these remained largely clan based, with the notable exception of the pan-Arab Independence Party (1932).[154] While vocal in their criticism of the older leaders, the new generation remained loyal to the established leadership of the national movement.[155] Indeed, the line between the traditional elite and the new middle class was blurred; the sons of the landed elite increasingly opted for professional careers, while middle-class members of "lesser" families, who accumulated wealth, frequently purchased land and/or married into the landed elite.[156] Thus, the middle class was "organically linked" to the traditional leaders.[157] More important, however, they remained dependent on the elite's family connections, prestige, control over religious institutions, and other assets; they were still unprepared to strike out on their own.

While the old and new generations of notables debated what to do, other leaders were working among the ranks of the dispossessed. Radical and ready to take up arms, they sought to mobilize the destitute migrants expanding the shantytowns around Palestine's cities and the peasants who were threatened with displacement. They found both segments receptive, as the traditional leaders, who made no effort to organize or mobilize the rural population due to their aversion to peasant organizations, had neglected them.[158] Most prominent of the new radical leaders was the Syrian cleric Sheikh Izzidin al-Qassam who endeavored to transform the sporadic violence into an organized revolutionary insurrectionary movement. Twice he was believed to have made contact with the Arab leader Haj Amin al-Husseini to coordinate an armed rebellion—he from the slums of Haifa in the north, al-Husseini from his base in Jerusalem in the south—and was twice rebuffed by the cautious al-Husseini who continued to prefer diplomacy.[159] Al-Qassam nevertheless launched a rebellion in 1935 that, although ill fated and ending with his death, would reverberate throughout the history of the national movement for its daring at a time when traditional leaders remained passive. It would also give rise to Qassam-inspired rebel groupings that would instigate numerous actions outside the control of the traditional leaders, revealing a chasm between the politics of the urban-based elite and the rural peasants.[160]

The dispossessed did not wait for the notable leaders to act, as attacks on Jews and rioting revealed. One such attack in April 1936 would result in the imposition of a state of emergency. In response, what would become the longest general strike in Middle Eastern and European history would be declared, initiated by militant organizations that had formed "national committees" throughout the towns. The strike would galvanize the notable leaders who, fearing its repercussions, sought to bring it under their control.[161] Their initial impulse to send a delegation to London was abandoned three days later for an alternative route that saw the convergence of the political parties, including that of the Nashashibis, the national committees, and traditional leaders into the Arab Higher Committee (AHC) with Haj Amin al-Husseini as its president.[162] The prudent al-Husseini, who one year earlier had spurned Qassam's more militant approach, was now leader of the movement that was heading toward full-scale insurrection. Cognizant of the prevailing mood of the populace, the notable leaders were forced to infuse their rhetoric with greater militance in order to harness the rebellion that was rapidly forming. They also sought to deflect growing popular anger against some of their members who had been implicated in land sales to Jews.[163]

In the name of the AHC, the national committees took on the administration and organization of every aspect of town and village life during the strike, including food distribution, defense, and community mediation.[164] In May, a congress of the national committees adopted a plan for active civil disobedience that included the nonpayment of taxes. Arab businesses and transportation came to a standstill, and schools, factories, and even the port of Jaffa were shut down. Arab government employees were permitted to contribute a tenth of their salary rather than join the strike for fear of their replacement by Jews and loss of this limited access to government.[165] In the countryside, organized peasant militants, many self-identified as "Qassamites," battled British forces with the assistance of armed pan-Arab volunteers from the north under the leadership of the Syrian Fawzi al-Qawuqji. With the rebels effectively controlling the countryside, the AHC persisted with diplomacy to achieve Palestinians' "national demands": a halt to Jewish immigration during negotiations, a ban on land sales, and the establishment of an independent national government.[166] The government's announcement of new immigration quotas in May, perceived as a deliberate rebuff, unleashed a new wave of violence and met with renewed British repression, including the demolition of large sections of Jaffa. In September, martial law was declared. Repression, the realization of additional Zionist economic gains during the strike, and the onset of the harvesting season—a major concern for the wealthy citrus plantation owners among the notables—combined to compel the AHC to seek an end to the six-month strike.[167] They would require the assistance of the Arab rulers of Iraq, Transjordan, and Saudi Arabia to convince the people to agree to such a halt in October.

The population awaited the outcome of the Arab kings' promise to intervene with the British on their behalf and, of course, the fruits of the general strike itself.[168] They were optimistic because a fifty-day general strike by Syrian nationalists had secured significant concessions from the French.[169] The British response would materialize in July 1937 in the Peel Commission recommendation for the partition of Palestine into Arab and Jewish states. Partition was rejected by the Arabs, including the Nashashibis.[170] Two months later, a second wave of resistance erupted in what became known as the Great Revolt.

The British authorities banned the AHC and arrested and deported leaders and activists. In 1937, al-Husseini escaped to Lebanon, where he would attempt to continue to lead the movement. With the notable leaders exiled or in prison, the rural rebels assumed control.[171] In the summer of 1938, at the peak of the rebellion, insurgents controlled most of the highlands, and by September the government had lost control over the urban areas.[172] A joint rebel command issued a declaration that went beyond the notables' "national demands," including a moratorium on debts, a rent freeze on urban housing, and other claims that revealed a class dimension to the peasant and urban workers' nationalism.[173] Indeed, described as a period of "revenge of the countryside," peasant rebels asserted their authority within the cities, prompting thousands of wealthy Palestinians to leave the country to wait out the events from a safe distance elsewhere in the region.[174]

With the possibility of war looming in Europe, the British launched a major counteroffensive to reassert control over Palestine. They were aided by the Nashashibis in the creation of "peace bands" of villagers who had suffered from the high-handed tactics of the rural rebels.[175] The Zionist Hagana contributed special units for night attacks on rebel bases.[176] And following the signing of the Munich Agreement in 1938, an additional British division was freed to serve in Palestine bringing the number of British troops in the country to 20,000.[177]

British suppression of the Revolt would be fierce and effective. However, in order to free troops now required in Europe and to secure regional Arab cooperation, the British reverted to diplomacy. In March 1939, they issued a white paper declaring the government's opposition to Palestine becoming a Jewish state, a ceiling to Jewish immigration of 75,000 during the following 5 years, the regulation of land sales, and the promise of independence in ten years, contingent on Arab and Jewish approval, with self-governing institutions in the interim.[178] Arab leaders, fearful of the provision of Jewish approval and wary of trusting the British once again, rejected the proposal.[179] Zionists would oppose the white paper with even greater vehemence.

The self-sufficient Zionist colonies were well poised for an offensive. In contrast to policies imposed on Arabs, the colonial government permitted the Jewish community autonomy, which they used to set up elected administrative bodies, including a general assembly and executive (Va'ad Haleumi), a powerful trade union federation (Histadrut), an effective military arm (the Hagana), and, with aid from abroad, economic self-sufficiency and viability.[180] Although the various waves of Jewish settlers were not homogenous, and the Zionist movement was not monolithic, Zionist institutions prevailed. Indeed, upon their arrival, immigrants had no recourse but to turn to

Zionist-dominated institutions for employment, housing, and services, as well as access to the colonial government. Self-segregated in colonies deliberately intended to isolate the community from the native inhabitants, the dependence of immigrants on Zionist agencies was virtually complete.[181] As such, immigrants, who in many cases only sought a haven, became unwitting and later willing participants in Zionist conquest.[182]

Although Zionists would owe their successful conquest of Palestine to the British, it was now their turn to experience British duplicity. British concessions to the Arabs, made to secure Arab cooperation for the duration of the war, enraged Zionist leaders. They were in a position to respond. Ironically, they had made important gains during the general strike and revolt as they filled the vacuum created by the suspension of Arab economic activity.[183] Moreover, through their assistance in quelling the rebellion in Palestine and in the war effort in Europe, they secured additional arms from the British—both openly and illicitly.[184] They were thus prepared to launch an assault, first against the British, then against the Arabs.

British suppression of the Arab rebellion in 1939 struck a blow to the Palestinian national movement from which it would not recover in time to respond to the Zionists' rapidly materializing offensive. Weakened by repression, the general strike, and the exile of its leaders, the Palestinian national movement was in complete disarray. The organization of peasants and workers would prove unable to withstand either British repression or the Zionist assault that would follow.

Land, Labor, and Palestinian Exclusion

Peasants made up nearly three-fourths of the Arab population of Palestine, and included small landowners, tenants, and hired laborers on the estates of the elite.[185] Villagers emerged from the First World War devastated by the Ottoman's wartime extraction of resources and conscripts. Under the British mandate they would experience further pauperization as a result of the combined effect of British land laws and taxation, and Zionist land purchases.[186] The registration of land under the Ottoman Land Code of 1858—introduced in order to raise revenue for the debt-ridden Empire—stimulated the transformation of state land *(miri)* into individual ownership *(mulk)* and the erosion of peasants' rights of access to communal land *(mushā),* giving rise to a new class of large landowners.[187] In order to escape taxation and conscription, peasants often deliberately refrained from registering land that had been cultivated by their families for generations or registered it in the name of the local *sheikh* or powerful landowner-patron.[188] Landlessness was exacerbated further by the colonial state's more efficient collection of taxes, increasing peasant indebtedness and eventually forcing small owner-cultivators to sell the parcels in their possession.[189] There was little hope of their purchasing back the land as prices skyrocketed with the increased demand that accompanied Jewish immigration.[190] Zionists could pay, and two segments of Arabs, often one and the same—money lenders and landowners—benefited. By 1930, combined with inheritance practices that reduced the viability of land in their possession, 30.7 percent of rural families were landless, and more than an additional one-third of peasants owned less than the minimum required for subsistence.[191] The average size of Palestinian holdings decreased steadily from 75 *dunums* in 1930 to 45.3 *dunums* in 1936.[192]

Dispossessed peasants migrated to the cities in search of employment, where they confronted limited Palestinian industry and Jewish exclusivity in the more advanced Jewish industrial sector. Competition from the more developed British and Jewish enterprises, European imports, and the granting of economic concessions to Jews rather than to Arabs[193] impeded the development of Arab industry, the Palestinian bourgeoisie,[194] and a Palestinian proletariat.[195] As a result, Palestinian migrants were, for the most part, relegated to a class of menial workers and day laborers. Some fortunate enough to enjoy village-based connections with urban notable families did secure employment in the public sector in construction, public utilities, and on the railroads and ports. In the public sector, however, Arab workers confronted a government policy of "civilized labor," which granted Jewish workers wages that exceeded those of non-Jews.[196]

Jewish industry and employment expanded with immigration. The various waves of immigrants, however, had a differential impact on the development of the *yishuv*—the Jewish community in Palestine—and on the indigenous population. As noted by Khalidi, the "pragmatic and unideological settlers" of the first wave of immigrants (1882–1904) contributed to "disappropriating [Palestinian peasants] but in most cases not fully dispossessing them," and thus behaved similarly to Arab landowners in that there was the possibility of peasants leasing back some land or obtaining work on it.[197] It was a markedly different situation that followed the second wave of immigrants (1904–14) who were ideologically committed to the "conquest of labor" and intent on excluding native labor.[198] This policy gained impetus with the socialist Zionists of the third wave (1919–22)—the future early leaders of Israel—who would achieve the goal of "Hebrew labor only." A fourth wave of immigrants (1930s), induced by the Nazis' rise to power in Germany, brought immigrants who infused enormous amounts of capital into the Zionist project, thereby substantially expanding the absorptive capacity of the Jewish sector.[199] Despite struggles between proponents of varying strands of Zionism, Labor Zionists succeeded in asserting their hegemony over the settler project and their vision of an exclusively Jewish entity. Although the extent to which the two economies were indeed separate is debated—given that, through taxation and discriminatory policies that favored Jews, the colonial state was implicated in the transfer of surplus from the Arab to the Jewish sector[200]—the Zionist leadership was clearly intent on the exclusion of the indigenous population from the Jewish state they envisioned. The only notable challenge to this vision within the Jewish community came from the anti-Zionist communists.

In 1922, the Palestine Communist Party (PCP) was formed out of the remnants of Jewish organizations decimated by British deportation of leftists. One year later, at the PCP's Second Congress, the Party adopted a position of support for the Arab national movement as a movement opposed to British imperialism, and denounced Zionism as a movement of the Jewish bourgeoisie allied to British imperialism.[201] The PCP's anti-Zionist program gained the Party membership in the Comintern the following year even though there were no Arab members. "Arabization" of the Party demanded by the Comintern was not resisted, however, coinciding as it did with the expulsion of the PCP's workers' wing from the Histadrut on charges of subversion, thereby effectively closing off the Party's most significant access to Jewish workers.[202]

It was no small task for Jewish communists to place themselves in opposition to the mainstream of the Jewish labor movement. Palestinian wage workers were a small segment of the country's working class, and colonial stunting of Arab industry, coupled with Jewish exclusivity in the larger and more advanced Jewish industries, meant that they would remain so. The PCP's anti-Zionism would alienate the majority of Jewish workers at a time when the Jewish working class was making important strides in the struggle against Jewish capital. Moreover, Jewish workers demonstrated a highly developed class consciousness, were organizationally strong, and were steeped in socialist ideology developed in their countries of origin. One indication of their relative strength was the ideological dominance of a "socialist-Zionism" or "proletarian-Zionism" in the Zionist movement as it began to evolve in Palestine.[203]

Committed to the anticolonial struggle, the PCP would become the first organization to strive to cross the sectarian divide. The Party's support for peasant resistance to evictions would be lauded by Arabs and denounced by Zionists.[204] However, the Party soon found that it could not work with the conservative elite leaders of the national movement.[205] In 1928, the PCP was released from this mission when the Comintern's policy shift required the Communist movements to assert their political independence from the bourgeois nationalist movements with which they had previously allied.[206] Now the PCP denounced the Arab Executive as reactionary and Palestinian notable families as sell-outs to British imperialism.[207] In the years to follow, the Party splintered repeatedly as communists struggled over positions on the Palestinian national movement, the Zionist-dominated Jewish labor movement, and the relationship between the two communities in Palestine. In 1944, the younger Arab members broke away to form an Arab communist party—the National Liberation League (NLL).

The NLL retained its links with Jewish communists and called on the Palestinian national movement to cooperate with non-Zionist Jews and recognize Jews as a national minority. It would build a base of support among intellectuals and workers but would not have enough time to consolidate, emerging as it did only four years before the partition of Palestine.[208] More important, as Beinin notes, communists' efforts among Arabs suffered from the close association of socialism with Zionism under Labor Zionists's hegemony.[209] The weakness of the NLL, however, was also due to the weakness of the Arab working class itself.

Palestinian attempts to organize trade unions began in 1923 among railway workers in Haifa where Arab workers were concentrated. Previously, workers relied on traditional channels and the intercession of notables or "personalities" (*shakhsiyat*) to resolve labor disputes; means that were hopelessly ineffective with British and Jewish employers.[210] This, coupled with their banning from the Histadrut, compelled Arab workers to form new organizations.[211] Within two years the first true trade union was established— the Palestinian Arab Workers' Society (PAWS)—whose earliest actions were directed at Arab industrialists.[212] In addition to obstacles erected by Arab employers, Arab workers also had to contend with the colonial government's nonrecognition of Arab unions and Histadrut machinations throughout this period.[213]

Arab union leaders were keenly aware of workers' marginality in the national movement, noting that none of the various Arab conferences, convened to address the national question in the late 1920s, addressed their plight.[214] Following the first Arab Workers' Conference in 1930, new unions appeared and disappeared in rapid succession, lacking essential experience, funds, and cadres.[215] Racked by internal dissent over communist involvement and highly politicized as rival political groupings sought to use the unions to expand their political influence, workers' grievances were neglected.[216] Union membership would expand, however, during the 1936 general strike as unions carried the strike across economic sectors.[217] But unemployment during the Great Revolt thinned the ranks of workers and union membership as workers turned their concentration to the political battles engulfing the country.[218] Eventually, Arab unions would suffer the fate of the national movement as a whole as British repression, which included the incarceration of union leaders, brought the Great Revolt to a halt in 1939.[219] The Second World War, however, found the colonial government granting permission for new industrial activity, expanding transportation lines, and setting up military camps, all of which generated substantial employment opportunities.[220] By 1946, urban Palestinian workers, estimated at 130,000, were employed in workshops, industry, construction, railways, ports, and public utilities. Approximately 20 percent were organized.[221]

Union organizing experienced renewed vigor with the emergence of the PCP as a legal organization in 1942. While the PCP worked through the PAWS, dissident members of the PCP formed the rival Federation of Arab Trade Unions and Labor Societies (FATULS). As Hiltermann explains, the communist FATULS adhered to a "workerist" line and to the attainment of socialism as the means of freeing Palestine from the imperialist stranglehold, while the more nationalist and social-democratic PAWS directed its energies toward redressing the inequality between Arab and Jewish workers.[222] These reflected the divergent understandings of what constituted the primary threat: imperialism or Zionism.

The relationship between the Arab labor movement and the traditional leadership of the national movement was far from harmonious, due in large measure to the latter's undemocratic character and persistent attempts to bring unions under their control. Although the working class managed to preserve some autonomy from the main factions of the traditional leadership, union activity suffered as a result of the traditional leaders' meddling, including the assassination of two union leaders.[223] Squeezed by a hostile national leadership on one side and the powerful Histadrut on the other, the nascent Palestinian labor movement had little hope of becoming a significant force within the national movement anytime soon.[224]

At the close of the Second World War, the two communities were on the threshold of a confrontation. Palestinians had been incapacitated by the repression of the 1930s. The only political organization in existence was the NLL. From his base in Lebanon, Haj Amin al-Husseini attempted to lead. But his support for Germany during the war alienated those leaders who remained in Palestine.[225] New political formations were emerging, including a reconstituted AHC in 1946, but they did not have sufficient time to coalesce.

After a number of attempts to reconcile their conflicting promises and the two communities' competing demands, the British were induced to abandon the predicament they had created and turned the matter over to the UN. In April 1947, the UN recommended partition. Jews, less than one-third of the population and in possession of approximately 7 percent of the land, were granted 5,500 square miles of the territory; Arabs were to retain only 4,500 square miles; Jerusalem was to be administered internationally.[226] The Arabs of Palestine rejected the plan outright, hoping to prevent its implementation; Zionists accepted it, making preparations to extend the boundaries of the portion allotted for a Jewish state.

In 1947, on the eve of the partition of Palestine, a large segment of the Palestinian leadership—those who had escaped exile by the British—and prosperous and middle-class Palestinians (estimated at 30,000) began to leave the country in anticipation of the events.[227] Palestinian resistance organizations had yet to recover from the blow of the 1930s, peasant communities remained divided and isolated from each other, and the urban workers remained organizationally weak. Arab armies would enter Palestine in 1947 but they would fail to thwart the more numerous and better equipped and trained Jewish forces.[228] Deprived of leadership and organization, Palestinian communities also had to contend with the collapse of services and institutions that had been under British control, while Jewish communities benefited from the self-sufficiency they had been permitted to develop.[229] The poorly armed and disorganized Palestinian communities disintegrated under the Zionist assault. In May 1948, the day the British forces evacuated Palestine, the state of Israel was proclaimed, encompassing 77 percent of the area of Palestine.[230] Eighty-five percent of the Palestinian population inside the territories captured by the Zionists was exiled by force of war or, that failing, by force directly.[231]

Explaining Failure

A reluctant Palestinian leadership was thrust onto a national movement whose mass base was by far more radical. The traditional leaders were considerably more at ease with pulling patronage strings from their urban bases than leading a national movement of the disinherited. Certainly, they had no conception of or interest in mass mobilization or organization. In fact, they were fearful of peasant and worker organizations that could potentially target them. Significantly, neither the general strike of 1936 nor the Great Revolt of 1936–39 were initiated by the elite leaders.[232] Nevertheless, recognizing what was at stake, the notables lost no time in asserting their leadership over the rebellion by forming the AHC, thereby bringing together rival factions of the notable elite. Their cooperation, however, was only temporary, and factionalism resurfaced to hamper a unified national response. Importantly, Muslim-Christian divisions were overcome, and the movement remained fundamentally a secular one, but clan and regional factionalization were not transcended because kinship and clan remained the basis of social organization, and clan alignments prevailed as the principle mode of political organization, to the detriment of the national movement.

The continued salience of kinship and clan in Palestinian social organization reflected the remarkable extent to which Palestinian society remained intact. The limited interpenetration of the settler and indigenous economies meant that to a significant extent, the latter had been spared the degenerative economic effects of Zionist colonization. This was, of course, with the exception of peasants dispossessed of their land. The indigenous economy and social relations remained largely coherent and self-reproducing throughout most of this phase of the Palestinian national movement, even as it remained subordinate to the more advanced Jewish sector as it was evolving in Palestine. It is important to note that Jewish settlers did not introduce capitalism to Palestine; they merely had the capital, technology, skills, and colonial government support that enabled them to capitalize on its prior existence. Thus, with the direct support of an imperial power, land could be purchased, industries established, and jobs monopolized without having to resort to arms—at least in the initial phase of conquest.

The preservation of traditional Palestinian social relations and organization explains why the mass of the population—the peasants—accepted the urban elite as their leaders. There had been a history of challenge to the notable leaders, intensified further as members of the Palestinian landed elite became implicated in land sales to Jews. And significantly, those peasants evicted from land and freed from dependence on the landed elite looked less and less to the notables for leadership. The mass of the peasantry, however, remained dependent on the urban-based elite as sharecroppers, laborers, or as debtors; urban migrants among them turned to the elite for access to state-sector jobs.[233] Important segments of the middle class too, in many cases the offspring of the notables or related by marriage, remained linked to and dependent on notable patronage for access to coveted posts within the mandate bureaucracy. While radical middle-class nationalists eventually emerged in this period to challenge the elite's domination of the national movement, the middle class remained too weak to wrest control from the elite.

Yet a new social force of landless peasants had formed—one that did not wait for traditional leaders to initiate resistance to the Zionist settlers. Although "depeasantized," their transformation into an urban proletariat remained incomplete due to the underdeveloped state of Arab industry and exclusion from Jewish-dominated industrial development in the country,[234] as well as continued access to land through kinship in their villages of origin.[235] What did occur was in the realm of government projects that did not involve leverage within the Zionist settler project. Thus, although a new social force was being created, it lacked leverage. Indeed, while peasants and migrant workers could wreak havoc through rioting, they lacked leverage with which to force either the British or the Zionists into aborting their colonization designs. What they had was the means to pressure their traditional leaders into increasingly more militant stands, eventually forcing members of the notable elite to compete with each other in espousing the most militant anti-British and anti-Zionist rhetoric, even while behind the scenes many cooperated with the British.

British success in manipulating the early leaders was due in part to the leaders' inability to conceive that Britain could give their country away. Naive about the relationship between British imperialism and the Zionist movement, they imagined that they could persuade Britain to abandon its support for Jewish colonization of Palestine. They may have been shrewd patrons but they were not politicians. Ever intent on a solution from above, to avoid radicalization of the mass base below, the early leaders were easily duped by British concessions meant only to secure their cooperation until a particular wave of unrest had passed. The problem, ultimately, was the elite's ambivalence regarding British imperialism, armed and organized peasants, and non-Zionist Jews. The notable elite leaned toward an accord, and many even toward a partnership with British imperialism; they desired a pacified peasantry[236] and rejected cooperation with non-Zionist Jews because of their left politics. These tendencies hampered any possibility of whatever success was attainable under the existing conditions.

Alternatives to the notable-led and factionalized political bodies did emerge in this period: the Independence Party, the NLL, trade unions, and rebel groupings, among others. But these organizations remained either marginal to the mainstream of the national movement or unable to compete with the clan-dominated politics, thereby attesting further to the strength and continued viability of traditional relations.

By the 1940s, as attention focused on developments in Palestine, the role of non-Palestinian Arabs outside of Palestine became more pronounced.[237] Initially, Palestinians aspired to incorporation within a larger Arab entity. The elimination of this option forced Palestinians to turn inward to Palestine while continuing to maintain contacts with the region's peoples and leaders. Palestinians were determined to retain Palestine as an Arab— though not specifically Muslim—entity integrated within the region. At the level of the elite, Arab leaders were actively involved in Palestine's notable-dominated politics, extending support to one or the other of the factions. However, even at the level of the mass base, the role of non-Palestinian Arabs in the national movement attests to the sense of pan-Arab identification that existed. Two of the most militant and popular leaders—al-Qassam and Qawuqji—were non-Palestinian Arabs. But while Palestinians sought and gained some security from their relationship to the larger entity, that relationship was not unproblematic. The rulers of the newly created states were themselves entangled with the imperialist powers and rapidly developing vested interests in the newly established entities with ambitions beyond.[238] With the dismemberment of Palestine, the Arab dimension would assume even greater significance in subsequent phases of the Palestinian national movement.

Failure of Elite-Led Movements

The formative phase of the national movements in South Africa and Palestine was dominated by the respective elites of the indigenous populations—the "natural" leaders of the communities who relied on traditionally recognized bases of authority. The political organizations established by the elites were cautious and nonconfrontational in both cases. Both believed that, as representatives of the majority populations, they could successfully plead their peoples' cases to the new rulers. Most accounts emphasize the elites' ideological predispositions to account for the patience and cooperation they displayed and their faith in British liberalism. There were, however, better explanations for their irresolute opposition to the ruling powers for much of this phase.

The elites enjoyed privileges that they were reluctant to risk in confrontations with the state. Chiefs were becoming increasingly dependent on the state for their survival, while middle-class Africans were reluctant to jeopardize the franchise, urban residence, and free-hold rights that distinguished them from the mass of Africans. In Palestine, posts in the mandate administration reinforced the elite's authority through the patronage that their access to the government enabled them to dispense. A second factor that would mitigate a confrontational approach to the ruling powers was the apparent conflicts and contradictions between Britain—the imperial power—and the nationalist settlers—Afrikaners and Jews. Both elites believed that through cooperation with the British and, in South Africa, through cooperation with English-speaking liberals among the whites, they would secure British support for the indigenous populations' rights that were threatened by the more nationalist settlers. But perhaps the most significant factor that accounts for their cooperation was their desire to avert more radical approaches by the populace that might either spill over to internal challenges to the elites' authority or threaten their access to the state.

Indeed, the elites were caught in a number of contradictions. They were intent on proving to the ruling powers that they could be trusted to protect their interests, while they claimed to be acting as pressure groups on those very powers. In addition, they were intent on preserving traditional social relations and bases of authority, while those were responsible for delaying the emergence of potentially more effective bases of resistance. The most fundamental contradiction was that while the elites objectively served as instruments of control over the indigenous populations, they believed they could use their access to the state in the service of the national movement that sought to free itself from that very control. The indigenous elites failed to resolve these contradictory positions.

The elite-led movements suffered from their reliance on traditional bases of organization and identification that were inherently fragmented, centralized, conservative, and lacked leverage within the settler society. Although making strides in terms of African and Arab "unity" that traversed linguistic and sectarian lines, respectively, for the most part this was achieved only at the level of the elites. Resolute attempts by the elite-led national organizations to organize and mobilize workers and peasants were limited in both cases. Organizational efforts by the African leaders took a backseat to the strategy of appeals, deputations, and reliance on white liberals in government circles; paid membership in the ANC was sufficient. The landed Palestinian elite feared mass mobilization more directly, particularly that influenced by radical ideologies. Unable to restrain their followers, however, the elite leaders were forced into adopting militant stands for which they were unprepared. Although the significance of traditional elites is their promise to restrain their followers, this says nothing about their actual ability to deliver on that promise to the ruling powers. Their inclinations and interests are toward restraint, but they may be forced to act. The Palestinian experience demonstrates that when elite leaders are in fact forced to act, their ambivalence and class resources render them incapable of mounting an effective challenge to settler-colonial projects. Indeed, at every turn Palestinian leaders sought to assert their control over the mass actions that did erupt, and did so to the detriment of the movement.

New social forces were in the making. These remained relatively weak, however, given that they were in a very real sense the victims of colonialism: African migrant laborers and the dispossessed Palestinian peasantry. Moreover, because these new social forces continued to depend on their village-based communities for their survival, they were not yet fully emancipated from the traditional bases of social organization or identification that they carried into resistance efforts in the new settings. However reduced, their continued dependence permitted the tribal African elite and the landed Palestinian elite to continue to exert authority over these segments.

Nevertheless, while traditional relations remained salient, both elites saw their authority eroding as a result of political and economic dynamics. The evident inability of the elites to secure meaningful gains for the population, whose interests they purportedly represented, reduced their authority. Economic dynamics reinforced this process; as elite-controlled resources, on which the population depended, eroded, so too the dependence of the mass of the population on traditional leaders. These dynamics, however, were not uniform in the two cases, reflecting the differential impact of inclusion and exclusion of indigenous labor in the settler projects.

The economic base of the African reserves was deteriorating rapidly as a result of the interpenetration of the colonial and indigenous economies. Importantly, Africans had already been dispossessed, and the settlers already a reality for hundreds of years. White settlers conquered first militarily, then economically through capitalist penetration of the indigenous societies and the incorporation of indigenous labor. Thus began the process of dissolution of indigenous tribal social relations. As the ability of African migrant workers' families to secure subsistence at home diminished, the new social force of migrant workers would increasingly look elsewhere for survival and eventually for leadership.

In Palestine, too, peasants rendered landless by eviction and economic processes became less dependent on the landed elite. But while segments of Palestinian peasants were being freed from such dependence, their full proletarianization was largely obviated by their exclusion from the settler economy—the locus of the country's rapidly expanding industries. The size and recentness of the settler society and continued Palestinian ownership of the majority of the land of Palestine no doubt reinforced Palestinians' commitment to existing social relations. These factors, coupled with exclusion and limited Arab industrial growth, meant that the process of transformation of Palestinian peasants remained incomplete: peasants' continued access to at least some land through kinship, their retention of homes in the villages, and preservation of family ties further delayed the process. Nevertheless, like their counterparts in South Africa, those segments outside the sphere of dependence on the urban-based notables began to look elsewhere for leadership.

Incidents of confrontation and resistance outside the control of the elite erupted continuously throughout this phase of both national movements. Numerous organizations formed as alternatives to the elite-led movement organizations, some by more radical elements of the middle classes, others by workers, peasants, religious leaders, communities, and others. The relationship between efforts that emerged outside the control of the elites and the political organizations of the elites was not harmonious. The elites jealously guarded their leadership of the national movements from competitors. The persistence of unbridled conflicts over cooperation, coordination, and goals enfeebled both national movements.

Of particular significance was the emergence in both cases of communist parties that presented ideological challenges to the national leaders and crossed the racial and sectarian divides in practice. These began as white and Jewish organizations that were critical of the national movements, but the parties were "Africanized" and "Arabized," eventually joining and/or expressing support for them. The parties' anti-imperialism and their championing of workers' struggles threatened the conservative elites who sought an accord with British imperialism and, in the Palestinian case, a docile working class. In both cases, communists would make invaluable contributions to trade union organization.

As faith in the elites began to give way, new, more radical, middle-class elements appeared to challenge the leaders of the national movements. At this point, however, they were in the process of forming their challenges to the elite. The relative weakness of the traditional African elite compared to its Palestinian counterpart had enabled the African middle class to assert itself to a far greater extent in this phase than the Palestinian middle class had succeeded in doing. In both cases, however, developments that would usher in a new phase of resistance would bring new middle-class leaders to the fore as both populations confronted dramatic evidence of the failure of their elites to protect them.

4

Middle-Class Hegemony and the Containment of Class, 1940s to 1970s

In 1948, both Africans and Palestinians confronted dramatic evidence of the failure of their national movements to thwart their opponents' objectives and the consequences of their differential inclusion/exclusion. The introduction of apartheid in 1948 reflected whites' determination to preserve their access to cheap black labor, that is, inclusion, while reinforcing the political and social exclusion of blacks from "white South Africa." The establishment of the state of Israel in 1948 was accompanied by the expulsion of Palestinians, reflecting the dispensability of Palestinian labor to the Zionist settler project and the goal of colonizing the land while excluding the people.

In South Africa, inclusion would entail increasing black dependence on the white-dominated economy, growing dependence of that economy on black labor, and the erosion of traditional African social relations. In Palestine, exclusion would involve the complete separation of the Israeli and, with the exception of a small community, Palestinian economies and societies; the dispersal of the Palestinian population throughout the region; and the preservation of Palestinian social relations in what remained of Palestine outside Israeli control in the West Bank and Gaza Strip.

Failing to protect their communities, the indigenous elites that had led the national movements in their formative phase would be discredited and for the most part abandoned. The mass of the African and Palestinian populations had yet to recover from the blow dealt to them at the end of the previous phase. Significant segments of African urban residents would be forcibly resettled in the impoverished reserves now reconstituted as "homelands," highlighting the precariousness of their residential rights within

South Africa. The majority of Palestinians from what became Israel were now refugees scattered across the West Bank, Gaza Strip, and neighboring Arab states and dependent on UN assistance. Members of the middle classes, who, in the early phase of resistance, had cooperated with their respective elites, would seek alternative courses of action. Both middle classes were radicalized by conditions that they now shared with the mass of their populations: middle-class Africans by the elimination of privileges that had distinguished them from the majority of Africans, and middle-class Palestinians by their statelessness. In both cases, members of the African and Palestinian middle classes would displace the elites in the leadership of the national movements and usher in a new phase of resistance.

Middle Classes, Organization and Resistance

With the failure of elite leadership, the opportunity for new contenders arises. Under conditions of settler colonialism, however, the possibility that an indigenous national bourgeoisie will be capable of asserting itself is remote. The economics of settler capitalism and the nationalism of settlers obstruct the rise and/or viability of an indigenous bourgeoisie, even as compradors. The colonial stunting of this class means that working classes within the indigenous economy remain concomitantly weak. Instead, members of the fragmented and heterogeneous middle classes are the most likely to displace elites as leaders of national liberation movements that survive their formative phase.

Members of the middle class who cooperated with or tolerated the elite leaders during the previous phase of the national movement are now free to press forward in new directions. Popular disillusionment with the defeated leaders renders followers amenable to alternatives. Their receptivity is reinforced by the erosion of the economic underpinnings of elite-dominated social relations—an inevitable consequence of their defeat and their opponents' gains—which frees other classes from dependence on the elite, whether that independence is sought or not. No longer as beholden to the elites or dependent on elite-controlled resources, middle classes and working classes may now pursue alternative approaches toward securing their national rights.

Although the elites take pains to demonstrate their capacity to restrain their people, middle-class leaders must show that they can activate them if they are to be taken seriously by their opponents. The inclination is to seek accommodation from above, but that being blocked, they turn to organize below. Mobilizing, activating, and leading organized resistance is the middle-class leaders' contribution to national liberation movements. To that end, they bring to bear class resources of various kinds: knowledge and expertise in the realms of organization, administration, propaganda, and law, among other things. Although not as directly threatened as elites by the potential disruption to social relations accompanying mass mobilization, they too will seek to retain control from above of the "masses" they activate below.

Yet, given that indigenous subordinate classes (workers and peasants) are not dependent on middle-class resources as a matter of survival, their acceptance of new leaders is less certain than it had been for the elites. Broadly conceived, there are two important distinctions within the middle class in dominated societies: self-employed (i.e., own means of production, control own labor, involved in individual production) and employees (i.e., own skills, do not control own labor time, involved in social production). While by virtue of the ownership of the means of production those who are self-employed enjoy greater freedom from both settlers and indigenous elites than employees, neither stratum employs others. In other words, middle classes may possess assets of value to the dominated population, but they do not control resources upon which other indigenous classes depend for their existence. Thus, in contrast to indigenous elites who are able to exercise their authority through their control over resources vital to other classes (usually land), middle-class leaders require organizational or institutional extensions through which to first wield their influence and then exercise their hegemony. They do this through political organizations that tout democracy and accountability as the basis of their claim to leadership of the entire nation. First and foremost that means laying claim to leadership of the popular sectors, their ticket to leverage.

In contexts of settler colonialism, indigenous middle classes lack leverage, even when inclusion of indigenous labor prevails. Their only significance to the settler-dominated society in the realm of production is a derivative or secondary one: members of the indigenous middle classes may function as agents of control (i.e., administering, supervising, policing). Under inclusion, the development of middle classes is constricted by the settlers' monopoly over administrative and professional occupations. Indeed, when the dominant group is able to maintain control over the indigenous population, the indigenous middle class becomes dispensable. Settlers will seek to co-opt segments of the indigenous middle class only when an effective challenge has formed. In seeking to restore order, they first turn to those segments that remained aloof from the national movement. Eventually, however, they may be forced to deal with those who have demonstrated an ability to deliver control over the challenge itself: the very goal of the movement's leaders.

The middle class, however, cannot pose a challenge on its own in either contexts of inclusion or exclusion of indigenous labor. As a class, it is incapable of disrupting the normal functioning of the settler society to an extent sufficient to induce their opponents into meaningful concessions. And, as noted, in contexts of settler colonialism characterized by inclusion, the expansion of this segment of the middle class is inhibited by the state's discriminatory policies favoring the settler community. Indeed, under conditions of inclusion, leverage derived from the relationship between the dominant and dominated exists as a potential resource in resistance, while the accumulation of assets is impeded. Exclusion, however, which entails relative freedom for the dominated from the dominant group, permits the accumulation of assets as a resource while precluding leverage. Therefore, accompanying inclusionary settler colonialism is a weak indigenous middle class, while exclusionary settler colonialism leaves the possibility of a strong middle class arising beyond the settlers' control; each entails implications for resistance.

Yet, in both cases, the middle class remains at a disadvantage in terms of leverage within the settler-dominated society as well as in terms of a class-based means of asserting its influence within the indigenous population. As such, members of indigenous middle classes who aspire to leadership of a national movement must make themselves relevant in both societies: theirs and their opponent's. They endeavor to accomplish both through political organizations under their hegemony.

South Africa, 1949 to Early 1970s

In 1948, the NP was narrowly elected by an alliance of classes that included agricultural capital, white workers, the Afrikaner petty bourgeoisie, and a small class of aspiring Afrikaner capitalists in finance, commerce, and manufacturing.[1] Each of these classes had their particular grievance with the previous ruling party, the United Party (UP), which represented the interests of British-dominated monopoly capital. During the economic expansion that accompanied the war years, the UP oversaw the relaxation of job color bars and influx controls to compensate for labor shortages in the rapidly expanding industrial sector.[2] Accompanying these developments was heightened militance among black workers. The UP supported limited recognition of black trade unions to stem such militance. These and other policies angered white farmers who were suffering labor shortages and provoked white workers who were unwilling to tolerate any erosion of the occupational color bars.[3] Elements of the Afrikaner petty bourgeoisie resented competition posed by Indians in particular.[4] These classes, together with the small class of Afrikaner capitalists left out by UP policies that favored monopoly capital, would turn to the NP. The NP consolidated its class alliance through its antimonopoly rhetoric, commitment to improving the material welfare and political power of Afrikaners, commitment to the separation of the races, and refusal to accommodate the black labor movement.[5] An ideology of Afrikaner nationalism and a program of apartheid cemented the class alliance. As the government demonstrated its ability to control labor, even industrialists abandoned their earlier calls for concessions to black workers to curb their growing militance.[6]

Apartheid policies were intended to reconcile competing demands for indigenous labor while redressing the increasingly apparent contradictions of economic inclusion in its particular form of migrant labor: ever growing dependence on a labor source that was becoming progressively less profitable as a combined result of workers' resistance and the diminishing capacity of the reserves to supplement wages.[7] Thus, apartheid legislation was aimed at regulating the supply of African labor and keeping it cheap by impeding Africans' ability to organize.[8] For African workers, inclusion under apartheid would mean intensified exploitation, accompanied by a more determined policy of political and social exclusion. Other black classes were also targeted as the white petty bourgeoisie resolved to eliminate its competition. Through the blanket assault on African rights irrespective of their class, as well as on Indians and coloreds, apartheid would create the potential for new political alignments within the oppressed sectors of the population.

The African middle class's response to the ascendence of Afrikaner nationalists and the class alliance that brought them to power would be to forge a cross-racial alliance with their counterparts among other black groups and white democrats and to strengthen the political organization's links with the people. Ironically, the policies of "apart-ness"—the political and social separation of blacks and whites as well as blacks from each other—would form the basis of unity among Africans and beyond.

"Africanism" and Passive Resistance, 1949 to 1960

The 1940s witnessed the first steps in the transformation of the ANC from an elite political pressure group into a "mass national liberation movement."[9] This transformation has been attributed to the growth and militance of the black labor movement during the Second World War, which had demonstrated new potentials for resistance, and the emergence of young militant African nationalists who recognized the failure of the old methods.[10] However, only with the NP's electoral victory and the institutionalization of apartheid would the call for more militant action by new leaders be adopted. Finding that appeals to the white minority rulers had accomplished nothing, the ANC would "[turn] consciously to the masses to stimulate political action and to arouse their fighting spirit," thus representing "a sortie from a politics of conformity and persuasion to a politics of confrontation."[11]

The impetus behind the ANC's radicalization came from two sources. First, as noted, the evident failure of reliance on petitions, deputations, and protests to redress African grievances bolstered those calling for more direct action. The second impetus was the more concerted assault on African middle-class privileges and obstacles erected by apartheid to middle-class advancement. In the search for resources and allies, the ANC would turn toward the mass of dispossessed Africans, the middle-class-led political organizations of Indians and coloreds, and communists. The state's policies pushed the ANC—even if reluctantly—in these directions. The road to "unity in struggle," however, was arduous.

Inclusion and Apartheid "Social Engineering"

Government and business concurred that the political implications of the economic inclusion of African workers would have to be controlled. Apartheid was to remedy the contradictions created by the economic inclusion of African workers without their integration. In the process, apartheid social engineering would penetrate every sphere of the black population's lives.

Beginning with the assault on remnants of integration, the 1950 Population Registration Act, the 1950 Group Areas Act, and the 1954 Black Resettlement Act together sanctioned residential segregation based on color. Nonwhites were forcibly removed to racially designated alternative sites at a distance from the "white cities." Pass laws were expanded under the Natives Act of 1952 and empowered local authorities to remove "surplus" Africans. The 1951 Bantu Authorities Act established the entities—eventually named "Bantu homelands"—that would receive the "surplus" population: unemployed men and women, the elderly, and children who, from capital's perspective, were no more than a superfluous burden that fueled workers' demands for higher wages.[12] To circumvent those who might resist resettlement, influx controls were tightened through the Natives Laws Amendment Act of 1952 and the Native (Urban Areas) Amendment Act of 1955, which tied African urban residential rights even within African urban "locations" or "townships" to employers' needs, controlled through labor bureaus.

The African population destined for the homelands or "bantustans" confronted yet another sort of segregation. Apartheid ideologues decreed the segmentation of the indigenous population into ten distinct "nations," each of which, they would eventually argue, warranted a "homeland." Arbitrarily created on less than 13.7 percent of South Africa's land area, the patchwork of geographically and ethnically fragmented bantustans would become the cornerstone of the apartheid strategy of "separate development": controlled economic inclusion combined with social and political exclusion of Africans.[13] The homeland scheme evolved from a series of hastily conceived measures. The impetus for its evolution was the apparent failure of the system of migrant labor to maximize the profitability of the inclusion of African workers through access to resources in the subordinate sector of the South African economy.[14] The diminishing product to which workers could have access not only rendered the migrant labor system less profitable but also provoked discontent. Homeland schemes were envisioned to remedy both.

The 1959 Promotion of Bantu Self Government Act took the "retribalization" project begun in 1951 further, declaring tribal authority as the basis of rule in the territories reserved for Africans. The goal of preserving the precapitalist economy in the rural territories necessitated the preservation of the associated relations of production, hence the "cultural, ethnic, national, and racial" character of the government's policies.[15] In the process, the state endeavored to cultivate collaborators among the traditional elite for its policy of indirect rule over the African population relegated to the bantustans. Traditional leaders were offered a stake in apartheid through the preservation and extension of their traditional roles, institutions, and authority within the confines of the ethnic creations. Entrusted with administrative and social control functions, rebellious chiefs were dismissed and replaced by compliant ones or lesser headmen. Tribal authorities thus became agents of the state in policing and pacifying capital's reserve army of labor. The combination of state manipulation of the chieftaincy and the eroding viability of the subsistence economy—forced to provide for a growing population on a fixed area of the country's most marginal land—undermined the authority of the traditional elite and the population's access to and dependence on indigenously generated resources.

These developments did not go on unresisted. Homeland residents opposed the chiefs who betrayed their traditional obligations to protect and serve their communities. Rural revolts in Sekhukhuneland (1958), Zululand (1959), and most notably in Pondoland (1960), among others, would force the state to reassess its bantustan strategy.[16] But the homelands' impoverished populations, geographically distant from the centers of economic and state power and poorly organized, were no match for the state. "Bantustanization" would proceed and assume even greater import at a later stage.

In the urban townships, residents actively resisted their forced resettlement. The prospects of what was tantamount to banishment to a homeland,

and the ever dwindling rural resources that were no longer sufficient to sup-plement migrant workers' wages, fueled discontent. Forced to make do with increasingly inadequate wages, workers had no recourse but to seek their survival requirements within the urban economy. Additional apartheid legis-lation, however, targeted the organizational capacity of urban African work-ers. The 1950 Suppression of Communism Act was used to cripple existing nonracial and black trade unions by removing many of its key leaders.[17] The 1953 Native Labour Settlement of Disputes Act outlawed strikes by African workers.[18] The 1956 Amendment to the Industrial Conciliation Act pro-scribed the registration of new "mixed" (nonracial) trade unions and at-tempted to impose segregated structures within existing nonracial unions and executive committees composed only of whites.[19] The Act further pro-hibited unions from political affiliation.[20] Accompanying these measures was the extension of the job color bar to industry that reserved skilled jobs for whites. Black workers responded with renewed militance and intensified strike activity.[21]

Middle-class Africans would lose even the nominal concessions they se-cured from the previous government.[22] Blacks were now prohibited from owning property or operating businesses within "white areas." This spelled the end for black businessmen and professionals who nurtured any illusions regarding marketplace competition with whites as the road to their full incorporation into the country's economic life at all levels. Africans and Indians—many prosperous traders particularly among the latter—were now confined to conducting business in the townships. Exemptions from the onerous pass and curfew laws earlier enjoyed by middle-class Africans were revoked. Most avenues for black advancement were now blocked by the reservation of jobs for whites under the 1956 Industrial Conciliation Act as the state pushed for "Afrikanerization" across sectors.[23] Moreover, blacks who aspired to upward mobility through education now encountered the 1953 Bantu Education Act and the 1957 Extension of University Education Act, which barred blacks from attending "white institutions." In the process, black education was to be underdeveloped through government appropria-tion of control over the liberal missionary institutions and introduction of programs consistent with its strategy of the "retribalization" of Africans.[24]

Entire communities resisted these and other measures that accompa-nied the onslaught of apartheid. In Sophiatown, where Africans had enjoyed freehold rights, residents actively fought their eviction and the breakup of their once-vibrant community (1953).[25] Cato Manor's black residents resist-ed their removal from the mixed African, Indian, and white community that had been established on Indian-owned land (1959).[26] Alexandra township residents organized the legendary bus boycotts to protest fare increases (1955–57).[27] And in the Eastern Cape and East Rand townships parents launched school boycotts following the government's assault on African education (1955).[28] These are only a few examples of the defiance that characterized black urban communities' responses to apartheid. Most, but not all, were efforts organized and initiated locally. The most notable national, issue-specific action was that launched by women who fought the extension of the pass laws to them (1955–56).

As the assault on communities swept the country, their members were caught up in defensive actions on many fronts simultaneously. The ANC would define its task as one of channeling efforts to achieve national objectives.

Mass Defiance and the African Middle Class

The elimination of the middle class's advantages, together with the corruption of traditional institutions, combined to force the middle-class leaders of the ANC to turn actively to the mass of the population. As Gerhart explains: "The more rigid the ceiling barring African mobility into the dominant society, and the more harsh the leveling process imposed . . . the more the recognition of an identity of interests between all strata of African society was bound to develop."[29] Although the specific nature of this "identity of interests" was neither self-evident nor inevitable (it was actively contested by the various strata represented in the organization), ANC leaders did, indeed, turn to the mass of the African population.

The ascendant leaders were African nationalists who came out of the ANC's Youth League (YL), formed in 1943. These were young, educated Africans from a more numerous middle class, who had established themselves professionally and who commanded respect among Africans for their skills and the positions they had attained.[30] They had been vocal critics of the leaders and tactics of the ANC in the previous phase. However, only with the conspicuous failure of earlier methods would they succeed in obtaining the organization's endorsement of their more militant approach.

In 1949, after fierce internal debates, the ANC adopted the Programme of Action in its quest to achieve "freedom from White domination" and "political independence" consistent with the African people's "right of self-determination."[31] This was no irredentist movement, however, and certainly not a movement that sought the seizure of state power. The program called merely for "the right of direct representation in all the governing bodies of the country—national, provincial and local," and the "abolition of all differential institutions or bodies specially created for Africans," which meant a boycott of the NRCs, the source of so much contention earlier.[32] The "weapons" to be employed were "immediate and active boycott, strike, civil disobedience, non-cooperation and such other means" required to achieve their aspirations.[33] The vagueness of the Programme of Action enabled the organization to accommodate the divergent degrees of militance that existed.[34] The new Executive was a mixture of old moderates, African nationalist Youth Leaguers, and communists.[35] Noncommunist ANC leaders ranged from the more conservative to the more militant and tended to share both an antipathy to communists as well as a distrust of other racial groups.[36]

With the radicalization of its leadership, the middle-class-led ANC began to look more seriously beyond its confines toward other African classes. Moreover, as many of the African middle class became unwilling to take the risks involved in the ANC's more confrontational approach, and as other Africans joined, the organization's composition began to change.[37] However, while more radical than their predecessors, ANC leaders continued to preach nonviolence and remained reformist in their aims, only now they turned to the masses to achieve them rather than continuing to rely on appeals to the white rulers.

The ANC sought to channel the various local struggles into more effective pressure on the central government through national campaigns. Guided by the Programme of Action, the ANC embarked on its new course, and declared as its first act a one-day national stoppage of work. Eventually, that day would be set for June 26, 1950, but at the time of its adoption, ANC conferees could not have foreseen that it would be conducted jointly with Indian and communist organizations. Indeed, by and large, ANC leaders, and particularly the Youth Leaguers among them, were proponents of African exclusivity in the struggle for liberation, suspecting Indians and communists of opportunism.[38] But events created conditions for new political alignments, as they would throughout the history of the movement. This was one example and represented the beginning of a process that would fundamentally alter the ANC's ideology and program.

On May 1, 1950, the Transvaal branch of the ANC, in which communists were heavily represented, and the CPSA organized a one-day suspension of work. Youth League leaders Oliver Tambo and Nelson Mandela actively opposed the action and the date's internationalist connotations and accused the CPSA of seeking to seize the initiative away from the ANC, which had already announced its intention to call for a national stoppage of work.[39] The event proceeded, however, and proved a success with more than half of all African workers in the Johannesburg area remaining home in response to the call.[40] A police assault resulted in numerous deaths, and a day of mourning followed, which would see an unprecedented accord between the YL and the CPSA. On May 14, the ANC and the YL met with the CPSA and the SAIC "in an atmosphere of cool mutual suspicion" to form a national coordinating committee for what would become the ANC's first national action in its history: a workers' "stay-away" set for June 26, 1950 to protest the Suppression of Communism Bill introduced in parliament, which was recognized as a blanket assault on political activity, and to mourn those killed on May 1.[41]

The jointly organized National Day of Protest was immensely successful as Africans and Indians throughout the major cities of the country participated en masse. The tremendous response by Indians was not lost on the ANC.[42] One month later, the ANC and SAIC formed a Joint Planning Council to prepare for peaceful campaigns of passive resistance. This would mark the beginning of joint, mass actions across racial groupings.

The Defiance Campaign of 1952 was the most successful of the ANC's nationally coordinated campaigns of mass action. Volunteers across the country were instructed to violate laws pertaining to curfews, passes, segregated facilities, and the like, and in so doing compel the authorities to arrest them. By inundating the prisons and courts beyond their capacity, the campaign was intended to demonstrate their ability to impair the functioning of the system, and, it was hoped, achieve the repeal of the oppressive laws.[43] The call for 10,000 volunteers produced more than 8,500.[44] Although repression and organizational problems put a halt to the campaign, the ANC had nevertheless succeeded in enlisting widespread participation, producing within a few months a massive increase in its dues-paying membership from 7,000 to 100,000, as well as the politicization of entire communities across the country.[45] Ironically, one indication of the success of the mobilization was that it contributed to the NP's ability to secure a solid electoral victory in 1953, running as it did on a promise that no repeat of the Defiance Campaigns would occur.[46]

With the experience of 1952–53 to draw on, the middle-class ANC leaders were more determined both to sink political roots firmly in the mass of the dispossessed population, and to extend them beyond through cross-race alliances. As the state turned its attention to stripping Indians and coloreds of what rights they enjoyed, their political organizations—the SAIC and the Coloured People's Congress (CPC) (1953)—underwent the same transformation from elite-led reformist organizations to one led by more militant middle-class elements who sought to organize a mass base.[47] Furthermore, the 1950 anticommunist legislation which equated all calls for change with acts of subversion and communism, laid the foundation for joint action between the newly reconstituted underground South African Communist Party (SACP) (1953) and the ANC.[48] With the urging of the ANC (which remained open only to Africans), white progressives, among them communists, initiated the formation of the South African Congress of Democrats (SACOD) (1953) to enlist the support of whites.[49] These, together with the newly formed nonracial South African Congress of Trade Unions (SACTU), joined forces in what came to be known as the Congress Alliance.

The Congress Alliance

Through the Congress Alliance, the national movement embarked on a new course, one that would witness a "cross-fertilization" between communist and nationalist ideologies and organizations, the incorporation of organized workers into the national liberation movement through SACTU, and a gradual shift from "Africanism" to "nonracialism." These, however, were achieved with considerable difficulty.

At its establishment in 1943, ANC-YL leaders were clearly unprepared for cross-race cooperation, even with Indians and coloreds:

> We support the co-operation of all Non-Europeans on certain issues. . . . But we maintain that Africans can only co-operate as an organised self-concious [*sic*] unit. Hence co-operation at the present juncture or state is premature. It can only result in chaos, ineffective action and mutual jealousies, rivalry and suspicion.[50]

By 1948, evincing greater confidence, the ANC-YL Manifesto declared that the time had arrived when "[t]he National Organisations of the Africans, Indians and Coloureds may co-operate on common issues."[51] Yet, the national liberation movement would have to be "led by the Africans themselves."[52] If now Indians—who the Manifesto insisted should not be regarded "as intruders or enemies"—and coloreds would be accommodated, whites remained a problem: The majority of "Europeans share the spoils of white domination," therefore, "Africans will be wasting their time and deflecting their forces if they look up to the Europeans either for inspiration or for help in their political struggle."[53] Indeed, the ANC-YL was committed to an African nationalism—the "national liberatory creed of the oppressed African people."[54] But there were "two streams" of African nationalism. The first, Garvey's "Africa for the Africans," based on the "Quit Africa" and "Hurl the Whiteman to the sea" slogans, was described as "extreme and ultra revolutionary."[55] The alternative "African Nationalism (Africanism)" that would be adopted by the YL was to "take account of the concrete situation in South Africa, and realise that the different racial groups have come to stay," while "insist[ing] that a condition for inter-racial peace and progress is the abandonment of white domination."[56] This brand of African nationalism dominated the thinking of the new middle-class leaders of the ANC who had emerged from the YL.

The move toward an alliance with communists was the most tortuous as the ANC searched for allies and resources. African nationalists within the ANC railed against "foreign ideologies" that had no place in Africa, rejecting the focus on class as divisive, and the goal of socialism as diversionary.[57] Struggles to oust communists from the ANC were led by such figures as Oliver Tambo and Nelson Mandela who accused communists of seeking to hijack the movement toward ulterior agendas.[58] The CPSA, for its part, denounced the ANC's "vague, often contradictory, and at times conciliatory" aims,[59] the "meagerness and crudity" of its program,[60] and its "organizational weakness," which they attributed to "the nature of the leadership, the vacillations, the lack of clarity—of the petty bourgeoisie,"[61] symptomatic of its "economic dependence on the white ruling class, and its isolation from the workers."[62] Accompanying these tendencies, communists argued, were the "beginnings of a Non-European racialism, matching the racialism of the Europeans,"[63] whose "basic assumption is that *all* Europeans are the enemies of the Non-Europeans, that no European can be trusted to fight wholeheartedly all the time for the liberation of the Non-Europeans, and that their liberation can be achieved only through exclusively Non-European organisations."[64] The CPSA asserted instead that nationalism "*need not* be synonymous with racialism, but it can avoid being so only if it recognises the *class* alignments that cut across racial divisions."[65] This typified the exchange between communists and ANC African nationalists. Two impetuses, however, would alter the direction of their relationship: the 1950 Suppression of Communism Act and in 1953 the adoption by the Communist Information Bureau (Cominform) of a "national democratic" strategy that meant that communist parties would no longer "challenge the leadership of the bourgeoisie in national struggles or fight for an alternative leadership by the working class."[66]

Only somewhat less contentious was the alliance with Indian organizations. Joint action between the SAIC and the ANC had been initiated in 1947 and reinforced two years later in the wake of riots in Durban that had been triggered by an incident involving an African and an Indian and left 142 dead. The Durban riots alerted African and Indian leaders to the need to address the animosity that existed between their communities.[67] Yet an alliance with Indian organizations was complicated by persistent tensions between sections of the African petty bourgeoisie and their comparatively successful Indian counterparts who competed with them in the townships.[68] An alliance with the ANC, however, became possible under the SAIC's communist-influenced leadership, which acknowledged the centrality of the ANC in the national struggle.

The ANC enjoyed the least success in drawing the colored population into the national movement under its leadership. The coloreds' relatively advantaged position—the last among the black population to be targeted by apartheid—complicated matters. Initial efforts for joint action revolved around defense of the colored population's franchise; a right already revoked from Africans and Indians. The formation of the Franchise Action Committee brought the colored APO together with the ANC and SAIC to oppose the Separate Representation of Voters Bill that eliminated the colored vote in the Cape Province in 1951.[69]

The direct participation of Indians, coloreds, and whites in the struggle led by the ANC reinforced African leaders' initial steps toward cooperation with other racial groupings, ultimately contributing to their commitment to nonracialism.[70] Resentment and suspicion of white and Indian paternalism persisted to some extent, but by evaluating the experience and conditions of struggle of the 1950s, leading ANC Africanists realized the benefits of a cross-racial alliance. No doubt the need for resources was a factor of considerable weight in deliberations concerning cross-race alliances.[71] Like its constituency, the ANC suffered from limited assets and tremendous constraints on mobility. The ANC's meager financial resources meant limited staffing and no national paper, while SACOD issued a newspaper and several journals, which devoted considerable and consistently favorable coverage to the ANC.[72] Moreover, SACOD leaders were highly experienced in political and trade union organizing and, as whites, they were mobile and enjoyed assets (affluence, education, and skills) of value to the relatively resource-poor ANC.[73]

On the workers' front, the trade union confederation SACTU (1955) enlisted workers to the national movement, thereby initiating a tradition of political unionism in South Africa.[74] The government's relentless assault on African political and trade union activities brought the ANC and nonracial unions together.[75] Countering charges of "populism," SACTU leaders insisted that to remain aloof from the political struggles of the day would "condemn the Trade Union movement to uselessness and to a betrayal of the interests of the workers."[76] Ever threatened by "workerism," the ANC was keen on "correcting any misconceptions that the trade unions had nothing to do with politics," alerting even political leaders that they had to support the growth of trade unions because *"the struggle of the people depends on the workers."*[77] In the prevailing climate of repression and economic recession, SACTU leaders recognized the recruitment potential of an alliance with the ANC as unions were not in a favorable position to make good on promises as a way of expanding their union base.[78] Moreover, African workers remained largely unskilled and easily replaceable in mining, thus what leverage they possessed was fragile. Political unionism was a double-edged sword, however. Although unions would draw many more members precisely where they pursued political action,[79] key SACTU unions were inundated and unable to consolidate organizationally, let alone achieve members' workplace demands.[80] For its part, the ANC's turn to workers was stepped up as urban workers demonstrated their capacity to pull off actions such as the stay-away in demand of a minimum wage in 1957.[81] Thus, the middle-class-led political movement and nonracial section of the labor movement came together in the hope of availing themselves of each other's strength and resources. ANC and SACTU leaders exhorted their members to join the other's ranks in what would become a melding of the political and trade union movements.[82] And while tensions between SACTU and ANC leaders were apparent during joint actions, SACTU remained a loyal ANC ally, eventually becoming the workers' wing of the organization.[83]

On June 25–26, 1955, these members of the Alliance came together in a Congress of the People to put forward their vision for a future South Africa. Year-long preparations by the Congress allies saw the holding of mass community meetings throughout the country articulating grievances and demands. Representatives of all races as well as all African classes were among the 3,000 delegates who convened in Kliptown.[84] The proceedings were forcibly terminated by the police, but not before the gathering had endorsed the Freedom Charter.[85] Among other things, the Freedom Charter projected a nonracial future South Africa that "belongs to all who live in it, black and white," and whose "national wealth . . . shall be restored to the people."[86]

The formation of the Congress Alliance and adoption of the Freedom Charter brought to the fore the tension between African nationalism and nonracialism that would remain throughout the history of the movement. Leading ANC figures were moving gradually from Africanism to nonracialism as the state stepped up its assault, their experience with other groupings deepened, and as the need for others came to be recognized. "Africanists" in the ANC rejected both what they considered to be a dilution of the African claim to the country suggested by the Freedom Charter's vision of a nonracial South Africa, and an alliance with communists.[87] They split off in 1958 to form the Pan Africanist Congress (PAC).

The PAC would claim that the ANC had deviated from the principles articulated in the YL Manifesto and would present itself as the true representative of the African people. PAC leaders tended to be of rural origin where they had limited social contact with whites,[88] and in comparison to ANC leaders were both younger and more likely to be drawn from the lower middle class.[89] Faced with this new challenge to its leadership of the African national movement, the ANC moved cautiously toward implementing nonracialism within the organization. Indeed, it took the ANC a year before it was to adopt the Freedom Charter. According to then Secretary-General Walter Sisulu, "timing was of the essence": "[w]hen you know that your struggle, your mobilization is based on black oppression, you don't want to minimize it, and although there were whites who were taking part, they were doing so as individuals. There was the danger of [the PAC] exploiting this" for their "claim to be the legitimate representative of the black people."[90]

The ANC was organizing its biggest campaign yet, a national anti-pass day scheduled for March 31, 1960. The PAC preempted the ANC by launching its protest of pass laws ten days earlier. The rather poor national response to the PAC's call was obscured by the police's actions in two Cape-area townships—Sharpeville and Langa.[91] There police fired upon demonstrators, killing 69 people—most of whom were shot as they fled from the attack—and wounding 186 others. This single act of protest would generate manifold consequences. Riots erupted across the country, and a state of emergency was declared. International condemnation of the apartheid state assumed new proportions, and foreign capital withdrew—at least temporarily.[92] In the wake of the events, the ANC and PAC were outlawed.

Nonracialism and the Armed Struggle, 1961 to Early 1970s

Forced underground, the ANC and SACP jointly established what would later become the military wing of the ANC—Umkhonto we Sizwe (MK). With the formation of MK in 1961, the ANC would soon join the ranks of national liberation movements pursuing a course of revolutionary armed struggle. MK would begin with a campaign of sabotage "to make a break, in revolutionary practice, with the previous half-century of non-violent politics."[93] The ANC's ambivalence regarding the new approach was evident from its leaders' oft-repeated references to the elimination of alternative avenues, as well as the early concealment of the links between the ANC and MK.[94] Indeed, ANC leaders—among them Mandela—who supported the shift in tactics, proceeded with caution because many veteran ANC leaders—including ANC President Chief Albert Luthuli—and leaders among Congress allies would not support the turn to violence.[95]

The MK's short-lived campaign of sabotage produced over 190 attacks within twenty-one months of its establishment.[96] A raid on the farm in Rivonia, from which the attacks were coordinated, netted key ANC leaders. They, along with Mandela who was already in detention, were sentenced to life imprisonment in 1963. ANC leaders and MK trainees who were abroad at the time, preparing for an underground existence, escaped prison but were trapped in exile.

The Struggle from Exile

Its structures inside the country decimated, the ANC now concentrated on building its External Mission. First established in London in 1960, the mission's initial duties were fund-raising, diplomatic relations, and preparations for military training of MK recruits. With the incarceration of ANC leaders inside the country, the External Mission effectively became the center of ANC leadership.[97] Under Deputy President-General Oliver Tambo, the mission was moved to the African continent and headquartered in Tanzania, a considerable distance from South Africa.[98]

On the diplomatic front, the ANC began by turning to the African states. It would obtain assistance from the Organisation of African Unity (OAU) formed in 1963 and its African Liberation Committee. OAU resources, however, were insubstantial and undependable.[99] In any case, African states were hard pressed themselves for financial resources, forcing the ANC to turn further abroad. The SACP was particularly instrumental in securing Soviet bloc assistance, which became the main source of the organizations' financial, military, and diplomatic support.[100] Eventually, considerable Scandinavian assistance for the ANC's nonmilitary activities would also be forthcoming. Access to these alternative sources of resources would enable the ANC to remain relatively aloof from inter-African state rivalries and manipulation, and to preserve a substantial degree of independence from host countries.[101]

From 1961 well into the 1970s, the ANC's strategy revolved around "the development of a popular armed struggle for the seizure of state power."[102] According to Barrell, the impetus for this "Guevarist 'detonator' approach" came from a combination of the particular variant of Marxist-Leninist theory of revolution that guided the ANC and SACP since 1961, contemporary examples of revolutionary liberation movements, and the rank and file's desire for retribution.[103] However, in view of the destruction of structures in South Africa and conditions of exile, the lack of options was undoubtedly an additional factor: the organization of armed struggle would eventually become a means through which the exiled liberation organization could assert its relevance and draw recruits from inside the country.

But MK faced formidable obstacles to the infiltration of its insurgents into the country, not the least of which was that at this time front-line states were closed off to the liberation movement, being themselves under South African occupation (Namibia), white minority (Zimbabwe) or colonial rule (Mozambique and Angola), or South African economic domination (Botswana, Swaziland, and Lesotho). This, however, also meant that the ANC had counterparts with which to ally in Zimbabwe, Mozambique, Namibia, and Angola.

Joint military campaigns with the Zimbabwe African People's Union (ZAPU) were carried out during 1963–69 when MK sought to infiltrate South Africa. As SACP General-Secretary Joe Slovo explained, the purpose of the incursions was "to demonstrate that we were able to hit the enemy" as a means of "helping to stimulate the process of political regeneration."[104] The most notable of the armed campaigns, the Wankie Campaign that was launched jointly with ZAPU in 1967, ended disastrously when MK guerrillas were intercepted by Rhodesian and South African forces.[105] The experience generated a reappraisal of strategy within the ANC. Unwavering advocates of armed struggle would emphasize the lessons learned regarding proper preparation and the future potential of such campaigns, others would emphasize the objective difficulties of waging armed struggle through unfriendly states.[106] Ultimately, the former would prevail because of the absence of alternative means through which the liberation organization based in exile could make itself relevant to the mass of the population inside the country.

In 1969, these and other concerns, including growing disaffection within MK ranks, were addressed at the Consultative Conference held in Morogoro, Tanzania. The leadership admitted that the ANC's organizational existence inside the country had been virtually eliminated and that difficulties were encountered in establishing contact with what survived of the organization.[107] The Conference adopted the document "*Strategies and Tactics of the ANC*," which reaffirmed the ANC's commitment to armed struggle as "the only method left open" to the organization.[108] Now, however, rather than endeavoring to "'spark off' guerrilla warfare" through armed actions by individuals, the organization would seek to "extend and consolidate an ANC underground machinery" for mass mobilization.[109] The conferees adopted a program for the escalation of guerilla warfare toward a "future all-out war" and the "conquest of power" that emphasized the necessity of political education and mobilization inside the country to ensure the survival of armed insurgents who infiltrated successfully.[110] A Revolutionary Council was established that was entrusted with the task of overseeing both military and political mobilization inside the country.

The Morogoro Conference also saw the ANC's adoption of the theory of "Colonialism of a Special Type," which defined the South African liberation struggle as fundamentally "anti-colonialist."[111] Colonialism in South Africa, however, manifests "special" features, most important of which is the fact that the oppressed and oppressor share the same territory.[112] As such, the theory asserts, the colonizers cannot be induced to turn power over to the colonized and retreat to their "metropolitan country," as is the case with other colonial states.[113] Thus, "[t]he struggle of the South African people has therefore centred on the abolition of the colonial white state and the creation in its stead of a democratic state *based on the principle of majority rule*."[114] However, "[b]ecause of the total inter-penetration of racial oppression and capitalist exploitation, the South African struggle also necessarily has a class dimension," hence the clauses in the Freedom Charter that "envisage the seizure of economic assets."[115]

Yet another significant development was that while the primacy of the African people's oppression and their contribution to the struggle for liberation were reaffirmed, whites, Indians, and coloreds were now admitted as members in the ANC's External Mission. This reversal of policy regarding membership applied only in exile and was not inclusive of membership on the NEC.[116] The Revolutionary Council, however, would be open to all.

For much of the 1960s and 1970s, cut off from their potential constituency inside the country, and hard-pressed for recruits, ANC leaders worked on foreign relations. While continuing to wrestle with the correct strategies and tactics, by and large this was a period of waiting: The conquest of state power could not be accomplished without the people.

Quiescence inside the Country

The incarceration, banning, and exile of leaders in 1963 dealt a crushing blow to the organization inside the country. Ten years earlier, anticipating the eventuality of an underground existence, Mandela initiated the formation of cells known as the M-Plan. Due to opposition from ANC conservatives, however, the M-Plan was implemented only in some regions, most notably in the Eastern Cape.[117] Inadequately prepared to operate as a clandestine organization, the ANC faded from political existence inside the country.

Indeed, although SACTU was not banned, it too ceased to function as a result of the loss of so many of its cadres and leaders. SACTU affiliates had been prominent in the Defiance Campaigns,[118] and its trade unionists had been heavily represented in many of the ANC's regional and branch leadership structures.[119] The links went further as SACTU leaders took over regional MK commands across the country and used their positions within unions to recruit for MK.[120] SACTU's leadership was felled in the roundup that followed the banning of the ANC. This experience would leave its mark on the labor movement for decades as many trade unionists blamed the political movement for exposing the labor movement to crippling repression before it could protect itself, thereby setting back trade union organizing among black workers.

As the ANC's vocal supporters were silenced and popular resistance quelled, people turned away from overtly political struggles to struggles of survival. The last armed action inside South Africa was in 1963.[121] Repression produced a quiescence on both the political and labor fronts that would prevail for nearly a decade. International capital, which had retreated in the wake of the Sharpeville unrest, returned, reassured by the state's restoration of order.[122] South Africa enjoyed an economic boom made possible by the suppression of both the black political and labor movements. Apartheid appeared to be successful.

Explaining Failure

By demonstrating a new level of white intransigence, apartheid stimulated support for and permitted a more radical leadership to assert itself within the ANC. Through the advocacy of mass defiance, the middle-class leaders took the national movement in a new direction; one that was an important departure from the politics of appeals and deputations of the previous phase. Despite the heightened mass struggle and new, bolder leadership, however, in the first period of this phase the ANC remained intent on reform rather than revolution, and "continued to call upon whites to 'share' power, to 'extend' freedom, and to allow nonwhites to participate as 'partners' in government within the system as it stood."[123] Although more militant in its rhetoric, the ANC's "perspective was not so much to deploy pressure from below as to incite a 'moral re-awakening' from above," still hoping that the ruling powers would see reason.[124] Moreover, while affirming the importance of mass mobilization, ANC leaders continued to neglect the organization of workers where inclusion gave them leverage—that is in the workplace. Instead, the ANC sought to mobilize Africans as an undifferentiated mass.[125] And once leaders were identified and paralyzed through banning, detention, imprisonment, and exile, the movement came to a halt.

The ANC's organizational presence inside the country was eliminated but not before considerable experience with and a commitment to a multiracial and cross-class approach had been gained. Through the withdrawal of advantages that had hitherto differentiated blacks along lines of color and class, apartheid-engineered divisions created conditions for joint struggles. As their communities came under assault, organizations from each of the oppressed communities turned to the others in search of support and resources. Tensions and mutual suspicions persisted as the state manipulated status and legal differences between the three groups. Moreover, residential segregation hampered mobility between communities thereby rendering cross-racial community organizing virtually impossible. Thus, while advocating nonracialism in principle, the Congress Alliance organized around racial groupings. Significantly, the only exception to this was SACTU.[126] The turn by African leaders of the ANC to alliances with other groups, including white democrats, was not unproblematic; one repercussion was a split in the movement and the formation of an "Africanist" rival, the PAC.

No less momentous a development in this period was the integration of an important segment of organized black labor into the national movement. SACTU, however, would become a subordinate partner in the alliance with the ANC; the implications would fuel debates well into the future. Opposing the subordination of the labor movement to the political movement, many unionists and intellectuals criticized SACTU's leadership. Despite some organizational advances in key industries, SACTU's preoccupation with township and community campaigns was blamed for dissipating unions' limited resources and energies as workers' organizational efforts were directed at the achievement of political strength outside the workplace rather than leverage within it.[127] Others have argued that SACTU's involvement was both necessary and unavoidable: for trade unions to have remained mere observers of the events that engulfed black communities would have hurt the unions as well as left the political movement without organized working-class input.[128] Moreover, as a member of the Congress Alliance, SACTU ensured that working-class demands were placed on the alliance's agenda. Both assessments were correct; it would be some time before the labor movement could become capable of preserving its autonomy while engaging politically in the struggles against apartheid.

With the banning of the ANC, a second period in this phase of the national movement was initiated, involving a turn to armed struggle. Exile conditions under which the organization was now forced to operate reinforced the ANC's nonracialism as well as its alliance with the SACP. The strategy was to use armed struggle as a means of activating a popular revolutionary movement inside the country. But this approach also failed, in part because of conditions of exile, difficulties of access, and crippling repression inside the country. More important, social forces that were capable of insurrection, let alone revolution, were absent inside South Africa. Ironically, the economic boom, which the repression of the black political and labor movements permitted, would stimulate the emergence of such social forces. Attempts to catalyze them into existence from abroad would not be sufficient.

By the end of the decade, there was very little reason for optimism regarding the prospects of the national movement to eliminate apartheid. The movements' structures inside the country had all but disappeared while the organization outside remained essentially powerless. So successful was the suppression of African political organizations that the history of the ANC would not be known to virtually an entire generation of Africans inside South Africa. This phase of the national movement under the leadership of middle-class leaders in both its approaches—mass defiance and armed struggle—had clearly failed.

Palestine, 1949 to Mid-1970s

For Palestinians, 1948 would become known as the year of "the Catastrophe" *(al-nakba)*. Palestinians not only failed to prevent the partition of their homeland, but the UN resolution that called for two states would yield only one. In the war that ensued, Jewish forces occupied territories well beyond those allotted by the UN partition plan, encompassing three-fourths of Palestine.[129] A military strategy of shelling, terrorism, rumors, and forced expulsions[130] produced the massive exodus of some 85 percent of the indigenous population from the territories that would form the Jewish state.[131] With only 100,000 Palestinians remaining, Israel would be free to consolidate its presence unencumbered by a serious "Arab problem."[132] The new Israeli state would organize the "in-gathering" of Jews; the "disappearance" of the indigenous population was "a miraculous simplification of the problem."[133] Palestinian homes, businesses, and land were transferred to the new Jewish immigrants.[134] The goal of exclusion had been successfully executed to its logical conclusion; a new diaspora was created as a result.

Jewish organizations behind the colonization drive prior to 1948 proved adept at state building. The para-statal institutions established by the Histadrut provided the foundations of the state.[135] The election of a Labor government reflected the labor movement's prominence in the colonization drive, and its contribution to the realization of the Zionist goal of a Jewish state. All fell in line, including Jewish communists. While the Communist Party of Israel (CPI) continued to reject the precepts of Zionism and supported the creation of an Arab state, it would not attempt to cross the national boundaries erected by the 1949 armistice lines. Nation building would revolve instead around the integration of *mizrachim* into the state already dominated by *ashkenazim.*

Palestinian exclusion took the form of expulsion, exile, and/or irrelevance. The founding of Israel left some 780,000 Palestinian refugees in its wake[136]—somewhat more than half of the Palestinian population.[137] One year later, less than 10 percent of Palestinians remained in what became Israel.[138] Cut off from other Palestinians and marginalized from Palestinian political developments for nearly two decades, they would receive Israeli citizenship while being placed under a military government until 1966. Given the size of the population, their inclusion would prove to be unproblematic for the Jewish state.[139]

The influx of refugees into Palestinian territories not seized by Israel—the West Bank and Gaza Strip—doubled their populations virtually overnight. These territories made up 20.5 percent and 1.5 percent of Palestine, respectively.[140] In the aftermath of the 1948 war, the West Bank was annexed by Transjordan, thereby fulfilling King Abdallah's ambition of a larger state,[141] while the Egyptians took over the administration of the Gaza Strip without annexing it. Palestinians were now divided between Israel (10 percent), the West Bank (52 percent), and the Gaza Strip (20 percent), while the remaining 18 percent of the Palestinian population was spread across Lebanon, Syria, Transjordan, Egypt, and Iraq.[142] Israeli leaders were confident regarding permanent Palestinian exclusion: Palestinians were simply to be assimilated into the region with which they shared a common language, religion, and history.[143]

The Palestinian national movement, like its constituency, had become geographically fragmented. Led now by middle-class elements, Palestinians' search for resources, both for reconstituting their communities and for securing "the Return" *(al-'awda),* first took them to the Arabs of the region. The lack of leverage within Israel, the forced economic and political reorientation of the remaining Palestinian territories toward Transjordan and Egypt, the Palestinian people's dispersal throughout the region—in short, the consequences of exclusion—were conducive to such an approach and, indeed, to dependence on Arab resources.

Arab Unity and War of Liberation, 1949 to 1967

In the wake of the 1948 calamity, the entire Arab region experienced dislocations and upheavals. The loss of Palestine was considered an Arab loss, certainly by Palestinians who had good reason to suspect Arab leaders' resolve during the war,[144] but also by the Arab populace. A series of military coups removed governments in Syria (1949), Egypt (1952), and Iraq (1958).[145] Arab politicians and intellectuals, as well as the highly politicized popular sectors, struggled with the implications of an Arab world carved up by colonial powers and rapidly coalescing American ambitions in the oil-rich region. New and newly reinvigorated Arab movements and political formations emerged: pan-Arab, communist, and pan-Islamic. Secular Arab nationalism prevailed as people throughout the region affirmed the slogan, "Arab unity is the road to the liberation of Palestine."[146]

Arab nationalism was bolstered by a coup that carried Gamal Abdel-Nasser to power in Egypt in 1952. Four years later, Egyptian resistance to the tripartite—British, French, and Israeli—invasion of the Suez Canal would cement Nasser's popularity as a pan-Arab leader. In 1958, the merger of Egypt and Syria in the United Arab Republic (UAR) brought Arab nationalists' aspirations of unity even closer to realization. But unrelenting geopolitical and ideological conflicts between Arab states, in large measure revolving around Cold War alignments, frustrated the attainment of unity. Given their dispersal throughout the region, Palestinians could not avoid becoming entangled in such conflicts.

Separated from each other by borders of five different Arab states, Palestinian communities were dependent on the sufferance of Arab governments and the solidarity of their people. Tensions emerged between making the best of it within their host countries, which required a certain amount of allegiance to their host governments, and reconstituting themselves as a people distinct from other Arabs. The overwhelming majority of Palestinian leaders would seek to counter their people's fragmentation with Arab unity. But this was not without contradictions, given the often articulated Zionist strategy that envisioned Palestinian absorption into the existing Arab states as the ultimate solution.[147] Eventually, tensions would appear between Arab nationalism *(qawmiya)* and Palestinian nationalism *(wataniya),* but at this time middle-class Palestinians who aspired to leadership opted to compensate for their enfeeblement with Arab military strength as the mass of the Palestinian population concentrated on survival and reconstituting their society. So thorough was the eradication of "Palestine" that Palestinians were denied recognition as principals in the conflict. For decades their struggle would be subsumed within "the Arab-Israeli conflict" and their national movement reduced to a "problem of refugees."

Exclusion, Refugees, and Resettlement

UN resolutions passed annually that called for the repatriation of or compensation for Palestine's refugees went unheeded.[148] The United Nations

Relief and Works Agency (UNRWA) assumed responsibility for the welfare of Palestine's refugees until a political settlement could be reached. The irony would not be lost on Palestinians. The international body that had delivered their homeland to European settlers was now in charge of administering relief to the victims. That UNRWA's biggest donors were the countries most instrumental in the creation of the Jewish State—the United States and the United Kingdom—only deepened suspicions regarding the true aims of the Agency.[149] UNRWA's mission, intended to be temporary, would be renewed perpetually for half a century in large measure because of its importance "for peace and stability in the area."[150] Although never stated explicitly, the organization's mandate moved gradually from relief to resettlement. Refugees were to be provided with skills that would enable them not only to be included but, indeed, to become integrated into their Arab host countries.[151]

Fearing that integration was tantamount to permanent resettlement and, as such, to the surrender of their claim to Palestine, Palestinians vehemently opposed resettlement schemes. Refugees launched demonstrations, strikes, and protests against UNRWA actions, including the construction of dwellings.[152] They would do with the wretched camp conditions and even dependence on the organization they suspected of being an agent of absorption and pacification but would not jeopardize their refugee status, which entitled them to the "Right of Return" *(haq al-'awda).*

In an attempt to create some semblance of normalcy, camp populations initiated vigorous efforts to organize the tent communities around their villages of origin. Such efforts would eventually prove to be a powerful source of "Palestinianism," but they would also preserve traditional leaders and bases of authority in the process. Indeed, Palestinians expended tremendous energy on preserving traditional social organization as a matter of survival; their Arab host governments supported this as a means of social control. Old patronage relations were reestablished between camp populations and their traditional leaders residing outside the camps.[153] Drawing on Arab government patronage themselves, the remnants of the old Palestinian elite assisted refugee families to negotiate their survival in the new settings. Traditional leaders' determination to preserve their standing brought them into conflict with the middle-class youth who offered the camp communities services, upliftment, and support in the refugees' resistance to resettlement schemes, all the while exhorting against succumbing to the "refugee mentality" of dependence.[154] These early contacts with camp refugees by future leaders would prove consequential.

Not all Palestinian refugees, however, were destined for the camps;

approximately one out of five refugees managed to escape the deprivations and humiliations of camp life.[155] Those with means secured residence and employment within the various Arab capitals or towns of the West Bank and Gaza Strip.[156] Timing was critical. Arab state formation and economic development required those with skills, and Palestinians enjoyed relatively high rates of education.[157] The improved prospects of inclusion of middle-class Palestinians stimulated further commitment to educational attainment and produced an expansion of this class in the region.[158] Education came to be seen as the lifeline out of the refugee camps: "one could be dispossessed of one's land, but never of one's education" would be echoed from one generation to the next. Camp refugees began to place tremendous pressures on UNRWA to provide more education services. But such demands were not unproblematic as the absorption of Palestinians in the region was consistent with Israeli and American solutions for the "refugee problem."[159] Indeed, the Palestinian diaspora steadily extended deeper into the Arab region and further abroad, that is, away from Palestine and resistance to Israel. By 1970, 48 percent of Palestinians no longer resided in Palestine.[160] Exclusion was working.

Arab Unity and the Palestinian Middle Class

The Palestinian middle class would respond, but not before the previous leadership had taken its last breath. In 1948, Haj Amin al-Husseini made a feeble attempt to establish an All-Palestine Government in the Gaza Strip, but was eventually exiled to Lebanon. Traditional Palestinian leaders, like the mass of the population, were dispersed, and while they were spared the fate of the camps, they were now entirely dependent on their hosts.

It was perhaps inevitable that the dismemberment and dispersal of Palestinian society would produce an ideologically and politically fragmented leadership. As members of the middle class, they could either support their hosts' ruling elites or turn to the mass of their population—the refugees and peasants. The Palestinian middle class split into three: those co-opted by Arab governments through posts and entitlements; radicals who supported revolutionary movements for the overthrow of conservative Arab regimes as the necessary step toward the liberation of Palestine; and those who called for an independent route in the form of Palestinian nationalism. For the most part, competition between middle-class leaders at this time was between the co-opted and radical elements. Palestinian nationalists were only just beginning to develop an alternative approach.

The co-opted segments of the Palestinian middle class could be found throughout the region's burgeoning political and economic institutions.[161]

They were proof that benefits could be derived from inclusion in the Arab region. The largest single segment was that absorbed into the Jordanian government and administration of the West Bank. These were liberal modernizers, intent on making the best of the opportunities that Jordanian citizenship conferred, opportunities denied other Palestinians of the diaspora.[162] Among them were nationalists who were extremely influential in the 1950s. In 1955, the Jordanian government decision to join the Anglo-American-sponsored Baghdad Pact, aimed at containing Soviet influence in the region, triggered violent demonstrations throughout the kingdom. In the process, two governments fell and the King was forced to retreat and recognize a nationalist government the following year.[163] The new prime minister Suleiman al-Nabulsi—an East Bank Jordanian of Palestinian origin—was elected on a platform that included severing ties with Britain, full democracy, unionization rights, and freedom for political parties. His would be the first Arab government in which communists were elected.[164] One year later, under American pressure, the King imposed martial law, suspended the constitution, dissolved the government, and was rewarded financially for doing so.[165] This experience dealt a blow to middle-class Palestinian liberals who believed it was possible to make it through existing systems.

The radicals, comprising university students, intellectuals, and professionals, supported the militant alternatives such as the Arab Nationalist Movement (ANM), the Ba'th party, and various Arab communist parties. None of these were Palestinian organizations, although Palestinians figured prominently among their leaders and ideologues, particularly those of the ANM. Differences revolved around the relationship between the liberation of Palestine from Israel and the liberation of the Arab region from Western imperialism. The ANM and the Ba'th (the ruling party in Syria and Iraq) concurred on the need for a revolutionary transformation of those Arab regimes that impeded Arab unity and facilitated Western penetration of the region; they disagreed on priorities, with the ANM's chief concern being the achievement of unity for the liberation of Palestine. While both enjoyed substantial followings in the region, and the ANM particularly so in the West Bank and Gaza Strip, they were unable to compete with Nasser's appeal. "Nasserism," an amorphous nationalism with no organizational existence, was supported by the broadest array of Arab classes. In popular perception, even communists could add very little to Nasser's opposition to Western imperialism and its feudal Arab accomplices in the region. Moreover, communist parties had yet to surmount popular indignation over their support of the partition plan and the Soviet Union's immediate recognition of the State of Israel.[166]

Although considerably less popular, pan-Islamic alternatives also existed. The most prominent organization within the Islamic movement, the
Egypt-centered Muslim Brotherhood, enjoyed substantial support in the
impoverished Gaza Strip.[167] In Jordan, where the Muslim Brotherhood was
the only political party permitted to operate after 1956, the organization
made inroads among refugees and the poor, in large measure owing to the
establishment of schools and social services.[168] Nevertheless, popular support for the Brotherhood was mitigated by the organization's detente with
the Jordanian and other conservative Arab regimes.[169] Even though religious
ideologies and organizations gained new adherents whenever people became
disillusioned with nationalist leaders and parties, Palestinian politics remained
firmly secular.[170]

To varying degrees, the various radical currents shared a commitment
to the restoration of unity—whether Arab or Islamic—as the means of foil-
ing imperialist designs for the region. They differed with regard to the
transformations they sought for the region and their alliances with existing
regimes. They also shared the view that the liberation of Palestine would require a unified military effort. Palestinian refugees were entrusted with a
symbolic contribution to the liberation of their homeland by remaining in
the camps and resisting permanent resettlement. These positions regarding
regional unity, social transformation, and a role for Palestinian refugees in
the liberation struggle, distinguished the radical nationalists from Palestinian nationalists who were beginning to coalesce. The latter would gain impetus in 1956.

Besides propelling Nasser to the forefront of pan-Arab efforts, the invasion of Suez in 1956 proved to be a turning point for Palestinian nationalists. Resistance to the Israeli forces that invaded the Gaza Strip inspired and
emboldened Palestinians elsewhere. In rapid succession, new and specifically
Palestinian formations emerged. Fatah, the General Union of Palestinian
Students (GUPS), and Palestinian branches in existing pan-Arab parties
were formed, and a number of Arab regimes initiated the establishment of
Palestinian organizations.[171] Even inside Israel, Palestinians formed al-Ard
(The Land) in 1959 to protest military rule, land confiscation, travel restrictions, and discrimination, among other things.[172] A specifically Palestinian
approach was in the making. But these political formations were not yet capable of competing with Nasser's sweeping popularity. Moreover, given
Palestinians' lack of leverage vis-à-vis Israel, most dismissed the early notions
of Palestinian self-reliance as foolhardy.[173] Conspicuous Palestinian weakness within those areas of Palestine free from Israeli control—the West Bank
and Gaza Strip—did not help the cause of Palestinian nationalists either.

"Jordanization" of West Bank Palestinians
and "Palestine" in the Gaza Strip

The experience of exclusion differed markedly for Palestinians in the West Bank and Gaza Strip. For West Bank Palestinians, exclusion took the form Israel had hoped for: the full political, economic, and social incorporation of Palestinians into another entity. Later, Israeli leaders would declare that "Jordan is Palestine."[174] They were mistaken. Palestine continued to exist in the Gaza Strip. Excluded from Israel, isolated and cut off from all other Palestinian communities, and only nominally tied to Egypt, Palestinians in the Gaza Strip fervently retained their claim to the last vestige of Palestine.

The merger of what came to be known as the West Bank and the East Bank of the Jordan River, the institutionalization of Jordanian authority, as well as the granting of Jordanian citizenship to West Bank Palestinians were intended to erode Palestinians' identification with the usurped homeland. Certainly the Jordanian monarchs believed this to be possible. If so, it portended well for the Israeli state: political and economic opportunities in Jordan might divert Palestinian energies away from resistance to exclusion and toward advancing their inclusion in the new alternative framework. Where the appeal of such opportunities did not prove sufficiently enticing, the Jordanian monarchs were capable and willing to apply force.[175]

"Jordanization" would reduce the West Bank to an appendage of Jordan, underdevelop its economy, and involve the active suppression of its Palestinian identity.[176] "Jordanization" also entailed the integration of all West Bank institutions—economic, social, political, religious—into the Jordanian framework where none were permitted to preserve "Palestine" in either name or in content.[177] Camp refugees, with the most immediate interest in carrying on the liberation struggle, were scattered over twenty-four camps and under constant surveillance. Jordanian forces actively obstructed their attempts to infiltrate Israel.[178] The combination, it was hoped, would erode Palestinian interest in resistance as generations that did not know Palestine would come to identify themselves as Jordanians.

The exclusion experience of Palestinians in the Gaza Strip held no such promises for the Israeli state. Egypt could not afford to incorporate them into its sizeable population and already sorely strained economy.[179] In the absence of attempts at "Egyptianization," Palestinians remained in Palestine and under rulers that did not begrudge them that claim. Instead of incorporation into an alternative entity, exclusion took the form of a militant population directly on the border of Israel with very little to do or to lose except wait for or create the means to battle Israel. A majority population of refugees, Palestinians in the Gaza Strip identified with the territories of their origin.[180] This was demonstrated forcefully when an American-sponsored, UNRWA- and Egyptian-supported scheme to permanently resettle refugees in the Sinai desert was successfully resisted by the refugees.[181] Moreover, Egyptian neglect of institution building kept the Gaza Strip institutionally poor but Palestinian in name and content.[182] Even more disconcerting for Israeli exclusion designs was the fact that Palestinians in the Gaza Strip were ruled by a regime whose president claimed the mantle of pan-Arab leader, which required that Egypt confront both Israel (the most obvious symbol of Arab powerlessness) and its Western allies. But Palestinians' demands for arms and training to respond to Israel's raids went unheeded until Egypt's leaders deemed it beneficial in 1955.[183]

These differences notwithstanding, there were significant similarities in the experience of Palestinians in the West Bank and Gaza Strip. In both cases the administrations endeavored to preserve existing social relations and traditional social organization rooted in the institution of kinship and clan.[184] While the traditional Palestinian elite as a whole had lost considerable influence among Palestinians, they continued to be prominent in the organized life of their local communities as a result of: (1) their absorption into the municipal, and in the West Bank, state levels of the Jordanian and Egyptian administrations; (2) old prestige, wealth, and property upon which many peasants continued to depend; and (3) the absence of an alternative, viable class capable of substituting itself in the new framework.[185]

Members of the West Bank elite who obtained state and municipal posts lacked a West Bank–wide constituency and therefore were not capable of acting as a West Bank–wide leadership.[186] The Jordanian monarchs made certain of this. The ranks of the prominent Jerusalem notables were thinned by their exodus on the eve of the 1948 war, and with Amman as the capital, the diminished administrative status of Jerusalem meant that those who remained enjoyed only local influence.[187] Members of the traditional elite who did remain were split along lines of allegiance to the Jordanian monarchy.[188] The Husseini family, which opposed annexation and Hashemite rule, and whose head, Haj Amin, continued attempts to assert his leadership of a Palestinian movement, was singled out for isolation.[189] The kings did this by supporting the Husseinis' erstwhile rivals, the Nashashibi family.[190] By rewarding supporters and punishing opponents, Jordanian rule thus reinforced interfamilial rivalries among the Palestinian elite. In the context of integration into the Jordanian framework, such rivalries were conducted in the municipal structures of the West Bank. In some West Bank towns the distribution of administrative positions among the various local notable families became virtually inherited.[191] In other towns, open rivalry continued unabated while competition persisted between the same families.[192] Even in towns where members of the young, educated middle class gained positions in the municipal administrations, they were generally members of local elite families.[193]

Egypt pursued the same approach in its administration of the Gaza Strip. Relying on Gaza's elite, administrative appointments were granted to members of the old, wealthy, landed families.[194] The highest post of mayor of Gaza city has rotated between the same four families since the days of the British mandate.[195] Egyptian manipulation of interfamilial rivalries reinforced existing conflicts and competition.[196] With Egypt moving leftward, however, Egyptian leaders made an active attempt to create a countervailing force to the conservative, Palestinian, traditional elite through the creation of a new class of merchants permitted through the expansion of trade.[197] But this class remained divided between those who sought to use their access to the Egyptian authorities in order to secure their immediate economic interests and those who sought to confront the Egyptian rulers;[198] compliance was the norm.

In short, the Palestinian societies of the West Bank and Gaza Strip withstood the dismemberment of Palestine and remained intact to a remarkable extent. The continued prominence of their elite was reinforced by their cooptation into administrative posts as well as persistent local recognition of old bases of authority among wide segments of the population.[199] They exercised their authority through the manipulation of old familial and clan linkages even as these now remained confined to their immediate locale.[200] But the productive sectors of the economy were not expanding to a degree capable of absorbing the existing workforce and reestablishing internal dependencies on new bases.[201] As such, refugees were "depeasantized" without being proletarianized: losing their skills as peasants was not compensated for by the acquisition of new nonfarming skills and employment.[202] Instead, camp refugees remained dependent on UNRWA assistance and seasonal employment in agriculture when it existed.[203] Importantly, in the West Bank, resentment was defused to a certain extent through migration to the East Bank and further abroad.[204] In the Gaza Strip, resentment could not so easily be defused due to the lack of opportunities in Egypt and, as noncitizens lacking internationally recognized travel documents, opportunities for emigration were limited.

In the West Bank and Gaza Strip, as elsewhere in the region, radicalized middle-class elements succeeded in mobilizing popular sentiment around their nationalist and anti-imperialist stances despite repression, factionalization, and a largely underground existence with weak organizational extensions. This would not go unnoticed by Arab governments and leaders intent on curbing the radicalization of Palestinians.

Competing Nationalisms: Arab and Palestinian

Two political developments would stimulate a strategic reassessment by Palestinians. In 1961, the failure of the unity experiment between Egypt and Syria dashed hopes that inclusion within a larger Arab entity would deliver the liberation of Palestine anytime soon. As evidence of state nationalism *(qutriya)*, the dissolution of the UAR, it was argued, presaged disaster for the Arab world in general and the liberation of Palestine in particular.[205] Indeed, Palestinian inclusion in several weak states would reinforce rather than offset their fragmentation with no promise of concerted Arab efforts toward the liberation project. The second impetus for a Palestinian strategic reassessment was the Algerian defeat of the French in 1962. Their success presented an alternative approach to liberation based on "people's revolutionary war."[206] These developments bolstered those who espoused Palestinian self-reliance as the route to the long-awaited Return.

Existing Palestinian formations that had emerged after 1956 gained ground. In the 1960s, another spate of organizations was added to Fatah, GUPS, and the various branches of existing Arab parties.[207] New underground organizations were established, and distinctly Palestinian branches of Arab nationalist organizations were formed. Recognizing both the advantages and limitations of inclusion within the region, they negotiated the terrain between Arab nationalism and Palestinian-specific national interests, identity, and objectives with caution. The emergence in the late 1950s of Fatah—a name that is derived from the initials of the Palestinian National Liberation Movement in reverse—would prove particularly consequential.

Fatah leaders, for the most part, emerged from the Palestinian middle class of teachers, municipal employees, and engineers employed in the Gulf.[208] Inspired by the national liberation movements of the day, with funding from Kuwait and Qatar, they organized military training bases in Syria and launched the Palestinian armed struggle on January 1, 1965. Impatient and disillusioned with Arab efforts to liberate Palestine, Fatah envisioned the use of armed struggle to induce the "entanglement" of the reluctant Arab regimes in a war with Israel.[209] They would also reverse the popularized slogan regarding Arab unity and the liberation of Palestine to assert that "the liberation of Palestine is the road to Arab unity."[210] Fatah's scathing attacks on Arab regime hypocrisy resonated for Palestinians across the region. Rejecting the divisiveness of competing ideologies that seemed only to sap energies and delay action, they promoted a "nonideological

Palestinian nationalism."[211] They sought to galvanize the most destitute—the camp refugees—who suffered the most from the loss of Palestine as their prospects for inclusion in the Arab region were the dimmest.

The Establishment of the PLO

Growing Palestinian impatience and the appeal of underground organizations that called for armed struggle prompted Arab regimes to consider the establishment of a "Palestinian entity" to harness Palestinian aspirations and forestall both Palestinian interference in Arab politics as well as manipulation of the Palestinian cause by competing Arab states.[212] In 1964, a meeting of the Arab League delegated Ahmad Shuqairi—a Palestinian career diplomat who, among other things, had been Saudi Arabia's representative to the UN—the task of presenting a proposal for such an entity at the next meeting of the League that year. Instead, Shuqairi appeared with a fait accompli.[213] Over two months, Shuqairi attended mass conferences in most of the major Palestinian concentrations to explain the concept, vague as it was: a political formation that was to channel and combine Palestinians' contribution to the liberation of their homeland.[214] The idea generated tremendous support from the popular sectors across the region; it was received less enthusiastically by the embryonic underground resistance organizations such as Fatah.[215]

Reactions to the establishment of the PLO among Palestinian political leaders were notably mixed. The ANM and other Arab nationalists, ever suspicious of anything that smacked of state nationalism, interpreted the formation of the PLO as a first step toward the relinquishment of Arab responsibility for the liberation project. Fatah leaders suspected it of being yet another Arab ploy aimed at controlling Palestinians and their political future.[216] Aware of such misgivings, others, mostly independents, saw potential in the PLO: If Palestinians participated, it might become a serious force; if they did not, it would remain an instrument of the Arab regimes.[217]

Not surprisingly, the original leaders of the PLO did not represent political groupings; they brought themselves without a mass following.[218] Indeed, the militant elements that were galvanizing popular interest for armed struggle were deliberately bypassed.[219] Instead, the early leaders were "personalities" with varying histories of political activity.[220] As well-educated professionals they were endowed with the class resources appropriate for setting up and administering institutions rather than mass organizations. However, these "statesmen" had no interest in the armed struggle;[221] they envisioned the establishment of a Palestinian army to parallel the armies of Arab League member states. Objections from Jordan and elsewhere, however, led to the

Palestine Liberation Army (PLA) being confined to brigades within Arab armies under separate commands in Egypt (Gaza Strip), Syria, and Iraq.[222] Resigned to dependence on their Arab host governments and Arab military strength, the PLO promoted the PLA as the vanguard of the Arab armies that would liberate Palestine.

But there was no Arab plan for the liberation of Palestine. Nasser admitted as much.[223] Underground Palestinian leaders chafed and persisted with raids into Israel that achieved more for the organizations' popularity than they did in terms of effectiveness against Israel.[224] Through such actions, underground organizations, and Fatah in particular, sought to step up pressure on Nasser to act. Palestinian refugees waited. The apparent stalemate would be shattered by a war with Israel that would dramatically alter the course of the conflict.

In June 1967 Israel occupied what remained of Palestine as well as Syrian and Egyptian territories. Over half of the Palestinian population now fell under Israeli rule. The notion of reliance on Arab assets to secure the liberation of Palestine was obliterated in the six days of war. Palestinian nationalists were poised to fill the vacuum.

Palestinian Nationalism and the Armed Struggle, 1968 to Mid-1970s

The loss of the West Bank and Gaza Strip in 1967 proved to be a turning point for the Palestinian national movement. Proponents of the inevitability of reliance on Arab strength for the liberation of Palestine—through "progressive fronts" or through existing regimes—were hard pressed to defend such a view following the defeat of three Arab armies in less than one week. Palestinian political leaders would converge on the notion of a specifically Palestinian formation, and Fatah, as the first to espouse such an approach, was well positioned to take the lead.

In the aftermath of the 1967 debacle, Shuqairi came under attack from Palestinian resistance organizations as well as from members of the PLO's Executive Committee (EC), who denounced his leadership as "no less damaging to the Organization than external factors," and declared an "accountable" and "collective leadership" imperative.[225] The growing popularity of the "freedom fighters" (fida'yin) among the Palestinian and Arab masses could not be ignored. Support for their integration into the PLO was one way for Arab regimes to defuse widespread indignation and demands for accountability.[226] In December of the same year Shuqairi yielded and a new transitional president was named.

Before his departure, Shuqairi initiated contacts with the underground organizations. Ever wary of constraints to their autonomy, it took some months for Fatah leaders to be convinced of the advantages of entering the PLO.[227] Negotiations over representation in the Palestinian National Council (PNC)—what became the Palestinian parliament in exile—were conducted over the following months and a new (the fourth) PNC was convened in Cairo in July 1968. A new charter was adopted that committed the PLO to "Armed struggle as the only way to liberate Palestine," the contribution to which became a condition for organizations seeking membership.[228] While upholding the distinction between Jews and Zionists, and reaffirming the commitment to battle the latter, the PNC adopted a program that envisioned "a progressive, democratic, non-sectarian Palestine in which Christian, Moslem and Jew will worship, live peacefully and enjoy equal rights."[229] Quotas were negotiated for representation of the organizations of the *fida'yin* in the PNC, and unions as well as independents were allotted a specified number of seats.[230] In February 1969, the fifth PNC elected Yasser Arafat (the head of Fatah) chairman of the PLO. This would mark the beginning of the transformation of the PLO from an organization headed by politically unaffiliated Palestinian figures, known for their education and family names but with no organized following, into one headed by relatively unknown, young, professional figures from "lesser families" who brought with them popular support through their as yet embryonic resistance organizations.[231]

In Search of a Base

The search for a base began immediately. Indeed, within months of the Israeli occupation, Arafat himself infiltrated the West Bank for the purpose of setting up cells for the armed struggle. Finding very limited receptivity to the call to arms, Arafat left the territories discouraged by the prospects of igniting a popular revolutionary armed struggle under the occupation.[232] Other political organizations in exile, at least in part, shared Arafat's disillusionment and would, like Fatah, concentrate their efforts on the population with the most to gain from liberation—the refugees. Thus, the Palestinian national movement would develop as a movement outside its homeland, drawing both its purpose and its forces from the exiled refugee population.

The *fida'yin* set about organizing recruits and mass organizations in Jordan, which had both the largest concentration of Palestinians and the longest border with Israel. They would get a chance to demonstrate what they could do on March 21, 1968, when 300 Fatah fighters defended the Jordanian village of Karameh, the center of *fida'yin* forces, inflicting heavy losses on an estimated 15,000 invading Israeli troops.[233] Karameh, which means pride in Arabic, became the symbol of a new Palestinian awakening.

Thousands—Palestinians and other Arabs—converged on Amman to join the *fidāyin,* who asserted their authority openly on the streets of the capital.[234] In 1970, tensions between the popularly supported resistance fighters and the Jordanian government erupted in a military confrontation to resolve whose authority would prevail.

Assured of the support of the Palestinian majority of the country, Fatah leaders sought to avoid a confrontation and were willing to tolerate the "dual authority" that prevailed.[235] Other organizations would argue that such a confrontation was both inevitable and necessary, given the need for unimpaired armed incursions into the occupied territories from Jordan and the nature of the Jordanian monarchy.[236] Defeated in their last stronghold in Jarash, the PLO forces were forced to evacuate Jordan in 1971.

The defeat of the PLO and the organization's expulsion from Jordan deprived the resistance organizations of a strategic location from which to conduct the armed struggle. The PLO relocated to Lebanon, which was by far less favorable both in terms of the size of the Palestinian community and the length of its border with Israel.[237] Lebanon, however, had a weak state. Moreover, in 1969, Palestinian uprisings in the refugee camps in Lebanon led to the signing of the Cairo Accords between the Lebanese government and the PLO, granting the latter control over the refugee camps and the right to operate from southern Lebanon.[238]

The *fidāyin* organizations were welcomed by the Palestinian refugee population, which had endured two decades of repression at the hands of the Lebanese internal security apparatus, the Deuxième Bureau, in the sixteen grossly neglected refugee camps. Treated as "alien residents," the predominantly Sunni Muslim Palestinians faced limited prospects for a future in Lebanon as their inclusion threatened to upset the precarious confessional basis of government that favored Christians even after they had become a minority.[239]

Popular participation of both Palestinians and Lebanese was enlisted in the building of the resistance organizations. Tremendous enthusiasm and revolutionary ideals particularly inspired the younger generation of camp residents who were eager to take up the PLO's call for armed struggle as the means of securing the Return: a generation that had no experience of Palestine, but whose parents retained keys to their homes long occupied by Jewish immigrants or reduced to rubble, as was the case with some 400 Palestinian villages and towns.[240] The call would reverberate throughout the Palestinian communities of the diaspora, as well as within Palestine, as recruits left their studies, jobs, and families to join the movement rapidly reconstituting itself in Lebanon.

The popularity and the number of *fidāyin* organizations continued to grow. Fatah, the pioneer of the notion of Palestinian self-reliance, remained the largest, inspiring particularly the poorer camp residents for whom inclusion in Lebanon entailed no relief. Formed as a movement, Fatah's Palestinian nationalism drew supporters from the entire spectrum of ideological perspectives; Palestinian and Arab nationalists, socialists, communists, and Muslim militants all found a home in Fatah. To varying degrees they shared a disillusionment with the Arab regimes' contribution to the liberation of Palestine and would remain vigilant against Arab attempts to usurp Palestinian independence in decision making.[241] Ironically, Fatah, the most disdainful of Arab nationalism and the most vehement about Palestinian independence, obtained the greatest Arab financial support, particularly from the conservative oil-rich states. This has been variably interpreted as "conscience money" or compensation for relieving the Arabs from the burden of liberating Palestine or a deliberate attempt by the conservative regimes to divert the movement from its revolutionary potentials.[242] More important was Fatah's espousal of "noninterference in the internal affairs of the Arab states"[243] at a time when other organizations called for the revolutionary overthrow of the reactionary Arab regimes and developed relations with their opposition movements with the aim of forming progressive Arab fronts.[244]

Competing with Fatah were the Marxist-Leninist Popular Front for the Liberation of Palestine (PFLP) and the Democratic Front for the Liberation of Palestine (DFLP). Formed in late 1967, the PFLP grew out of the ANM. Without abandoning its pan-Arab nationalism, the PFLP adopted Marxism-Leninism in this now specifically Palestinian formation. Palestinians, and particularly the workers among them, were to form the vanguard of the Arab people in the confrontation with Israel. The DFLP, which split from the PFLP in early 1969, criticized the latter for being too nationalist and not sufficiently Marxist. Both would remain vocal critics of Fatah's "Palestinian chauvinism" and petty-bourgeois leanings. These, along with Fatah, would form the largest and most important of the organizations of the PLO; Fatah was by far the largest. Eventually, a total of eight organizations would come to operate under the umbrella of the PLO, brought together by a commitment to the armed struggle to liberate Palestine.[245]

But, as would happen repeatedly throughout the history of the Palestinian national movement, regional developments introduced new constraints. In October 1973, Arabs launched a war against Israel: Egypt sought to regain the Sinai, Syria the Golan Heights. Remarkably, backing the war effort was a united Arab front that included the conservative oil-producing

Gulf states employing the "oil weapon" for the first time.[246] If the joint effort revived Palestinian hopes for Arab unity as the road to the liberation of Palestine, developments that followed the cease-fire quashed them. Out-maneuvering both the UN and the Soviets, the United States wrested control of diplomatic initiatives and sidelined Palestinians. The U.S.-mediated disengagement agreements implied de facto Arab recognition of Israel.[247] Israel further gained American assurances regarding the isolation of the PLO, and discussions of a comprehensive peace plan were based on UN Resolution 242, which treated Palestinians as merely a "problem of refugees" once again.[248] Moreover, there were indications that Egypt, militarily the strongest Arab country, was prepared to break with Arab ranks to pursue a separate peace with Israel.

The PLO's response would be to move on the diplomatic front. Within less than a decade, the Palestinian leaders would shift from the goal of liberating "all of Palestine" to the establishment of a "secular democratic state" to the creation of a Palestinian "national authority" in 1974.[249] The PLO would now embrace any territory liberated from Israeli control, thereby signaling the acceptability of the West Bank and Gaza Strip—that is, less than the homeland in its entirety—for the reconstitution of the Palestinian nation.

The majority of Arab states encouraged the PLO's new position and, indeed, the guerrilla leaders' transformation into statesmen.[250] Arab leaders were themselves eager to be rid of the popularly based resistance organizations' radicalizing influence upon their populations.[251] In October 1974, the PLO obtained Arab League recognition as "the sole legitimate representative of the Palestinian people."[252] One month later, the liberation organization gained international recognition when Arafat addressed the UN General Assembly and the PLO was granted UN observer status. Both were significant achievements for a population whose very existence continued to be denied by Israeli leaders. PLO concessions and compromises achieved nothing, however, and Israel remained as unyielding as ever.[253] This, coupled with the relaxation of the commitment to revolutionary armed struggle implied by the new course of diplomacy, produced a period of marked internal dissension led by the PFLP-headed "Rejectionist Front."[254] Worse yet, Lebanon, the site of the PLO's center of operations, was on the brink of a civil war.

In April 1975, the Lebanese civil war erupted with an attack on a bus carrying Palestinian civilians home through a Christian quarter of Beirut. Fatah sought to stay out of the Lebanese conflict while other Palestinian factions joined the fighting along the side of the Lebanese National Movement (LNM).[255] Within one year, the annihilation of Palestinian refugee camps and neighborhoods in the areas under right-wing Lebanese control compelled Fatah to commit actively to the fighting.[256] In 1976, Syria—ever intent, opportunistically, on preserving a balance between opposing forces in Lebanon—intervened on behalf of the right-wing forces, dealing a severe blow to both the PLO and the LNM. The PLO would become a central participant in a war that would persist for fourteen years.

Within six years of its transformation from an appendage of the Arab League into a mass-based resistance movement, the PLO had obtained Arab acceptance of a Palestinian voice among Arab states as well as international attention to the Palestinian cause after decades of neglect and obstruction. These were not insignificant gains. Yet, as an exile organization that drew both its members and its purpose from refugees, the organization lacked leverage within Israel. A sizeable constituency, however, remained within the homeland: Palestinians in the West Bank and Gaza Strip.

Resistance Quelled under Israeli Occupation

Palestinians' initial response to the Israeli occupation of the West Bank and Gaza Strip reflected their preparedness to act. In the Gaza Strip, the presence of PLA forces as well as trained and armed civilians—neither of which had been permitted in the West Bank—enabled Palestinians to resist actively.[257] Moreover, with their access to Egypt hindered by the Sinai Desert, and the only land routes to Jordan traversing Israeli territory, relatively few people were displaced by the war from the Gaza Strip.[258] Resistance was, therefore, fierce and carried out directly within communities as the Israeli army bulldozed avenues through the densely populated refugee camps to permit the free movement of military hardware.[259] It took approximately three years to quell resistance in the Gaza Strip, a land area 28 miles long and five miles wide in total.

By contrast, Israeli occupation forces encountered relatively little armed resistance in the West Bank.[260] Already subdued by the Jordanian regime, the Israeli authorities conquered a largely pacified population. Their task of rounding up potential resisters was simplified by the appropriation of security files amassed by Jordanian intelligence networks in the West Bank.[261] And the exodus of some 250,000 Palestinians to the East Bank, many becoming refugees for a second time, facilitated Israeli control further.[262]

Early Israeli administration of the occupied territories relied on the administrative institutions prevailing before 1967, which were largely preserved and in some cases reinforced.[263] Content with their Jordanian credentials, the Israeli authorities reactivated West Bank municipal and village councils, and mayors, *mukhtars,* and other functionaries who remained continued in their previous roles. Jordanian laws were kept in force, as well as the circulation of the Jordanian currency and financial links between the municipalities and the Jordanian government, which continued to pay the salaries of its civil servants. In the Gaza Strip, the Israeli occupation continued to apply the British Mandatory regulations, and appointed members of Gaza's notable families to the civilian posts.[264]

Municipal and village leaders now maintained patronage relations with residents based on a combination of access to the Israeli military authorities and Jordanian funds.[265] Their localistic roles suited Israel's policy of preserving a fragmented leadership; their functions and authority were circumscribed strictly within the municipality or village.[266] Relying on each locale's most influential families, the Israeli administration sought collaborators among them and relied on the inherent conservatism of others.[267] In return for a continued role in local matters, the occupiers required that they assist in preserving calm, while the Israeli security forces took charge of suppressing organized Palestinian resistance activity.

In 1972, the occupation authorities proceeded with West Bank municipal elections as scheduled. Fearing the appointment of military personnel, which Israeli leaders threatened in the event of an election boycott, the Jordanian government supported participation; the PLO appealed to residents to refrain.[268] The elections would go ahead and for the most part reinstated the conservative, pro-Jordanian incumbents and elected new members who shared the old guard's apolitical approach to the role of municipalities.[269]

In the relative calm that prevailed, the Israeli occupation authorities executed their plans for the territories. In the immediate aftermath of the war, East Jerusalem was annexed. By 1975, sixty Israeli settlements had been established in the occupied territories.[270] Bridges linking the West Bank to Jordan remained open, permitting the continued passage of goods and people, thereby also facilitating Palestinian emigration to Jordan and beyond.[271] And with a policy of "open borders" between Israel and the occupied territories, the latter were rapidly becoming exporters of cheap and unorganized labor and importers of Israeli goods.[272]

Palestinians did not watch passively. Indeed, within the first year of occupation, efforts by Jerusalem's religious and municipal leaders to organize Palestinian civil disobedience resulted in the deportation of 514 leaders.[273] Renewed Palestinian attempts to form an internal leadership led to the formation of the Palestinian National Front (PNF) in 1973, which obtained the PLO's endorsement.[274] While representing a wide array of social and political forces, communists—those with the most extensive experience in mass organizing—figured prominently in the PNF, something that would prove problematic for the more conservative elements of the PLO.[275] The semi-clandestine PNF presented itself as the political arm of the PLO inside the occupied territories and declared as its objective the establishment of a Palestinian state through diplomatic means.[276] In the following two years, the PNF would lead demonstrations and protests, thereby demonstrating the potential that existed for mass action.[277] But PLO ambivalence regarding leadership inside the territories, combined with Israel's deportation of PNF leaders, rendered the PNF's contribution short lived.[278]

Attempts to form internal leadership structures notwithstanding, for the most part this was a period of waiting, first for the international community and then for the liberation movement in exile to secure an Israeli withdrawal from the territories. The liberation movement existed only as an exile force; Fatah and PFLP attempts to establish cells for armed activity inside the territories floundered.[279] And while students and young professionals began to initiate community-based efforts, the organized political forces of the PLO in exile did not take such undertakings seriously.[280]

By the mid-1970s, the prospects of the Palestinian national movement appeared bleak. Arab dealings aimed at mollifying the United States bypassed the PLO, a civil war loomed in Lebanon where the organization was headquartered, and Palestinian resistance to the Israeli occupation remained feeble. Palestinians under occupation, and particularly the youth, carried out demonstrations and protests, but showed no signs of a sustained resistance movement. The costs to Israel of containing Palestinian resistance proved tolerable and freed Israel to "create facts" on the ground to prevent a reversion to the status quo ante. As hope for a speedy Israeli withdrawal receded, a new threat emerged: substantial emigration of Palestinians from the territories.[281]

Explaining Failure

The Arab defeat in 1948 produced the dismemberment of Palestine and the dispersal of its people. It also entailed freedom from Israeli rule for the majority of Palestinians. The loss in 1967 presented the possibility of reintegration for Palestinians in the West Bank, Gaza Strip, and Israel but under Israeli rule. Each entailed particular constraints and potentials for the Palestinian national movement.

The first defeat resulted in Palestinians' complete exclusion and dependence on other Arabs. For the dispersed and vanquished refugee population it was inconceivable that the liberation of Palestine could be secured without Arab resources. This necessitated, in turn, an ideology that placed the question of Palestine at the center of Arab concerns. Whether in the form of Arab nationalism, communism, or Islam, the most popular ideologies were those that transcended the inherent divisiveness of state nationalism. That Arab nationalism prevailed (which in addition inveighed against sectarian and class divisions) testifies to the strength of appeal of "unity." Ironically, Arab unity, elusive as it was, delayed the emergence of Palestinian-specific political formations: Arab nationalism, aimed at overcoming the liability of separate Arab states, was an unlikely sponsor of the creation of a new one—Palestine.[282] Thus, relying on Arab political formations and/or Arab states, Palestinians sought to keep "Palestine" alive within the Arab nation.

But Palestinian reliance on Arab resources to liberate Palestine failed in 1967. Without abandoning the turn to Arabs entirely, Palestinians began to be receptive to those advocating self-reliance. Examples internationally of national liberation movements successfully utilizing revolutionary armed struggle gave additional impetus to such a turn. Initially, mainstream Palestinian leaders envisioned employing armed actions to "entangle" Arab states into a war with Israel. The occupation of the West Bank and Gaza Strip stimulated a new understanding, and attempts were initiated to generate popular revolutionary armed struggle under occupation that met with limited success. Following the October War, the movement's mainstream relegated the armed struggle to a largely symbolic position. But while recognizing its limitations under Palestinian conditions, they could not abdicate the armed struggle; the popularly supported *fidāyin,* armed and mobilized, attested to the organization's existence and vigor, as well as to the movement leaders' relevance. Yet, by concentrating on the diaspora—where PLO leaders were able to exert control—the movement remained vulnerable to Arab manipulation and neglected the occupied territories. Indeed, as Tamari astutely points out, "there was a lack of congruence between a national project that sought the liberation of the Palestinian territories occupied in 1967 but relied exclusively on refugees who originated from territories lost in 1948 to achieve it."[283]

In both periods, members of the Palestinian middle classes led attempts to revive a Palestinian national movement decimated by the population's expulsion and dispersal. But the middle classes' inherent fragmentation was exacerbated by exile. Interestingly, "Palestinianism" originated among Palestinians employed in the distant Gulf states, where Palestinians confronted the greatest obstacles to integration.[284] For middle-class Palestinians in Jordan, Syria, and many Christian Palestinians in Lebanon, integration was possible and held tangible benefits. And while both the landed elite and dispossessed peasants suffered from the loss of the means of production in

1948, members of the middle class thrived professionally in a region under-going substantial economic development. Thus, middle-class Palestinian refugees were the ones in a position to initiate political action. Initially, they applied their class resources to existing Arab political formations and only later to specifically Palestinian organizations.

Neither reliance on Arabs nor armed struggle conducted from exile were sufficient to induce Israel to retreat from the newly occupied territories, let alone from all of Palestine. The PLO's new goal of achieving a "national authority" reflected recognition of this. And while the PLO enjoyed an enormous following in exile, exclusion meant that Palestinians lacked lever-age within Israel—or so it seemed, as most Palestinians inside and outside the territories did not question their powerlessness. Encountering a tolerable level of resistance to their rule, the Israeli occupation forces proceeded with their plans for the territories unhindered.

Failure of Middle-Class-Led Movements

In the formative phase of their national struggles, the African and Pales-tinian middle classes could not dismiss the authority wielded by the indige-nous elites. In the phase that followed, they asserted their autonomy from the discredited and ineffectual leaders. They were now free to do so because of the failure of elite leadership and the elites' loss of control over resources that constituted the basis of their standing as an elite. But middle classes are not homogeneous. Confronted with the new political realities, various segments of the middle class—intellectuals, professionals, and civil servants, among others—responded differently. What is important, however, is that elements that aspire to leadership of a national movement can only hope to succeed through alliances that enable them to compensate for their resource weak-ness vis-à-vis both their opponents and their potential constituency. Whom they seek out is a function of what they conceive their class interests to be and who exists with an interest in supporting them. They may turn to the indigenous elite, indigenous popular classes, external parties, or seek accom-modation with the ruling powers. In contexts of settler colonialism, where the settlers' only interest in inclusion is confined to labor, collaboration by the middle class, which seeks the elimination of domination, is not likely as long as settlers are capable of ensuring control over labor on their own.

Inclusion and exclusion generated different constraints and possibilities for the African and Palestinian middle classes, weakening the former while permitting the expansion of the latter. By circumscribing rights to property, employment, education, and residence, apartheid legislation undermined the existing African middle class and impeded the social mobility of those who aspired to join them. The Palestinian middle class, however, expanded dramatically in this period. Excluded from Israel's economy and society where they too would have confronted the discriminatory policies that obstructed the upward mobility of the small number of Palestinians who became citizens of Israel, Palestinians secured opportunities in the Arab states.[285] Arab countries in the process of state building and economic expansion actively incorporated Palestinian talent even while giving preferential treatment to their own citizens. The loss of the means of production in 1948, UN assistance aimed at integrating Palestinians into their host countries, and employment opportunities in those countries created powerful incentives for educational attainment. Thus, while the class-specific aspirations of the African middle class were being frustrated, their Palestinian counterparts found prospects for advancement despite their statelessness. As a result, the efforts of significant segments of middle-class Palestinians were diverted away from the movement by the availability of options that did not exist for their counterparts in South Africa.

The search for resources through alliances by members of the African and Palestinian middle classes who aspired to leadership of the national movements produced two periods in the consolidation phase of resistance. In South Africa, this phase began with the new leaders of the ANC turning actively to mass mobilization and cross-race alliances (1949–60). The ANC's search for allies eventually led to the formation of the Congress Alliance, which brought together middle-class leaders of all the oppressed communities—African, Indian, and colored—as well as sympathetic, largely middle-class, whites. From unity of Africans in the early phase, they moved toward unity of other oppressed groups and white democrats. Through the middle-class-dominated Congress Alliance, mass-defiance campaigns were organized nationally to resist apartheid laws. As the mobilization failed to withstand state repression, however, and the organization was banned, a second period was initiated with the turn to armed struggle (from 1961 onward). Armed struggle represented another way in which the middle-class-led political organization sought to gain both leverage within the white-dominated society and followers among the oppressed.

The consolidation phase of the Palestinian national movement also consisted of two periods. In the first period, Palestinian leaders turned to Arabs and a military solution for the liberation of Palestine (1949–67). Would-be Palestinian leaders sought to compensate for the fragmentation of Palestinian society with Arab unity. Dispersed throughout the region, middle-class Palestinians pursued different routes and alliances within different geopolitical contexts and constraints. They shared, however, the view that the liberation of Palestine could only be accomplished through some form of joint Arab effort and were prominent in the various Arab political formations of the time. An alternative approach was in the making, however, which would come into its own but only after the failure of reliance on Arab unity. That failure came in the June War of 1967 when the Arab armies were defeated by Israel, resulting in the occupation of the remainder of Palestine. A new period was ushered in by Palestinian leaders who espoused a distinctly Palestinian nationalism and initiated the armed struggle (from 1968 onward). Again, armed struggle was the middle-class leaders' attempt to create both leverage that could be wielded against their opponents and the basis for their claim to leadership of the national movement among its constituency.

The consolidation phase is a transitional one in a number of respects. First, although asserting their autonomy from their traditional elites, middle-class leaders still lacked the power of an activated mass base behind them. Whereas the elites's relevance to the ruling powers is derived from their ability to restrain mass resistance, middle-class leaders must demonstrate their capacity to activate it. In this phase of resistance they are well on their way to asserting their hegemony over the movements—evident in the popular support for their programs—but the resistance potentials of the mass base remained uncertain. The middle-class leaders' approach to that mass base, however, begins to take shape with implications for the subsequent phase of the national movement.

Second, the two movements converged on the necessity of armed struggle, although from different starting points: the ANC following decades of unsuccessful nonviolent struggle and hope in white liberals; the PLO following decades of futile appeals to the UN and reliance on Arab capabilities. Revolutionary armed struggle becomes the middle-class leaders' alternative to the elite's ineffective and vacillating leadership, and yet before the popular sectors seize the initiative in resistance in the last phase.

Finally, the implications of inclusion/exclusion shaped the political objectives adopted by the mainstream of both national movements. The forced African dependence on the white-dominated economy and the limited viability of what remained of an indigenous economy were conducive to a vision of a unitary South Africa. Nonracialism and the incorporation of whites in the program for a future South Africa reflected both recognition of the extent of dependence forged and the lack of appeal of an African state composed of fragments of destitute territories. Moreover, for significant segments of middle-class Africans and workers, the rural economy was irrelevant as their reproduction depended on the urban, white-dominated sectors of South Africa's economy. In contrast, exclusion meant that Palestinians remained free of dependence on Israel and could thus envision a future independent of Jews. Prior to 1967, exclusion had permitted the preservation of the indigenous resource base and social relations in the areas not occupied by Israel, areas insulated from the degenerative dynamics of Israel's advanced capitalist economy. As a result, African inclusion and Palestinian exclusion came to be reflected in the political objectives of the mainstream of both national movements: inclusionary of whites and exclusionary of Jews. The limited appeal of African and Palestinian organizations that espoused alternative views—exclusionary of whites and inclusionary of Jews—reflected their respective middle classes' readings of possibilities through the lenses of their class interests. These divergent objectives were reinforced further by regional realities.

ANC recognition of African states' limited means and the PLO's access to substantial Arab state resources were consequential. Reliance on African states, which were themselves racked with economic and political struggles, remained limited. Moreover, despite the appeal of African nationalism in the Garveyist vein, there was no history of a unified African entity that spanned the continent from which to draw mobilization power. Thus the pan-Africanist challenge to the ANC's nonracialism drew insufficient financial support from African states or emotive resonance from history. In contrast, Arab state resources were plentiful and those vying for leadership of the region invoked the history of unity that spanned centuries and continents with tremendous effect. Eventually, however, Palestinian leaders gave up on unified Arab action. Then their struggle became one of carving out a distinct Palestinian national entity and identity from centuries-old Arab and/or Muslim ones. That is, while the South African movement advocates a South African entity that is inclusive of their opponents, upon whom they are dependent, the Palestinian movement seeks first to make Palestine the heart of the definition of "Arab," then failing in this turns to create a Palestinian national entity and identity exclusive of their opponents, from whom they are independent. As such, the South African liberation struggle presents nonracialism as a negation of the exclusionary white or Afrikaner nationalism, while Palestinians come to mirror the exclusionary Jewish nationalism with an exclusionary Palestinian nationalism. Both are symptomatic of inclusion/exclusion dynamics and structural possibilities as they are read by the respective middle-class leaders.

5

Merging Class and Nation in the Expansion of Popular Struggles, 1970s to 1990s

With African and Palestinian resistance quelled, both South Africa and Israel would enjoy a period of relative stability and prosperity. Repression had generated economic gains as no political or trade union organizations stood in the way of putting black and Palestinian workers to work on South African and Israeli employers' terms. Signs of renewed militance, however, began to appear. New, defiant social forces began to coalesce, aided by the nature of South Africa's economic expansion and the integration of the Palestinian territories' economies with Israel's.

With the first signs of the resurgence of resistance, struggles would ensue within the South African and Israeli ruling groups regarding the nature of the relationship to the populations they dominated and the implications of inclusion and exclusion. South Africa's economic expansion collided with apartheid constraints: as numerous authors have noted, when apartheid worked, it kept black labor cheap but poor and therefore unable to consume what was being produced; and it kept it dependent and compliant, but unskilled and therefore unable to meet the changing labor needs of an evolving and expanding economy. Renewed resistance would become both symptomatic and transformative of the exigencies of South African capital. The *verligte* or "open-minded" wing in government would introduce reforms: the inclusion of certain segments of urban blacks would be expanded while the exclusion of the rural population would be reinforced. Palestinian resistance in the mid-1970s would force an Israeli reappraisal of their rule in the territories. Rather than reforms, however, the new hawkish Israeli government would endeavor to restore order by force, thus ending the "liberal" period of

Israeli rule. The new government was openly committed to the annexation of the territories; Palestinian resistance was used as a pretext to step up repression and efforts to induce emigration. The differences in the South African and Israeli approaches reflected differences in their relationship to the dominated population. In South Africa, capital required stability as well as the cooperation of black workers for continued economic expansion; something that repression alone could not secure. Israeli dependence on Palestinian labor was considerably less, thus coercion was not mitigated by the need for cooperation. Indeed, it had the additional benefit of inducing emigration.

In both cases a new phase of resistance would be forged by mass-based organizations, asserting the popular sectors' contribution to the national liberation project. The renewal of popular struggles provides the ANC and the PLO with the long-awaited opportunity to pressure their opponents on the internal front. In both cases, the political organizations in exile would have to catch up to developments inside the country; both would be caught by surprise by the resurgence of resistance in the 1970s and a decade later by the full-scale uprisings that would shift the momentum of both movements from exile into South Africa and Palestine directly.

Workers, Leverage, and Resistance

In contexts of settler colonialism, the most effective resistance resource is leverage derived from dependence of the dominant group on a function performed by those they dominate. That function is variable and so too is its organization. The organization of production and its attendant structures permits certain forms of leverage and not others and facilitates the exercise of some forms and not others. Workers may develop the leverage they possess or it may remain an unrealized potential source of power. When workers recognize their leverage, struggles ensue within the national liberation movement over who will wield this power and to what end.

Inclusion of indigenous labor in early or extractive settler economic enterprises (farming and mining) permits leverage whose use is difficult to activate. This is so because workers with the requisite skills are in abundance, rendering them easily replaceable, while the organization of production hinders their combination. Not dissimilar is inclusion in the form of unskilled labor in an industrialized capitalist economy, particularly in sectors such as construction or low level services. Scattered in small-scale settings, minimally skilled, and difficult to organize, workers' leverage is limited and what exists is hard to mobilize. Nevertheless, inclusion even in this form generates dynamics that begin to erode indigenous social relations and organization and, as such, free the movement's mass base from indigenous dominant classes. Leverage is maximized in industrial settings. Concentration and acquisition of skills required by industrialization render the organization of the withholding of labor more easily accomplished. Indeed, leverage is greatest when workers are skilled, in concentrated settings, and organized. But leverage is a resource that may be applied to variable ends.

In the context of national liberation struggles, asset-rich yet leverage-poor middle classes seek to compensate for their resource weakness by harnessing the working class's leverage. They do this by continuously pressing for workers to adopt the liberation project as a priority over their class-specific interests. National liberation movement leaders realize that only the threat of activation of popular resistance makes them viable players in a game their opponents dominate. Recognizing that the movement's power lies in an activated mass base, they search for ways to mobilize the "masses" from above and seek to wield the leverage of workers in negotiations with their opponents. The key to a successful challenge to their opponents, however, lies not in leaders' ability to activate the movement's mass base, but in the mass base gaining the capacity to mobilize itself.

Historically, union politics have exhibited tremendous variability. Workers may eschew participation in the national movement as too risky or they may commit actively. They generally opt to navigate between the two: class and national interests. Factors that influence which course workers adopt include the strength of indigenous dominant classes, the strength of working-class formations, and their opponents' readiness to co-opt. These factors, in turn, are shaped by inclusion and exclusion.

Through the incorporation of indigenous labor, inclusionary settler colonialism endows indigenous workers with leverage. By freeing the working class from indigenous dominant classes, inclusion also contributes to democratizing political action through the introduction of potentially new bases of identification and organization that transcend inherently narrow traditional forms (e.g., ethnic, clan, and religious) under the control of dominant classes. The persistence of traditional identifications and formations reduces the effectiveness of working classes' leverage by locating organization at a distance from their opponents' point of vulnerability—that is, in production. Thus, through the transformation of indigenous economic relations, inclusion simultaneously introduces new bases of identification and organization and undermines the old that impede effective forms of combination and action.

Exclusionary settler colonialism neither permits indigenous workers leverage, nor contributes to the erosion of traditional formations that delay the emergence of more effective forms of mass political action. At best not all-inclusive, at worst divisive, traditional organizations rooted in kinship and clan, ethnicity, or religion are not conducive to cross-group, mass participation and the empowerment of the mass base. This is not to say that traditional organizations are not beneficial; they may serve important survival functions of protection and security for workers and communities. Their persistence, however, is at a cost, particularly where the working class is ethnically heterogeneous. Indeed, opponents actively cultivate competing indigenous identifications and formations as a means of undermining unity within the working class.

The struggle for workers becomes one of recognizing their class's leverage, organizing to exercise it, and actually applying it in ways and toward ends that address not only their class interests but that assert their class interests as hegemonic within the national liberation movement beyond the workplace. Once an alliance has been struck between indigenous dominant and working classes, they compete over the movement's precise objectives as each struggles to assert their class-specific national objectives. The effectiveness of workers' contribution to the democratization of the liberation project and its outcome is a function of the strength of working-class formations within such alliances. Organization from below of workers in strong, democratic trade unions renders the expansion of the mass base of political participation more effective as leverage becomes a direct source of power wielded by those who are endowed with it. Such organization also increases the likelihood of a democratic outcome; rather than acquiescing to what would be at best a representative democracy in which workers are asked to rely on middle-class representatives, workers produce a participatory democracy in which they assert and safeguard their interests themselves. The bases of each is laid in this phase of resistance.

South Africa, 1973 to 1990

In the decades since 1948, apartheid-driven economic growth had proven both rapid and supremely profitable. Under the state's patronage, Afrikaner business had succeeded in penetrating the heights of historically English-dominated monopoly capital.[1] A confident Afrikaner bourgeoisie was now well ensconced in all sectors.[2]

By the mid-1960s, industrial capital was ascendant with manufacturing contributing a greater share of the GDP than mining and agriculture combined.[3] Mechanization, introduced in the 1960s boom years, made a skilled and stable workforce increasingly necessary even in mining and agriculture.[4] Apartheid inclusion, however, presented impediments to further growth:

acute shortages of skilled labor despite an abundance of work-seekers, a relatively small domestic market despite a substantial population lacking all types of goods, and massive pressures on the industrialized center by victims of the apartheid underdevelopment of the rural periphery. Apartheid kept African labor poor and unskilled and was doing so at considerable cost.[5] Thus, for capital, the system of inclusion of African labor required modifications; black resistance would make such modifications imperative. Just as in 1946 and 1960, that is, during crises involving massive worker unrest, employers touted reforms while behind the scenes they chafed for the government to restore order. This time, however, stability would be elusive, and black resistance would considerably raise the stakes of biding time.

The End of Quiescence: Challenge in Formation

In retrospect, the strike wave that rocked the Durban area in 1972–73 would mark the beginning of the end of the decade of quiescence and, eventually, the system that had exacted it.[6] The surge of strike actions that traversed numerous industries and regions would be the biggest to hit the country since the Second World War.[7] Concurrently, though not by design, black university students initiated actions across black university campuses in 1972–73.[8] Defiant workers and students who emerged in parallel would make their way to each other uneasily, and only later to the wider community of the oppressed.

Industrial expansion had altered the character of the working class as workers in industry increased and as employers, driven by the exigencies of production, violated apartheid employment stipulations by permitting in practice what continued to be prohibited by law: the acquisition of skills by African workers.[9] This rendered workers less easily replaceable with new leverage at their disposal. However, as they gradually discovered their leverage, they exercised it cautiously and resorted to strikes only after exhausting existing channels for redress of grievances related to wages and working conditions.[10] Workers' actions remained confined to workplace settings where they were strong in numbers and purpose and were not carried over into the townships.[11] Lacking organization and identifiable leaders, strikers were protected, as not everyone could be jailed.[12] In the process, the strikes succeeded in securing relatively substantial wage increases, thereby inaugurating the renewal of black trade unionism.[13]

Another source of challenge had formed on black university campuses. The need of industry and services for a better educated and skilled workforce compelled the state to expand African education.[14] Over a single decade (1960–70), African secondary school and university enrollment more than

doubled to 122,489 and 4,578, respectively.[15] University enrollment continued to expand dramatically through the 1970s, even while enrollment rates
relative to the size of the population remained dismal and the quality of education poor.[16]

Student organizations that had been affiliated with the ANC and PAC
in the 1950s remained banned, thus for most of the 1960s black students
worked through the liberal and white-dominated National Union of South
African Students (NUSAS). In 1968, citing white paternalism, black students announced "that a time had come when blacks had to formulate their
own thinking, unpolluted by ideas emanating from a group with lots at
stake in the status quo" and broke away from NUSAS to form the South
African Students Organisation (SASO).[17] African, Indian, and colored students declared, "we are BLACK students and not black STUDENTS," thereby
rejecting their "nonwhite" classification to assert instead a "black" identity
that encompassed the three oppressed groups in what became known as the
Black Consciousness Movement (BCM).[18] As Anthony Marx notes, the
"BC sought a middle ground between the exclusiveness of the [Africanist]
PAC and the inclusiveness of the [nonracial] ANC."[19] Initially, this development was welcomed by the government. The break up of the multiracial
NUSAS and assertion of black distinctiveness from whites was consistent
with the prevailing ideology of apartheid and political exclusion.[20] They
were slow to recognize the potential of BC to break down barriers between
"nonwhites" and its implications.[21] Indeed, BC would have a tremendous
influence on black students in the townships who were "conscientized"
around the notion of cultural and psychological liberation from white domination. Activists throughout the country, who would later abandon the emphasis on "blackness" to adopt a nonracial perspective, would trace their
early politicization to their experience in the BCM.

Although workers and students set out at the same time, mutual, class-
based suspicions kept them apart for much of the decade. Struggles in the
workplace were conducted in parallel to the newly emerging student ac-
tivism in the universities and township schools. For one thing, BC had no
tolerance for trade unionists' class focus, which they believed to be divisive
of blacks.[22] The BC's idealist perspective and de-emphasis on material concerns, which they insisted diverted attention from the more fundamental issues of cultural and psychological liberation, prevented the BCM from making significant inroads among workers through their trade union arm the
Black Allied Workers Union (BAWU)(1972).[23] Indeed, while BC sought to
use race to empower blacks,[24] democratic trade unionists were only too well
aware of the divisiveness of race in their efforts to empower workers.

In June 1976, both views would be tested when a strike by Soweto school students protesting the imposition of Afrikaans as the medium of instruction in schools provoked a full confrontation with the state. The BCM-inspired uprising provided powerful and surprising evidence of the potential for collective action that existed within the townships.[25] It also revealed its limits as the death of 575 youths in nine months and the state's ruthless suppression of the BCM would prove.[26] Among the numerous lessons student activists would draw was the need for more than the solidarity of others; mobilization of entire communities was required.[27] Recognition of the need to combine efforts grew as repression took its toll. The process of convergence of struggles, however, which becomes the hallmark of this phase of resistance, had yet to reach fruition. The Soweto uprising revealed that convergence was missing; the state would endeavor to ensure that it remained that way.

Reform, More Social Engineering, and Repression

The resurgence of popular opposition in South Africa was paralleled by momentous regional developments. The collapse of Portuguese rule in Angola and Mozambique in 1974 and their replacement by Marxist governments, the routing of the South African forces in Angola in 1976, the impending transition to majority rule in Zimbabwe, all intensified the prevailing unease in South African government and business circles. The ANC and PAC were emboldened by the new opportunities these developments afforded for armed struggle. The state's "Total Strategy" (1978) response to this "total onslaught" was an amalgam of a steady course along well-entrenched apartheid lines and a sweeping destabilization campaign in the region combined with reforms at home.[28]

The increasingly apparent inadequacy of the migrant labor system, coupled with the upsurge of resistance, compelled the state and employers to consider altering the terms of inclusion of African workers. The new approach would be to seek to stem urban unrest and avert the formation of a national, black political force by creating divisions between privileged urban "insiders" and excluded rural "outsiders."[29] The strategy was clear: to enlist one segment of the African population in the continued exclusion of the other by predicating the former's progress on the denial of access to others. This was combined with a new strategy of fostering the emergence of a compliant African middle class, which, motivated by a stake in free enterprise, might inject a "moderating" influence into black politics.[30] Thus, while persisting in divide and rule based on race and ethnicity, new divisions were introduced in the form of socially engineered class differentiation that reversed decades of active leveling of African society. The aim was to meet capital's new requirements while thwarting unity among the majority.

Reinforcing Exclusion, Escaping Exclusion:
The Marginalization of the Bantustan Population

As the cornerstone of the state's policy of political exclusion, bantustaniza-tion was pursued more vigorously. The Bantu Homeland Citizenship Act (1970) declared Africans "citizens" of one of ten bantustans, where African political aspirations were to be confined.[31] By 1976, eight bantustans had at-tained the status of "self-governing" territories.[32] The events of 1976 inject-ed new urgency and eventually new substance into the old policy of separate development: between 1976 and 1981 four bantustans were declared "inde-pendent republics." In the process of attaining "independence," approximate-ly eight million Africans were stripped of their South African citizenship,[33] reducing South Africa's de jure African population by half.[34] Eventual "in-dependence" was envisioned for all the African "national states" as a potential-ly less objectionable—internationally and domestically—means of perma-nently excluding the indigenous population.[35] Over time, the combination of forced removals[36] and forced incorporation of entire communities across bantustan borders[37] relegated an ever-larger percentage of the country's African population to the marginal territories: 39.5 percent in 1960; 47.3 percent in 1970; and 54.0 percent in 1980.[38]

Bantustanization was intended not only to permanently "relocate" and "externalize" Africans and their political aspirations, but also their rapidly looming potential revolutionary challenge.[39] New, more stringent influx controls were combined with measures to keep the unemployed and unem-ployable population inside the bantustans. Ten sets of relatively powerful African bureaucrats would eventually be entrusted with "efflux" control.[40] The state actively fostered these and other class forces, which were willing, at least implicitly, to abandon the goal of a unitary South Africa and acquiesce to permanent exclusion in exchange for dominance within the "ethnic fief-doms." Among the new, cooperative, if not collaborative, social forces was a small class of African capitalist farmers that was promoted through changes in laws pertaining to land tenure, which now permitted the privatization of land.[41] A sizeable class of African businessmen, which operated relatively free from restrictions that had stifled black commercial activity inside South Africa proper, now prospered. Together with traditional leaders who were absorbed into the governing structures of the bantustans as salaried func-tionaries, these formed a new bantustan elite that shared an immediate stake in bantustanization while being spared the fate of the overwhelming majority of the residents.

"Self-rule" and "independence" brought no relief to the majority of the population barely able to eke a living in the overcrowded, destitute, and fragmented territories.[42] As the privatization and concentration of land undermined communal land tenure and exacerbated landlessness, survival necessitated employment outside the territories more than ever,[43] at a time when opportunities for the largely unskilled laborers were bleaker than ever.[44] In the desperate search for jobs, many "illegal" workers found it economically more advantageous to combine employment for part of the year in South Africa's economic centers with jail terms for the remainder of the year than to remain inside the bantustans.[45] In order to stem the flow of African work seekers into "white South Africa," the state eased restrictions on international investment in the bantustans to create the economic underpinnings of what was merely a political shell. Even South African companies were offered new incentives, which were "among the most generous in the world" to advance the old policy of decentralizing industrial locations to border regions.[46] While incentives included doing away with even "the doubtful labour standards of South Africa itself," the policy fell far short of expectations in generating jobs.[47]

With their material underpinnings virtually eliminated, the paternalistic and communal nature of traditional social organization and authority were being supplanted by bureaucratic relations bolstered by repression. However, traditional social relations as a mode of social control were artificially preserved through dependence on patronage dispensed by bantustan bureaucracies via the tribal structures. Residents came to depend on such patronage in every aspect of their lives: securing employment outside the territories, arable land, pensions, licenses, passes, and the like.[48] Resentment of traditional leaders, who functioned as local authorities, was exacerbated by their corruption. With Pretoria's urging, local authorities compensated for the inadequacy of resources,[49] both for service provision and self-enrichment, by extracting all they could from the already destitute population.[50]

Despite its failure to achieve either economic viability or political legitimacy, bantustanization was succeeding in insulating the central government and South Africa's economic centers from the discontent of over half of the country's African population. While producing abominable conditions, bantustanization did not create the class forces capable of eliminating the system of domination in the rural territories, let alone in South Africa as a whole. The working class of the bantustans was divided over ten territories and under ten administrations. Significant segments of this class were permanently absent from the territories,[51] while commuters,[52] those employed locally, and the unemployed, endured divergent conditions and constraints.[53] Women formed a disproportionate share of the population, left to carry both the burden of survival[54] and care for the overwhelmingly large young population and the elderly.[55] As such, the population relegated to the bantustans was virtually powerless and incapable of altering the conditions they themselves confronted, let alone conditions affecting Africans nationally. Inspired by the BCM, the sizeable population of youth was the most politically active sector, but it too was divided by bantustan administrations and lacked leverage within them. Lacking leverage and ruled by social forces with a direct stake in bantustanization and control over the means of repression, the bantustan residents could do very little. Moreover, if bantustan governments demonstrated vigilance in keeping the population in, they kept influences out with even greater vigor.

Social forces developing in South Africa proper represented a threat to bantustan leaders.[56] Already in South Africa's economic centers new forms of organization challenged traditional leaders' authority despite employers' decades-long strategy of control via traditional leaders.[57] Bantustan leaders were alarmed by the prospect of militant workers organized in democratic popular organizations that transcended ethnicity, spreading their influence and organizational extensions into the leaders' traditional strongholds. Bantustan governments and the resident bourgeois aspirants were keen on keeping union influence out in order to attract investments.[58] These social forces converged on the need to suppress alternative bases of identification and organization inside the bantustans and to suppress resistance showing signs of coalescing.

While the new bantustan elite had a vested interest in bantustanization and, perhaps, even in abandoning claims to a unitary South Africa, the dominated certainly did not. Bantustanization had little hope of attracting the mass of residents when the gap in standards of living and economic opportunities was so glaring.[59] Mounting repression and lack of economic viability of the territories contrasted further with "reforms" and privileges now held out for Africans who enjoyed residency rights in South Africa's urban townships.[60] The strategy was clear: permanent exclusion of one-half of the African population was to be the price of "reforms" held out to the other.

Controlling Inclusion, Using Inclusion: Urban Workers and Leverage

Popular opposition in the late 1970s stimulated a spate of commissions of inquiry and government white papers addressing old concerns with new urgency: black labor and population concentrations in "white South Africa."

Three years following the Soweto uprising, two commissions recommended the expansion and modification of inclusion of certain segments of urban Africans who were "acknowledged universally as a permanent and indispensable element in the national economy."[61] Legislation spawned by Riekert Commission recommendations proffered definite gains including permanent residency, unrestricted geographic mobility, preferential access to jobs, and leasehold rights inside the townships to urban residents fortunate enough to qualify for Section 10 classification.[62] In 1982, an estimated 3.5 million, or 65 percent of the urban African population qualified for Section 10 rights.[63] Touted as major political reforms by the government, these were essential components in capital's strategy for meeting its requirements for a skilled and stable workforce and domestic market.

The state sought to defuse its volatile relationship with township residents by combining reliance on "apolitical" or "neutral" market mechanisms with indirect rule, thereby "depoliticizing" and "decentralizing" control over the African majority.[64] Control over the African urban population, which forced removals and influx controls had failed to reduce in numbers,[65] was now to be exercised through the markets: labor, housing, and service markets would determine mobility rather than overt coercion.[66] Indeed, depoliticization was understood as giving free enterprise free rein. The gradual elimination of those elements of apartheid that fettered capital accumulation and fueled discontent would be combined with reliance on market forces to reproduce the well-entrenched white domination. Decentralization of control over urban Africans meant that authority over township affairs, including the extraction of resources, would be transferred to elected black councilors who would function as a buffer insulating the state from popular resentment.[67] The combination of reliance on markets and indirect rule required and produced a stratum of urban Africans with an interest in cooperating, if not in collaborating.

With the urging of liberals among white business, a number of avenues were opened up for the expansion of an African middle class. The 1977 Community Councils Act granted community councilors powers of control over a variety of resources—council funds, allocation of housing and business sites, and student scholarships, among other things—and permitted unbridled corruption among councilors.[68] Furthermore, a number of obstacles to black businesses within the townships were removed and businesses expanded.[69] This was consistent with Wiehahn Commission recommendations for "giving all population groups a stake in the system" that would "ensure a common loyalty to both the system [of free enterprise] and the country."[70] The aim was to create a class within the townships that could be counterpoised to the increasingly class-conscious African working class that was vehemently opposed to capitalism. As one white advisor to the National African Federated Chambers of Commerce (NAFCOC) counseled: "the Black businessman has a social responsibility" that includes "influenc[ing] the political thinking of their own people to promote free enterprise."[71] Importantly, the place being readied for the newly emerging African petty bourgeoisie was inside the black community, rather than alongside its white counterpart.

The extent of the expansion of the African middle class and the political role it might be expected to play were vigorously debated by supporters of the national liberation movement. One perspective dismissed the extent of this class's expansion as insubstantial and concessions aimed to secure its co-optation as too meager to pry it away from its national interest in the elimination of apartheid.[72] Another view saw the expansion and gains of the African petty bourgeoisie as substantial enough for it to develop interests in the status quo and, if not in outright collaboration, certainly in opposing the national movement's more radical economic objectives.[73] Both views were correct: the extent of the expansion of the African petty bourgeoisie was, relatively speaking, substantial for some class fractions,[74] but for the most part, gains remained within the framework of segregated economic structures, thereby constraining the further expansion of this class and mitigating against its full support for the status quo. Equally important was the question of the locus of reproduction of this class and its persistent dependence on the state. Those co-opted into community councils, like the new bantustan elite, were entirely dependent on state resources and, therefore, more likely to collaborate; businessmen who had managed to establish independent economic bases within the townships were more likely to support the national movement.[75] Such qualifications notwithstanding, both government and business had clearly succeeded in creating an African class with an interest in capitalism, even if not in apartheid. Indeed, organizations such as NAFCOC, which grew substantially during this period, defended capitalism undistorted by apartheid.[76] However, through organs such as NAFCOC, the African petty bourgeoisie, like the urban working class, rejected bantustan "independence," which they saw not only as fracturing and weakening their strength as a class, but also as irrelevant given that the locus of their production and reproduction as a class lay in the advanced sector of the South African economy.[77]

A strategy of co-optation was directed at workers as well. By improving the terms of inclusion of some workers, while bolstering the exclusion of others, the state and employers sought to subvert the potential unity and efficacy of the nonracial and militant trade unions. The Wiehahn Commission had noted that under the status quo, democratic trade unions "are subject neither to the protective and stabilising elements of the system nor to its essential discipline and control; they in fact enjoy much greater freedom than registered unions, to the extent that they are free if they wished to participate in politics and to utilise their funds for whatever purposes they see fit."[78] The Commission thus recommended recognition and registration of these nonracial trade unions and the granting of limited rights to strike, among other things, as a means of replicating the depoliticization that characterized unions in the advanced industrialized economies of the West.[79] For their part, employers conceded wage raises and incorporated some blacks into managerial positions, thereby signaling their readiness to consider unfastening their economic interests from their apartheid moorings.[80] The creation of a relatively privileged stratum of black workers with something to lose was intended to prevent the working class from coalescing into a unified political force. As Nolutshungu explains, the new approach was to "serve the twofold aim of keeping 'politics' out of industry and preventing the political use of the massive potential power of Blacks in industry."[81] In addition to race and ethnicity, new, potential political fissures were cultivated with the aim of setting migrant against permanent,[82] skilled against unskilled, and unemployed against employed workers.[83]

Workers' response would be decisive but not immediate. Recognition stimulated the growth of democratic trade unions.[84] In 1979, the Federation of South African Trade Unions (FOSATU) was formed, whose leadership was first and foremost committed to worker unity and to developing the organizational capacity of trade unions. They chose to utilize the new space to expand their union base and shop-floor structures rather than to extend union activity into struggles emerging beyond the workplace in the townships. Concentrating on strengthening their workplace presence, union leaders guarded against control by the state and employers (as evidenced by the struggles over registration) as well as interference by the political forces of the national movement. Citing the experience of SACTU,[85] they eschewed political affiliations as "divisive of the national worker unity that ha[d] been developed," although they sought "to build an effective and powerful worker organisation within the wider liberation struggles."[86] Moreover, these "orthodox" trade unionists preached against "populism," arguing that workers' interests would suffer were unions to enter into broad-based popular alliances engaged in political battles before workers had developed their organizational strength.[87] The political role of the working class was projected to some future date when unions were strong enough both vis-à-vis their opponents as well as their allies to ensure the protection and realization of workers' class objectives.[88] ANC and SACP leaders in exile would endeavor and fail to persuade FOSATU leaders, whom they derisively dismissed as "workerists," to alter their course.[89] Indeed, concentration on the shop floor was consistent with the state's objective of keeping politics out of the workplace and workers' strength out of township struggles. Nevertheless, FOSATU's commitment to worker unity enabled it to avert divisions cultivated by the state and employers, and the Federation's concentration on building shop-floor structures enabled it to establish powerful shop-steward councils. For most of the 1970s, this key segment of the democratic labor movement was absent organizationally from the political struggles that were emerging, although their members were active as residents of the beleaguered townships.

The state's new policies meant that the costs of the inadequate and unequal services in African townships were now to be borne by the residents themselves. Citing budgetary constraints induced by the recession, the state stepped up pressure on the impoverished township residents. Community councilors and township police charged with extracting payments became easily targeted representatives of the state.[90] Township residents responded with the only weapon at their disposal—boycotts. A new community-based organizational phenomenon, the "civics," emerged in townships throughout the country. Unable to secure compliance or restore order, the community councilors called in the state's repressive apparatus, thereby exposing themselves to even further derision.[91]

Depoliticization and decentralization had clearly failed. Indeed, they would simultaneously politicize communities and present accessible targets within their reach. Once African urban residents obtained permanent residency rights they could no longer be expected to displace their demands for housing, affordable rents, services, and schools to the bantustans, even while their political and citizenship demands might be thus transferred. Moreover, traditional relations and the rural economy became increasingly irrelevant for new generations of township residents. In the past, in keeping with the view of the urban African population as "temporary sojourners," and in order to inhibit the influx of rural Africans, the state had deliberately perpetuated the townships' deplorable living conditions.[92] Now, having recognized that conditions were fueling discontent, the state turned to address the needs of a stable and cooperative urban working class.[93] But the government's feeble efforts to address communities' needs riled rather than pacified communities. Moreover, permanent residency rights emboldened residents no longer threatened by removal and the threat of banishment to the bantustans.[94] Their dependence on the urban economy and government services meant that they would target these to meet their survival requirements and improve their horrendous living conditions.

These social forces would come together, push apart, and struggle with the ANC, which sought to bring them together in a common front under its leadership. By the early 1980s, a wide range of organizations, structures, and activists were in place with experience in testing and forcing the limits of the available space. Missing, however, was the convergence of these divergent organizations and forces, as well as the basis for translating their sector- or locale-specific efforts into a national politics of liberation. The ANC, from its bases hundreds of miles away, would contribute the political cohesion that would bind these divergent groups and class forces together.

The ANC in Exile

Virtually an entire generation of South Africans was largely unaware of the situation of the liberation organizations in exile. Government censorship prevented the new generation of blacks from learning about the ANC and PAC, and veterans of the 1950s campaigns who attempted to pass on the organizations' history of resistance seemed anachronistic in a time when virtually no evidence of their struggles remained. Soweto changed this, but the uprising was clearly BC-dominated. While the BCM contributed to educating youth about the history of black resistance and political organizations, they presented the contemporary ANC and PAC as irrelevant and dismissed their leaders "enjoying the easy life" abroad.[95] Ironically, it would be precisely the BCM-inspired Soweto uprising that would generate both new opportunities and new recruits for the banned liberation organizations.

The government's suppression of the BCM created a political vacuum in the black community. The brutal assault on school students demonstrating peacefully seemed to be a glaring confirmation of the ANC assessment that armed struggle was "the only method left open."[96] Young black militants turned their attention abroad to the organizations they came to know through illicit radio broadcasts. In the year following the Soweto uprising, more than 4,000 black youths left the country to join the exiled liberation organizations.[97]

The ANC External Mission used the years in exile to prepare for armed struggle as well as cultivate international support for the isolation of the minority government and the application of sanctions. The organization's most weighty achievements on these fronts, however, were yet to be realized. Nevertheless, the events of Soweto rendered the international community more attentive to the national liberation organizations and more generous as an appreciable increase in support from a variety of sources followed.[98] Determined to maximize support and avoid becoming enmeshed in East-West rivalries, the ANC sought help from any and all governments opposed to apartheid, both capitalist and socialist.[99] In particular, however, substantial assistance would be obtained from the Soviet Union and East Europe, largely owing to the efforts of its ally, the SACP.[100] Financially, the Scandinavian countries—particularly Sweden—would become the largest contributors to ANC-approved, nonmilitary projects and organizations inside South Africa.[101] By the mid-1980s, the ANC operated with an annual budget of $100 million divided nearly equally between military and nonmilitary expenditures.[102]

Regionally, the ANC depended on Zambian, Angolan, and Tanzanian hospitality where its headquarters, training camps, as well as health and education facilities came to be established.[103] The community of exiles, however, was never sizeable, even after 1976.[104] The organization did not invest much effort into cultivating its relationship with the OAU, whose aid remained limited and unreliable.[105] But regional developments, particularly in southern Africa, were consequential to the liberation organizations' ability to maneuver. In the late 1970s, conditions appeared encouraging as the national liberation movement's allies replaced colonial regimes in Angola and Mozambique (1975), and would soon do so in Zimbabwe (1980).[106] Yet, the front-line states' vulnerability to South African military and economic coercion made ANC and PAC hopes short lived. Even the FRELIMO (Frente de Libertação de Moçambique/Front for the Liberation of Mozambique) government in Mozambique would eventually be forced to sign a nonaggression pact with Pretoria involving the closure of ANC bases in 1984.[107] The net would soon tighten around the liberation organizations' bases, but not before the ANC had registered important advances on the internal front.[108]

The 1976 uprising caught the ANC surprised and unprepared.[109] The organization would be reinvigorated, however, by the absorption of the majority of the new recruits who brought fresh knowledge of the resurgence of popular struggles taking shape inside the country.[110] The following year, bases were set up in Angola for the training of the new recruits eager to carry the armed struggle back into South Africa.[111]

The resurgence of popular resistance stimulated a reappraisal of strategy during 1978–79. As Barrell explains, "the militarist vanguardism of the past [having] manifestly failed," the ANC recognized the need to "'turn to the masses'" in order to remain relevant.[112] Now, rather than relying on armed activity to generate an internal political base capable of carrying out the revolutionary armed struggle toward the seizure of state power, political means would be pursued to achieve the same objective.[113] One of the strategic recommendations adopted was the pursuit of a broad-based national front of existing organizations inside the country. Tensions within the ANC and SACP regarding the correct relationship between the political and military structures and forms of struggle would persist, however.[114] Moreover, the armed wing would continue to predominate due to a combination of factors that included the preference of recruits for joining MK, resource allocation decisions, and difficulties in preparing political cadres for the underground.[115] As a result, armed incursions increased,[116] including a number of spectacular attacks.[117] The armed struggle, however, would remain limited in effectiveness because of difficulties encountered in crossing borders, in securing local support at their destination,[118] and, most important, the limited internal adoption of the armed option in action.[119]

Nevertheless, inside South Africa, the ANC's prospects were improving, and to a large extent owing to the armed actions: "armed propaganda" was succeeding in popularizing the ANC.[120] In 1981, the ANC underground was also expanded by the release of activists who had completed their five-year prison terms. Most of these militants had been recruited away from BC by an elaborate ANC network that operated within the prisons, particularly on Robben Island where the top leadership, including Nelson Mandela, was being held.[121] Upon their release, many became MK operatives within the country, others were integrated into the community organizations forming inside the townships, while others worked through the democratic trade unions. Indeed, one of the conclusions of the strategic review had been the need to extend the ANC's influence and support to the mass-based organizations emerging inside the country.[122]

Throughout South Africa a wide array of local and national organizations were beginning to coalesce. The political organization in exile would seek to assert its hegemony over the growing movement inside the country. It lacked, however, the organizational resources to do so directly; organizationally, the ANC still had only a small, though growing, number of cadres in position in its "underground machinery."[123] Local initiatives inside the country, by politically unaffiliated but decidedly anti-apartheid community leaders, saw linkages between organizations beginning to be constructed for the purpose of national political action. The ANC signaled its endorsement of such initiatives and the idea of creating a united front composed of the disparate forces prepared to confront apartheid.

In keeping with the "national democratic" stage of the liberation struggle, both the ANC and SACP sought the broadest-possible coalition of forces committed to the elimination of apartheid: ethnic and religious community leaders; student, youth, and women's groups; various sections of the petty bourgeoisie; and even some bantustan leaders would be approached. It was with some of the strongest democratic trade unions, however, that the ANC encountered the most difficulty. Through exhortations from exile and through their underground, the ANC and SACP pressed these unions to join the political struggles that were escalating.[124] Sections of FOSATU's leadership, particularly whites among them, were assailed for undermining black workers' involvement in the political struggle.[125] Even the SACP, which might have welcomed FOSATU's role in inculcating a commitment to socialism among a sizable segment of the working class, dismissed its leaders as "adventurist, leftist, workerist" for prioritizing the class struggle over the national democratic struggle.[126] ANC recruits and supporters operating within trade unions pushed for their unions' adoption of the Freedom Charter (a symbolic identification with the ANC) and participation in township struggles. Indeed, the ANC would seek to make the Freedom Charter the basis of an alliance that would cross both the class and racial divides, thereby forging a united front to achieve the elimination of apartheid in South Africa.

Convergence of Struggles and Movements

Initiatives to form a national front were given impetus by the government's 1982 announcement of constitutional proposals for the establishment of a tricameral parliament. As part of the government's strategy of reform, the new constitution was aimed at co-opting Indians and coloreds as a means of preserving both the political exclusion of Africans and white control. By August 1983, over 300 civic, trade union, youth, students', women's, religious, and ethnic organizations came together to form the United Democratic Front (UDF). A combination of influential ANC stalwarts, ANC sympathizers, and independents were behind the formation of the UDF.[127] Virtually every organization represented, however, was autonomous from the ANC. The following year, making full use of the space permitted for debate on the constitutional initiative,[128] the UDF coordinated a successful boycott campaign of the parliamentary elections, thereby defeating this experiment in controlled political inclusion aimed at driving a wedge between blacks.[129] One month later, what began as local protests over rent increases and other township grievances related to living conditions in the Vaal Triangle, spread to townships throughout the country. Through the efforts of the UDF and its affiliates—now numbering 600 organizations[130]—stay-aways, boycotts, street battles, and other mass actions would merge to form an uprising that would engulf the country for two years.

The community organizations that had emerged at the close of the 1970s and that now sustained the uprising shared a number of important features. Significant numbers were organized around immediate local problems such as rent, housing, and services, thereby enabling township residents to develop their organizational capacities and experience directly around matters of daily life.[131] Despite tremendous regional variation they proliferated throughout the country, including the bantustans.[132] And due to the imprisonment or exile of veteran ANC, SACP, and other national liberation leaders and activists, the new grassroots organizations had to produce their own leaders.[133] They benefited from the presence of trade unionists who brought organizational experience and a commitment to democratic procedures and accountability—the hallmark of the democratic trade union movement in the 1970s.[134] Community leaders thus emerged out of an active, experienced, and politicized social base, and one that issued the mandates and demanded accountability of its leaders.[135] Moreover, when the state's refusal to compromise "transformed local urban struggles into campaigns with a national political focus," organizations were in place that were capable of carrying their mass base into what became national campaigns.[136] Indeed, through rent boycotts, for example, township residents presented a direct challenge to the state by "undermin[ing] the fiscal foundations of township administration."[137]

The UDF provided the framework within which the numerous local acts of resistance could be combined, coordinated, and forged into national political campaigns.[138] Moreover, the UDF succeeded in mobilizing organizations across the racial divide: Indian, colored, and white organizations were active in the formation of the Front and were prominent in its leadership. The UDF demonstrated adeptness at organizing mass action on a national scale through decentralized structures that preserved the autonomy of its affiliates.[139] Its decentralized organization permitted the Front to make inroads even in the bantustans where UDF-affiliated youth initiated action. The loose coalition of hundreds of diverse organizations sought to combine struggles in the workplace with struggles in the townships, but the most prominent trade unions were slow to join.[140]

Following years of struggles within the labor movement over questions of registration and government reforms, the Congress of South African Trade Unions (COSATU) was formed in 1985. The trade union federation brought the major democratic unions together in a new "political unionism."[141] While its predecessor, FOSATU, had shunned alliances with political organizations as potentially divisive of worker unity, COSATU did not. Pressures from the rank and file and successful lobbying by ANC and SACP unionists would eventually carry even FOSATU unions to the center of the movement to eliminate apartheid.[142]

For its part, the ANC in exile sought to foster the growth of the UDF and the incorporation of unions as an important element in its strategy of attaining a revolutionary capacity to seize state power. The armed component was considered integral to this strategy of building toward "people's war." But the Nkomati Accord (1984), which curtailed MK's access through Mozambique, combined with the expulsion of ANC members from Lesotho, Swaziland, and Botswana, impaired the organization's ability to extend support to the movement inside.[143] These and other pressures on the External Mission, including a mutiny in the training camps in Angola in 1984,[144] augmented the ANC's dependence on forces inside the country.

In June 1985, the ANC held its fourth consultative conference in Kabwe, Zambia, to strategize for the new conditions presented by the revolt inside South Africa. The NEC Report submitted to the delegates reiterated the need to "concentrate on political mobilisation and organisation so as to build up political revolutionary bases" as "the foundation of our people's war."[145] The armed struggle remained "one of the vital elements in helping prepare the ground for political activity and organisation," but was deemed "secondary" to political struggle at this juncture.[146] For the first time, membership on the NEC would become open to non-Africans, reflecting the strides made in the application of nonracialism by the movement inside the country.[147] Growing ANC hegemony over the mass movement inside South Africa was becoming increasingly apparent; support for the ANC eclipsed that for the PAC as well as for the BC offshoot, the Azanian People's Organisation (AZAPO). The NEC Report noted, however, the insufficient advance registered in the enrollment of workers—"the undisputed motive force" of the revolution—as members in the ANC and MK.[148]

Limited worker membership within the ANC notwithstanding, by 198/ COSATU's adoption of the Freedom Charter and alliance with the UDF,[149] and soon thereafter with the ANC directly, reflected its recognition of the ANC's political hegemony among the rank and file of its affiliates.[150] However, when COSATU allied with the ANC, it did so without losing its autonomy: unionists were prepared to join in struggles outside the workplace, something that apartheid had necessitated, but they would not do so on terms dictated by the national liberation organization.[151] Thus, while aligning with the popular national movement, thereby contributing to "a convergence of workplace and township forms of struggles," it did so on terms favoring the interests of black workers, making it clear that it would not be willing to subordinate those interests to the interests of other black classes.[152] Thus, the community and trade-union forms of struggle—two forms previously waged parallel to each other—could be combined.[153] But rather than workers subordinating their class interests to "national" ones and see them, as a result, dissipate into a "populist" formulation of movement interests, workers were able, through COSATU, to make their mark on the alliance with community organizations, both in terms of leadership and in the vision of the post-apartheid order.[154] Bolstered by their experience in struggle and their vigorous class consciousness, the formidable organizational capacity that unions had constructed during the 1970s could not easily be circumvented by alliance partners. In what can be considered a vindication of "workerism," it was those unions that had developed their shop-floor strength that now brought to the movement control over the most significant resource of all: leverage within the economy.[155] The combination of self-organization, autonomy, democratic practices demanded by workers in particular, and accountability of leaders instituted by trade unionists enabled the organized segments of the black working class to assert themselves inside the national movement, shifting the momentum of the movement back into the country, thereby also posing a more serious challenge to their opponents.

In the late 1980s, COSATU's existence proved vital for what came to be known as the Mass Democratic Movement when the state succeeded in suppressing UDF-affiliated community organizations and the uprising.[156] The state and employers were no doubt reluctant to use armed force within the workplace; townships, however, were not spared. Their suppression was brutal in large part because it was less costly: battles could be easily contained within the townships, at safe distances from white communities. Three states of emergency permitted the decimation of structures behind the resistance inside the townships.[157]

The state's response to the challenge combined intensified repression with piecemeal reforms. The uprisings in 1984–86 revealed the dismal failure of Riekert- and Wiehahn-inspired reforms to depoliticize and pacify the black population. Indeed, the unremitting influx of rural "squatters" and the increasingly apparent economic nonviability of the bantustans demonstrated the failure of exclusion; the continued growth of the democratic trade unions and their politicization and convergence with popular organizations was evidence of the failure of inclusion. Internal pressures were augmented by the international application of economic sanctions, exacerbated further by spiraling foreign debt in the context of a global recession.[158] South Africa's costly military containment activity in the region was an added drain of state resources.[159] Through organizations such as the Urban Foundation, segments of capital were compelled to appeal to the state to abandon more of apartheid in order to rescue the economy.[160]

In 1986, the government initiated a number of reforms in rapid succession: a new policy of "orderly urbanization" permitted black residence in and around certain urban centers;[161] pass laws were abolished; and the Restoration of South African Citizenship Act permitted Africans to apply to regain South African citizenship.[162] Moreover, the economic reincorporation of the bantustans that had begun in 1981 was accelerated as part of a regional development strategy that recognized the nonviability of the ethnic entities.[163] In addition, some of the more odious laws, such as the prohibition on intermarriage, were scrapped. Reflecting recognition of the failure of both exclusion and inclusion, the state now sought to control what had begun to be recognized as inevitable: integration. However, like the experiment in controlled inclusion, only wavering and partial steps were taken toward controlled integration; steps that, like inclusion, would meet with failure. While the state played around with half-hearted reforms, the representatives of capital, foreseeing the consequences of the state's feebleness, pursued their own course for averting disaster by initiating contact with the national liberation movement in exile.

Beginning in 1985, various representatives of capital descended upon ANC headquarters in Lusaka to inquire into the organization's position regarding future arrangements, particularly with regard to the economy.[164] They had reason for concern: "the failure of South African capitalists as a whole to dissociate themselves from apartheid—as distinct from criticising it in times of crisis—[had] strengthened the socialist element in black nationalism."[165] Indeed, the national liberation movement was presenting the ruling powers with two challenges: one to the political structures of apartheid domination and the other to the economic structures of capitalist exploitation, generating internal struggles between vested interests anchored in each. Government attempts to subvert the mass democratic movement continued unabated: assassinations of leaders at home and abroad, the arming of township vigilantes, and the backing of the Natal-based alternative (Inkatha) were among a range of tactics that were pursued but to no avail.

It had become clear that ANC leaders in exile could not be bypassed: the government's strategy of creating an alternative leadership had failed dismally, and the ANC had succeeded in asserting its hegemony over the movement that had formed inside the country. Indeed, in addition to the democratic labor movement, the ANC could count on the political support of the organized sections of African youth, township residents, and business, as well as Indian, colored, and white democrats. Even traditional leaders opposed to apartheid began in 1987 to organize themselves under the banner of the UDF through the Congress of Traditional Leaders of South Africa (CONTRALESA). But the ANC's hegemony was not absolute. The organization lacked the resources that would be required to assert its control.[166] It also had to contend with organizations that had emerged independently.[167] Attempts to impose policies from exile were effectively resisted.[168] Indeed, for the most part, ANC success in securing the support of what were autonomous mass organizations may be attributed to the organization's articulation of political programs and demands that were consistent with those articulated inside the country. Adept leadership or not, the ANC clearly had no choice but to accept the autonomy of the labor movement and COSATU as well as the loose coalition of hundreds of organizations that composed the UDF. These had emerged as politically unaffiliated bodies that did not develop a dependence on ANC resources. Ultimately, the preservation of their autonomy and accountability to their constituencies strengthened these organizations and their contribution to the movement to end apartheid—precisely what the ANC needed.

Under mounting international pressure, the government took steps toward a negotiated settlement. In 1990, the ANC, SACP, and other national liberation organizations were unbanned, and restrictions were lifted from COSATU and the UDF. Nelson Mandela was released from Robben Island and preparations for negotiations commenced three months later. While this was no "conquest of power" via a "people's war," the edifice of white political domination had been irreparably fractured and the stability and future of capitalism in South Africa placed in jeopardy. The democratic labor movement had delivered its leverage to the national liberation movement to achieve the end of apartheid. Now, through COSATU, it would participate directly in determining how that leverage would be wielded in negotiations over the postliberation order: the democratic forces would be represented jointly by the ANC, SACP, as well as COSATU in negotiations.

Evaluating Success

The mass struggles of the late 1970s to 1980s were initiated and sustained by township residents who were entirely dependent on the state and white-dominated economy for their survival—the population that had been freed from social relations in bantustans.[169] Despite forced "citizenship" and family extensions, traditional social relations in the bantustans became increasingly irrelevant for those segments of the township communities born in the metropolitan townships or with decades-long residence and employment outside the bantustans. More important, as subsistence could no longer be derived in the areas allotted for the homelands, and as urban communities became entirely dependent on meeting their survival needs in the advanced sector of the South African economy, workers and communities had no choice but to develop their challenge there once they had decided to challenge at all.

Although the bantustans were not immune, resistance there was more limited where the co-optation of leaders and an African petty bourgeoisie, combined with suppression of organized activity, had been largely effective in marginalizing the population from events in the country. With the upsurge of mass resistance in the 1980s, however, bantustans became the sites of a number of rebellions that hastened the disintegration of apartheid on all fronts.[170] However, the more limited resistance in the bantustans must be explained, given that the urban township and bantustan populations are comparable in numbers, and the very high population densities of the latter belie their classification as "rural." More important, greater resistance in and around South Africa's urban centers cannot be explained by greater deprivation: the population relegated to the bantustans has lived on the brink of starvation for decades. The explanation lies in the fact that in contrast to Africans in the bantustans, the population in the urban townships: (1) was freed from dependence on social relations that were dominated by a conservative—even collaborating—elite; (2) was endowed with leverage derived from the dependence of whites on black labor; and (3) had formed alternative bases of organization and identification that had, to a large extent, transcended traditional bases that were inherently divisive. That is, inclusion in the dominant economy had produced an African working class with no choice but to direct its demands at the dominant group that controlled the means of workers' survival. Through their powerful trade unions, workers exercised the leverage they derived from the system's dependence on their labor. The population of the bantustans lacked all three factors while they suffered even greater deprivations. Moreover, it is in the bantustans that the government successfully preserved and co-opted traditional leaders, created an African middle class and bourgeoisie with a vested interest in the status quo, and preserved the population's dependence as a matter of survival on patronage dispensed by bantustan leaders and bureaucrats. Importantly, the only viable challenge to the ANC—Inkatha—emerged precisely where traditional leaders remained the strongest.[171] If there was any doubt about most bantustan leaders' position vis-à-vis the national liberation struggle, it became clear during the uprisings as bantustan governments actively suppressed UDF, youth, civic, and trade union formations in the areas under their control.[172]

In its strategy of controlled inclusion, the state had miscalculated on two accounts. First, <u>recognition and integration of democratic trade unions</u> <u>into the industrial relations system had been intended to achieve the de-</u><u>politicization of trade unions as it had in the West</u>. An essential component in this policy in the West, however, was the franchise and political inclusion that served to contain and depoliticize workplace struggles and displace working class politics beyond the realm of production. The continued political exclusion of urban black workers and the irrelevance of bantustan political structures meant that politics would be practiced where workers were: in the workplace and townships. Second, by expanding inclusion to an African petty bourgeoisie, the state and employers sought to create a class that could serve as a buffer against the mass of the township residents. They were correct in attributing to the middle class such a role in reestablishing stability; they were wrong in believing that just any segment of the middle class could accomplish this. Apartheid had created a powerful working class and had politicized township residents; the only segment of the middle class they recognized as a legitimate representative was the one that had championed the political struggle: those leading the national liberation movement. Business recognized this; now the government needed to do so. Both would call on the ANC to restore stability. Ultimately, both would decide that a democratic political order was not too high a price to pay with the economic order—capitalism—at stake in South Africa.

Palestine, 1976 to 1991

Nearly a decade of occupation showed unmistakable signs of Israel incorporating what remained of Palestine: Palestinian neighborhoods in annexed East Jerusalem had been demolished en masse to make way for Jewish housing; a network of Israeli settlements encircled the West Bank and Gaza Strip; and the territories' infrastructure was being steadily diverted to Israel. Ultimately, Israel's "creeping annexation" was intended to achieve the integration of the territories but without its people. In the meantime, however, there were immense benefits to be derived from rule over more than one million Palestinians: Israeli producers prospered from the conveniently located and captive market; employers profited from the pool of cheap, unorganized labor; and the resulting expansion of industry and services permitted Israeli workers to advance into better and higher-paying jobs, abandoning those least desired to Palestinian workers from the newly acquired territories.[173] Thus, the early nationalist slogan of "Hebrew labor only" was set aside as divergent Israeli classes converged on the benefits of Palestinian economic inclusion. Israeli "expansionism," however, had to be reconciled with Jewish "exclusivism," which Moshe Dayan, Israel's earliest architect of policies in the occupied territories, assured the public could be done.[174] Thus, Palestinian economic inclusion took the form of migrant labor: their stay in Israel ended with the workday and their political exclusion remained complete.

Palestinians in growing numbers would be propelled onto Israel's labor market by the occupiers' economic policies in the West Bank and Gaza Strip. Gradually, they would develop a dependence on such employment as a matter of survival. But West Bank and Gaza Strip Palestinians, no less than Israelis, were committed to political exclusion from the Israeli state. Rather than seeking political inclusion they would demand independence.

The Status Quo Disrupted: The 1976 Municipal Elections

Anticipating a repeat of the previous elections, Israel proceeded with municipal elections in the West Bank in 1976. In retrospect, the military government had missed signs of maturing Palestinian nationalists ready to challenge the old guard.

Traditional leaders' failure to prevent Israel from "creating facts" aimed at rendering the occupation irreversible undermined their standing in their communities. Early Israeli backing of these compliant figures had backfired. Indeed, it was one thing to draw patronage from Jordan and Egypt, quite another from Israel.[175] Concomitantly, Israeli economic policies undermined the elite further as confiscation of land, denial of import and export permits, and exorbitant taxation, among other things, constrained Palestinian employers' prospects and control over resources.[176] Deterred by the prevailing conditions from investing inside the territories, the Palestinian bourgeoisie for the most part left for or invested in Jordan.[177] Thus, the occupiers' economic policies undermined the very class forces on which they had relied to preserve order.

Popular resentment of and reduced dependence on the conservative elite would assume political expression in the outcome of the West Bank municipal elections of 1976. A massive West Bank–wide mobilization carried vocal PLO supporters into offices of mayor and municipal councils in several West Bank towns, in the process displacing the traditional elite from the only representative bodies permitted to function under the occupation.[178] The new leaders were younger and better educated than their predecessors, mostly professionals with active links to existing professional and community associations.[179] While in most cases they too were members of elite families, they actively disassociated themselves from their pro-Jordanian and conservative family members and were elected on new bases: open support for the liberation organization in exile and Palestinian self-determination.[180]

The momentous mobilization of West Bank residents that made the 1976 municipal elections outcome possible had been facilitated in part by an Israeli amendment to the Jordanian Municipal Law (1955) that permitted women and propertyless men to vote in municipal elections for the first time.[181] More important, in contrast to 1972, this time the elections received the PLO's endorsement. Indeed, the PLO and Jordanian Communist Party (JCP), as well as independent community leaders, actively mobilized for the elections through the semi-clandestine PNF. Although Israeli repression and PLO politics in exile resulted in the demise of the PNF one year later, it had, during its brief existence, demonstrated the potential that existed for mass mobilization.[182]

The politicization of the municipal system and radicalization of office holders frustrated Israel's strategy of indirect rule. A number of municipal councils were suspended, powers of municipalities were revoked and funds withheld, a number of municipal members were placed under house arrest and others would later be expelled from the West Bank.[183] This was the last time that municipal elections would be permitted in the West Bank.[184] Nevertheless, in itself, the mobilization that produced the election outcomes represented a milestone in the relationship between the occupied and occupiers, both of whom shifted their subsequent course of action as a result.

The End of Indirect Rule: "Civil Administration" and the "Iron Fist"

In 1977, Israel's Labor Party lost its first election since the establishment of the state of Israel in 1948. The new Likud coalition government brought together disparate social forces disaffected by Labor rule: the *mizrachim* by the *ashkenazi*-dominated Labor Party's early treatment,[185] business by Labor's welfare state policies, and religious groupings by Labor's secular politics. The new government was openly annexationist, declaring that "Judea and Samaria" (the West Bank's Biblical names) would never be relinquished.[186] Despite its vitriolic rhetoric, geopolitical constraints—not the least of which was the presence of over one million "non-Jews" in the territories they claimed—would force the Likud to delay outright annexation. Former cabinet secretary Arye Naor captured the dilemma astutely: Israeli goals of a Jewish, democratic, and large state were irreconcilable; any two could be met, but never the three simultaneously.[187]

Palestinians were at the core of Israel's dilemma, although the creation of Israel and what followed had fragmented that core: Palestinians were refugees in diaspora, under military rule in the West Bank and Gaza Strip and Israeli citizens in Israel. The Jewish state had accommodated itself to two segments: the small community of Palestinians who remained in Israel

("Israel's Arabs") and the majority of Palestinians who remained fully excluded. West Bank and Gaza Strip Palestinians, however, presented a quandary for Israel. Likud leaders awaited propitious conditions for either Palestinian self-removal, through emigration, or, as some euphemistically advocated, their "transfer" across the border to Jordan could be realized.[188] In the meantime, two approaches were pursued: a heavy hand against the new pro-PLO urban leaders and the cultivation of an alternative leadership in the countryside with the aim of impairing linkages between the majority of the West Bank population, which was rural, and the increasingly politicized towns.[189] Both gained momentum following the signing of the Camp David Accords with Egypt in 1978. As the Accords revealed, the most that Palestinians could hope for was "self-autonomy": a peculiar form of rule that would permit Palestinians to run their "affairs" exclusive of the land and its resources, while their citizenship and entity ambitions remained "externalized" to the state of Jordan.[190] In this way "self-autonomy" was, in fact, to function as a means of "externalizing" Palestinians who could not be removed from the land coveted by the occupiers.

Manipulating Inclusion, Enduring Inclusion: Proletarianization and "Steadfastness"

The Israeli government asserted its claim to "Greater Israel" by accelerating land confiscation and the construction of settlements.[191] By 1980, through various means of land expropriation,[192] Palestinians would lose control over 27 percent of the West Bank's land, exclusive of East Jerusalem, and one-third of the Gaza Strip, where population density was already among the highest in the world.[193] Settlements were now established inside and surrounding Palestinian population concentrations in such a way as to inhibit the expansion of Palestinian villages and farms and to ensure command of the towns' heights.[194] Likewise, road networks were designed to serve Jewish settlements and bypass Palestinian communities, thereby superimposing an exclusionary physical and spatial reality onto the occupied territories.[195]

The West Bank and Gaza Strip were rapidly becoming Israel's colonial periphery: while millions of dollars worth of Israeli goods were conveyed daily in one direction, thousands of Palestinian workers poured in daily in the other, obscuring the boundaries between Israel and the occupied territories. The territories would become Israel's second largest market after the United States.[196] Paradoxically, the resulting decline or stagnation of the productive sectors produced high unemployment and labor scarcity: few jobs were generated for skilled labor and university graduates, while local wages for manual labor were too low to retain the workforce.[197] Palestinian responses to these double pressures were emigration, viewed as temporary, of family members with marketable skills, or migration to jobs in Israel. Access to both was continuously manipulated by the occupation authorities to secure cooperation.

Beginning in the mid-1970s, Palestinian emigration from the West Bank experienced a five-fold increase and remained at an annual average of 13,500 persons, or 1.9 percent of the population, through 1981.[198] Employed in oil-producing Arab states for the most part, emigrants remitted their earnings to their families, who stayed behind, thereby contributing to their ability to remain in the territories.[199] Those without prospects abroad traveled daily to jobs in Israel. Between 1970 and 1975, West Bank and Gaza Strip Palestinians employed in Israel through official channels more than tripled, accounting for nearly one-third of the territories' employed work force in 1975.[200] Including workers who circumvented the Israeli labor exchanges would increase the officially cited figures by an estimated 25 to 30 percent.[201] The combination of emigration and migration of substantial segments of the Palestinian workforce rendered the territories dependent on external sources of income.[202] In this way, Palestinian residents of the territories were permitted relief from the deterioration of conditions at home, while simultaneously relieving the occupiers of having to address these.

Landless refugees, small holding peasants, village artisans, and petty traders were undergoing proletarianization. In 1970, 49.3 percent of the West Bank and 60.0 percent of the Gaza Strip labor force were employed for wages; by 1982 the percentages had increased to 57.3 percent and 67.6 percent, respectively.[203] This transformation, however, was occurring inside the Israeli economy rather than at home, and increasingly so. In 1970, 24.8 percent of West Bank and 16.5 percent of Gaza Strip wage workers were employed in Israel; by 1982, the percentages had increased to 51.1 percent and 63.9 percent, respectively.[204] The impact on the territories' agricultural economies was direct: between 1970 and 1982, the occupied territories lost nearly 80 percent of their agricultural wage workforce, and, in 1982, twice as many Palestinians migrated daily to labor on farms in Israel or on Israeli settlements than remained employed in local agriculture.[205] Accompanying this was a 19 percent reduction in the land area under cultivation since the onset of the occupation.[206] Furthermore, seniority in employment in Israel was associated with declining cultivation of family plots and sharecropping back home.[207] In view of Israeli confiscation of fallow land, the interruption of cultivation became a source of tremendous Palestinian anxiety. Indeed, by 1983 the West Bank area in Israeli possession had increased to 44 percent.[208]

Palestinian political organizations were now resigned to their inability to halt the daily stream of workers into Israel. Given Israeli annexationist designs, they began to consider employment in Israel as preferable to an exodus from the territories. Thus they watched as Israeli labor offices organized the daily transport of Palestinian workers to their places of employment in Israel. Permits issued by the Labor Exchanges had to be renewed every four months, which served as a useful mechanism for dismissing workers when either employers or politicians deemed it beneficial. In Israel, workers were channeled into the lowest levels of the Israeli employment structure, relegated to jobs least attractive to Jewish workers,[209] with over half employed in construction.[210] Workers were prohibited from forming independent unions, they were denied membership in the Histadrut, and unions in the occupied territories were not permitted to represent them with their Israeli employers.[211] They received, on the average, half the wages received by Israeli workers for the same labor—wage differentials that could not be accounted for by differences in skills or productivity.[212] They did not obtain a wide range of benefits (including old age, survivors', disability, and unemployment benefits) although deductions amounting to 20 percent of wages were taken.[213] The exploitation of laborers employed illegally was even more acute, and by withholding social and health benefit payments to the government on "illegals" in their employment, Israeli employers saved an additional one-third of their labor costs.[214]

Proletarianization combined with high rates of emigration of those with capital, skills, and/or education, contributed to "homogenizing" the Palestinian social structure under the occupation.[215] Increasingly, those who remained inside the occupied territories were migrant workers, women, children, and the elderly, in what has been characterized as the "bantustanization" of the occupied territories.[216] A new array of class forces, endowed with different resources and potential to engage in resistance, was coalescing. But potential needs to be realized, and constraints to organizing persisted, not the least of which were those internal to Palestinian society.

Decline of Traditional Leaders

The proletarianization of various segments of the Palestinian workforce through economic inclusion in Israel was contributing to the erosion of traditional social organization and authority back home. Employment in Israel contributed to: (1) altering relations within villages by reducing income and status differentials as even landless peasants secured incomes that compared favorably to those derived within villages; (2) eroding the authority of village leaders as dependence on patronage they dispensed became less critical; and (3) in the absence of males from the villages, necessitating and permitting a greater participation of women in village life beyond the home and family plot.[217] The erosion of dependence on social relations within the rural economy was accompanied by challenges to traditional village leaders and the landed elite with whom they were connected through patronage relations.[218] Operating under constraints imposed by Israeli economic policies and the pull of higher wages in Israel, Palestinian owners of industries could not replace landowners as employers. The industrial sector suffered under the occupation where industries remained small in scale. In the mid-1980s, 97 percent of the West Bank (excluding East Jerusalem) plants, which numbered nearly 2,000, employed fewer than twenty workers, and only three employed more than one hundred workers.[219] Thus, relations of dependence within Palestinian society were being broken down without being reestablished internally. As the economic prospects of Palestinian workers and landless peasants became less tied to that of Palestinian employers, the latter's authority diminished. There were two important dimensions to this process: proletarianization was contributing to the radicalization of Palestinians but in distinctly national rather than class terms, as their transformation was occurring inside Israel rather than inside the Palestinian economy. However, because the locus of transformation was outside the home economy, it afforded those transformed some measure of newfound freedom from the dominant class forces back home.

Such profound changes notwithstanding, a number of factors operated to preserve traditional authority. The newly proletarianized peasants returned daily to their rural society and to a political and social milieu that proclaimed the preservation of idealized traditional rural relations as a form of resistance to Israel. In their efforts to galvanize communities, PLO nationalists themselves avoided defying the socially conservative status quo and traditional leaders at its apex; they only demanded their loyalty.[220] Fatah leaders, specifically, actively sought to wean traditional leaders away from Jordan and into their camp, and in so doing contributed to preserving the elite's political participation, although on new terms.[221] The Jordanian government also promoted the preservation of the traditional elite, whose dependence it had carefully cultivated and continued to manipulate. This dependence was encouraged by the occupiers who recognized the advantage of preserving Palestinian linkages to Jordan in facilitating Palestinian outmigration to the East Bank. Thus, through the elite, the residents of the territories were encouraged to turn to the Jordanian king for assistance, thereby further alleviating pressures on the occupiers to meet the welfare needs of the occupied population.[222] Finally, members of the traditional elite themselves resisted any erosion of their positions and were aided by these different benefactors to retain the local reins of patronage and, as such, some of their authority.

Palestinian determination to preserve their society intact engendered a policy of "steadfastness" *(sumud)* against Israeli encroachment: remaining on the land and resisting pressures to emigrate. The call was given clout by an Arab summit meeting in November 1978 that established an annual fund of $150 million for the occupied territories to be administered by a joint body of Jordanian government and PLO officials.[223] Between 1979 and 1988 the Jordanian-Palestinian Joint Committee (JPJC) dispensed a total of $446 million covering a wide range of needs and services that were properly the occupiers' responsibility under the Geneva Conventions.[224] In addition, Arab states contributed to municipality budgets through the twinning of Palestinian towns with Arab capitals.[225] With the persistent worsening of living conditions, Palestinians turned increasingly to the JPJC, Arab governments, and elsewhere for assistance[226] but would not direct their demands for the rescue of public sector services to the Israeli administration.[227] Combined with UNRWA, which entered its fourth decade of servicing the refugee population, a number of sources essentially subsidized the occupation and relieved the Israeli government from what might have been a crippling financial burden. Indeed, the occupation proved a financial boon for Israel as Palestinians covered the costs of their own occupation.[228]

Palestinian politics, however, was moving perceptibly beyond the municipalities: by clamping down on above-ground municipal politics, Israeli government policies drove increasing numbers to the more radical underground organizations in waiting. Whereas middle-class municipal leaders sought to mobilize from above using their status and institutional connections, the underground political organizations turned their attention to organization from below.

The underground organizations would get a chance to demonstrate their new found strength when failure to gain support for "self-autonomy" led the Israeli authorities to implement the Camp David agreements unilaterally by instituting "civil administration" in 1981. The cornerstone of this policy was to be the Village Leagues: a network of collaborators in the countryside charged with administering rural affairs. By forcing the rural population to turn to the Village Leagues for everything from work permits to "family reunification" permits, they intended to replicate traditional patronage relations but for the purpose of pacification.[229]

Palestinians responded to the "civil administration," which they regarded as merely a facade for the military administration, with an unprecedented wave of unrest that began in November 1981 and continued through March

1982.[230] Coordinating the massive demonstrations and acts of passive resistance was the National Guidance Committee (NGC), which was formed to organize a Palestinian response to the Camp David agreements in 1978. In a public meeting, the NGC elected an executive committee composed of mayors, representatives of unions, and a number of independents.[231] Until it was outlawed and disbanded in 1982, the NGC played an important role in coordinating Palestinian "steadfastness" efforts and was instrumental in organizing the demonstrations and strikes that delayed the implementation of "civil administration." Such a Palestinian mobilization was made possible by the underground political factions' organizational extensions into communities. These had their origins in the close of the previous decade.

Emergence of Political Factions

Fatah's nationalist appeal and relatively successful co-optation of the West Bank and Gaza Strip elite away from the Jordanian regime enabled it to assert its political influence through existing institutions that operated under elite patronage. These were inherited from the past, and in some cases as early as the British Mandate, and they shared particular characteristics. For example, welfare institutions operated by women's groups were elite led, urban based, socially conservative, and charitable in orientation.[232] In contrast, mass organizations and trade unions, the preserve of the JCP, and eventually of the PFLP and the DFLP, introduced a grassroots approach that sought to empower their constituencies.[233] What came to be known as a "war of institutions" erupted in the late 1970s driven by the deterioration of conditions under Israeli occupation,[234] the goal of establishing institutions free from Israeli control as the infrastructure of a future state, and competition between Palestinian political factions.[235]

The left became increasingly disturbed by Fatah's hegemony over PLO institutions abroad and control over funding for the occupied territories.[236] Municipalities, universities, schools, hospitals, factories, cooperatives, unions, and other institutions, as well as individuals, were among the recipients of JPJC funds. Given the composition of the JPJC, however, beneficiaries of such funds were, for the most part, those institutions and organizations associated with supporters of Fatah, the Jordanian King, or "independents"— those with no ties to the left.[237] In response, the organizations of the left intensified their efforts to establish mass organizations. The frenzy of organization building that ensued produced a proliferation of grassroots organizations among workers, students, women, and youth. Such organizations expanded participation by drawing people who otherwise feared joining the underground political organizations directly.[238] They differed from institutions already in existence in both form and content. Eschewing the urban bias of existing institutions, these operated directly in neighborhoods, villages, and refugee camps; they emphasized mass participation and democratic decision making; they promoted anti-imperialist and socialist politics; and they openly rejected Jordanian influence and dependence on funding from conservative Arab regimes.[239] In response, Fatah set up its own mass organizations. By the early 1980s there were four distinct trade-union, student, women, and youth "blocs" affiliated with each of the four main political currents.[240] The implications of the factionalization of Palestinian politics may be noted from an examination of the labor movement.

The JCP has been credited with the reactivation of trade unions in the West Bank, most of which had operated under its influence during the Jordanian period.[241] Through the General Federation of Trade Unions (GFTU), the largely JCP-controlled member unions confined their activities to the protection of West Bank workers employed in Palestinian-owned enterprises inside the territories. Among the unionists were Fatah, DFLP, and PFLP sympathizers, but they did not pose a challenge to the communists' domination of the Federation; at this point they continued to concentrate on building their organizations in exile and on armed struggle, both of which were dismissed in practice, if not in rhetoric, by the JCP. Beginning in the mid-1970s, however, the DFLP initiated vigorous attempts to establish mass organizations inside the territories.[242] On the trade union front it began to organize Palestinian workers employed in Israel. Until their efforts, migrant workers had been viewed as "traitors" by some political factions and as an unorganizable "lumpen" element by the JCP.[243] In 1978, based on its success among migrant workers, the DFLP established a trade-union bloc and sought entrance into the existing trade unions and the national federation dominated by the JCP. Not to be outdone, Fatah formed its own trade-union bloc. What Fatah organizers lacked in trade-union experience and a commitment to socialism, they made up with the organization's popular appeal as the dominant force in the national movement in exile and access to JPJC funds. It too began to present a challenge to the communists. The JCP's response to these two challenges—one based on strength among an important segment of the working class, the other based on populist appeal and access to patronage from abroad—was to close off individual unions to new members and the GFTU to new unions. JCP union leaders defended their actions by denouncing the new unions as mere fronts for political organizations that served only to divide the labor movement and jeopardize workers' class-specific interests.[244] The resulting confrontation between Fatah and the GFTU led to a split in the Federation in 1981 and to the formation of a separate GFTU by the Fatah bloc. Between 1981 and 1985, the JCP-dominated GFTU became paralyzed by infighting between the remaining factions of the PLO and the JCP. In 1986, the DFLP broke away and established a third, parallel federation. These dynamics and struggles were repeated in organizational efforts among students, women, youth, and professional associations.

The lack of unity in the labor movement notwithstanding, competition between the various factions contributed to the establishment of a number of new unions; a substantial expansion in union membership;[245] the organization of migrant workers in their places of residence, including villages; experience in relatively democratic and decentralized mass organizations; mass education on workers' rights; the provision of essential benefits for workers, particularly health care where no national health program existed; and the politicization of workers as union offices became meeting places.[246] However, a number of factors impeded the development of a proletarian class consciousness.

Palestinians employed in Israel were concentrated in unskilled and semiskilled jobs and in small, nonindustrial firms for the most part;[247] most were employed for daily wages; and Palestinian unions were barred from activity inside their places of employment in Israel.[248] As for Palestinian unions in the territories, a myriad of Israeli restrictions included the banning of trade unions in the Gaza Strip until 1979 followed by a freeze that restricted union membership to those workers enrolled prior to 1967.[249] Three additional factors contributed to delaying the emergence of a cohesive and class-conscious Palestinian working class.

First, the working class was bifurcated; half was dependent on Israeli employers while the other half continued to be employed inside the territories and confronted fundamentally different constraints and concerns. Second, the expansion of the working class was occurring without urbanization; prohibited from remaining overnight in Israel, virtually all workers returned daily to their homes dispersed throughout the occupied territories.[250] This, coupled with the precariousness of their employment in Israel, reinforced the workers' ties to their village communities, and in many cases to a plot of land as a security net.[251] Finally, Palestinian political organizations, including those of the left, supported the "freezing" of class struggles for the duration of the national liberation struggle.[252] Class alliances with Palestinian employers were defended in light of Israeli assaults on national industries, which, it was emphasized, hurt Palestinian workers as well.[253]

Despite rampant factionalism, coordination between efforts in the West Bank and Gaza Strip had begun; the national movement had penetrated the daily lives of the population; social institutions and welfare efforts were now endowed with political content as virtually all mass organizations and institutions were linked to a political organization; and leadership at the grassroots level was evolving.[254] These features of post-1978 organization made the unprecedented demonstrations and strikes of 1981–82 possible.

By 1982, the occupation authorities' failure to gain Palestinian support for "civil administration" and "self-autonomy" had become apparent. In response, the Israeli government implemented a two-pronged strategy aimed at suppressing Palestinian resistance once and for all. First, the NGC was outlawed and an "iron fist" policy of repression was launched in the West Bank and Gaza Strip. Municipal councils were shut down and Israeli colonels assumed direct control, thereby eliminating the "buffer" of municipal councils and "the facade of local rule."[255] Second, in June 1982, in an attempt to force Palestinians in the occupied territories to accept Israeli terms for a settlement, Israel invaded Lebanon with the goal of eliminating the PLO and destroying the linkages between Palestinians "inside" and "outside."[256]

Integration and Exile: 1948 Palestinians

The fragmentation of Palestine had produced a reality much more complex than that captured by the distinction between "inside" and "outside." This may be noted from a comparison of the divergent experiences of two segments of 1948 Palestinians: those who obtained Israeli citizenship and experienced integration—albeit on exceedingly unequal terms—as distinct from mere inclusion, and diaspora Palestinians who experienced the ultimate exclusion of exile. By deflecting criticism of the Jewish State, the integration of a small segment of 1948 Palestinians as citizens no doubt eased the way for Israel's persistent exclusion of the majority of Palestinians. Palestinians inside Israel were proletarianized fully and integrated politically, if only as voters; those in exile were free from Israel's exploitation but also lacked any leverage inside Israel. Neither community would be capable of accomplishing the national liberation project. Indeed, their experiences reveal some of the neutralizing effects of both political inclusion and economic exclusion for the waging of national liberation struggles.

For Palestinians who managed to remain within what became Israel, continued residence in the homeland held limited comfort and virtually no promise: Israeli citizenship spared them neither land expropriation nor military rule.[257] For decades, a profound demoralization and paralysis prevailed among Palestinians who became citizens of Israel. Military rule was finally lifted in 1966 when Israeli labor needs mandated unimpeded movement of Palestinian workers to Jewish towns.[258] Alternative mechanisms of subordination and control, however, would prove equally effective.[259] Co-optation of traditional leaders, classic divide-and-rule strategies to prevent the coalescing of a unified Palestinian or Arab identification,[260] and active persecution and obstruction of political activists and organizations enfeebled Palestinians politically. Economic dependence and the underdevelopment of the Palestinian sector merely reinforced their communal paralysis. Blatant discrimination in government funding for public services, housing subsidies, and municipal budgets perpetuated their impoverishment.[261] And their exclusion from the parastatal "national institutions"—including the Israel Land Authority that controls 92 percent of the land of Israel—prevented their access to significant resources available to Jews.[262]

But Palestinians in Israel had the vote. Their first attempt to organize a political organization—al-Ard (The Land) in 1959—found its organizers banished to Jewish cities and its activities suppressed until it was finally outlawed by the Minister of Defense in 1965, when the organization sought to take part in elections.[263] Without a national party and with communities dependent on government funding, the Palestinian vote went predominantly to Mapai—the senior partner in the governing Labor coalition. Mapai actively manipulated its control over government financing and, prior to 1966, the military administration, to this end. Because they did not permit Arab membership, Zionist parties up to the mid-1960s set up separate Arab lists composed of traditional leaders who delivered their clans' vote.[264] Following the end of military rule, the Palestinian vote went increasingly to the Israeli Communist Party (Rakah), and from the mid-1980s to the Progressive List for Peace, both distinctly binational parties.[265] But despite some jockeying for the Palestinian vote, no Israeli government could ever be formed without a majority of Jewish parties, thereby neutralizing even this limited Palestinian voice.[266]

The occupation of the remaining Palestinian territories in 1967 proved to be a turning point, the implications of which began to become apparent by the mid-1970s. By this time, Palestinians began to channel their political voice through the non-Zionist Communist Party, which, from the early days of the creation of the State of Israel, had defended Palestinian rights fully, including the demand for an end to land expropriation and military rule.[267] In 1975, they succeeded in electing a communist Palestinian mayor of the only Arab city, Nazareth, thereby ending Labor's virtual monopoly over elected positions within Palestinian municipalities.[268] The following year, Rakah was successful in organizing resistance to a planned government seizure of new land. National Land Day has since been observed annually in the West Bank and Gaza Strip, as well as in the refugee camps in exile.[269]

A new generation of Palestinian intellectuals and activists had emerged. Among them were nationalists who initiated new organizations such as Abna' al-Balad (Sons of the Land).[270]

The renewed vigor of Palestinians in Israel was, to an important extent, a result of the restoration of contacts with Palestinians in the occupied territories; a population, which, as Lustick notes, "possessed a full-blown nationalist ideology, thriving urban centers, a variety of political organizations, and a widely respected nationalist leadership."[271] And while contacts would continue to develop and deepen and include the extension of assistance and support during the uprising, Palestinian efforts in Israel would remain focused on achieving civil rights and equality as citizens of Israel.

For the majority of 1948 Palestinians (refugees exiled from the homeland) freedom from Israeli domination held no comfort and very little promise. The experience did vary, however, by class, host country, and time. By 1981, there were nearly 1.9 million Palestinian refugees—both 1948 and 1967 combined—registered with UNRWA, 63 percent residing outside Palestine.[272] Time was on Israel's side and the realization of Israeli exclusionary goals as yet another generation of Palestinians was born in exile. For certain segments, residence in their Arab host states permitted prosperity impossible for Palestinians in Israel to achieve. A tremendously wealthy and influential Palestinian bourgeoisie could be found in the various Arab capitals, Europe, and even further abroad.[273] Relatively well integrated into their host countries, most were reluctant to risk their success by involving themselves in politics. Others were not, however, and contributed substantial resources to the liberation movement. Influential members of the Palestinian bourgeoisie have figured prominently on the board of the Palestine National Fund (the institution that oversees the PLO's financial affairs) and have enjoyed direct ties to Fatah's top leaders.[274] Their experience of exile has been a markedly different one than that endured by the most impoverished stratum of Palestinians, the refugee camp populations.

In midyear 1982, UNRWA continued to operate a total of sixty-two refugee camps with the largest housing 62,000 residents.[275] In 1981, the total Palestinian camp population was approximately 712,000, 59 percent residing in camps outside Palestine.[276] Exclusion for the camp populations meant a perpetual struggle to secure a livelihood, which kept them from the struggle to liberate the homeland. The PLO would offer them a way in which to address both living conditions and a role in securing the Return. Camp refugees would provide the *fidàyin* of the national liberation movement.

For the exiled Palestinian bourgeoisie, exclusion had permitted integration elsewhere and the development of class interests that they were reluctant to risk through political activity. For the camp refugees, exclusion entailed an unrelenting preoccupation with survival. Thus, Palestinian nationalism was the product of middle-class exiles who experienced the vulnerability of statelessness while also securing their material welfare through employment that their education and skills made possible. They would contribute the personnel, ideology, and organizational resources of the PLO.

The PLO in Lebanon: "A State within a State"

The 1976 mobilization of Palestinians in the West Bank, and the potential for popular action it revealed, caught the PLO leadership in exile by surprise.[277] For one thing, Palestinians who were exiled from the homeland remained the PLO's primary focus; for another, the PLO was embroiled in the Lebanese civil war that had been raging for over a year. With Israel's Lebanese allies seeking to expel the PLO from Lebanon, Palestinian forces engaged directly in the civil war, allied with the LNM. Eventually, the PLO's presence and authority became stronger than that of the Lebanese state in the areas held by the PLO-LNM alliance, forming what came to be regarded as a "state within a state." The organization's "state-like" behavior, however, was not confined to its control of the streets. The PLO constructed an extensive infrastructure of institutions and services. In the process, the Palestinian national movement became the single largest employer of Palestinians in Lebanon; one estimate suggests as much as 65 percent of Palestinians in 1982.[278]

The PLO had become a welfare state. Through the Institute for Social Affairs and Welfare of Families of Martyrs and Prisoners of War, families of victims were assured a monthly stipend, priority for PLO jobs, health care coverage, and university scholarships.[279] The PLO enabled 20–30,000 students to pursue studies abroad.[280] The Palestine Red Crescent Society provided medical services that rivaled those of the Lebanese government.[281] This period saw the improvement of camp conditions, establishment of factories, initiation of cultural and social programs, and introduction of a wide range of educational services. A plethora of PLO institutions—research centers, specialized departments, professional and trade unions, and media and broadcasting centers—drew thousands, many abandoning promising careers in the diaspora to join the resistance movement. And branches of the various unions—students, women, youth, writers, teachers, engineers, journalists, and doctors and pharmacists—were established to link Palestinian communities of the diaspora as far away as the United States and Latin America. Class interests were "betrayed" as individuals from divergent classes converged with the oppressed of the refugee camps. Politics were distinctly antisectarian as Muslims and Christians combined to defend secular political and class analyses of the region's traumas.[282] And democracy, it was asserted, would ultimately differentiate the future state of Palestine from existing Arab states. Indeed, measured solely in terms of freedom of expression and tolerance of political opposition, the Palestinian national movement was a democratic movement.

The substantial PLO presence in Lebanon could not have been sustained without enormous infusions of money. The "corruption of the revolution," or, in a play on words, what came to be coined as "wealth without revolution" *(al-tharwa bila al-thawra)* was and continues to be fervently debated.[283] Initially, between 1964 and 1969, sums contributed by Arab governments through the Arab League were largely taxes collected from Palestinians employed in the oil-producing states and distributed by the Palestine National Fund to the various institutions of the PLO.[284] After 1973, petrodollars became abundant and the 1978 Baghdad Summit committed Arab states to providing $300 million annually to the PLO and the occupied territories.[285] In addition, Arab governments began to bypass the Arab League and court one or a number of the eight Palestinian organizations with undisclosed payments. By far the largest recipient of Arab money was Fatah, which received amounts that surpassed even those to the PLO.[286] In the process, a dependence developed between the PLO and its donors on the one hand, and between the refugee population and the PLO on the other; dependencies that would constrain both, with implications well into the future.

The frenzy of institution building was accompanied by the bureaucratization of the movement.[287] The left places the blame squarely on Fatah, which, owing to its populist appeal and control over PLO institutions, lacked the incentive to develop genuinely mass-based organizations. Fatah's middle-level leadership resembled state functionaries more than revolutionary cadres; and its preoccupation with the militia and military, necessitated in part by the Lebanese civil war, reinforced its hierarchical and autocratic approach to the movement's mass base.[288] However, it must be added that in a context where PLO money was flowing, there was limited pressure from below to alter the organization's approach, and once dependence developed, limited interest in risking access. Moreover, family and kinship persisted as the primary basis of social organization.[289] Both were symptomatic of the nonclass nature of refugee social relations and the weakness of working-class formations specifically.[290] Destitute, vulnerable, and noncitizens in a hostile host state, camp refugees could not escape dependence on the PLO and UNRWA. Rampant factionalism at the mass base within the ranks of work-

ers, women, youth, and others, further reduced these sectors' collective ability to pressure PLO leaders.

The left was not immune to the shortcomings of Fatah. Struggles between the various factions of the PLO, which revolved around funding and
representation *(tamwil* and *tamthil)*, were deftly manipulated by Fatah leaders who controlled the purse strings. By the admission of PFLP and DFLP
leaders, the organizations of the left were less successful than Fatah in drawing the oppressed sectors into their ranks.[291] The explanation lay, in part, in
the more rigorous membership requirements and political education demanded by the PFLP and DFLP; Fatah required a minimum and controlled
the movement's resources.[292] But there was also a problem of relevance and
resonance of Marxism-Leninism in the context of the class fluidity that characterized the refugee population. "Democratic centralism" superimposed on
a traditional social structure, and a distorted one at that, merely reproduced
the hierarchical and paternalistic authority structures of old in new form,
even while they infused these with new political content. Thus, "clannish,"
"patriarchal," and "autocratic" behavior permeated relations between leaders
and followers and merely reproduced the traditional authority in the new
form of political organizations: "the new tribalism."[293] This would prove
detrimental to the development of participatory democracy in the Palestinian movement.

Nevertheless, the PLO in Lebanon had succeeded in generating and
amalgamating a Palestinian national movement out of a geographically fragmented population; one that would survive a fourteen-year civil war, three
Israeli invasions, and Israeli assassinations of key leaders. Palestinians were
back on the political map as attempts to "melt" them into the region were
resisted and failed. This was no mean accomplishment. The PLO had revived and sustained the Palestinian "cause." But the greater part of the
Palestinian national movement's energy and resources had been directed to
the institutions and structures assiduously constructed in Lebanon. The
PLO had neglected the occupied territories.

The Israeli invasion in June 1982 altered things dramatically. A three-
month-long Israeli assault forced the PLO to retreat from Lebanon. The
American-brokered evacuation in August saw the relocation of the organization's headquarters to Tunis, and its armed units dispersed further than
ever from the front with Israel. With its forces stranded in camps, and its
headquarters removed from the area, the organization was cut off not only
from its base of support in the occupied territories but also from its main
constituency, the exiled refugee camp populations. The PLO entered a period of disarray and Fatah suffered a nearly devastating insurrection and

Syrian-backed split. In search of a way out of the PLO's predicament, Arafat sought a rapprochement with King Hussein, which culminated in a joint Palestinian-Jordanian peace initiative in 1985. In protest, the PFLP and DFLP suspended their membership in the PLO Executive Committee. Declining morale and evident disorientation damaged the PLO's ability to operate. Its powerlessness in the mid-1980s was apparent when Palestinian camps in Lebanon were targeted once again by Lebanese forces in what came to be known as the "War of the Camps." Ironically, however, with the destruction of the PLO's infrastructure in Lebanon, the organization was both forced and free to turn its attention to Palestinians under Israeli occupation as the last remaining hope for the national movement. This shift in focus would contribute to an unprecedented resurgence and convergence of struggles inside the territories that would, in fact, bring about the long-awaited internal challenge to the Israeli occupation.

Convergence of Factions and the Intifada

On December 8, 1987, an Israeli Defense Forces (IDF) tank transporter crashed into a van returning Palestinian workers to the Gaza Strip at the end of a workday, killing four workers instantly and injuring seven. Rumors spread that the collision had been deliberate. Funerals for the dead on the following day, three of whom were residents of the Jabalya refugee camp, turned into mass demonstrations denouncing the occupation. Israeli forces opened fire on the demonstrators killing a youth who became the first "martyr" *(shahid)* of what was to become a major uprising or *intifada* in the West Bank and Gaza Strip.

Within a few weeks, a number of aspects were particularly striking about the uprising. Demonstrations engulfed virtually the entire West Bank and Gaza Strip. Its momentum was sustained by "popular committees" that sprang up at the level of neighborhoods inside towns, refugee camps, and villages. And Israeli occupation forces were unable to quell the unrest. Between 1988 and 1993, a total of 1,481 Palestinians would be killed, of whom 29.2 percent were refugee camp residents, 34.8 percent residents of towns, and 35.8 percent villagers.[294] Students and workers would make up approximately 40 percent and 30 percent, respectively, of deaths.[295] Street battles between stone-wielding youth and heavily-armed government forces were only one notable aspect of the *intifada*. Workers boycotted jobs in Israel; farmers fed beleaguered towns and villages; shopkeepers turned back Israeli goods, stopped paying taxes, and shut down; and industrialists expanded production to support the boycott of Israeli goods.[296] Eventually, even Palestinians within Israel would contribute to the uprising.[297] IDF commanders were at a loss to explain the surprising intensity of this challenge to Israeli rule or to contain it.[298]

Two events facilitated the shift in the momentum of the Palestinian national movement to the occupied territories and, as a result, the genesis of the *intifada.* First, in April 1987, the eighteenth session of the PNC concluded with the reunification of the PLO. The collapse of Arafat's agreement with King Hussein the previous year paved the way for the reactivation of the PFLP and the DFLP's membership in the PLO's EC.[299] In addition, the JCP—renamed the Palestinian Communist Party (PCP)—became a member organization of the PLO. Thus, after nearly five years of dissension and disarray, the PLO was reunited. This unity was immediately translated into efforts within the territories and foreshadowed the emergence of a rotating, underground leadership in the West Bank and Gaza Strip—the Unified National Leadership of the Uprising (UNLU).[300] Second, topping the agenda of the November 1987 Arab Summit meeting was the "Iranian threat" in the Gulf. This was the first time since the establishment of the Arab League in 1945 that the "Palestinian problem" did not dominate an Arab Summit meeting. Palestinians interpreted this as a sign of shifting Arab priorities and a deliberate snub of the PLO.[301] These two events occurred against a backdrop of persistent deterioration in living conditions under Israeli rule[302] at a time when recession in the Gulf states dramatically reduced both opportunities for emigration and JPJC and other Arab funding.[303] Now, even graduates of Palestinian universities were being forced to join manual laborers in Israel as an alternative to remaining unemployed.[304]

Political organizations inside the territories, no less than their leaders in exile, were surprised by the intensity of the mass actions that erupted twenty years after the onset of occupation.[305] They were quick to act, however, through their organizational extensions. Owing to the proliferation of mass organizations, experienced organizers were in place who were capable of directing and extending what had begun as a spontaneous expression of indignation into a full-scale uprising.[306] Within a month, an effective underground leadership was established that included one representative of each of the four main political factions, the first body in which Fatah representatives did not predominate. In the Gaza Strip, in addition to the four main organizations, the Islamic revivalists were represented. This new phenomenon, whose unimpeded development can be traced to the Israeli authorities' need for a countervailing force to the PLO,[307] was beginning to assert itself in the territories. Through leaflets *(bayanat)* issued regularly and distributed surreptitiously by underground networks, the UNLU translated local efforts into coordinated actions that traversed the territories. Leaflets provided analyses, guidelines, and specific calls for action, including general strikes, on specified days coordinated throughout the territories. Popular response to the calls was overwhelming,[308] in large measure because the directives were perceived as realistic and demonstrated a sensitivity on the part of the underground leaders to the specific constraints confronting each sector. Casualties mounted as the Israeli forces stepped up repression, in the process drawing unprecedented international criticism of Israeli actions and attention to Palestinian demands for self-determination and an independent state. Despite repression, the *intifada* continued unabated, rooted as it was in the democratic local structures of the "popular committees" that organized defense, procurement, and distribution of goods for communities under siege, the resolution of internal disputes, and the like in neighborhoods and communities across the territories.[309] When in 1988 the Israeli occupation forces imposed a ban on the popular committees, a discernible decline in popular participation resulted, but the *intifada* persisted.

From its headquarters in Tunis and its regional offices, the PLO leadership searched for a direct role. Ironically, given Israeli goals, the 1982 invasion of Lebanon placed the PLO in a better position to oversee and direct efforts inside the occupied territories through contacts from Jordan where the PLO was permitted to establish offices for the first time since 1971.[310] A Fatah-controlled *intifada* fund was established, thereby reintroducing the divisiveness of competition over resources.[311] PLO leaders also began to demand greater control, including that leaflets should be faxed for prior approval.[312] Mockingly, critics of this policy coined the phrase "revolution by fax." Such short-sighted interference was resented by the underground leadership, including Fatah's representatives.[313] But the UNLU's ranks were being thinned by the massive hunts, detentions, expulsions, and assassinations conducted by the occupation forces. A new layer of leaders was produced each time, but one that was less experienced and therefore more likely to succumb to pressures from their leadership abroad to turn over decision making to them.[314] Although an impressive level of coordination and cooperation between the political factions had been demonstrated, the reintroduction of PLO exile politics undermined this once again. Eventually, the PLO leadership in exile was able to assert its control. The impact and implications have been debated: one view suggests that the uprising was already on the decline due to fatigue, the banning of popular committees, and absence of concrete gains; another that the intervention of PLO leaders, and Fatah's in particular, weakened the uprising. Indeed, since the establishment of the PNF in 1973, PLO leaders consistently demonstrated an aversion to the consolidation of a unified leadership, even one that was solidly pro-PLO, inside the territories.[315] Either way, the *intifada* began to lose its popular character and relied even more on a vanguard cut off from its base as people's exasperation with factionalism undermined their confidence and returned them home.[316]

Nevertheless, the uprising would continue for six years and would prove extremely costly for Israel, both economically and in terms of international opinion.[317] Due to their limited inclusion, however, Palestinians never had the capability of shutting down Israel's economy; less than 10 percent of Israel's labor force was drawn from Palestinians in the occupied territories.[318] Some sectors, however, most notably construction, where Palestinians from the occupied territories constituted 48.9 percent of Israel's wage workforce in 1987, came to a virtual halt.[319] In light of their partial dependence on Palestinian labor, the Israeli economy had the capacity to adjust to their exercise of leverage. Yet the costs entailed were sufficient to force Israel into seeking a negotiated end to the uprising. This, in turn, required the uprising's recognized leaders—the PLO.

After two decades of attempts to bypass, create alternatives to, and eradicate the PLO, its ability to deliver the restoration of order in the territories gained the organization a part in negotiating a permanent settlement to the conflict. Through their unwavering, though not uncritical, support of the PLO, Palestinians under the occupation gave the organization a new resource to wield with their opponents. In 1991, Israeli officials began negotiating with a joint Jordanian-Palestinian delegation that included no PLO officials but enjoyed PLO approval. The following year, a new Israeli government brought Israeli leaders who recognized the inevitability of negotiating directly with their opponents' representatives. Palestinians had succeeded in asserting their chosen leaders in negotiations for a settlement to a conflict that had been waged for the better part of a century. The question that now loomed was how well those leaders could be trusted to represent Palestinians' interests.

Evaluating Success

Following decades of relatively contained resistance, the West Bank and Gaza Strip became the site of Palestinians' most important challenge since the 1930s. All the parties to the conflict were caught by surprise, even the underground activists who had worked for nearly a decade to extend the reach of the exile-based political organizations into the camps, villages, and towns of the occupied territories. Israel's oppressive occupation, Arab regimes' manipulation, and calamities befalling their beleaguered counterparts in exile, spurred the new round of resistance. Collective eruptions of indignation were common under the occupation; the duration and extent of its replication across the territories that was exhibited this time were not. By expanding channels for popular political participation, the mass-based organizations in place since the late 1970s made the *intifada* possible.

Palestinian resistance to the occupation was shouldered by a configuration of class forces produced by the subsumption of the territories' economies into Israel's. Economic decline induced the proletarianization of numerous segments of the labor force, in the process bringing together within the same exploitative labor market disparate social forces that shared an inability to secure adequate livelihoods within their home economy. Indeed, landowners, undermined economically, were no longer the main source of employment for the landless, and landownership for small holders was no longer a guarantee of security. These changes saw migrant workers' ties to their villages weakened, status differentials less salient, generational clashes more common, and, most important, a certain amount of freedom from the conservative village and community leaders possible. Constraints to the expansion of Palestinian industry precluded the rise of a Palestinian industrial bourgeoisie capable of replacing landowners as significant employers.[320] And the expansion of the middle class was being impeded directly by Israeli control over the administration of the territories and, indirectly, by the outcome of their policies. Under these conditions, and with emigration rapidly disappearing as an option, Palestinian factions found tremendous receptivity to their organizing efforts.

Although economic inclusion contributed to the erosion of traditional social relations and organization, and with it the authority of traditional leaders and their village proxies, the process remained incomplete. A number of factors contributed to retarding their dissolution. Threatened by land confiscation and displacement, Palestinians invested tremendous effort into maintaining their society intact; internal struggles against capitalist exploitation and patriarchal domination were for the most part "frozen" for the duration of the national liberation struggle, and the nationalist wing of the PLO co-opted and preserved the Palestinian elite. Indeed, "steadfastness" proposed to thwart Israeli depopulation schemes and retain the basis for a future state through the preservation of existing Palestinian institutions.

The contribution of the various political factions was critical to the politicization and organization of Palestinians under occupation, even though such efforts began late. Stimulated by competition, political organizations established a variety of mass-based organizations that traversed the territories. These organizations introduced a new activist approach that emphasized democratic participation organized directly within communities. They represented a break from both the members of the elite who led prior to 1976, as well as the pro-PLO, middle-class community leaders who became prominent after 1976. While the latter organized from above through municipalities, social service institutions, and professional associations, as well as through bodies such as the PNF and NGC, the new leaders organized from below. Working underground and directly among their constituencies, they proved to be both less vulnerable to detection and more effective.

But while the mass base of political participation expanded within the territories, the political leadership in exile was ultimately able to assert its control, thereby aborting the experiment in participatory democracy already debilitated by Israeli repression. The centralized approach to mass organization, characteristic of the PLO in exile, was carried into their relationship with the movement inside the territories. The extent of the external organizations' influence is noted from the degree to which the factionalization of Palestinian politics inside the territories reflected political struggles in exile.[321] While the Israeli invasion of Lebanon in 1982 hastened and facilitated the convergence of the movements' "inside" and "outside" components, factionalization delayed the convergence within sectors "inside," thereby delaying the unification of workers', students', women's, and youth's "blocs" under the occupation.

Competition over resources funneled into the territories exacerbated factionalization. The matter of resources, however, did not end there. As conditions worsened under occupation, residents turned to family members employed outside the territories, the JPJC, UNRWA, the PLO, and Arab governments—anywhere but the Israeli administration for the resources they required. Indeed, to demand of the occupiers anything—fair wages, the rescue of basic services, badly needed expansion of government-run facilities—short of full independence from occupation was deemed unacceptable as it was tantamount to granting recognition to the occupiers.[322] In this way, Palestinians not only indirectly assisted in subsidizing the occupation, but also released Israel from its responsibilities under the Geneva Conventions, thereby giving up an important source of potential pressure. The existence of alternative resources combined with the continued viability of the territories' economies reinforced Palestinians' determination to avoid directing such demands to the occupiers. However, as externally derived resources diminished—both "steadfastness" funding and family remittances—and conditions worsened, Palestinians had fewer options. This undoubtedly fueled the mass resistance even further.

The uprising proved costly but not devastating for Israel. Due to the limited extent of their inclusion, Palestinians lacked sufficient leverage with which to induce an Israeli withdrawal; Israeli dependence on Palestinian labor did not render the Israeli economy sufficiently vulnerable to Palestinian leverage. Limited inclusion meant that Palestinians wielded limited leverage within Israel's economy and that organizational forms necessary to effectively exercise what leverage they possessed remained weak. Palestinian trade unions were, for the most part, surrogates for political organizations, and most organizations were dependent on PLO resources. Yet Palestinians were able to disrupt Israel's comfortable rule of the territories sufficiently to necessitate Israeli action. Repression slowed down the *intifada* but did not halt it. The only means left available to Israel was to negotiate a cessation. This would require involvement of the uprising's recognized leaders: the PLO had asserted its relevance.

The Expansion of Popular Struggles and Movement Success

In the 1970s, both national liberation movements were on the threshold of a new phase of resistance. As the liberation organizations developed their scenarios of revolutionary action in exile, a phase of movement expansion would soon be initiated by new social forces coalescing inside South Africa and Palestine. This phase would culminate in the 1980s with mass uprisings that would astonish even the liberation organizations with their intensity.

The mass uprisings of the 1980s had antecedents. The strike wave of 1972–73 and the 1976 Soweto uprising revealed a glimpse of the potential for black resistance in South Africa; the mobilization around the 1976 West Bank elections and 1981 response to Likud rule revealed Palestinian potentials for action. Up until this point, both the ANC and PLO had underestimated the potential for resistance on the internal front, and overestimated the centrality of armed struggle conducted from exile. The limited effectiveness of armed struggle notwithstanding, it had succeeded in inspiring and galvanizing popular support for the exiled liberation organizations.[323] It may also be suggested that, operating from exile, the liberation organizations persisted with armed struggle because it was the only means of action directly within their control. The problem is that "when the only tool you have is a hammer, you tend to see all problems as nails,"[324] and a military approach to the liberation struggles in both cases delayed leaders' recognition of non-military potential inside South Africa and Palestine.

In both cases, a new phase of the national movement is ushered in by mass-based organizations rooted in new social forces produced by economic inclusion. By undermining the traditional elites, economic inclusion also enabled the new social forces to consider alternative means of organization and action, in the process expanding the mass base of political participation in both South Africa and the occupied Palestinian territories. Importantly, the mass organizations and actions that developed continents apart resembled each other to a remarkable extent: the "civics" in South Africa had their counterpart in the "popular committees" in the West Bank and Gaza Strip; and stones, barricades, and boycotts were the weapons of the communities in revolt in both cases. The fundamental difference between the two uprisings lay in the contribution of their respective labor movements.

In both cases this phase is marked by the increasing leverage of the working class within their opponents' camp: in South Africa, in the form of dependence of industrial enterprises on an urban, stable, and semiskilled and skilled black workforce; in Palestine, in the form of migrant workers employed in Israel or on Israeli settlements in the occupied territories. Yet the differences were consequential: the particular character of economic inclusion produced a proletariat with revolutionary potential in South Africa, while it did not in Palestine. South African workers were concentrated in enterprises of scale and exhibited a keen class consciousness. Their organization into powerful, democratic trade unions enabled them to recognize and use their leverage effectively. Their residential concentration reinforced their new identification and permitted them to extend their influence to others within the urban townships. In contrast, Palestinian workers employed in Israel remained in small-scale services and construction for the most part, remained easily replaceable, and returned daily to homes dispersed throughout the territories. Moreover, Palestinian workers demonstrated a strong national consciousness but weak class consciousness; their unions reinforced the former and not the latter.

Indeed, while in South Africa the success of resistance in the 1980s was based on the convergence of workers' and community struggles, the lesson may be that when workers organize first on shop floors and then turn to struggles beyond, their contribution is more effective than when they organize politically from a weak workplace presence. That is, although addressing workers' oppression as members of subordinate national groups may mobilize more workers than if only economic concerns are addressed, when confined to the former the process of organization and mobilization does not develop workers' full capacity to contribute. Organizing first as workers in strong, democratic trade unions enabled black workers to bring more to the national movement once they joined. Although South African trade unionists debated the appropriate strategy for decades, when they finally turned to national political struggles they were strong enough to ensure a distinct contribution and organizational presence. In the process, they had developed both their capacity to use their leverage, as well as a class consciousness regarding the political ends to which they would apply this.

In the Palestinian case, workers were organized by political organizations directly. Addressing their concerns as workers was treated, for the most part, as a means to a political end: that of mobilizing for the national movement. Although trade unions whose agendas prioritized liberation from Israeli occupation were more successful in enrolling members than those that focused on economic and workplace grievances, the labor movement's limited organizational capacity was undoubtedly a function of its weak workplace presence. Objectively, the Palestinian workers' stunted leverage reinforced this. Thus, while FOSATU unions concentrated on workers' shop-floor strength, temporarily eschewing political action, Palestinian unions submerged workers into the liberation struggle while neglecting their workplace interests. COSATU melded the two, but was successfully able to do so no doubt because of FOSATU's effective preparation of unions.

Differences between the two communities were equally significant. For the overwhelming majority of blacks in South Africa, dependence on the state was complete, and emigration, ANC or regional resources were never viable alternatives. Addressing daily needs, such as decent housing and affordable rents and fares, became matters of struggle that brought township residents face to face with the state. In the process, communities acquired experience and confidence in their capacity to resist. In contrast, for Palestinians, alternatives to dependence on the occupiers were relatively abundant; in the search for resources, Palestinians could endure temporary emigration or turn to the JPJC, UNRWA, Arab governments, or the PLO directly. These alternatives served as pressure-release valves for Palestinians and, by allowing for the externalization of Palestinian demands, reduced pressures on Israel to address the needs of the population under their occupation. Significantly, the upsurge in Palestinian resistance to the occupation coincided with the waning of alternatives in the mid-1980s.

The response of ANC and PLO leaders in exile to the assertion of popular political will inside differed markedly. In contrast to ANC leaders' receptivity to the UDF, PLO leaders verged on being hostile to bodies such as the PNF and NGC, which they saw as potential rivals that Israel could exploit. To some extent the difference may be explained by the fact that the ANC had no choice but to accept the UDF, given that its constituency remained inside the country. In contrast, a sizeable section of the PLO's constituency was outside the territories with demands that were distinct from those of Palestinians who remained inside Palestine. But this is not the entire picture.

Paradoxically, in several respects the ANC's disadvantage worked to the organization's favor and the PLO's advantage to its own detriment. The ability of the ANC in exile to impose its will on organizations inside the country was limited; the majority had formed and developed independently of the liberation organization. Trade unions and civics, not to mention churches and other community formations, were established by the sectors themselves, and even while individuals had ANC sympathies, the majority did not act on ANC instructions. This required the ANC to actively cultivate support to achieve its political hegemony over institutions that had independent origins. The combination of difficulties of access, due to the organization's distance from South Africa, and relatively limited financial resources, rendered the ANC incapable of exerting direct control. Ultimately, this worked to the ANC's advantage by enabling UDF affiliates to develop along lines that were responsive to their constituencies, thereby expanding their reach and effectiveness while also producing local leaders. In contrast, with the exception of the Communist Party, Palestinian organizations and bodies that emerged in the late 1970s were linked directly to the factions of the PLO in exile to whom they turned actively for leadership, programs, and resources. This facilitated PLO control over organized efforts inside the territories, thereby hampering the emergence of an effective Palestinian leadership inside the territories.

These differences notwithstanding, in both cases the popular sectors that mobilized through mass organizations produced unprecedented challenges to the South African and Israeli states. Repression having failed, both governments were compelled to turn to the uprisings' recognized leaders—the national liberation organizations—to restore order. In South Africa, the gravity of the challenge to business interests propelled business leaders to the ANC headquarters in exile. In Palestine, the Israeli government more reluctantly called on the PLO. In both cases, the national liberation organizations' principal resource was the leverage contributed by the mass-based challenge. ANC and PLO leaders were eager to use that leverage in negotiations with their opponents. Whether or not representatives of their respective working classes would participate in strategizing for negotiations, if not in negotiations directly, reflected the relative strength of workers within the broader movements of national liberation. Indeed, the relationship forged between leaders and followers, the political and labor movements, and the "inside" and "outside" components of the two movements during the process of national liberation would come to be reflected in the process of negotiations and the outcomes they would produce in both cases.

Conclusion

In the early 1990s, several decades after other national liberation movements had attained governance, black South Africans and Palestinians would begin to govern themselves. Both movements, which emerged in the 1910s, owed this accomplishment to massive uprisings in the 1980s that substantially raised the costs of maintaining white minority rule in South Africa and Israeli military rule in the West Bank and Gaza Strip. In both cases, a well-organized mass base delivered leverage to their respective liberation organizations, which the latter carried into negotiations with their opponents to secure democracies long promised South Africans and Palestinians. Despite notable parallels in their development over time, and the greater relative success of both movements in the 1980s, South Africans would prove more successful than Palestinians in achieving their declared objective. Indeed, as in the process of liberation, so too in the product of negotiations, the South African national movement would surpass the Palestinian national movement.

The ANC: From Seizing Power to Power Sharing

Negotiations between the ANC and the NP began in 1990. Significantly, the democratic forces were represented by a triple alliance composed of the ANC, SACP, and COSATU, revealing the weight of the working class within the national movement.[1] Negotiations were conducted behind closed doors, in the process generating tremendous criticisms of the ANC and its partners. Democratic trade unionists were particularly vocal as such secrecy flouted the very principles and practices they had fought to establish and protect over decades. Expectations were high and accusations regarding a possible sellout in the works came to be heard from a variety of quarters. SACP General-Secretary Joe Slovo would be the boldest in his sobering assessment: having neither demolished the state nor developed the capacity to seize state power, the movement was "not dealing with a defeated enemy."[2] Moreover, with "never a prospect of forcing the regime's unconditional surrender across the table,"[3] a transitional period would be required before majority rule would be achieved, hence a "'sunset' clause" in the interim constitution that provided for a period of power sharing.[4]

As news of accommodation and concessions to the previous rulers made their way to the streets, union and community leaders and activists called for the reactivation of mass action. Indeed, for a significant segment of organized labor the "national democratic" stage was a transitional one toward the attainment of socialism. A number of internal developments, however, weakened the organized capacity of the mass base and its ability to act.

In 1991, a conference was convened to determine the fate of the UDF as an organized body. One view was that as an effective organ of "people's power" the UDF should be retained. Proponents of this view envisaged the UDF's role as one of watching over the government, remaining prepared to activate mass action if the need should arise. Many leaders and activists emphasized that the preservation of the UDF was imperative to ensure that participatory, rather than merely representative, democracy prevailed in South Africa. The opposing view suggested that the legalization of the ANC had eliminated the need for the UDF. Popular participation, they argued, would be preserved through ANC membership at various levels in branches throughout the country. Yet others questioned whether, in view of the fatigue that prevailed, it was realistic to seek to sustain the level of popular mobilization that had characterized the UDF once a friendly government was installed. The conferees voted to disband the UDF.[5]

Yet another development that would devitalize the mass base and its ability to effectively carry out organized action was the wholesale transfer of leaders and cadres from the democratic mass organizations and trade unions into the various leadership levels of the ANC. As the ANC prepared to govern, the organization faced a dearth of experienced and skilled personnel. The shortage of personnel made the ANC's ability to assume control over the various apparatuses of the state, which were retained rather than dismantled, let alone the economic enterprises of the country, virtually impossible. No attempt would be made to displace their white incumbents, even those directly responsible for administering apartheid.[6] Apartheid inclusion had retarded the development of a black middle class of administrators, managers, professionals, and other segments with what were deemed requisite skills. Indeed, while apartheid had forged a revolutionary working class capable of national liberation, it had stunted the development of a black middle class capable of running the state apparatuses inherited by the movement. As such, ANC recruitment for government positions deprived trade unions, community and mass organizations, and other black institutions of their most able leaders and cadres.

Ironically, corporations also came to siphon black talent away from the organizations of the mass democratic movement. Corporate leaders, eager both to stave off government intervention and to accelerate the cultivation of blacks with a stake in capitalism to do battle with the unions, incorporated some blacks into the various levels of the country's economic enterprises. This included the creation of partnerships in joint investment schemes that have transformed a number of prominent union leaders into corporate executives who now tout "labor capitalism" or capitalism with a "human face."[7] In the process, COSATU and its affiliates lost a number of its key leaders.

Nevertheless, in 1994, a political democracy was achieved in South Africa. The transitional power sharing arrangements ended two years later when the new constitution was ratified and the NP withdrew from the Government of National Unity to become an opposition party. Moreover, a bill of rights, recognized internationally as particularly progressive, was adopted and the government committed itself to an ambitious, comprehensive Reconstruction and Development Programme (RDP). Importantly, in large measure these were secured by the democratic labor movement and popular sectors through their vigilant and direct participation in political developments both before and since the 1994 elections. Indeed, at a number of points during the negotiations, mass actions proved decisive.[8] The problem remains, however, that for the successful implementation of the RDP or application of the bill of rights, political will is insufficient. In the absence of economic power, these will remain unrealizable.

Indeed, there has been minimal adherence to those clauses in the Freedom Charter that referred to the disposition of the country's economic resources: privatization, rather than nationalization, is the current policy, and World Bank–inspired land reform limps along irresolutely. Only two years after taking office, the ANC reversed its policy on World Bank and IMF aid, which it had previously rejected,[9] and adopted the market-driven, macroeconomic Growth, Employment, and Redistribution (GEAR) strategy, which once again burdens workers while relieving big capital, in the process undermining the RDP.[10] Thus, while a political democracy has been attained, the economic structures as well as white ownership and control remain intact; political power sharing has ended but economic power sharing is still being sought. ANC leaders hope to use political power to foster "black economic empowerment" within the system they inherited as the Afrikaners had done so effectively after coming to power in 1948, ignoring consequential differences in the two cases and time periods that will inevitably confine gains to an elite. In 1997, black companies controlled only 8 percent of the equities listed on the Johannesburg Stock Exchange, although blacks constituted over 80 percent of South Africa's population.[11] In comparison to 1995, however, this represented a phenomenal increase from 0.3 percent.[12] Despite such a growth rate, there is room at the top for only a small number, black or white, while the overwhelming majority of blacks must contend with 40 percent unemployment and the legacy of horrible inequalities.[13] If the situation of other countries is any indication, the ANC's courting of World Bank and IMF favor and the focus on self-enrichment of an elite—albeit a black elite—dooms the majority to this fate.

What then of the success of the national movement in South Africa? A political democracy has been achieved, and the potential remains for the working class and poor to safeguard and expand the political space they secured. But developments since 1994 have gradually reduced the capacity of South Africa's participatory democracy to breach the barriers to economic power for the benefit of the majority. Indeed, for the majority of South Africans, the South African success only becomes obvious when compared to the Palestinian case.

The PLO: From Liberation to Submission

In September 1993, Israel and the PLO signed the Declaration of Principles, culminating the so-called Oslo process, named after the secret location in which Israeli and PLO officials hammered out the agreements. The negotiations were conducted in such secrecy that even Palestinian officials engaged in negotiations with their Israeli counterparts in Washington were kept completely unaware. Indeed, Arafat proceeded without consulting the PLO's EC—not even his own organization's representatives—and later dismissed calls for the convening of the PNC.

Arafat's flagrant violation of democratic norms was widely denounced. Palestinians were vocal in their demands for a say on an issue of unrivaled magnitude to the Palestinian people: the fate of the West Bank and Gaza Strip. But, once again, while PLO democracy tolerated free and open expressions of outrage and criticisms of leaders, such a democracy would achieve nothing. Importantly, criticisms of Arafat were neither confined to fringe Palestinian organizations that rejected any compromise with Israel, nor to the organizations of the left, which had a history of opposition to Arafat's leadership. Critics now included Fatah leaders and supporters who recognized Palestinian weakness, and the inevitability of compromise with their opponents, but rejected what they considered to be Arafat's inept and irresponsible negotiating, which had squandered the national movement's greatest resource—the *intifada*.[14] Indeed, the prevailing explanation for the haste with which Arafat readily surrendered fundamental Palestinian demands points to his eagerness to preserve control over the movement and its future at all costs. In the wake of the punitive reduction of financial resources to the PLO that followed the Gulf War, Arafat had cause to fear the disintegration of a PLO bureaucracy and clients who had served him well.

In defending their meager gains, supporters of the Oslo accords popularized the slogan "Gaza-Jericho First"—a reference to the two areas in which self-rule was first implemented. They pointed out that just as Zionists had been able to expand their initial gains to achieve a state, so would Palestinians. Indeed, on the eve of the Israeli elections in May 1996, Labor leaders indicated that they were amenable to the eventual establishment of a Palestinian state. The dubious nature of this state aside, the newly elected Likud government put a brake on the implementation of the agreements already signed, let alone permitting any advance toward a Palestinian state of any sort. Thus, not only did PLO leaders sign a questionable agreement, they did so without securing guarantees that it would be binding from one Israeli government to the next.

Teams were set up to negotiate the specifics of the Oslo agreement. The Palestinian negotiators chosen were a combination of PLO bureaucrats from exile and middle-class professionals, academics, and other "personalities" from the West Bank and Gaza Strip—figures with no organized following. Importantly, the *intifada*'s grassroots leaders were bypassed and no representative from the Palestinian trade unions was included.[15] Even the general secretary (a Fatah supporter) of the PLO's exile-based General Union of Palestinian Workers (the body representing Palestinian workers worldwide) was excluded.[16] This was a conspicuous reflection of the weakness of workers in the Palestinian national movement. Indeed, Arafat entered negotiations with his opponents as a traditional leader rather than one heading an organization with a constituency to which he was accountable. Moreover, as a traditional leader, he deftly brought around individual heads of "lesser clans" (member organizations of the PLO) in the process inducing splits within each—one section moving "with Arafat" and the other remaining incapacitated by the split.

Negotiations produced an agreement for the redeployment of Israeli forces, as distinct from withdrawal, and Palestinian self-rule, but no state.

Ironically, Israeli leaders had already conceded both self-rule and the rede-ployment of forces in the Camp David Accords signed with Egypt in 1978. The difference between the two agreements, however, was that in 1978 Israeli leaders were not willing to see Palestinian self-rule administered by the PLO. The Palestinian *intifada* altered that, making it necessary to incor-porate their recognized leaders as enforcers of the new arrangements.

Thus far, the redeployment of Israeli forces has been confined to major Palestinian population concentrations—3 percent of the West Bank and 60 percent of the Gaza Strip. A Palestinian National Authority (PNA) now oversees the affairs of Palestinians in the West Bank and Gaza Strip in the areas of health, education, and municipal services and functions. Travel into and between the two territories, as well as between major Palestinian popu-lation concentrations inside the West Bank, remain entirely under Israeli control and is manipulated continuously as a form of collective punishment by Israel. The already fragmented territories are being splintered even fur-ther in what may be described as an intensification of the "bantustanization" of the West Bank and Gaza Strip. One consequence is that linkages between Palestinian institutions and grassroots organizations within and between the West Bank and Gaza have become so tenuous as to prevent any possibility of a repeat of the *intifada*.

Objectively, the PLO's weakness in negotiations was due in large mea-sure to the limited leverage that Palestinians wielded with Israel. Palestinian leverage has not been sufficient to induce a complete Israeli withdrawal from the territories occupied in 1967. But there are other sources of weakness: the power of the PLO leaders and the inability of the movement's mass base to demand and secure their leaders' adherence to democratic norms. This can be traced to the weakness of the popular classes and the organizations they constructed in the 1980s, which factionalization prevented from coalescing effectively. Although the dynamics of inclusion enabled Palestinians to over-come regional, clan, and other communal obstacles and freed them from tra-ditional elite leaders who had hampered their uprising in the 1930s, political factionalism and a factionalized leadership came to undermine their upris-ing in the 1980s. Moreover, while by virtue of inclusion Palestinians enjoyed leverage in the 1980s they did not possess under exclusion in the 1930s, working-class formations remained underdeveloped. Indeed, the Palestinian experience did not contribute to the emergence of a strong, organized work-ing class, let alone a revolutionary working class capable of national libera-tion. It did, however, permit the flourishing of a middle class and bour-geoisie in exile capable of running a state. Were a Palestinian state to be established, Palestinian capital and expertise abounds. Significant segments of the diaspora Palestinian bourgeoisie, however, have already expressed no interest in operating under Arafat's rule; other Palestinians have no choice.

Self-rule in the limited areas from which Israeli forces have redeployed has entailed new and additional hardships, including unparalleled levels of poverty and unemployment, and Palestinian-administered repression.[17] Accompanying the 1996 election of Arafat as President of the PNA has been the construction of an immense Palestinian security force comprising seven distinct apparatuses, all of which answer directly to Arafat. The security forces have shown complete disregard for political freedoms, freedom of the press, and human rights.[18] Indeed, an Israeli precondition for PLO rule was the suppression of opposition to Israel—although it continues to occupy the majority of the territories—and to the agreements signed. Thus, Israel's previous policing role has now devolved to the PLO, thereby seriously impugning the democracy that Palestinians have attained. The persistent weakness of the Palestinian working class and popular sectors more generally renders the prospects for democratization bleak.

In short, the differences in the democracies produced by the national liberation movements in South Africa and Palestine can be traced to differences that were already apparent during the process of liberation. The prevailing configuration of class forces and the relationship between leaders and the movements' mass bases—that is, the extent of the democratization of the liberation movements—would effectively determine the nature of the democracies the two movements would produce.

Liberation and Democratization

The progressive democratization and effectiveness of both national movements is noted from their development over three phases. Neither movement was successful when traditional elites dominated or retained significant influence over their societies in the formative phase of the national movements (1910s to early 1940s). The elites preferred cooperation with the ruling powers to mass mobilization, thus they often acted to restrain rather than promote popular formations. In the phase of movement consolidation, a radicalized middle class came to dominate in both cases (late 1940s to early 1970s). While turning explicitly to activate the "masses," the movements remained top-down efforts, subordinating the mass base and sector-specific struggles to the middle-class leadership of the national movements and the national struggle. The latest phase of movement expansion was launched by the popular sectors, who asserted new and more effective forms of resistance while aligning with the liberation organizations in exile (late 1970s to1980s). The now bottom-up mass organizations reflected newfound capacities of the popular sectors to act. The evident democratization of both movements through the expansion of the mass base of political participation was responsible for the greater effectiveness of both movements in their latest phase of resistance.

While expanded popular participation produced the successes registered by both movements, differences between the two movements were critical in explaining the comparatively more limited success of the Palestinian national movement. This can be traced to the weakness of Palestinian workers and mass organizations and, as a result, to the more limited democratization of the Palestinian movement as compared to the movement in South Africa. This weakness is the product of the history of Palestinian exclusion prior to 1967, and the limited extent of Palestinian inclusion since 1967.

In contrast to exclusionary forms, inclusionary settler colonialism in South Africa and Palestine since 1967 generated dynamics for the democratization of both national movements. It did so by weakening the indigenous elites and leveling social and class differences through the transformation of various segments of both societies into workers for the settler projects. Thus, by eliminating or eroding obstacles to the popular classes—elites above and differences below—inclusion facilitated the convergence of forces at the mass base and their capacity to identify and act on their interests, in the process introducing dynamics conducive to democratizing both national movements. The character and extent of blacks' inclusion meant both that their indigenous elites were weaker and their working class was stronger, hence prospects for democratization greater. Nevertheless, even in Palestine, the organization of resistance became more effective when the *intifada* forced movement leaders to yield to the movement's mass base.

Significantly, inclusionary settler colonialism introduced dynamics for the democratization of the relationship between the national movement and their opponents as well. Inclusion in South Africa ultimately rendered both blacks and whites amenable to an inclusionary democracy: white dependence on black labor made political democracy imperative; black dependence on expertise and capital hitherto monopolized by whites made it equally so. In contrast, the more limited inclusion of Palestinians in the West Bank and Gaza Strip, and complete exclusion of Palestinians in exile, rendered neither Palestinians nor Israelis interested in pursuing inclusionary democracies: Israeli dependence on Palestinian labor was too limited to require this as a means of pacification; Palestinian expertise and capital were sufficient to obviate this as an imperative of survival. However, failure of the Palestinian national movement to secure an independent state, coupled with the persistence of economic arrangements that bind Israel and the PNA, will mean the perpetuation of dynamics typical of inclusion. Both sides resist this: Israel's determined search for alternative sources of labor in the form of foreign, guest workers and Palestinians' determination to unlink from Israel are manifestations of both sides' resistance to the implications of inclusion. Thus, for the foreseeable future, the political formations in both cases—Israel and Palestine—can be expected to remain exclusionary of each other.

In short, and paradoxically, exclusion permitted Palestinians greater independence from their opponents as compared to blacks in South Africa, but it also deprived them of leverage to wield as a result. Their limited inclusion after 1967 permitted them some leverage but preserved class forces and relations that were not conducive to fully democratizing their resistance movement, hence the limited effectiveness in the use of what leverage they enjoyed. Indeed, inclusion permitted blacks in South Africa class resources required for liberation but not for state building, while exclusion enabled Palestinians to develop class resources for state building but not for liberation. Black inclusion produced a revolutionary proletariat capable of threatening the apartheid project where it was most vulnerable—the economy. Inclusion, however, prevented the formation of a substantial black middle class of technocrats, administrators, and managers (let alone a class of capitalists) that would have enabled blacks to take over existing state functions and consider proceeding without whites. In contrast, the Palestinian working class was weak, substantially migrant, and divided between a stagnant, yet viable, indigenous economy and nonindustrial employment in Israel. Palestinians' relative freedom from Israel, however, permitted the growth of a middle class and bourgeoisie with a range of skills and expertise, as well as capital, even while this class became concentrated in the diaspora. But with the failure to gain an independent state, the PLO will fail to attract diaspora Palestinians who are required for state building, thereby further reinforcing Palestinian dependence on Israel. At some point in the future, this dependence and intensified inclusion may well generate dynamics conducive to integration comparable to those in South Africa.

Timing

What remains to be explained is the similarity exhibited by these movements in the timing of the shifts from one phase to the next. There was certainly nothing inevitable about either the shifts or their timing. Examples abound of national movements that were suppressed, aborted, or successfully co-opted at various moments in their history. The explanation for the parallel development of the South African and Palestinian national movements lies in the global political and economic dynamics that impinged on these similarly aligned states and movements.

Both movements emerged in response to actions by the preeminent imperial power of the day, Britain. The launching of the ANC followed Britain's support for the consolidation of white control and the formation of the Union of South Africa in 1910 with complete disregard for Africans' interests. The first Palestinian-specific political bodies were formed in response to the imposition of British rule in Palestine, which began in 1917, and British support for Jewish colonization of Palestine. For decades, black South African leaders and Palestinian leaders who saw themselves as loyal British allies believed it was only a matter of time before Britain would recognize the injustice of supporting their opponents' designs. Thus, through its backing of white and Jewish colonization, British imperial actions catalyzed the formation of national movements by the indigenous peoples of South Africa and Palestine.

The Second World War impaired Britain's ability to assert its will globally. For South Africa and Palestine specifically, the war entailed additional reverberations. In South Africa, Afrikaner nationalists long disaffected by English domination of the country's economic and political power shattered the precarious white accord that existed by rejecting support for Britain's war effort.[19] By 1948, an Afrikaner challenge to English domination had sufficiently coalesced to win them the elections, in the process initiating the country's descent into apartheid. That year, Zionist forces were strong enough to induce the British into withdrawing from Palestine and militarily asserted their control over most of the country. The Second World War had facilitated Zionists' access to additional arms, and war-related economic expansion reinforced their economic foothold in Palestine. Thus, by 1948, global developments had strengthened the opponents of both national movements, enabling them to defeat both.

Accompanying Britain's postwar decline was the rise of the United States as the preeminent hegemonic power, as well as the consolidation of its communist rival. From the 1950s onward, the Cold War between the United States and the USSR, and the rivalry between capitalism and socialism more generally, formed the principal backdrop to the South African and Palestinian national movements and, indeed, to struggles for self-determination worldwide. To stem the expansion of Soviet influence, the United States vigorously cultivated regional surrogates. South Africa and Israel—both adamantly anti-Soviet, developed capitalist economies in economically underdeveloped regions—were exemplars in the U.S. strategy of containing the spread of communism. One avenue of Soviet penetration was nationalist governments, another was national movements that fought colonial or unpopular regimes tied to the West. For the following three decades, the socialist bloc, through significant political and military support, helped to sustain movements worldwide, including the South African and Palestinian national liberation movements.

In the early 1970s, the global recession that followed the sharp rise in oil prices reached South Africa and Israel, although both had just emerged from a period of exceptional economic growth: South Africa's successful suppression of the political and labor movements in the preceding decade had been rewarded with substantial Western investments; the occupation of the remainder of Palestine in 1967 stimulated tremendous economic expansion in Israel. A period of economic recovery in the late 1970s was cut short by the onset of another global recession in the 1980s. In South Africa, the government's response to the recession, which was aggravated by sanctions, was to squeeze blacks even more to meet their survival needs. For Palestinians, the global recession reduced both external "steadfastness" resources and options such as emigration to oil-producing states undergoing economic contraction themselves. In both cases, the genesis of the unparalleled uprisings of the 1980s can be attributed to the exacerbation of perennial political grievances by new economic strains.

In the late 1980s and early 1990s, the demise of the USSR and fracture of the socialist bloc would reverberate internationally with the full extent of repercussions yet to be realized. The loss of the socialist bloc's material and political support for both national movements, and the waning of the Soviet challenge to capitalist hegemony more generally, modified the roles required of South Africa and Israel as regional surrogates for Western interests. With the threat of communism receding into history, the new imperative for the United States would become regional stability for capital. This required the taming of both states and the movements that challenged them. Western government pressures were applied on South Africa and Israel to negotiate resolutions to the conflicts. The loss of socialist bloc support placed pressure on both national movements to accelerate the move toward negotiations, which they sought in any case. In the early 1990s, both national movements and their opponents embarked on negotiations, the outcomes largely determined by the extent of each movements' success in maneuvering within the parameters already circumscribed by inclusion and exclusion. The story continues, however, as South Africans, Israelis, and Palestinians turn to negotiating their futures within parameters circumscribed by an international form of inclusion: globalization.

Notes

1. The South African and Palestinian National Liberation Movements in Comparative Perspective

1. ANC constitution in Karis and Carter, *From Protest,* vol. 2, 204.

2. See Graham Usher, "Palestinian Authority, Israeli Rule," *Nation,* 5 February 1996, 15–18. According to former Israeli Prime Minister Benjamin Netanyahu, Labor leaders intended that "Arafat will be [Israel's] subcontractor to fight terrorism." Serge Schmemann, "Israeli Opposition Chief Making Comeback," *New York Times,* 30 March 1996.

3. Until the 1950s, the program of the Herut Party—the party of former prime ministers Menachem Begin and Yitzhak Shamir—envisioned a Greater Israel that included areas east of the Jordan River. Neuberger, "Nationalisms Compared," 72.

4. See, for example, Hunter, *Israeli Foreign Policy;* Beit-Hallahmi, *Israeli Connection;* and Joseph, *Besieged Bedfellows.*

5. See, for example, Abramowitz, *Jews, Zionism and South Africa;* and Curtis, "Africa, Israel and the Middle East."

6. Moleah, "Israel and South Africa," 2.

7. See Ashmore, "Israel and South Africa"; Jabbour, *Settler Colonialism;* Lee, "Ethnicity, Militarism and Human Rights"; Stevens, "Israel and Africa"; and Stevens and Elmessiri, *Israel and South Africa.*

8. See McTague, "Israel and South Africa," 107; and Connor, "Ethno-nationalism," 23, 25.

9. SAIRR, *Race Relations Survey, 1989–90,* 35.

10. On the eve of the Palestinian uprising in 1987, the combined population was 3.6 million Jews and 2.3 million Palestinians. CBS, *Statistical Abstract, 1988,* table ii/1, 31 and table xxvii/1, 705.

11. The pre–June 1967 Palestinian population in Israel, the West Bank, and Gaza Strip constituted 63.4 percent of Palestinians worldwide. Khalidi, "Palestinians," 10.

12. Abu-Lughod, "Demographic Transformation," 141, 153.

13. Interview with *Sunday Times,* London, 15 June 1969, cited in Farsoun, "Settler Colonialism," 17.

14. Clyde Haberman quoting Yitzhak Shamir, "U.S. Comment on Old Issue Inflames Israelis," *New York Times,* 15 May 1992.

15. Adam, "Israel and South Africa," 38.

16. Palestinians residing in the West Bank and Gaza Strip accounted for 37.6 percent of the post–June 1967 Palestinian population and 27.0 percent in 1987. Khalidi, "Palestinians," 10.

17. See, for example, Stork, "Israel as a Strategic Asset."

18. Frank Collins, "Borrowing Money for Israel," *Washington Report on Middle East Affairs* 10, no. 6, Dec. 1991/Jan. 1992, 33.

19. Adam, "Israel and South Africa," 35.

20. Raphael Danziger, "Indyk: 'Evenhandedness' Is Not in Our Lexicon," *Near East Report XLII,* no. 8, 20 April 1998, 30.

21. Mandaza, "Southern Africa," 112. For a provocative discussion of the limits and contradictory effects of external pressures applied on South Africa, see Cohen and Cobbett, *Popular Struggles,* 2–4.

22. For a review of the numerous occasions in which the triple veto in the UN Security Council rescued South Africa, see IDAF, *Apartheid,* 114–15.

23. See Moore, "Politics of Beleaguered Ethnic States," 33–36. On Zionism, see Said, *Question of Palestine,* 56–114; Taylor, "Vision and Intent"; and Zogby, *Palestinians,* 7–18.

24. Sayigh, "Palestinian Cause," 17. Similarly, the ANC surpassed South Africa in international recognition with a total of 33 offices in various world capitals in the late 1980s. ANC, Department of International Affairs, August 1994, Johannesburg.

25. U.S. State Department, *Patterns of Global Terrorism: 1986,* January 1988, 32.

26. According to former Prime Minister Yitzhak Shamir, Jews were justified in using terrorism to win statehood while Palestinians were not. "Congress Likely to OK Bush Request, Delay Guarantees to Israel," *San Francisco Chronicle,* 6 September 1991, A4.

27. For a history of the introduction of particular tactics in the conflict over Palestine, see Khalidi, *Critical Juncture.*

28. Ibid., Appendix, 23–28. Khalidi further found a 1:1 ratio of military to civilian Israeli deaths as a result of PLO or Palestinian violence; and 1:5 ratio of military to civilian Palestinian deaths as a result of Israeli violence. All figures exclude the 1967 war and the 1982 Sabra and Chatilla massacres.

29. See Aronson, "Israel's Policy," 81, 83.

30. CBS, *Statistical Abstract, 1988,* table ii/1, 31; and Khalidi, "Palestinians," 10.

31. See Ryan and Will, *Israel and South Africa;* Davis, *Israel: Apartheid State;* Chazan, "Israel and South Africa"; and Shahak, "Israeli Apartheid."

32. These include "national institutions" such as the Jewish National Fund, the Jewish Agency, and the Land Development Administration. Lustick, *Arabs,* 97.

33. Ryan and Will, *Israel and South Africa,* 7–8.

34. See, for example, Chazan, "Israel and South Africa," 10; and McTague, "Israel and South Africa," 106, 108.

35. Adam has argued that the South African state's greater "sophistication" in its selective use of repression against activists should have been more effective than Israel's indiscriminate use of collective punishment in the occupied territories. "Israel and South Africa," 31.

36. McTague, "Israel and South Africa," 106.

37. Migdal offers Israel as an example of a quintessentially "strong state." The measures of state strength he uses, however, apply equally to the South African state. Moreover, he identifies ways in which the Labor Party's legacy contributed to the erosion of some state control. *Strong Societies,* 171.

38. McTague, "Israel and South Africa," 105.

39. Numerous Palestinians interviewed for this project, among them current and past PLO leaders, volunteered that the ANC had proven to be a more capable organization.

40. Cainkar cites the following university enrollment rates per 100,000 population for the early 1980s: 464 Palestinians in the West Bank, 660 Palestinians in Jordan, 3.3 Africans in South Africa, and 1,777 whites in South Africa. "Patterns," 36–37.

41. Palestinians in the West Bank and Gaza Strip are 96 percent Muslim. Heiberg and Øvensen, *Palestinian Society,* 43.

42. In 1989, blacks accounted for 86.4 percent of South Africa's population: 27.5 million Africans; 3.2 million coloreds; and 0.9 million Indians. SAIRR, *Race Relations Survey, 1989–90,* 35.

43. See, for example, Neuberger, "Nationalisms Compared," 72–73.

44. Khalidi, *Critical Juncture,* Appendix, 23–28. Recall the figure excludes the 1967 war and the 1982 Sabra and Chatilla massacres.

45. The newly emergent Islamic organizations, such as Hamas, are not part of the Palestinian national movement. They emerged precisely in response to the failure of the national movement to secure Palestinian independence. Hamas terrorism is therefore the exception that proves the rule: they resorted to such a course of action when alternative means (e.g., elections, strikes, *intifada*) of influencing their opponents were absent or eliminated, and through their actions they have sought to demonstrate their relevance to a demoralized constituency. Such a strategy hinges on continued Israeli intransigence and PLO enfeeblement to render Palestinians desperate enough to become attentive to their alternative approach.

46. Ironically, those critical of such actions were undermined by the palpable international gains that resulted. Nabil Amr, former PLO ambassador to the Soviet Union/Russia between 1988 and 1993 and member of Fatah's Central Council, notes, for example, that after the 1972 attack in Munich, the PLO obtained an office and representative in Bonn. Interview, Amman, 19 April 1994.

47. Interview with Abu-Ali Mustafa, deputy general-secretary of the PFLP, Damascus, 24 February 1994.

48. The Popular Front for the Liberation of Palestine hijacked an El Al plane and flew it to Algeria on 23 July 1968. Jureidini and Hazen, *Palestinian Movement,* 77.

49. The Palestine Liberation Front.

50. Interview with Abu-Ali Mustafa, Damascus, 24 February 1994.

2. Liberating the Nation

1. See McAdam, *Political Process,* 25.

2. Moore, *Social Origins,* 418, 422.

3. Democracy, according to Moore, serves to replace the "arbitrariness of rulers" and rules with "just and rational ones," ensuring the possibility of participation by the "underlying population" in their making. Ibid., 414.

4. O'Donnell and Schmitter, *Transitions,* 27, 50.

5. Ibid., 18.

6. Ibid., 27, 70.

7. Ibid., 38.

8. The authors identify a "procedural minimum," and distinguish between "limited" and "more 'complete' democracies." Democratization, in their definition, involves the "application," "expansion," or "extension" of rules and procedures of citizenship— "[d]emocracy's guiding principle"—to new groups, issues, and/or institutions. Ibid., 7–9.

9. Ibid., 62.

10. Ibid. See 28–32, 62–64.

11. Ibid., 27, 63–64, 69.

12. Ibid., 69.

13. Rueschemeyer et al., *Capitalist Development,* 46.

14. Ibid., 287.

15. Ibid., 270.

16. Ibid., 283.

17. Ibid., 270, 282.

18. Ibid., 272, 283.

19. Ibid., 49.

20. The authors distill democracy to universal suffrage and state accountability to an elected parliament, reinforced further by the protection of civil rights. Ibid., 43–44.

21. Oberschall, for example, includes "anything from material resources—jobs, income, savings, and the right to material goods and services—to nonmaterial resources, authority, moral commitment, trust, friendship, skills, habits of industry, and so on." *Social Conflict,* 282. See also Marwell and Oliver, "Collective Action," 15; and McCarthy and Zald, "Resource Mobilization," 1216.

22. McAdam, *Political Process,* 22–23, 25.

23. Ibid., 31.

24. Piven and Cloward, *Poor People's Movements,* 24.

25. McAdam, *Political Process,* 30.

26. The leverage derived from such tactics depends on the significance of the disruption, whether those targeted have the means to make concessions, and whether the insurgents are capable of protecting themselves from retaliation. Piven and Cloward, *Poor People's Movements,* 25.

27. Tarrow, *Power,* 85. Consequential changes in political opportunity structures include the widening of political space for participation, instability in the prevailing political alignments, access to significant allies, and divisions within and among elites (86–89).

28. See McAdam, *Political Process,* 21–22, 25.

29. See Burawoy, "State and Social Revolution," 108–9 and "Capitalist State," 292.

30. In the absence of such an economic imperative, settlers have tended to eliminate rather than dominate indigenous peoples.

31. Wright, *Interrogating Inequality,* 39–43.

32. Wright adds a third condition—that the exclusion "is morally indictable"—to eliminate cases in which unequal property rights result from competitions for prizes. Ibid., 39.

33. Ibid., 40 (emphasis in original).

34. Ibid., 41.

35. Ibid.

36. Nor, of course, are all oppressors exploiters.

37. Wright, *Interrogating Inequality,* 40 (emphasis in original).

38. Shafir, *Land, Labor.*

39. Simons and Simons, *Class and Colour;* and Wolpe, *Race, Class.*

3. Merging Elites as Nation and Movement Formation, 1910s to 1940s

1. In the twentieth century, there were only two notable attempts at armed African resistance: the Bambata Rebellion in 1906 and Pondoland in 1960. Karis and Carter, *From Protest,* vol. 1, 10.

2. Marks and Trapido, "Politics," 2, 8. Whether the preservation of African territories was a result of successful African resistance or part of a deliberate policy of pacification by the settlers is still debated.

3. The following acts drew particular protest: the Mines and Works Act of 1911 erected color bars restricting skilled and supervisory jobs to whites; the Dutch Reformed Church Act of 1911 excluded blacks from the church; the Native Labor Regulation Act of 1911 established unfavorable recruitment terms for African workers; and the Defence Act of 1912 established an all-white citizen militia force. Indians were also targeted with the Immigrants Restriction Act of 1911. Meli, *South Africa,* 34–35.

4. See Legassick and Wolpe, "Bantustans"; Wolpe, "Capitalism"; and Wolpe, "Theory."

5. Established as the South African Native National Congress (SANNC) on 8 January 1912, the organization changed its name to the ANC in 1923.

6. For African political organizations that preceded the formation of the ANC, see Carter, "African Nationalist Movements," 152.

7. Quoted in Walshe, *Rise of African Nationalism*, 34.

8. Ibid., 387; and Meli, *South Africa*, 38–39.

9. Walshe, *Rise of African Nationalism*, 36.

10. Ibid., 32, 210, 387; and Simons and Simons, *Class and Colour*, 135. Walshe adds that tribal connections were often crucial for the careers of middle-class professionals, such as lawyers (32).

11. Walshe, *Rise of African Nationalism*, 209.

12. Gerhart, *Black Power*, 34, 47–48; and Marks and Trapido, "Politics," 6.

13. See Karis and Carter, *From Protest*, vol. 1, 53; and Fine and Davis, *Beyond Apartheid*, 47.

14. Macah Kunene quoted in Fine and Davis, *Beyond Apartheid*, 47.

15. Walshe, *Rise of African Nationalism*, 45, 81; and Gerhart, *Black Power*, 25 n. 4, 110.

16. Quoted in Walshe, *Rise of African Nationalism*, 34.

17. Quoted in Karis and Carter, *From Protest*, vol. 1, 72.

18. From the SANNC Constitution in ibid., 76.

19. Simons and Simons, *Class and Colour*, 131.

20. Ibid. The authors add that by eliminating tenancy rights, the Act was also intended to equalize access to African labor among white farmers.

21. ANC secretary-general Solomon T. Plaatje quoted in Meli, *South Africa*, 46.

22. Ibid.

23. Stanbridge, "Contemporary African Political Organizations," 68.

24. The Pact government was a coalition of the National and Labor Parties representing Afrikaner capital and white labor, respectively, that united against English-dominated mining capital. See Davies, et al., "Class Struggle."

25. The job color bar was first applied in mining in 1897 and later reinforced by the 1911 Mine and Works Act. Davies, et al., *Struggle*, vol. 1, 10.

26. Magubane, *Political Economy*, 308.

27. Meli, *South Africa*, 84. According to Butler et al., as late as 1974 only 80 percent of the allotted land had been transferred. *Black Homelands*, 12.

28. Benson, *South Africa*, 65; and Gerhart, *Black Power*, 35 n. 18.

29. Walshe, *Rise of African Nationalism*, 128, 420–21.

30. Karis and Carter, *From Protest*, vol. 1, 153–54; and Davies, et al., *Struggle*, vol. 2, 285.

31. Luckhardt and Wall, *Organize*, 65–66.

32. Marks and Trapido, "Politics," 41.

33. See Pahad, "South African Indians," 87; and Gerhart, *Black Power*, 102. See Frederikse for an interview that recounts the difficulties encountered by young Indian militants of the time who sought to convince their conservative community leaders of the need to cooperate with Africans. *Unbreakable Thread*, 29–31.

34. See Marks and Trapido, "Politics," 28–32.

35. Meli, *South Africa*, 84.

36. Ibid.

37. Ibid., 85; and Gerhart, *Black Power,* 40.

38. Carter, "African Nationalist Movements," 152–53.

39. Ibid., 152.

40. Ibid., 153.

41. Simons and Simons, *Class and Colour,* 501.

42. Walshe, *Rise of African Nationalism,* 263.

43. Ibid., 262, 418.

44. In Karis and Carter, *From Protest,* vol. 2, 217. The "Bill of Rights" included demands for land redistribution, equal opportunity in employment and education, and trade union rights (209–23).

45. Lodge, *Black politics,* 24–25; and Walshe, *Rise of African Nationalism,* 385.

46. Walshe, *Rise of African Nationalism,* 387.

47. The Pegging Act of 1943 and the Ghetto Act of 1946. Davies, et al., *Struggle,* vol. 2, 295.

48. Carter, "African Nationalist Movements," 153.

49. The Pact was named after its signatories, then ANC president Xuma and SAIC leaders Yusuf Dadoo and G. M. Naicker.

50. Karis and Carter, *From Protest,* vol. 2, 77.

51. Ibid., 91.

52. Magubane, *Political Economy,* 293.

53. O'Meara, "1946 African Mine Workers' Strike," 149.

54. Terreblanche and Nattrass, "Periodisation," 11, 13; and Holland, *Struggle,* 49.

55. O'Meara, "1946 African Mine Workers' Strike," 150.

56. Marsh, "Labor Reform," 49. From 1934–35 to 1936–37 African workers in manufacturing doubled from 66,503 to 134,233, respectively. White employees decreased from 41 percent of the manufacturing workforce in 1932–33 to 30 percent in the 1950s. Walshe, *Rise of African Nationalism,* 135.

57. According to 1936 census data, 45 percent of the African population resided in the reserves with 55–80 percent of the adult male population away as migrant laborers at any one time. Cited in Walshe, *Rise of African Nationalism,* 135.

58. O'Meara, "1946 African Mine Workers' Strike," 150.

59. The following discussion of the migrant labor system is based on Wolpe's work and in particular on "Capitalism."

60. Wolpe, "Capitalism," 440; and Walshe, *Rise of African Nationalism,* 136.

61. Davies, et al., *Struggle,* vol. 2, 322.

62. Baskin, *Striking Back,* 7.

63. Ibid. See also Bonner, "Black Trade Unions," 176.

64. Luckhardt and Wall, *Organize,* 42.

65. Friedman, *Building Tomorrow,* 12.

66. Baskin, *Striking Back,* 7.

67. Stanbridge, "Contemporary African Political Organizations," 68.

68. Davis, *Apartheid's Rebels,* 4.

69. Meli, *South Africa,* 67.

70. Luckhardt and Wall, *Organize,* 42–46.

71. Bonner, "Black Trade Unions," 175.

72. Baskin, *Striking Back,* 7.

73. Simons and Simons, *Class and Colour,* 285.

74. Ibid., 276, 287, 289. See also *South African Communists Speak,* 67–68.

75. Bunting in Roux, *S. P. Bunting,* 92.

76. Simons and Simons, *Class and Colour,* 289–90.

77. Ibid., 285, 299; and Mzala, "Revolutionary Theory," 46.

78. See Slovo, "South Africa," 158–59.

79. Simons and Simons, *Class and Colour,* 302.

80. See Slovo, "South Africa," 159–60; and Mzala, "Revolutionary Theory," 46.

81. Simons and Simons, *Class and Colour,* 406.

82. Jordan, "Socialist Transformation," 108.

83. See "Programme of the Communist Party of South Africa adopted at the seventh annual conference of the Party on January 1, 1929," *South African Communists Speak,* 104.

84. See Jordan, "Socialist Transformation," 107.

85. Roux, *S. P. Bunting,* 120; and Fine and Davis, *Beyond Apartheid,* 36.

86. Walshe, *Rise of African Nationalism,* 364; and Luckhardt and Wall, *Organize,* 60–61.

87. Davies, et al., *Struggle,* vol. 2, 322–23.

88. See O'Meara, "1946 African Mine Workers' Strike," 153; and Davies, et al., "Class Struggle," 23–26.

89. The success of the strike has been variably attributed to proletarianization and class consciousness, ethnic and regional mobilization, and even criminal elements. Compare O'Meara, "1946 African Mine Workers' Strike"; Beinart, "Worker Consciousness"; and Moodie, "Moral Economy."

90. Beinart, "Worker Consciousness," 296.

91. Bonner, "Black Trade Unions," 180.

92. Marks and Trapido, "Politics," 47.

93. Burawoy, "Capitalist State," 316; and Wolpe, *Race, Class,* 65.

94. A number of early ANC leaders were educated abroad, among them Seme who received degrees from Columbia University and Oxford in 1906 and 1910, respectively; Xuma who received his medical degree from Northwestern University in 1926; and Charlotte Maxeke, founder of the ANC's women's section, who graduated from Wilberforce University in Ohio in 1905. See Karis and Carter, *From Protest,* vol. 4.

95. ANC leaders expressed little interest in the AMWU even though the Union was led by J. B. Marks, an ANC leader and communist in the Transvaal. See Hirson, *Yours for the Union,* 187–88.

96. See Bonner, "Black Trade Unions," 175; and Karis and Carter, *From Protest,* vol. 1, 155.

97. Lodge, *Black Politics,* 68; and Karis and Carter, *From Protest,* vol. 4, 166.

98. Walshe, *Rise of African Nationalism,* 412, 417; and Gerhart, *Black Power,* 36.

99. Magubane, *Political Economy,* 274.

100. Gerhart, *Black Power,* 41–42.

101. Meli, *South Africa,* 44–45.

102. Mbeki, *Struggle,* 1.

103. See Davies, et al., "Class Struggle," 5.

104. For a discussion of differences between ANC branches in the four provinces, see Walshe, *Rise of African Nationalism,* 223–32.

105. Only present-day Lebanon, sections of western and northern Syria, and Mesopotamia (present-day Iraq) were explicitly to be denied independence.

106. Palestine was to be administered internationally because of the area's religious significance to Christianity. The secret agreement was exposed by the Soviets.

107. In the summer of 1919, the British Foreign Secretary Lord Balfour admitted to the irreconcilability of the promises, adding further that "the contradiction between the letter of the Covenant [of the League of Nations] and the policy of the Allies is even more flagrant in the case of the 'independent nation' of Palestine than in that of the 'independent nation' of Syria. For in Palestine we do not propose even to go through the form of consulting the wishes of the present inhabitants of the country. . . . The Four Powers are committed to Zionism." Quoted in Lesch, "Palestine Arab Nationalist Movement," 9.

108. Under Ottoman rule Palestine was administratively segmented. The north was attached to the province (*wilayat*) of Beirut and the south to the autonomous district (*sanjak*) of Jerusalem. The population, however, identified with a larger region known as Greater Syria within the Empire's eastern Arab provinces. Ibid., 14.

109. Abu-Lughod, "Demographic Transformation," 141. Between 1882 and 1914 land owned by Zionist institutions increased from 25,000 *dunums* to 420,700 *dunums,* and Jewish settlements increased from 5 to 47. P. Smith, *Palestine,* 33. (Four *dunums* equal one acre.)

110. Sayigh, *Palestinians,* 37. P. Smith further points out that between 1920 and 1935 Jewish immigrants brought the equivalent of 80 million Palestinian pounds into Palestine. The Mandate government budget for Palestine was 2 million Palestinian pounds annually, or no more than a total of 30 million between 1922 and 1935. *Palestine,* 45–46.

111. Israel Zangwill, quoted in Zogby, *Palestinians,* 7.

112. Mahatma K. Gandhi, "Jews in Palestine," 369.

113. Lesch, "Palestine Arab Nationalist Movement," 14.

114. Swedenburg, "Role of the Palestinian Peasantry," 179; and Lesch, *Arab Politics,* 90.

115. Swedenburg, "Role of the Palestinian Peasantry," 180.

116. For a review of early Arab and Palestinian attempts to reach an accommodation with the Zionists, see Hirst, *Gun,* 30–35; Mandel, *Arabs and Zionism;* and Lesch, "Palestine: Land and People," 31.

117. Lesch, *Arab Politics,* 60–61.

118. Peretz, "Palestinian Social Stratification," 406.

119. P. Smith, *Palestine,* 29.

120. Lesch, "Palestine Arab Nationalist Movement," 19–20.

121. From the "Report of the Third Arab Palestinian Congress," addressing the High Commissioner, 18 December 1920, Haifa, in UAR, *Malaf watha'iq,* Doc. 97, 277.

122. A 1936 British government survey of 322 Palestinian villages found that 0.21 percent of the population owned 27 percent of cultivated land, with holdings of at least 1,000 *dunums;* 8.0 percent owned another 36 percent, with holdings between 100 and 1,000 *dunums;* and 91.8 percent owned 37 percent, with holdings of less than 100 *dunums* or none at all. Sayigh, *Palestinians,* 31.

123. Migdal, "State and Society," 384.

124. Tamari, "Factionalism," 190–91.

125. Lesch, "Palestine Arab Nationalist Movement," 19.

126. Swedenburg, "Role of the Palestinian Peasantry," 185.

127. C. Smith, *Palestine,* 72.

128. Ibid., 71–72; and al-Hout, *Al-Qiyadat,* 71.

129. See Lesch, "Palestine Arab Nationalist Movement," 21–22, 28–29; and Tamari, "Factionalism," 192.

130. Lesch, "Palestine Arab Nationalist Movement," 8–9. For an inventory of the various occasions in which the British promised independence, see the "Memorandum of the First Palestinian Arab Delegation to the British Government Concerning Palestinian Arab National Demands," 12 August 1921, in UAR, *Malaf watha'iq,* Doc. 102, 297–301.

131. On the education of the Palestinian elite, see Swedenburg, "Role of the Palestinian Peasantry," 181; Tamari, "Factionalism," 187; and Peretz, "Palestinian Social Stratification," 405.

132. "Memorandum presented by the President of the Third Arab Congress to the British Foreign Secretary," 8 March 1921, in UAR, *Malaf watha'iq,* Doc. 99, 8 March 1921, 281.

133. "Memorandum of the First Palestinian Arab Delegation to the British Government Concerning Palestinian Arab National Demands," 12 August 1921, in UAR, *Malaf watha'iq,* Doc. 102, 297–301.

134. Lesch, "Palestine Arab National Movement," 10.

135. Ibid., 14, 16. The Third Arab Congress was held in Haifa in the winter of 1920–21. See "Memorandum of the First Palestinian Arab Delegation to the British Government concerning Palestinian Arab National Demands," 12 August 1921, in UAR, *Malaf watha'iq,* Doc. 102, 297–301.

136. See C. Smith, *Palestine,* 73–74; Lesch, "Palestine Arab Nationalist Movement," 21; and Waines, "Failure," 222–23.

137. Lesch, "Palestine Arab Nationalist Movement," 21.

138. Anglo-American Committee of Inquiry, *Survey,* vol. 1, table 1, 141.

139. For annual figures of Jewish land purchases, see PLO, Research Center, *Village Statistics 1945,* 25.

140. Granott, *Land System in Palestine,* table 32, 277. According to Khalidi's

calculations, 58 percent were absentee landlords who were not Palestinians. "Palestinian Peasant Resistance," 225. Between 1891–1920, the sale of a single Beiruti family's land-holdings in the Plain of Esdraelon resulted in the eviction of some 8,000 peasants and the loss of 22 villages. Hirst, *Gun,* 29.

141. For immigration statistics, see Anglo-American Committee of Inquiry, *Survey,* vol. 1, table 1, 185, 210.

142. See Waines, "Failure," 228; and P. Smith, *Palestine,* 67.

143. Quoted in Waines, "Failure," 228. The manifesto was signed by Musa Kazim al-Husseini, al-Haj Amin al-Husseini, Raghib al-Nashashibi, Mustafa al-Khalidi, and Aref Dajani.

144. Sayigh, *Palestinians,* 50; and Swedenburg, "Role of the Palestinian Peas-antry," 181.

145. Quoted in Lesch, "Palestine Arab Nationalist Movement," 31.

146. The Shaw Commission attributed the 1929 riots to the British government's disregard for the promises made to the Arabs and to Arab fears of domination by the eco-nomically more advanced Jewish sector. The Commission recommended controlling im-migration to avoid precipitating similar disturbances in the future. Waines, "Failure," 228–29. Citing the disturbing emergence of "a landless and discontented class," the Commission also recommended setting limitations on the amount of land that could be transferred to non-Arabs. C. Smith, *Palestine,* 90.

147. Sir John Hope-Simpson concluded that "The present position, precluding any employment of Arabs in the Zionist colonies, is undesirable, from the point of view both of justice and of the good government of the country." In Khalidi, *From Haven,* 307.

148. Based on two commissions' findings, the Colonial Secretary Lord Passfield rec-ommended more stringent regulations on immigration and land transfers, noting "there remains no margin of land available for agricultural settlement by new immigrants." Quoted in Waines, "Failure," 229.

149. See C. Smith, *Palestine,* 90–94.

150. Waines, "Failure," 229.

151. Lesch, "Palestine Arab Nationalist Movement," 32.

152. Ibid., 19; and Yasin, *Ta'rikh,* 123.

153. Lesch, "Palestine Arab Nationalist Movement," 20.

154. Swedenburg, "Role of the Palestinian Peasantry," 186; and al-Hout, *Al-Qiyadat,* 186. The Nashashibis dominated the National Defense Party (1934); the Husseinis sponsored the Palestine Arab Party (1935); and the Reform Party (1934) was established by the Khalidis, another prominent Jerusalem family. Swedenburg adds that the Independence Party, an offshoot of the Arab Independence movement of Faisal's days, and the only mass-based political party, succeeded in transcending clan factionaliza-tion, yet was racked by pro-Hashemite and pro-Saudi factional divisions (186). Whether or not the Independence Party could be considered the party of the Palestinian bour-geoisie is a matter of debate. See Tamari, "Factionalism," 196–97.

155. Lesch, "Palestine Arab Nationalist Movement," 20.

156. See Peretz, "Palestinian Social Stratification," 406.

157. This is Tamari's characterization of the relationship between the Palestinian bourgeoisie and the landed classes, which I suggest holds equally true for the middle class and the landed classes. See Tamari, "Factionalism," 199.

158. Al-Hout, *Al-Qiyadat,* 191.

159. Al-Hout, *Al-Sheikh,* 72.

160. See Sayigh, *Palestinians,* 52.

161. Swedenburg, "Role of the Palestinian Peasantry," 190.

162. Lesch, "Palestine Arab Nationalist Movement," 34.

163. According to C. Smith, al-Husseini's popularity was due in part to his early denunciation of Arab land sales, and his open criticism of the Arab Executive's inaction in the 1920s. *Palestine,* 94–95.

164. Lesch, *Arab Politics,* 116–17.

165. Lesch, "Palestine Arab Nationalist Movement," 35.

166. Ibid., 17. Lesch quotes one Arab observer who expressed the prevailing Arab viewpoint: "The feeling is *not* that if the British will go we will kill the Jews; the feeling *is* if the British go the Jews will be less arrogant and less grabbing and we will be able to live with them" (emphasis in original).

167. Swedenburg, "Role of the Palestinian Peasantry," 191.

168. Ibid.

169. Lesch, "Palestine Arab Nationalist Movement," 36.

170. C. Smith, *Palestine,* 98, 100.

171. Belatedly, the colonial government realized that through exile and arrest it had lost the very Arab leaders on whom previously it had relied to maintain order and control. Lesch, "Palestine Arab Nationalist Movement," 37–38.

172. Swedenburg, "Role of the Palestinian Peasantry," 192.

173. Ibid., 193; and Porath, *Palestinian Arab National Movement,* 267.

174. Swedenburg, "Role of the Palestinian Peasantry," 193.

175. Ibid. See also Porath, *Palestinian Arab National Movement,* for the implications of this factional split within the elite (254–55).

176. Porath, *Palestinian Arab National Movement,* 241.

177. C. Smith, *Palestine,* 101. In 1938 alone, the death count was 1,624 Arabs, 292 Jews, and 69 British.

178. Ibid., 105.

179. Khouri, *Arab-Israeli Dilemma,* 27.

180. Lesch, "Palestine Arab Nationalist Movement," 13; and Migdal, "Crystallization," 10, 16.

181. See Horowitz, "Before," especially 40–41; Migdal, "Crystallization," 16; and Weinstock, *Zionism,* 183.

182. See Khalidi, *From Haven.*

183. See Porath, *Palestinian Arab National Movement,* 175–77.

184. C. Smith, *Palestine,* 116–17. See also David Ben-Gurion in Khalidi, *From Haven,* 371–74.

185. Peretz, "Palestinian Social Stratification," 406. There was also a Bedouin

population estimated at 100,000 in 1922 that was reduced to 66,000 ten years later (406, 408). Bedouin leaders enjoyed patron-client ties with Jerusalem's families but were not integrated into the national movement. Sayigh, *Palestinians,* 41, 51.

186. P. Smith, "Aspects of Class Structure," 100–101.

187. See ibid., 32, 84; and Swedenburg, "Role of the Palestinian Peasantry," 173.

188. In the process, some fell prey to the unscrupulous among the landlords who later denied the peasants' claims; others simply lost their tenure due to the lack of record of ownership. Ruedy, "Dynamics," 124; and Zureik, *Palestinians,* 40.

189. New taxes and new methods of assessment for old taxes meant peasants now paid an average of 25–50 percent of their already insufficient incomes, effectively driving peasants into debt en masse. P. Smith, *Palestine,* 52–53. According to Carmi and Rosenfeld, in 1930, an average Arab peasant family's debt was at least equal to its annual income. "Origins," 472.

190. P. Smith, *Palestine,* 52–53.

191. Sayigh, *Palestinians,* 32. These figures exclude the landless migrants already in the cities.

192. Ibid., 36.

193. Lesch, "Palestine Arab Nationalist Movement," 13.

194. See al-Ameri, *Al-Tatawwur,* 121–24; Migdal, *Palestinian Society,* 35; C. Smith, *Palestine,* 95; and P. Smith, *Palestine,* 29.

195. In 1942, Arab-owned industrial firms employed an average of 5.7 workers as compared to 19.8 in Jewish-owned industries. This excludes self- or family-operated workshops, which accounted for 28.1 percent of Arab industry and 6.7 percent of Jewish industry. Al-Ameri, *Al-Tatawwur,* 142.

196. In 1918, British officials granted the Zionist Commission to Palestine's request for differential salaries, accepting the argument that as Europeans, Jews had greater living expenses than Arabs. The Jewish Agency later secured half of the public works jobs for Jews, despite the fact that at no time did the Jewish population exceed 30 percent. C. Smith, *Palestine,* 68, 95.

197. Khalidi, "Palestinian Peasant Resistance," 215.

198. Ibid., 215, 228.

199. Between 1932 and 1936, German immigrants brought the equivalent of near-ly 10 percent of the Palestine government's total expenditure over that period. Waines, "Failure," 225.

200. See Asad, "Class Transformation," 4–8.

201. Beinin, "Palestine Communist Party," 6.

202. Ibid., 6. Beinin explains that between October 1929 and 1934 the PCP concentrated on recruiting Arab members, many of whom were sent to Moscow for training. Not content with the pace of Arabization, however, the Comintern dissolved the PCP's Central Committee and appointed a new one with an Arab majority in October 1930 (9).

203. See Beinin, *Red Flag,* on working class hegemony asserted in the 1930s (67–68).

204. Ibid., 7; and Swedenburg, "Role of the Palestinian Peasantry," 187.

205. Beinin, "Palestine Communist Party," 7.

206. Ibid., 8.

207. Ibid.

208. In 1948, the NLL would unite with the Communist Party of Israel (MAKI) in the areas allotted for a Jewish state in the partition plan, while in the areas designated for Arabs—including those under Israeli rule—it would continue as the NLL. Beinin, *Red Flag,* 52.

209. Ibid., 11–12.

210. Yasin, *Ta'rikh,* 118.

211. Hiltermann, *Behind the Intifada,* 58.

212. Sayigh, *Palestinians,* 53.

213. Yasin, *Ta'rikh,* 130.

214. Opening statement of the first Arab Workers' Congress (1930) in al-Budeiri, *Tatawwur,* 156. Yasin notes that in 1928–29, in addition to the Seventh National Conference, students, women, businessmen, and villagers held national conferences. *Ta'rikh,* 124.

215. Yasin, *Ta'rikh,* 131.

216. Budeiri, *Palestine Communist Party,* 54; and Lesch, *Arab Politics,* 64.

217. Hiltermann, *Behind the Intifada,* 59.

218. Yasin, *Ta'rikh,* 131, 133.

219. Ibid., 133.

220. Ibid., 134.

221. Hillal, "West Bank and Gaza Strip," 34.

222. Hiltermann, *Behind the Intifada,* 59.

223. Tamari, "Factionalism," 195–96. Two general secretaries of PAWS were assassinated: Michel Mitri in 1936 and Sami Taha in 1947. Both assassinations were widely attributed to al-Husseini whose leadership of the national movement they opposed. The PAWS disintegrated in the aftermath of the assassination of Sami Taha. Al-Hout, *Al-Qiyadat,* 519, 526–27.

224. Sayigh, *Palestinians,* 53.

225. Interestingly, he shared this stand, and the logic behind it, with the extremist Zionist Stern Gang, which expressed willingness to assist Germany and Italy, the enemies of Britain, during the Second World War. C. Smith, *Palestine,* 121.

226. Ruedy, "Dynamics," 134; and Khouri, *Arab-Israeli Dilemma,* 53–54.

227. Peretz, "Palestinian Social Stratification," 410.

228. By the final phase of the war, Arab forces numbered 40,000 and Jewish forces 60,000. Flapan, *Birth of Israel,* 189–99; and Rodinson, *Israel,* 35.

229. Ibid.

230. Ruedy, "Dynamics," 135.

231. Abu-Lughod, "Demographic Transformation," 161.

232. Sayigh, *Palestinians,* 52.

233. See Tamari, "Factionalism," 190.

234. By 1942, the Jewish sector accounted for 55 percent of firms, 75 percent of

workers, 83 percent of wages, and 60 percent of capital in industry. The Arab industrial sector's share was as follows: 44 percent, 17 percent, 17 percent, and 10 percent. Trabulsi, "Palestine Problem," 65 n. 27.

235. See Carmi and Rosenfeld, "Origins."

236. See Waines on the implications of Arab leaders' "inability and unwillingness" to throw their lot in fully with the peasants to secure the end of the mandate. "Failure," 228.

237. For a discussion of the role of Arab and Muslim countries up to 1939, see Lesch, *Arab Politics,* 131–54.

238. As revealed subsequently, King Abdallah of Transjordan, the grandfather of the current Jordanian king, had colluded with the Zionists in the division of Palestine. Under the guise of entering the war to prevent Zionist occupation, he secured a portion of Palestine for his kingdom, an act for which he was later assassinated. See Flapan, *Birth of Israel,* 125, 127.

4. Middle-Class Hegemony and the Containment of Class, 1940s to 1970s

1. Davies, et al., *Struggle,* vol. 1, 19, 140.

2. See Davies, et al., "Class Struggle," 25–26.

3. Ibid., 27.

4. Wolpe, "Changing Class Structure," 148. See also O'Meara, *Volkskapitalisme,* 167–71.

5. Davies, et al., *Struggle,* vol. 1, 20.

6. Bonner, *Black Trade Unions,* 181.

7. See O'Meara, *Volkskapitalisme,* 174.

8. Marks and Trapido, "South Africa," 8.

9. Davies, et al., *Struggle,* vol. 1, 285.

10. Ibid.

11. Magubane, *Political Economy,* 298.

12. See Magubane, *Political Economy,* 146–47; and Legassick and Wolpe, "Bantustans," 98–99, 104–5; and Smith, *Apartheid,* 38–39.

13. See Rogers, *Divide and Rule,* 10.

14. See Wolpe, "Capitalism," 440.

15. Wolpe, "Theory," 244 and "Critique," 9, 13.

16. Bundy, "Land," 275–77. See also Mbeki, *South Africa,* 111–34.

17. Luckhardt and Wall, *Organize,* 273.

18. Ibid.

19. Fine and Davies, *Beyond Apartheid,* 157.

20. Ibid. The prohibition applied equally to white workers in "essential industries."

21. The number of strikers and strikes by black workers more than doubled between 1954 and 1955, continued at high levels through 1958, and declined thereafter. Ibid., table 7.1, 159.

22. For a list of the concessions made by the Smuts UP government, see Gerhart, *Black Power,* 110.

23. Some indication of the impact may be noted from the following: In 1946, Africans accounted for 14.1 percent (62,056) of all professional, administrative, clerical, and sales workers; 10.8 percent (58,967) in 1951; increasing again to 13.7 percent (102,724) in 1960. Calculated from Wolpe, "Changing Class Structure," table 1, 153. If service workers are included, as Wolpe does in his analysis, the percentages are as follows: 56 percent, 1946; 52 percent, 1951; and 49 percent, 1960 (table 1.1, 154).

24. Gerhart, *Black Power,* 86; and Marks and Trapido, "Politics," 21. The number of African university students, including correspondence students, was extremely small over this entire period: 811 in 1951–52; 2,151 in 1957; 1,901 in 1960; and 2,413 in 1965. Wolpe, "Changing Class Structure," table 6, 157. In 1954, university enrollment ratios per 1,000 population for all groups were as follows: Africans, 0.06; Colored, 0.19, Indians, 1.13; and whites, 6.9. SAIRR, *Survey of Race Relations, 1954–1955,* 189–90.

25. Benson, *South Africa,* 165.

26. Lodge, *Black Politics,* 147.

27. Ibid., 153–87.

28. Ibid., 114–38.

29. Gerhart, *Black Power,* 110.

30. Ibid., 111. Gerhart notes that, for the most part, the respect accorded to middle-class Africans by their communities was due to "their success in becoming 'like whites.'"

31. In Karis and Carter, *From Protest,* vol. 2, 337–39.

32. Benson, *South Africa,* 136.

33. In Karis and Carter, *From Protest,* vol. 2, 337–39.

34. Lodge, *Black Politics,* 69; and Gerhart, *Black Power,* 90.

35. Benson, *South Africa,* 129.

36. See Gerhart, *Black Power,* 87–88; and Holland, *Struggle,* 63.

37. Mbeki, *Struggle,* 70–71. Another factor was the repression of trade unions in the late 1940s which propelled unionists into the leadership structures of the ANC. Luckhardt and Wall, *Organize,* 72.

38. See Gerhart, *Black Power,* 87; Benson, *South Africa,* 137; and Karis and Carter, *From Protest,* vol. 2, 406.

39. Karis and Carter, *From Protest,* vol. 2, 406; and Lodge, *Black Politics,* 33.

40. Benson, *South Africa,* 130.

41. Ibid., 131. The Act defined a communist as anyone who aimed "at bringing about any political, industrial, social or economic change within the Union . . . by unlawful acts." Quoted in Gerhart, *Black Power,* 91.

42. This event helped reduce suspicions of Indians as many risked and lost their jobs only to be replaced by Africans. Ibid., 132.

43. See Lodge, *Black Politics,* 41–42. The six laws were: Pass Laws, Group Areas Act, Suppression of Communism Act, Separate Representation of Voters Act, Bantu Authorities Act, and Stock Limitation regulations.

44. Benson, *South Africa,* 159.

45. Ibid., 150.

46. Karis and Carter, *From Protest,* vol. 2, 405.

47. Gerhart, *Black Power,* 56, 102; and Lodge, *Black Politics,* 38–39.

48. Magubane, *Political Economy,* 297.

49. Lodge, *Black Politics,* 69; and Gerhart, *Black Power,* 106.

50. Letter from the Transvaal branch of the ANC Youth League to the secretary of the Progressive Youth Council, Ruth First, 16 March 1945. In Karis and Carter, *From Protest,* vol. 2, 316.

51. "Basic Policy of Congress Youth League." Manifesto issued by the National Executive Committee of the ANC Youth League, 1948. Ibid., 329.

52. Ibid.

53. Ibid.

54. Ibid., 324.

55. Ibid., 328.

56. Ibid.

57. Lodge, *Black Politics,* 71; and Benson, *South Africa,* 130.

58. Walshe, *Rise of African Nationalism,* 357, 392; and Gerhart, *Black Power,* 117.

59. CPSA, "Nationalism and the Class Struggle," Central Committee report to the National Conference of the Communist Party in Johannesburg on 6, 7, and 8 January 1950 in *South African Communists Speak,* 208.

60. Ibid., 209.

61. Ibid., 210.

62. Ibid., 209.

63. Ibid., 210.

64. Ibid. (emphasis in original).

65. Ibid. (emphasis in original).

66. Fine and Davies, *Beyond Apartheid,* 128–29.

67. Benson, *South Africa,* 123–24.

68. Lodge, *Black Politics,* 37–38; and Gerhart, *Black Power,* 104.

69. Lodge, *Black Politics,* 40; and Karis and Carter, *From Protest,* vol. 2, 411.

70. Gerhart, *Black Power,* 101–2, 112.

71. On the significance of Indian resources, see ibid., 103–5, 118, 122; and Lodge, *Black Politics,* 38.

72. Lodge, *Black Politics,* 69.

73. Ibid., 69, 73.

74. Lambert and Webster, "Re-emergence," 21.

75. Baskin, *Striking Back,* 14.

76. From the SACTU Statement of Policy submitted to the First Annual Conference in Cape Town, March 1956, quoted in Luckhardt and Wall, *Organize,* 97.

77. Walter Sisulu, quoted in Luckhardt and Wall, *Organize,* 357 (emphasis in original).

78. Webster, "Rise of Social-Movement Unionism," 177; and Bonner, "Black Trade Unions," 184.

79. Lambert and Webster, "Re-Emergence," 21. Friedman notes that the "non-political" Federation of Free Trade Unions of South Africa remained smaller than SACTU. Friedman, *Building Tomorrow,* 27–28.

80. See Bonner, "Black Trade Unions," 184. SACTU members and affiliates grew as follows: 20,000 workers in 19 unions in 1956; 46,000 in 35 unions in 1959; and 53,000 in 51 unions in 1961. COSATU, *COSATU Education: Organisation File,* "Notes on the South African Congress of Trade Unions (SACTU)," 2 July 1987, from COSATU office, Johannesburg.

81. Friedman notes that whereas ANC leaders had to be persuaded to support the 1957 workers' stay-away, its relative success made ANC leaders eager to make use of such actions the following year. *Building Tomorrow,* 30.

82. Magubane, *Political Economy,* 302. Addressing the 1959 SACTU Conference, ANC President Chief Luthuli captured the relationship thus: "SACTU the spear, ANC the shield." Quoted in Luckhardt and Wall, *Organize,* 357.

83. For a discussion of the tensions and strains in the relationship between SACTU and the ANC during the 1958 call for a stay-away, see Luckhardt and Wall, *Organize,* 354–56.

84. Somewhat more than two-thirds of the delegates were Africans, and between 200 and 300 delegates participated from each of the Indian, colored, and white communities. Benson, *South Africa,* 175.

85. The nearly five-year long Treason Trials virtually incapacitated the ANC but ended with the acquittal and release of its 156 leaders. See Lodge, *Black Politics,* 76.

86. In Karis and Carter, *From Protest,* vol. 3, 205–6.

87. See Gerhart, *Black Power,* 158–59, 165.

88. Lodge, *Black Politics,* 81.

89. In 1960, the class origins of the 15-member PAC National Executive Committee (NEC) were as follows: 20 percent "professional elite," 53 percent "other middle class," 20 percent university students, and one trade unionist (7 percent). Among the 69 middle and lower level PAC leaders, none was drawn from the "professional elite," 41 percent were classified as "other middle class," and the remaining 59 percent were working class or trade unionists. As for the ANC/NEC, 70 percent of the 13 members were drawn from the "professional elite," 23 percent from "other middle class," with one trade unionist (7 percent) and no university students. Among the 84 middle and lower level ANC leaders, 49 percent were classified as "professional elite" or "other middle class," with the remaining 51 percent "working class and trade unionists." Gerhart, *Black Power,* 318–19.

90. Interview, Johannesburg, 15 February 1993.

91. Gerhart, *Black Power,* 236.

92. Marks and Trapido, "Politics," 52.

93. Slovo, "Sabotage Campaign," 24.

94. See Davis, *Apartheid's Rebels,* 15; Meli, *South Africa,* 147; and Karis and Carter, *From Protest,* vol. 3, 649–51.

95. Barrell, *MK,* 4–5. See also Slovo, "Sabotage Campaign," 24.

96. Barrell, *MK,* 15.

97. Lodge, *Black Politics,* 297.

98. For considerations involved in choosing bases for the organization on the continent, see Davis, *Apartheid's Rebels,* 37–38.

99. Barrell, *MK,* 19. Lodge notes that in 1967–68, the ANC received only $3,940 of the $80,000 pledged by the OAU through the Liberation Committee. *Black Politics,* 300.

100. Lodge, *Black Politics,* 304.

101. See ibid.

102. Barrell, "Turn to the Masses," 65.

103. Ibid., 67, 69.

104. Slovo, "Second Stage," 33.

105. See Barrell, *MK,* 20–24.

106. See ibid.

107. Lodge, *Black Politics,* 300.

108. ANC, *ANC Speaks,* 177.

109. Mzala, "Umkhonto we Sizwe," 21.

110. Ibid., 175.

111. ANC, "Apartheid South Africa," 2.

112. Ibid., 2.

113. Ibid., 1–2.

114. Ibid., 3 (emphasis in original).

115. Ibid.

116. Lodge, *Black Politics,* 301.

117. Davies, et al., *Struggle,* vol. 2, 286; and Karis and Carter, *From Protest,* vol. 3, 37–39.

118. Lodge notes that over 70 percent of the arrests during the 1952 Defiance Campaign were made in the Eastern Cape. Of these, over half were in Port Elizabeth alone. He adds that it was here too that African political leaders were predominantly working class. *Black Politics,* 46–47, 51.

119. According to Gerhart, while only one of the 13 ANC/NEC members was a trade unionist, 51.2 percent of the ANC Treason Trialists who made up the organization's middle- and lower-rank leaders between 1957 and 1960 were working class or trade unionists. *Black Power,* 319. See also Baskin, *Striking Back,* 14.

120. Barrell, *MK,* 9, 12.

121. Barrell, "Turn to the Masses," 72.

122. Benson notes that as U.S. and British investments expanded, 1964 became one of South Africa's most prosperous years, with investments experiencing an 18 percent increase over the previous year. Concomitantly, defense expenditures increased by 45 percent. *South Africa,* 267.

123. Gerhart, *Black Power,* 94.

124. Fine and Davis, *Beyond Apartheid,* 120. See also Lodge, *Black Politics,* 78.

125. Friedman, *Building Tomorrow,* 31.

126. See Slovo, "South Africa," 173–74.

127. Friedman, *Building Tomorrow,* 31–32; and Fine and Davis, *Beyond Apartheid,* 212–13.

128. Lambert, "Trade Unions," 234–36; Davies and O'Meara, "Workers' Struggle," 111–12; and Bonner, "Black Trade Unions," 184–86.

129. Ruedy, "Dynamics," 135.

130. See Morris, *Birth;* Flapan, *Birth of Israel,* 89; and Hitchins, "Broadcasts."

131. Abu-Lughod, "Demographic Transformation," 161.

132. 1948 Israeli census figures of 120,000 "non-Jews" included foreign Christian residents. Ibid., 160 n. 21.

133. Chaim Weizmann quoted in Flapan, *Birth of Israel,* 84.

134. The UN placed the total value of movable and immovable Palestinian property at 122,483,784 Palestinian pounds. Zuriek, *Palestinians in Israel,* 116.

135. Zionists referred to the Histadrut as "the State in embryo." Hanegbi, et al., "Class Nature," 17.

136. Besides those displaced from Israeli-held territories, an estimated 120,000 Palestinian residents in the West Bank and Gaza Strip lost their livelihoods (land and businesses) across the armistice lines. UNRWA recognized the refugee status of both groups. Abu-Lughod, "Demographic Transformation," 161.

137. Brand, *Palestinians,* table 1.1, 9.

138. In 1949, Palestinians remaining within Israel numbered 133,000, or 9.6 percent of Israel's population. Ibid.

139. By Abu-Lughod's calculations, by December 1948 less than 8 percent of all Palestinians remained within what became Israel. "Demographic Transformation," 160. Those who remained made up approximately 11 percent of Israel's population during the years 1957–65. CBS, *Statistical Abstract, 1988,* table ii/1, 31.

140. Aruri, "Dialectics," 5.

141. King Abdallah approached the British as early as 1937 to endorse his proposed annexation of Western Palestine in exchange for his support for a Jewish state. P. Smith, *Palestine,* 87.

142. Brand, *Palestinians,* table 1.1, 9.

143. Addressing the British Royal Commission in 1936, Ben-Gurion wrote: "Each Jewish soldier has a deep personal commitment to defending this country which is his home and the only one he knows he will ever have. The Palestinian Arab shows no such emotional involvement. Why should he? He is equally at ease whether in Jordan, Lebanon or a variety of places. . . . why should an Arab fight for this place? Because of specious propaganda attempting to prove his attachment to a mythical Palestinian nation?" Ben Gurion, *Memoirs,* 118.

144. See P. Smith, *Palestine,* 84–85, 88.

145. See Sharabi, *Nationalism,* 56.

146. Abraham, "Development," 396.

147. This notion appeared very early in Zionism. In 1895, Theodor Herzl wrote: "We shall try to spirit the penniless population across the border by procuring employ-

ment for it in the transit countries, while denying it any employment in our own country." *Complete Diaries,* vol. I, 88. In 1940, Joseph Weitz, Head of the Colonization Department of the Jewish Agency reaffirmed this: "The only solution is a Palestine . . . without Arabs. . . . And there is no other way than to transfer the Arabs from here to the neighboring countries, to transfer all of them; not one village, not one tribe, should be left." Quoted in Hirst, *Gun,* 130.

148. Article 11 of UN Resolution 194 issued on December 11, 1948. See Hirst, *Gun,* 264.

149. Fatah assailed "America's relief agency," which sought to "obliterate the Palestinian cause." *Filastinuna,* No. 8, May 1960, 8.

150. UN Resolution 393 of December 2, 1950 states: "the reintegration of the refugees into the economic life of the Near East, either by repatriation or resettlement, is essential in preparation for the time when international assistance is no longer available, and for the realization of conditions of peace and stability in the area." IPS, *United Nations Resolutions,* vol. 1, 21–22.

151. Sayigh, *Palestinians,* 109; Hirst, *Gun,* 264.

152. See Hirst, *Gun,* 266; Sayigh, *Palestinians,* 109; and Hillal, *Al-Diffa al-gharbiyya,* 61.

153. For UNRWA's role in reinforcing traditional Palestinian leaders see Badran, "Means of Survival," 56; and Sayigh, *Too Many Enemies,* 36, 50.

154. Interview with Shafiq al-Hout, the PLO Representative in Lebanon between 1964 and 1993, Beirut, March 22, 1994. Early Fatah leaders referred continuously to the need to begin by resisting the despair and helplessness that pervaded the refugee community. See *Filastinuna,* No. 10, September 1960, 24; and No. 15, March 1961, 19.

155. Hirst, *Gun,* 266.

156. See Badran on the pre–1948 preparations made by members of the Palestinian bourgeoisie in order to survive the catastrophe. "Means of Survival," 51–54.

157. Brand, *Palestinians,* 107; and Graham-Brown, *Education,* 35.

158. In 1976–77 the higher-education rate among Palestinians was 20 per 1,000 as compared to 4 per 1,000 for the Arab world as a whole. Hallaj, "Mission," 77.

159. Hirst, *Gun,* 264.

160. Brand, *Palestinians,* table 1.1, 9.

161. A perusal of the *Who's Who* reveals a substantial representation of Palestinian-born among the region's dignitaries. *Who's Who in the Arab World,* Beirut: Publitec Editions, various years.

162. Only Palestinians in Jordan became citizens of their host country. Syria granted Palestinians rights equal to Syrians, including employment in government service and the military, while permitting Palestinians to retain their identity. In Lebanon, they were denied public sector employment and were required to obtain a permit for many private sector jobs. Sayigh, *Palestinians,* 111–12.

163. Hillal, *Al-Diffa al-gharbiyya,* 67.

164. P. Smith, *Palestine,* 187.

165. Al-Ameri, "Socioeconomic Development," 88.

166. P. Smith, *Palestine,* 187.

167. Ibid., 189.

168. P. Smith, *Palestine,* 189–90.

169. Ibid., 189.

170. P. Smith, *Palestine,* 188.

171. For an excellent review, see Qassmiya, "Al-Haraka," 124–27.

172. See Zureik, *Palestinians,* 172–74.

173. This was particularly so with regard to armed activity. See Quandt, "Political and Military Dimensions," 165; and P. Smith, *Palestine,* 192.

174. Yitzhak Shamir, "Excerpts from Israeli Foreign Minister's speech," *New York Times,* 6 October 1981. See also Ariel Sharon, cited in Harkabi, *Israel's Fateful Hour,* 116.

175. In 1952, 80 percent of Jordan's political prisoners were West Bank Palestinians at a time when the latter made up less than a fourth of Jordan's total population. Hillal, *Al-Diffa al-gharbiyya,* 70.

176. On the eve of the merger, the West Bank was considerably more developed than the East Bank where nomadism remained extensive. This advantage would be reversed within a few years of the merger. See Mazur, "Economic Development," 240–41, 211–13; and Sayigh, *Economies,* 187–91, 196–97.

177. This began as early as March 1950 with a government ban on the use of "Palestine" in official documents. Migdal, *Palestinian Society,* 38.

178. See P. Smith on the establishment of a National Guard specifically for this purpose. *Palestine,* 102.

179. See Peretz, "Palestinian Social Stratification," 416–17.

180. Nearly half of the Strip's population resided in refugee camps as compared to less than 10 percent of the West Bank's population. CBS, *Census of Population, 1967,* Publication No. 1, table C, x.

181. The plan was to resettle some 50–60,000 refugees in northwest Sinai in 1953. Abu-Amr, *Usul al-harakat,* 16, 19.

182. See Peretz, "Palestinian Social Stratification," 417.

183. P. Smith, *Palestine,* 153. Smith notes that the decision to permit some Palestinians access to arms came after three days of rioting that followed a particularly fierce Israeli attack in February 1955.

184. Jerbawi and Abu-Amr, "Al-Sira," 7.

185. Migdal, *Palestinian Society,* 37.

186. Ibid.; and Mishal, *West Bank/East Bank,* 100.

187. Mishal, *West Bank/East Bank,* 101; and Migdal, *Palestinian Society,* 37.

188. See Migdal, *Palestinian Society,* 36–37; and P. Smith, *Palestine,* 89–91.

189. P. Smith, *Palestine,* 90.

190. Ibid.

191. Mishal, *West Bank/East Bank,* 103, 107.

192. Ibid.

193. Ibid., 104.

194. Thirty landowning families owned one-fourth of the Gaza Strip's agricultural lands. Jerbawi and Abu-Amr, "Al-Sira," 3.

195. Abu-Amr, "Muqadamma," 14.

196. Yasin, "Al-Haraka," 31.

197. See Abu-Amr, "Muqadamma," 4. There are a number of indications of the rapid expansion of this class, including the increase in the number of commercial shops from 2,000 in 1962 to 10,000 four years later (5).

198. Ibid., 14.

199. See Abu-Amr, "Muqadamma," 2–3.

200. In the case of the West Bank, see Mishal, *West Bank/East Bank,* 100.

201. See Migdal, *Palestinian Society,* 39–40.

202. Peretz, "Palestinian Social Stratification," 412.

203. It should be noted that by all accounts UNRWA assistance was always meager, forcing Palestinian refugees to seek employment wherever they could find it. This pool of surplus labor further depressed wages. See Hillal, "West Bank and Gaza Strip," 42, 62; and Abu-Amr, "Muqadamma," 8.

204. Plascov, *Palestinian Refugees,* 95–96.

205. See Cohen, *Political Parties,* 126–27.

206. See Hirst, *Gun,* 273.

207. Kadi notes that more than thirty Palestinian organizations were established in the wake of the breakup of the UAR in 1961. Kadi, "Origins," 129.

208. Saleh, "Genèse et évolution," 213–14.

209. Abraham, "Development," 396.

210. Ibid., 392.

211. Ibid., 393–94.

212. Interview with Khaled al-Fahoum, member of the PLO's first EC, president of the PNC, 1971–84, Damascus, 16 February 1994.

213. Frangi, *PLO,* 100. Interview with Bahjat Abu-Gharbiya, member of the PLO's first EC, Amman, 12 February 1994.

214. Al-Shuaibi, "Development," (Part 2), 50–54.

215. See Cobban, *Palestinian Liberation Organisation,* 31.

216. Abu-Jihad, second in command in Fatah until his assassination in 1988, revealed: "We considered the establishment of the Palestinian Liberation Organization on the part of the Arabs as nothing but an attempt to thwart the revolutionary tumult germinating inside Palestinians after stagnation, annexation, and dependency that lasted more than 16 years." Quoted in Hamza, *Abu-Jihad,* 308.

217. Interview with Bahjat Abu-Gharbiya, Amman, 12 February 1994.

218. See Quandt, "Political and Military Dimensions," 87.

219. P. Smith, *Palestine,* 192.

220. Khaled al-Fahoum points out that before 1969 the PLO-EC, of which he was a member, was a "committee of independents" with some political experience "but no military or revolutionary underground experience," while after 1969 all the members of the EC represented political factions. Interview, Damascus, 16 February 1994.

221. Indeed, early PLO leaders considered the actions of the underground groups as reckless because they hastened Israeli reprisals for which Arabs were ill prepared. Quandt, "Political and Military Dimensions," 68 n. 30.

222. Jordan would not permit PLA forces to be stationed in the West Bank.

223. In a meeting in February 1967, Nasser advised Shafiq al-Hout to "be patient with Shuqairi," because "we [Arabs] don't have the means to fight the Israelis." Interview with Shafiq al-Hout, Beirut, 22 March 1994.

224. Nevertheless, those raids have been cited as one impetus behind the war launched in 1967. Quandt, "Political and Military Dimensions," 157.

225. Mu'assasat al-dirasat, *Watha'iq,* 1009–10.

226. Interview with Khaled al-Fahoum, Damascus, 16 February 1994.

227. See Hamza, *Abu-Jihad,* 310.

228. Article 9 of the Palestinian National Charter. PLO, January 1980, 4. Obtained from the PNC Office, Amman.

229. Hirst, *Gun,* 292.

230. Seats on the PNC were distributed as follows: 33, Fatah; 12, Saiqa; 12, PFLP; 15, PLA and Popular Liberation Forces (PLF) combined. In protest, the PFLP, PLA, and PLF abstained from participating in the following congress, thereby facilitating Arafat's election as chairman. Quandt, "Political and Military Dimensions," 71.

231. Interview with Khaled al-Fahoum, Damascus, 16 February 1994. Saleh notes that whereas the original PLO leaders were either intellectuals or members of the "upper bourgeoisie," that is, descendants of leading urban families, the new leaders emerged from different fractions of the petty bourgeoisie and were of "modest" social background. "Genèse et évolution," 212–13, 215.

232. Arafat met clandestinely with former Nablus mayor Bassam al-Shak'a, to whom he expressed his disappointment regarding the prospects for armed action by West Bank Palestinians. Interview with Bassam al-Shak'a, Nablus, West Bank, 19 June 1994. See also Hirst, *Gun,* 281.

233. Cobban, *Palestinian Liberation Organisation,* 42. For a discussion of its impact, see Abraham, "Development," 398–99.

234. Fatah reported 15,000 Palestinian and other Arab volunteers in the immediate aftermath of Karameh. Suleiman Zabbal, "Follow me to victory . . . ," *Al-Arabi,* (Kuwait), 122, April 1969, 107 (Arabic). In May 1968, approximately 12,000 young Egyptians contacted Fatah's Cairo office to become volunteers. Cobban, *Palestinian Liberation Organisation,* 39.

235. Interview with Abu-Ali Mustafa, Damascus, 24 February 1994.

236. Interview with Abu-Ali Mustafa, Damascus, 24 February 1994.

237. Lebanon was the least attractive but neither Syria nor Iraq would permit the movement freedom of action. In Abu-Ali Mustafa's words, "the resistance movement was ready to resist, but no Arab capital was willing to become a Hanoi." Interview, Damascus, 24 February 1994.

238. Sayigh, *Too Many Enemies,* 25, 30.

239. Many Christian Palestinians fared better, approximately 40,000 of whom are

currently Lebanese citizens. Interview with Shafiq al-Hout, Beirut, 23 March 1994. Population estimates for 1975 place Lebanon's Christian population at 40 percent. Cobban, *Palestinian Liberation Organisation,* table 2, 64.

240. A total of 374 towns and villages, constituting 45 percent of Palestinian settlements in Palestine, were eliminated after the establishment of Israel. Jiryis, *Arabs,* 79.

241. Hamza, *Abu-Jihad,* 180.

242. Interview with Taysir al-Aruri, PCP Politburo member, Amman, 6 February 1994.

243. Abraham, "Development," 392.

244. Interview with Qais al-Samrai (Abu-Leila), DFLP Politburo member, Damascus, 21 February 1994.

245. Saiqa (early 1967) grew out of the socialist Syrian Ba'th party. The Iraqi's Ba'th equivalent was the Arab Liberation Front (ALF) (late 1968). The remaining three organizations were committed to a "working-class perspective" and the goal of socialism: the Popular Front for the Liberation of Palestine-General Command (PFLP-GC) (1968); the Palestinian Popular Struggle Front (PPSF) (1967); and later, the Palestinian Liberation Front (PLF) (1976).

246. The oil embargo was initiated thirteen days into the war after the United States allocated $2.2 billion for Israel and resupplied it with weapons. C. Smith, *Palestine,* 231.

247. See Abraham, "Development," 407.

248. See Cobban, *Palestinian Liberation Organisation,* 58–60, 66–67; C. Smith, *Palestine,* 231–36; and Abraham, "Development," 407.

249. The program was first enunciated by the DFLP in 1972.

250. Dakkak, "Back to Square One," 79.

251. For a discussion of the revolutionary implications of the Palestinian national movement, see Abraham, "Development," 403–4.

252. Cobban, *Palestinian Liberation Organisation,* 60.

253. Abraham, "Development," 416, 425.

254. See Cobban, *Palestinian Liberation Organisation,* 148–49.

255. Ibid., 66.

256. Ibid., 68.

257. Hillal, "Class Transformation," 10.

258. Abu-Lughod estimated that by December 1968 approximately 75,000 persons had been displaced. Excluded from the numbers are 25,000–50,000 persons abroad on the eve of the war. "Demographic Consequences of the Occupation," *MERIP Reports,* no. 115, June 1983, 13–17.

259. Taraki, "Development," 56–57; Locke and Stewart, *Bantustan Gaza,* 11–12.

260. Metzger, et al., *This Land,* 140.

261. Cobban, *Palestinian Liberation Organisation,* 37.

262. Abu-Lughod, "Demographic Consequences," 14. The estimates do not include persons known to have been outside the West Bank on the eve of occupation.

263. Al-Shuaibi, "Development," (part 2), 61–62.

264. Peretz, "Palestinian Social Stratification," 63.

265. Al-Shuaibi, "Development," (part 2), 61.

266. Ibid.

267. Aronson, "Israel's Policy," 81.

268. Sahliyeh, *In Search,* 37–38.

269. Ibid., 40.

270. Israeli military, paramilitary, and agricultural settlements numbered 49 in 1973, revealing the pace of expansion. Bull, *West Bank,* 137.

271. See Van Arkadie, *Benefits,* 32–34.

272. Ibid.

273. Sahliyeh, *In Search,* 33. Two bodies were formed and then forced to disband: the Islamic Higher Committee and the National Guidance Committee.

274. Dakkak, "Back to Square One," 75. The formation of the PNF received PLO support at the 11th PNC meeting held in January 1973.

275. Sahliyeh, *In Search,* 53, 57.

276. Ibid., 53, 56.

277. Dakkak, "Back to Square One," 78.

278. Sahliyeh, *In Search,* 58–63.

279. Interview with Walid Salem, a Palestinian journalist incarcerated numerous times on suspicion of being a leader of the PFLP underground, East Jerusalem, 7 April 1994.

280. Interview with Walid Salem, East Jerusalem, 7 April 1994.

281. Over a single year, 1974–75, a five-fold increase in emigration was experienced and remained at a high annual average rate of 1.9 percent of the West Bank population through 1981. Gaza's emigration rate displayed the same pattern. CBS, *Statistical Abstract, 1983,* table xxvii/1, 758.

282. Gresh, *PLO,* 18.

283. Interview with Salim Tamari, professor of sociology, Birzeit University, Ramallah, 22 May 1994.

284. Interview with Taysir Aruri, Amman, 1 February 1994.

285. A comparison of university enrollment rates within seven major Palestinian concentrations in the early 1980s reveals the lowest rates were those of Palestinians in Israel. Cainkar, "Patterns," 36.

5. Merging Class and Nation in the Expansion of Popular Struggles, 1970s to 1990s

1. See Marks and Trapido, "South Africa," 7–8; and Murray, *South Africa,* 24–25.

2. See Marks and Trapido, "South Africa," 7–8; and Mann, "Giant Stirs," 55.

3. Price, *Apartheid State,* 29.

4. Wolpe, *Race, Class,* 85–86.

5. See Price, *Apartheid State,* 32–34.

6. The strike wave had its antecedents. See Friedman, *Building Tomorrow,* 44; and Joakimidis and Sitas, "Study of Strikes," 105.

7. In the first three months of 1973 alone, 61,000 workers went on strike, exceeding the totals for the preceding eight years combined. Baskin, *Striking Back,* 17–18. This level of strike activity continued as more than 200,000 African workers participated in strike action between January 1973 and mid–1976. Mann, "Giant Stirs," 53.

8. See Hirson, *Year of Fire,* 84; and Marx, *Lessons,* 54.

9. Wiehahn Commission, *Complete Wiehahn Report,* 1.

10. WIP, "Strikes," 57.

11. See IIE, *Durban Strikes,* 100.

12. Bonner, "Black Trade Unions," 186.

13. IIE, *Durban Strikes,* 6, 45.

14. Wolpe, "Changing Class Structure," 163–64.

15. Marks and Trapido, "South Africa," table 1.1, 33.

16. In 1973, university enrollment rates per 1,000 population were as follows: whites, 22.79; Indians, 7.51; coloreds, 1.45; and Africans, 0.45. Calculated from SAIRR, *Survey of Race Relations, 1973,* 49, 332.

17. SASO, "SASO on the Attack: An Introduction to the South African Students' Organisation 1973," Durban, n.d., 4, Biko Collection, Howard Pim Library, University of Fort Hare.

18. Ibid., 7.

19. Marx, *Lessons,* 51.

20. Ibid., 49.

21. Ibid.

22. See Marx, *Lessons,* 57.

23. Ibid., 58.

24. For BAWU's criticism of white trade unionists, who formed a significant segment of the leadership of the emergent democratic trade union movement, see BAWU, "Call to organise and form Black Trade Unions in South Africa," excerpted in *Review of African Political Economy,* no. 7, September–December 1976, 115.

25. See Brooks and Brickhill, *Whirlwind,* 105.

26. A total of 5,980 people were arrested. Barrell, *MK,* 31.

27. Ibid., 105–6.

28. See Price, *Apartheid State,* 85–95.

29. See Morris, "State, Capital," 44.

30. Mann, "Giant Stirs," 55–56.

31. The fiction of homelands is noted from the following: Lebowa combines the Pedi and North Ndebele speakers; Gazankulu contains both Tsonga and Shangaan speakers; South Ndebele speakers, whose designated homeland is Kwandabele, are dispersed over several homelands; and Xhosas are divided in two separate homelands. Butler, et al., *Black Homelands,* 2–4.

32. Ibid., 2.

33. Murray, *South Africa,* 77.

34. The 1970 census enumerated 15.3 million Africans. Including only those residing inside South Africa's "new" 1985 "boundaries" would yield a population of 11.9

million in 1970, or a 22 percent reduction. In addition, in 1985, 177,000 fewer Africans resided within this area than in 1970. RSA, *South African Statistics,* 1990, 1.6.

35. See Zille, "Restructuring," 63.

36. The Surplus People Project estimates that between 1960 and 1982, at least 3.5 million people were forcibly relocated to bantustans. *Forced Removals,* vol. 1, 5.

37. See Collinge for how boundaries are redrawn to exclude African population concentrations. "Waging War," 18.

38. SPP, *Forced Removals,* vol. 2, table 1, 6. The de jure bantustan population in 1980, which includes migrant workers, accounted for 60 percent of the African population (6).

39. Keenan, "Reform," 120. Giliomee refers to the policy as one of "'ruralizing' the revolution" that was in the making. "Changing Political Functions," 50.

40. Keenan, "Reform," 122.

41. See SPP, *Forced Removals,* vol. 2, 12; Smith, *Apartheid,* 80; and Unterhalter, *Forced Removal,* 103.

42. In 1970, population densities ranged from 24.1 persons per hectare in Bophuthatswana to 68.5 in Kwazulu, as compared to 13.7 for South Africa as a whole. Only six years later the densities ranged from a low of 30.4 in Bophuthatswana to a high of 189.6 in Qwaqwa. Rogers, *Divide and Rule,* 48.

43. In 1980, migrants and commuters from the six "self-governing" bantustans contributed over three times as much as domestic sources to the territories' GDP, and accounted for nearly 80 percent of their gross national income (GNI). Smith estimates that the territories' per capita GNI of R488 in 1980 would have been reduced to R10 without these sources of income. *Apartheid,* 56.

44. One study indicated that in 1981, approximately 850,000 fewer workers were recruited from bantustans as compared to 1975. Cited in Keenan, "Reform," 120.

45. Murray, *South Africa,* 101–2.

46. ILO, *Special Report,* 1986, 51.

47. Ibid.

48. For the ways in which tribal authorities manipulated residents' needs, see McIntosh, "Rethinking Chieftaincy," 42, 44.

49. In 1983, the South African government spent only R2.2 billion, or approximately 9 percent of its budget, on the bantustans. Giliomee notes that the amount is not particularly high considering that approximately 60 percent covered education, health, and industrial infrastructure, amounts that the government would have had to spend anyway had the territories remained integrated. "Changing Political Functions," 56.

50. Keenan, "Reform," 124.

51. In 1980, migrant labor constituted the following percentages of the labor force: Venda, 56.5 percent; Transkei, 53.0 percent; Ciskei, 29.3 percent; and Bophuthatswana, 41.8 percent. Calculated, DBSA, *SATBVC Countries,* table 2.3, 45; table 3.3, 76; table 4.3, 106; and table 5.3, 136.

52. Commuters are those who travel daily to the cities, industrial zones, or rural areas inside "white South Africa."

53. According to DBSA estimates, in 1980, Bophuthatswana's labor force was divided as follows: 18.5 percent locally employed; 30.9 percent transfrontier commuters; 41.8 percent migrant; and 8.7 percent unemployed. The comparable figures for the Ciskei were: 33.4 percent; 19.9 percent; 29.3 percent; and 17.4 percent, respectively. DBSA, *SATBVC Countries,* table 3.3, 76 and table 5.3, 136.

54. In 1980, among those aged 20–64, there was an average of 57.9 males for every 100 females resident in the bantustans. The sex ratios ranged from a low of 35.9 in Venda to a high of 73.9 in Bophuthatswana. Calculated from DBSA, *Self-Governing Territories* and *SATBVC Countries,* various tables.

55. In 1980, dependency ratios for the four "independent" bantustans ranged from 485.9 (Bophuthatswana) to 531.4 (Transkei) per 1,000 population. Calculated, DBSA, *SATBVC Countries,* various tables.

56. For measures taken against "foreign" (i.e., South African) trade unions and other organizations based outside the bantustans, see Cooper, "Bantustan Attitudes"; and Keenan, "Counter-revolution," 146–47, 149.

57. For a description of how traditional relations through tribal *indunas* are exploited by mine bosses to intimidate and control African mine workers, see Sefako Nyaka, "Reaping the Whirlwind," *Weekly Mail,* 23–29 January 1987.

58. It should be noted that despite their dependence on Pretoria for resources, not all bantustan leaders did the government's bidding or supported its plans for "independence." Cobbett, et al., "Critical Analysis," 37.

59. In 1986, GNP per capita in South Africa as a whole was R3,754, while in the bantustans it ranged from R760 in Lebowa to R1,582 in Qwaqwa. Alan Hirsch, "A Bank Report the Homelands Won't Hurry to Okay," *Weekly Mail,* 19–25 January 1990.

60. For the implications of the loss of citizenship for bantustan residents, see Collinge, "Tampering," 29; and Kenyon, "Dumped," 20.

61. Wiehahn Commission, *Complete Wiehahn Report,* 38.

62. See Price, *Apartheid State,* 105.

63. Bekker and Humphries, *From Control,* 48.

64. See Wolpe, *Race, Class,* 97; Unterhalter, *Forced Removal,* 133; and Price, *Apartheid State,* 119–21.

65. While the rate of growth of the African urban population outside the bantustans decreased from 6.6 percent over the period 1946–51 to 2.2 percent between 1970 and 1980, the population continued to grow as a result of both natural increase and urbanization. The urban African population residing outside the bantustans increased as follows: 2.2 million in 1950; 3.4 million in 1960; 4.5 million in 1970; and 5.3 million in 1980. Unterhalter, *Forced Removal,* 46 and table 6, 143.

66. South Africa, *Report of the Commission of Inquiry,* 168.

67. Price, *Apartheid State,* 168.

68. Seekings, "Origins," 62.

69. In 1962, there were 7,850 registered businesses in African townships. By 1980 the number rose to approximately 40,000, and then to approximately 60,000 four years later. Pityana, "Black Middle Class," 7–8.

70. Wiehahn Commission, *Complete Wiehahn Report,* 7.

71. Professor Georg Marais, Director, School of Business Leadership, University of South Africa, in his Keynote Address to the Fourteenth Annual Conference of NAFCOC, Durban, 5 July 1978, 5, ANC archives at Mayibuye Centre, University of the Western Cape.

72. See, for example, Nolutshungu, *Changing South Africa,* 116–22; Z.P.J. [Jordan], "Black Middle Class," 27–28; and Mashinini, "Some Reflections," 14.

73. See, for example, Hudson and Sarakinsky, "Class Interests," 171, 182; and Wolpe, "Changing Class Structure," 151, 172. Wolpe, however, qualified his position by stating that this was at least the case "in the *present conjuncture*" and as it applied to the petty bourgeoisie in the bantustans specifically (emphasis in original).

74. Nzimande identifies four fractions of the African petty bourgeoisie: bureaucratic, trading, civil, and corporate. For his insightful examination of each, see "'Corporate Guerrillas,'" 69–93.

75. See ibid., 76, 81–82, 87–88, 92, 352.

76. NAFCOC membership increased from 2,000 in 1975 to 15,000 in 1986. Pityana, "Black Middle Class, 7–8. See also Hilary Joffe, "Black Business Ponders upon Its Own Impotence," *Weekly Mail,* 10–16 July 1987.

77. NAFCOC President, S. M. Motsuenyane put it thus: "Blacks should never allow themselves to be led astray to believe that they could set up viable independent economies of their own, outside the mainstream of the South African economy. . . . What we ought to strive to achieve is to secure for ourselves a fair share and full participation in the South African economy. This, however, cannot happen if we allow ourselves to be divided into mini-nations and mini-economies." Presidential Address delivered at the Fourteenth Annual Conference of NAFCOC, Durban, 6 July 1978, 5, ANC archives at Mayibuye Centre, University of the Western Cape.

78. Wiehahn Commission, *Complete Wiehahn Report,* 33.

79. Lambert and Webster, "Re-emergence," 23.

80. Bonner, "Black Trade Unions," 189; and Hindson, "Restructuring," 233.

81. Nolutshungu, *Changing South Africa,* 97.

82. In 1981, the legal status of the urban African labor force was as follows: 50 percent permanent (Section 10), 28 percent migrant (contract), and 22 percent commuters. Bekker and Humphries, *From Control,* table 6, 59.

83. See SALB, "Critique," 142–44, 149–50; Hindson, "Restructuring," 233; and Marks and Trapido, "South Africa," 30.

84. Wolpe, *Race, Class,* 79.

85. See Lambert and Webster, "Re-emergence," 22.

86. FOSATU, "An Introduction to the Federation of South African Trade Unions— FOSATU," June 1983, 6.

87. Joe Foster, FOSATU General Secretary, Keynote Address, "The Workers [*sic*] Struggle—Where Does FOSATU Stand?" Occasional Publication, no. 5, 1982, Durban, 22–24.

88. Ibid.

89. Interviews with John Nkadimeng, SACTU general-secretary in the 1980s, Johannesburg, 2 February 1993, and Jeremy Cronin, SACP Politburo member, Johannesburg, 18 July 1994.

90. Marx, *Lessons,* 163.

91. Seekings, "Origins," 65; and Price, *Apartheid State,* 168.

92. Price, *Apartheid State,* 102.

93. Ibid., 101.

94. See South Africa, *Report of the Commission of Inquiry,* 169.

95. Record of conversation between B. S. Biko and B. D. Haigh, second secretary, Australian Embassy, on 13 January 1977, Biko Collection, Howard Pim Library, University of Fort Hare.

96. ANC, *ANC Speaks,* 177.

97. Barrell, "Outlawed," 56.

98. Stanbridge, "Contemporary African Political Organizations," 93.

99. Barrell, "Outlawed," 56.

100. Lodge, *Black Politics,* 304.

101. See Lodge, "State of Exile," 238–39; and Davis, *Apartheid's Rebels,* 73.

102. Davis, *Apartheid's Rebels,* 72.

103. See Lodge, "State of Exile."

104. The United Nations High Commissioner for Refugees assisted approximately 9,000 South African refugees through the ANC in 1984. Ibid., 233.

105. Ibid., 243.

106. The ANC's firm backing of Robert Mugabe's rival organization complicated relations between the liberation organization and Zimbabwe's first president for a number of years.

107. Barrell, *MK,* 52–53. On the economic vulnerability of front-line states see Nolutshungu, "Strategy," 336–38.

108. On the expulsion of MK from front-line states, see Barrell, *MK,* 53–54; and Ellis and Sechaba, *Comrades,* 160–71, 174–76.

109. See Barrell, *MK,* 30; and Mzala, "Umkhonto we Sizwe," 21.

110. Barrell, "Outlawed," 56.

111. Lodge, "State of Exile," 233.

112. Barrell, "Turn," 85.

113. Ibid., 65, 89.

114. As Josiah Jelé, former secretary of the Politico-Military Council and NEC member, explained, developments inside the country would ultimately overtake the liberation organizations' efforts abroad to develop the correct balance between the two. Interview, Cape Town, 18 August 1994. For an excellent discussion of the debates and restructuring that followed, see Barrell, *MK.*

115. Barrell, "Turn," 79.

116. From 19 attacks in 1980, the number increased to 136 in 1985 and 118 in the first six months of 1986 alone. Lodge, "State of Exile," table 9.1, 230.

117. See Barrell, "Outlawed," 57.

118. Mzala, "Umkhonto we Sizwe," 23.

119. Barrell, "Turn," 74.

120. A survey of blacks in the Transvaal showed an increase in support for the ANC from 27 percent in 1977 to 42 percent in 1981, an increase attributed to the actions of MK. Barrell, *MK,* 46.

121. See Marx, *Lessons,* 97–100; and Swilling, "United Democratic Front," 96.

122. Barrell, "Turn," 86.

123. According to Tom Lodge, professor of political studies at the University of Witwatersrand, in the mid–1980s the ANC had no more than 500 MK guerrillas inside the country and much fewer nonmilitary cadres in touch with the ANC in exile. Interview, Johannesburg, 27 October 1992. See also Davis, *Apartheid's Rebels,* 209.

124. Interviews with John Nkadimeng, Johannesburg, 2 February 1993, and Jeremy Cronin, Johannesburg, 18 July 1994.

125. Interview with John Nkadimeng, Johannesburg, 2 February 1993. The ANC's official publication, *Sechaba,* expressed the organization's frustration with FOSATU's white leaders openly. See "Workers' Struggle" in which FOSATU is attacked for its "high handed methods of leadership which foster thoughts of racism and white domination." *Sechaba,* December 1980, 15.

126. Interview with Jeremy Cronin, Johannesburg, 18 July 1994. He added that the SACP was "wrong" in that it took some time for the Party to recognize the positive contribution made by these unions.

127. See Barrell, "Turn," 92.

128. Wolpe, *Race, Class,* 100.

129. According to UDF calculations, only 15.5 percent of Indians and 17.5 percent of coloreds eighteen years and older took part in the elections. Collinge, "United Democratic Front," 253.

130. Swilling, "United Democratic Front," 92.

131. See ibid., 93–94.

132. See ibid., 94–95; and Seekings, "'Trailing Behind'," 107–10.

133. See Swilling, "United Democratic Front"; Bloch, "United Democratic Front"; and Seekings, "'Trailing Behind.'" Seekings offers a more critical evaluation of the UDF.

134. Bloch, "United Democratic Front," 10.

135. See ibid., 9.

136. Ibid., 93–94.

137. Ibid., 106.

138. Swilling, "United Democratic Front," 93–94.

139. Bloch, "United Democratic Front," 11; and Marx, *Lessons,* 135–37.

140. Baskin, *Striking Back,* 43; Marx, *Lessons,* 138; and Swilling, "United Democratic Front," 93.

141. See Lambert and Webster, "Re-emergence."

142. See von Holdt, "Trade Unions," 71–72; and Lambert and Webster, "Re-emergence," 29.

143. Barrell, "Outlawed," 60; and Lodge, "'Mayihlome!,'" 232–38.

144. For insight into the organization's operations in exile and the relationship between leaders and recruits, see the report of the commission that was appointed to investigate the mutiny. ANC, "Report: Commission of Inquiry."

145. ANC, "Report of the National Executive Committee," 20, ANC archives at Mayibuye Centre, University of the Western Cape.

146. Ibid.

147. "Open Membership and Equal Participation," ANC National Consultative Conference in Zambia, 16–23 June 1985, part I, 1–2, ANC archives at Mayibuye Centre, University of the Western Cape.

148. ANC, "Report of the National Executive Committee," 3.

149. For the debates within COSATU leading up to the adoption of the Freedom Charter, see Marx, *Lessons,* 205–6.

150. See Seidman, *Manufacturing Militance,* 233.

151. Lambert and Webster, "Re-emergence," 32.

152. Ibid. Following a meeting with the ANC in Zimbabwe, COSATU General Secretary Jay Naidoo reported: "I told the ANC and SACTU delegations we did not want superficial changes or black bosses to replace white bosses, while the repressive machinery of state and capital remained intact. I expressed very clearly to them our commitment to see a society which was not only free of apartheid but also free of the exploitative, degrading and brutalising system under which black workers suffered." Quoted in Saul, "Class, Race," 222.

153. Lambert and Webster, "Re-emergence," 32.

154. Seidman, *Manufacturing Militance,* 251.

155. See Von Holdt, "Trade Unions," 13.

156. Seidman, *Manufacturing Militance,* 230, 250; and Bloch, "United Democratic Front," 10.

157. The first state of emergency, which covered 36 magisterial districts, was declared on 21 July 1985 and remained in force until 7 March 1986; the second was declared on 12 June 1986 and covered the entire country; and the third went into effect immediately following the expiration of the second. Barrell, "Outlawed," 87 n. 21.

158. See Price, *Apartheid State,* 230–32. Foreign debt increased from 8.4 percent of the GDP in 1980 to 26.8 percent in 1984; short-term loans constituted 66 percent of debts. Mann, "Giant Stirs," 76.

159. In 1986–87, defense expenditure had increased to account for 13.7 percent of the budget. Mann, "Giant Stirs," 73.

160. Cobbett et al., "Critical Analysis," 22; and Morris, "State, Capital" 48, 51.

161. See Cobbett, et al., "Critical Analysis," 25–26; and Hindson, "Restructuring," 242.

162. Price, *Apartheid State,* 140, 250.

163. In 1981, the government initiated a development strategy that conspicuously treated South Africa as an integrated territory, thereby implying an admission of failure in transforming the politically "independent" bantustans into economically viable entities. See Cobbett, et al., "Critical Analysis," 27–28; Smith, *Apartheid,* 77; and Alan

Hirsch, "A Bank Report the Homelands Won't Hurry to Okay," *Weekly Mail,* 19–25 January 1990.

164. See Barrell, "Outlawed," 63; and Lambert and Webster, "Re-emergence," 37.

165. Patrick Laurence, "White Capitalism and Black Rage," *Weekly Mail,* 13–19 September 1985.

166. As Jeremy Cronin explained, "ANC resources were sufficient to have an impact and influence inside the country but it couldn't dictate." Interview, Johannesburg, 23 August 1994.

167. With regard to trade unions and COSATU, see Saul, "Class, Race," 221.

168. For example, the ANC failed to convince unions to reject registration. Interview with Tom Lodge, Johannesburg, 3 December 1992.

169. Of course the process was uneven, varied by region, and in many cases remained incomplete.

170. See NLC, *Bantustans.*

171. According to Chief Sanso Patekile, CONTRALESA president, Natal contains approximately 500 chiefs, by far the largest number in any of the provinces in the country. Interview, Cape Town, 18 August 1994.

172. See Naidoo, "Internal Resistance," 190–93.

173. Semyonov and Lewin-Epstein, *Hewers of Wood,* 24.

174. Hirst, *Gun,* 245.

175. See Graham-Brown, "Impact," 229.

176. See Sahliyeh, "West Bank," 59–60; UN, *Living Conditions,* 37; and Tamari, "Palestinians," 98, 100.

177. On investments, see Gharaibeh, *Economies,* 120.

178. Al-Shuaibi, "Development," (part 3), 123.

179. Sahliyeh, *In Search,* 67. Sahliyeh points out that 28 percent of municipal council members elected in 1976 had a university education as compared to only 10 percent of those elected four years earlier. Among those elected in 1976, 40 percent were employed in white-collar occupations, 40 percent were businessmen and merchants, and 20 percent were farmers and landowners.

180. Ibid., 66–67.

181. Ibid., 64.

182. Dakkak, "Back to Square One," 78.

183. See Sahliyeh, *In Search,* 83; and Benvenisti, et al., *West Bank Handbook,* 156.

184. In the Gaza Strip, council members were appointed by the Military Governor and elections were prohibited. The last elections held in the Gaza Strip were in 1946. Al-Khaas, "Municipal Legal Structure," 102.

185. See Keller, *Terrible Days,* 59–60.

186. See Lustick, *For the Land,* 14; and Hirst, *Gun,* 220.

187. Cited in *"*From the Israeli Press,*" Journal of Palestine Studies* 18, no. 2, winter 1989, 162.

188. For a history of the idea of "transfer," see Shahak, "History," especially 31–33. On proponents of this view in the late 1980s, see Lustick, *For the Land,* 179.

189. Sahliyeh, *In Search*, 85; and Tamari, "Israel's Search," 378.

190. Kimmerling uses this term to describe Dayan's early policy of "functional division" of control between Israel and Jordan, with the former controlling the territory and the latter the people. "Boundaries," 279.

191. Between 1974 and 1983, Israel invested a total of $231 million in settlements, of which 88.7 percent was invested under Likud rule between 1978 and 1983. Benvenisti, *West Bank Data Project*, 53. This was accompanied by a substantial increase in the number of settlers: between 1968 and 1977, under the Labor government, the average annual increase in settlers was 770, while between 1977 and 1984, under Likud rule, the increase was 5,400 settlers annually. Benvenisti, *1986 Report*, 46.

192. See Benvenisti, *West Bank Data Project*, 30–35.

193. Gharaibeh, *Economies*, 60. In 1984, population density in the Gaza Strip was estimated at 1,300–1,400 people per square kilometer. Roy, *Gaza Strip*, 5.

194. Former deputy mayor of Jerusalem, Meron Benvenisti, cited in UN, *Living Conditions*, 13.

195. See Benvenisti and Khayat, *West Bank and Gaza Atlas*, 34–36.

196. In 1982, excluding diamond exports, $701.1 and $639.0 million worth of Israeli goods were exported to the United States and the occupied territories, respectively. Gharaibeh, *Economies*, table 7.3, 111.

197. Ryan, "Colonial Exploitation," 182; and Gharaibeh, *Economies*, 52.

198. Between 1969 and 1974, West Bank emigration averaged 2,700 persons annually or 0.4 percent of the population. Emigration from the Gaza Strip exhibited comparable rates and patterns. CBS, *Statistical Abstract, 1983*, table xxvii/1, 758.

199. On the role of remittances, see Graham-Brown, "Impact," 232–45.

200. Calculated from CBS, *Statistical Abstract, 1983*, table xxvii/20, 780.

201. Gharaibeh, *Economies*, 50.

202. In 1983, factor payments from abroad accounted for 27.1 percent and 44.1 percent of the GNP of the West Bank and Gaza Strip, respectively. Calculated from CBS, *Statistical Abstract, 1985*, table xxvii/6, 708–9. Gharaibeh notes further that wages constituted slightly more than half of the total exports of the occupied territories in 1982. *Economies*, 114.

203. CBS, *Statistical Abstract, 1983*, table xxvii/21, 781.

204. Ibid., table xxvii/21, 781 and tables xxvii/23, 784.

205. Ibid.

206. In 1966, a total of 2,073,000 *dunums* (512,031 acres) were under cultivation in the West Bank. Metzeger et al., *This Land*, 122 n. 76. In 1980–82, the cultivated area had been reduced to 1,636,000 *dunums* (404,092 acres). Gharaibeh, *Economies*, 61.

207. In 1977, 70 percent of West Bank heads of households employed in Israel did not cultivate land; the percentage increased with years of seniority from 62.4 percent of those employed two years or less, to 71.6 percent of those employed four years or more. Graham-Brown, "Economic Consequences," table 9.1, 237.

208. UN, *Living Conditions*, 1983, 14.

209. For a thorough discussion of work conditions for the period under examination, see ILO, "Report on the Conditions."

210. CBS, *Statistical Abstract, 1983,* table xxvii/21, 781 and table xxvii/23, 784.

211. Halsell, "Price," 11.

212. Tamari, "Palestinians," 91; and Semyonov and Lewin-Epstein, *Hewers of Wood,* 115.

213. Benvenisti, *1986 Report,* 12; and Graham-Brown, "Economic Consequences," 209.

214. Ryan, "Colonial Exploitation," 179.

215. Tamari, "Palestinians," 97 and "Building," 29.

216. The extent of emigration of males may be noted from West Bank sex ratios for 1984: 75.6 males per 100 females among those aged 30–44; and 73.9 among those aged 45–64. Calculated from CBS, *Statistical Abstract, 1985,* table xxvii/3, 705.

217. See Tamari, "Building," 21, 27, 33, 48; Arnon and Raviv, *From Fellah,* 196–98, 200; and Migdal, *Palestinian Society,* 67, 75–76. For an insightful examination of regional variations, see Migdal, *Palestinian Society,* 65–76.

218. See Migdal, *Palestinian Society,* 67–68, 70–72, 74–75; and Tamari, "Building," 29–30.

219. Benvenisti, *West Bank Data Project,* 16.

220. Jerbawi and Abu-Amr, "Al-Sira'," 7.

221. See ibid., 6–8.

222. Between 1978 and 1984, the Jordanian government spent $147.4 million on salaries and pensions, rent, assistance to municipalities, guarantees on loans by commercial banks, direct grants, education, and health in the West Bank. UNCTAD, *Palestinian Financial Sector,* table 39, 118.

223. Interview with Fuad Besseiso, former general-secretary of the JPJC, Amman, 23 June 1994.

224. JPJC, *Al-Lajna,* 14.

225. See Dakkak, "Back to Square One," 82.

226. Between 1978 and 1984, Arab and Islamic aid transfers to the occupied territories totalled $561 million. UNCTAD, *Palestinian Financial Sector,* table 39, 118.

227. Interview with Adel Ghanem, general-secretary of the original General Federation of Trade Unions (later JCP affiliated), Nablus, 19 June 1994 and Taysir Aruri, Amman, 6 February 1994.

228. See Benvenisti, *1986 Report,* 12, 18; and Bishara, "Uprising's Impact," 225–26.

229. See Tamari, "Israel's Search," 382; Sahliyeh, *In Search,* 85; and Graham-Brown, "Impact," 230.

230. Peretz, *Intifada,* 16–17.

231. Khalil and Dawwas, "Al-Haraka," 108.

232. See Hiltermann, *Behind the Intifada,* 128–131.

233. With regard to women's organizations, see ibid., 133.

234. On the deterioration of social services under Israeli control, see McDowall, *Palestine,* 113–14.

235. Interview with Lisa Taraki, assistant professor of sociology at Birzeit University, Ramallah, 17 July 1989. See also Hiltermann, *Behind the Intifada,* 65.

236. Hiltermann, *Behind the Intifada,* 65–66.

237. See ibid., 48–49, 65–66.

238. Interview with Lisa Taraki, Ramallah, 17 July 1989.

239. Interview with Lisa Taraki, Ramallah, 17 July 1989. See also Hiltermann, *Behind the Intifada*; and Khalil and Dawwas, "Al-Haraka."

240. See Khalil and Dawwas, "Al-Haraka," 109–16. The labor movement encompassed five blocs, one of which was affiliated with the Ba'thist ALF.

241. Hiltermann, *Behind the Intifada,* 61. The following synopsis of the Palestinian labor movement is based on Hiltermann's superb work.

242. Hilmi Mussa, a Gazan activist, observed that "an inverse relationship existed" between organizations' popular support and efforts to build mass organizations. Fatah initiated the establishment of mass organizations relatively late, while the DFLP's need for a mass base was the impetus behind its relatively early organizing efforts. The PFLP held the middle ground on both counts. Interview, Damascus, 24 February 1994.

243. Hiltermann, *Behind the Intifada,* 66.

244. Interview with George Hazboun, deputy general-secretary of the GFTU, Bethlehem, 11 May 1994.

245. According to Khalil and Dawwas, unionization of West Bank workers increased from 6 percent in 1978 to 20.7 percent in 1980. "Al-Haraka," 110.

246. See Hiltermann, *Behind the Intifada.*

247. In 1982, only 17.7 percent of West Bank and Gaza Strip Palestinians employed in Israel were employed in industry. CBS, *Statistical Abstract, 1983,* table xxvii/20, 780.

248. Halsell, "Price," 11.

249. Hiltermann, "Force for Change," 340.

250. In 1982, 80.4 percent of workers returned daily to their homes in the territories. CBS, *Statistical Abstract, 1983,* table xxvii/24, 785.

251. Tamari, "Building," 32 and "Palestinians," 93; and Abdul-Hadi, "Al-Tabaqa al-'amila," 127–28.

252. See Hiltermann, *Behind the Intifada,* 8, 63.

253. Hiltermann, "Force for Change," 339.

254. Interview with Lisa Taraki, Ramallah, 17 July 1989. See also Khalil and Dawwas, "Al-Haraka," 117; Pressberg, "Uprising," 42–43.

255. Lesch, "Palestinian Uprising," 3.

256. Cobban, *Palestinian Liberation Organisation,* 3, 136.

257. Classified as "present-absentees," their land, like the property of the refugees, was subject to disposal as Israeli authorities saw fit. By the mid–1970s, over 1 million *dunums* of land had been expropriated from Palestinian citizens of Israel. Jiryis, *Arabs,* 81.

258. Keller, *Terrible Days,* 93.

259. See Lustick, *Arabs;* and Zureik, *Palestinians.*

260. Palestinians are categorized as Christians, Muslims, Druze, Bedouin, and

Circassians, with each group being accorded differential rights and treatment. See Lustick, *Arabs,* 129–35.

261. For a comparison of government funding for Jewish and Arab municipalities, see Zureik, "Palestinians," 115. In 1990, 51.8 percent of Palestinians in Israel lived below the poverty line as compared to 10.9 percent of Jews; and while constituting approximately 18 percent of the population, Palestinians accounted for 55.0 percent of the poor in Israel. Sofian Qubba, "What Arabs get from the *aliyah,*" *Haaretz,* 7 December 1990 (Hebrew).

262. As of 1962, when state lands were consolidated with Jewish National Fund lands under the Israel Land Authority, land administered by the Authority became either completely inaccessible to non-Jews or available on terms that discriminated in favor of Jews who are granted 49- or 99-year leases while non-Jews are restricted to 1-year leases. Keller, *Terrible Days,* 90. For other such institutions, see Lustick, *Arabs,* 97–109.

263. The banning was upheld by the Supreme Court on the grounds that by recognizing the 1947 UN partition plan, al-Ard did not recognize Israel's 1965 borders. Keller, *Terrible Days,* 92.

264. Zureik, *Palestinians,* 167; and Kimmerling and Migdal, *Palestinians,* 171.

265. In 1965, the Israeli Communist Party split into two factions, Rakah and Maki; Arabs predominate in Rakah, Jews in Maki. Kanaana, "Survival Strategies," 7. One indication of the growing support for Rakah is noted from a comparison of voting outcomes in large Palestinian villages, where the Arab vote for Rakah increased from 23.1 percent in 1965 to 40.9 percent in 1973. Zureik, *Palestinians,* 169.

266. Keller, *Terrible Days,* 107.

267. Ibid., 93.

268. Kimmerling and Migdal, *Palestinians,* 177–78.

269. Dakkak, "Back to Square One," 81.

270. See Kimmerling and Migdal, *Palestinians,* 178; and Zureik, *Palestinians,* 175–80.

271. Lustick, *Arabs,* 240.

272. UNRWA, *Registration Statistical Bulletin,* table 1.0, 3 and table 4.0, 7.

273. For an excellent detailed discussion of the Palestinian bourgeoisie in exile, see P. Smith, *Palestine,* 112–43.

274. Hani al-Hassan, former member of the PLO's Central Council and Fatah's Revolutionary Council, explained that "We in Fatah attributed special importance to the national bourgeoisie . . . so in every PNC or Palestinian Central Council we allotted a quota for businessmen, capitalists, etcetera. Since 1968, no PNC has been held without their representatives' participation. And we made certain that they would always form the main force within the Palestine National Fund." Interview, Amman, 27 June 1994.

275. UNRWA, *UNRWA,* 82.

276. UNRWA, *Registration,* table 1.0, 3 and table 4.0, 7.

277. This was stated by every PLO leader interviewed for this project.

278. Sayigh, *Too Many Enemies,* 213.

279. Interview with the president of the Institute, Intisar al-Wazir, Amman, 2 February 1994.

280. Interview with Shafiq al-Hout, Beirut, 22 March 1994.

281. See TEAM International, *Health Services*. The Society operated nine hospitals in Lebanon until the Israeli invasion in 1982.

282. In this regard, it is noteworthy that the general secretaries of the PFLP and DFLP are of Christian origin, the latter also being Jordanian.

283. See Dakkak, "Back to Square One," 82.

284. Interview with Khaled al-Fahoum, Damascus, 22 February 1994.

285. Interview with Yusif Sayigh, leading Arab economist and PLO advisor, Beirut, 26 March 1994.

286. Interview with Khaled al-Fahoum, Damascus, 22 February 1994.

287. For an insightful discussion of the bureaucratization of the PLO and its implications, see Hillal, "PLO Institutions," 52–53.

288. Interview with Qais al-Samrai, DFLP Politburo member, Damascus, 21 February 1994.

289. For an excellent discussion of the role of families and kinship in relation to the national movement, see Sayigh, *Too Many Enemies,* 105–8.

290. It should be noted that the experience varied by country and refugee camp. For example, before the annihilation of the Tel al-Zaatar refugee camp in 1976, its 60,000 residents provided the workforce for a number of Beiruti factories.

291. Interviews with Nayef Hawatma, DFLP General Secretary, Damascus, 23 February 1994, and Abu-Ali Mustafa, Damascus, 24 February 1994.

292. Interview with Shafiq al-Hout, Beirut, 22 March 1994.

293. Interview with Shafiq al-Hout, Beirut, 22 March 1994.

294. Calculated from lists compiled by the Palestine Human Rights Information Center, East Jerusalem.

295. Ibid. Statistics are for the 1,402 killed whose occupations were known.

296. See Tamari, "What the Uprising Means"; and Saleh, "Effects," 49.

297. Tamari, "What the Uprising Means," 133.

298. See the following *Jerusalem Post* articles: Elaine Ruth Fletcher and Bradley Bruston, "Four Die As Strip Still Flares," 16 December 1987; David Landau, "PLO Behind the Unrest," 18 December 1987; Joshua Brilliant, "Rabin: Violence in Areas Indicates a 20-Year Build-Up of Tensions," 10 January 1988.

299. McDowall, *Palestine,* 36.

300. The UNLU was officially formed on 9 January 1988. Unity in exile also immediately led to unity talks among the various trade-union blocs. Hiltermann, *Behind the Intifada,* 119.

301. See Peretz, *Intifada,* 181; and Lesch, "Palestinian Uprising," 4.

302. On the eve of the 1984 Israeli elections, a Labor Party grouping submitted a paper warning of "a substantial danger for radicalization" engendered by the deterioration of economic conditions in the territories since 1981. Susan Hattis Rolef, "The Territories: an Economic Question," *Jerusalem Post,* 27 February 1986.

303. Emigration from the West Bank declined as follows: 1981, 15,700 persons; 1982, 7,900; 1983, 2,700; and remained at approximately 5,000 thereafter. A similar pattern characterized emigration from the Gaza Strip. CBS, *Statistical Abstract, 1988,* table xxvii/1, 705. Arab fulfillment of their financial commitment to the JPJC fund diminished steadily and dramatically from a high of nearly $85 million in 1981 to $9.5 million in 1986. JPJC, *Al-Lajna,* table 1, 60.

304. Carey Goldberg, "Palestinian Students Now Graduate into Uncertainty," *New York Times,* 31 July 1983.

305. This was expressed repeatedly by various underground leaders who were interviewed.

306. Tamari, "What the Uprising Means," 134–35.

307. See ibid., 137.

308. Between 1982 and 1987, Israeli authorities recorded a total of 3,000 "disturbances of peace," while in the first four months of the *intifada* 5,000 such incidents were reported. Smooha, "Israel's Options," 149.

309. Al-Madhoun, *Al-Intifada,* 31–44.

310. Fatah's second in command, Khalil al-Wazir, began almost immediately after relocating to Amman in 1983 to finance women's groups, labor unions, professional associations, newspapers, and the youth movement (*shabiba*). Marie Colvin, *New York Times Magazine,* 18 December 1988, 63.

311. Interview with Taysir Aruri, Amman, 2 February 1994.

312. Interviews with Taysir Aruri, Amman, 2 February 1994, and Mohammad al-Labadi, former DFLP and UNLU leader in the West Bank, Amman, 16 April 1994.

313. Interview with Ihab al-Ashqar, Fatah's UNLU representative in the Gaza Strip, Gaza, 15 May 1994.

314. Interview with Taysir Aruri, Amman, 2 February 1994.

315. Interview with Taysir Aruri, Amman, 6 February 1994, and Walid Salem, East Jerusalem, 9 May 1994. See also Dakkak, "Back to Square One"; and Sahliyeh, *In Search.*

316. Interviews with Haidar Abdel-Shafi, Red Crescent Society president and head of the Palestinian negotiating delegation, Gaza, 15 May 1994, and Walid Salem, East Jerusalem, 9 May 1994.

317. See Bishara, "Uprising's Impact," especially 227–29. One Israeli minister estimated that the initial three months of the uprising cost Israel's economy $300 million. Russell Watson, "Israel Wages Economic War," *Newsweek,* 28 March 1988: 40. In the first year alone, Israeli exports to the occupied territories dropped from $928 million in 1987 to $650 the following year; and the cost of fighting the uprising in its first year was $225 million. Joel Brinkley, "Israelis View a Battered Economy As Motivation for a Peace Effort," *New York Times,* 13 February 1989.

318. In 1982, they constituted 8.5 percent of Israel's workforce. Semyonov and Lewin-Epstein, *Hewers of Wood,* 28.

319. CBS, *Statistical Abstract, 1988,* table xvi/15, 480. Russell Watson, "Israel Wages Economic War," *Newsweek,* 28 March 1988, 40.

320. One indication of the meager expansion of industry in the Gaza Strip is noted from employment figures: 3,934 in 1969; 5,000 in 1980; and 6,383 in 1984. Roy, *Gaza Strip,* 58.

321. With the exception of the initial year of the *intifada,* this has been consistently the case. See Sahliyeh, *In Search,* 61.

322. Interestingly, a Palestinian demonstration for family reunification elicited this observation from the Israeli reporter covering the event: "It is rare for Palestinians from the territories to demonstrate at the site [of the Prime Minister's Office in Jerusalem], petitioning a government they consider a foreign occupier." Joel Greenberg, "W. Bank Arabs Demonstrate for Family Unification," *Jerusalem Post,* 6 April 1987.

323. Slovo captured this well when describing the impact of even failed ANC efforts: "It could be seen by everyone that the ANC was persisting in its efforts without end despite enormous difficulties. People were becoming aware that here was a committed and dedicated group . . . I think this was a very important side-product of the efforts most of which ended in failures." "Second Stage," 34.

324. This astute observation regarding the role of the PLO in exile vis-à-vis the movement inside the country was made by a former member of the PLO's Scientific Committee, which operated in Beirut prior to 1982. The interviewee requested to remain anonymous, East Jerusalem, 13 June 1994.

Conclusion

1. In a 1991 survey of 863 shop stewards, 70 percent believed that COSATU would best represent workers' interests in negotiations for a new constitution as compared to 21 percent who expressed support for the ANC and 9 percent for the SACP. Pityana and Orkin, *Beyond the Factory Floor,* 25.

2. Slovo, "Negotiations," 36.

3. Ibid.

4. Ibid. 40.

5. Interviews with Walter Sisulu, Johannesburg, 15 February 1993; Govan Mbeki, Port Elizabeth, 5 November 1992; Graeme Bloch, UDF leader in Western Cape, Cape Town, 30 November 1992; and Raymond Suttner, ANC Head of the Department of Political Education, Johannesburg, 2 February 1993.

6. Another reason was to deprive counterrevolutionary forces of potential supporters.

7. Gevisser, "Ending Economic Apartheid," 26.

8. See Cronin, "Sell-Out?," 9–10.

9. SALB, "World Bank," 23.

10. See Bond, "GEARing Up," 23–24, 27–28.

11. Gevisser, "Ending Economic Apartheid," 24.

12. Ibid.

13. See ibid. 25.

14. Arafat was also castigated for the lack of consultation with experts on land, water, and economic matters while negotiating these aspects with Israeli officials; the

vagueness of the agreements that permit Israeli reinterpretations; and the surrender of every Palestinian "card" without serious negotiation. See Said, "Mirage."

15. Interview with George Hazboun, Bethlehem, 11 May 1994.

16. Interview with Haidar Ibrahim, general-secretary of the General Union of Palestinian Workers, Irbid, Jordan, 1 July 1994.

17. Since 1993 the Palestinian unemployment rate is 15 percent higher and per capita income 20 percent lower. "Stretching Jerusalem," *The Economist*, 27 June 1998, 19.

18. See Usher, "Palestinian Authority."

19. Terreblanche and Nattrass, "Periodisation," 11.

Works Cited

Abdul-Hadi, Assad. "Al-Tabaqa al-ʿamila al-filastiniyya: Munaqasha li-dirasatay [Rose] Muslih wa [Mustafa] Jaffal" (The Palestinian working class: A discussion of the two studies of [Rose] Muslih and [Mustafa] Jaffal). *Shuun Filastiniya,* no. 121 (December 1981): 122–35.

Abraham, Sameer. "The Development and Transformation of the Palestinian National Movement." In *Occupation: Israel over Palestine.* Edited by Naseer H. Aruri, 391–425. Belmont, Mass.: AAUG, 1983.

Abramowitz, Yosef I. *Jews, Zionism and South Africa.* Washington, D.C.: B'nai B'rith Hillel Foundations, 1985.

Abu-Amr, Ziad. *Usul al-harakat al-siyasiya fi qitaʿ ghazza, 1948–1967* (The origins of the political movements in the Gaza Strip). Aka: Dar al-Aswar, 1987.

———. "Muqaddama fi dirasat al-tarkib al-tabaqi wa'l-nukhba al-siyasiya fiqitaʿ ghazza, 1948–1986" (An introduction to the study of class structure and the political elite in Gaza, 1948–1986). Paper presented at the Arab Thought Forum Centre, Jerusalem, 2 December 1986. Arab Thought Forum series, Jerusalem, May 1987: 1–20.

Abu-Lughod, Ibrahim. "Territorially-based Nationalism and the Politics of Negation." In *Blaming the Victims: Spurious Scholarship and the Palestinian Question.* Edited by Edward Said and Christopher Hitchens, 193–206. London: Verso, 1988.

Abu-Lughod, Janet L. "Demographic Consequences of the Occupation," *MERIP Reports,* no. 115 (June 1983): 13–17.

———. "The Demographic Transformation of Palestine." In *The Transformation of Palestine.* Edited by Ibrahim Abu-Lughod, 139–64. Evanston: Northwestern University Press, 1987.

Adam, Heribert. "Israel and South Africa: Conflict Resolution in Ethnic States." *Telos,* no. 82 (winter 1989–90): 27–46.

African National Congress. *ANC Speaks: Documents and Statements of the African National Congress, 1955–1977.* Underground publication, 1977.

———. "Apartheid South Africa: Colonialism of a Special Type." Lusaka, Zambia, n.d.

———. "Report: Commission of Inquiry into Recent Developments in the People's Republic of Angola." Lusaka, Zambia, March 1984.

———. "Report of the National Executive Committee Presented by the Secretary General Comrade Alfred Nzo." National Consultative Conference, Kabwe, Zambia, June 1985.

al-Ameri, Anan. *Al-Tatawwur al-ziráʿi waʾl-sináʿi al-filastini 1900–1970: Bahth ihsáʾiy* (Agricultural and Industrial Development in Palestine 1900–1970: A Statistical Study). Beirut: Manshurat salah al-din, 1974.

———. "Socioeconomic Development in Jordan (1950–1980): An Application of Dependency Theory." Ph.D. dissertation, Wayne State University, Detroit, 1981.

Anglo-American Committee of Inquiry. *A Survey of Palestine: Prepared in December 1945 and January 1946 for the information of the Anglo-American Committee of Inquiry.* 2 vols. Washington, D.C.: Institute for Palestine Studies, 1991.

Aronson, Geoffrey. "Israel's Policy of Military Occupation." *Journal of Palestine Studies* 7, no. 4 (summer 1978): 79–98.

Arnon, Isaac I., and Michael M. Raviv. *From Fellah to Farmer: A Study on Change in Arab Villages.* Rehovot, Israel: Agricultural Research Organization, 1980.

Aruri, Naseer H. "Dialectics of Dispossession." In *Occupation: Israel over Palestine.* Edited by Naseer H. Aruri, 3–27. Belmont, Mass.: AAUG, 1983.

Asad, Talal. "Class Transformation under the Mandate." *MERIP Reports,* no. 53 (December 1976): 3–8.

Ashmore, Robert B. "Israel and South Africa: A Natural Alliance." *The Link* 21, no. 4 (October–November 1988): 1–15.

Badran, Nabil A. "The Means of Survival: Education and the Palestinian Community, 1948–1967." *Journal of Palestine Studies* 9, no. 4 (summer 1980): 45–73.

Barrell, Howard. "The Outlawed South African Liberation Movements." In *South Africa: No Turning Back.* Edited by Shaun Johnson, 52–93. Bloomington: Indiana University Press, 1989.

———. *MK: The ANC's Armed Struggle.* London: Penguin Books, 1990.

———. "The Turn to the Masses: the African National Congress' Strategic Review of 1978–79." *Journal of Southern African Studies* 18, no. 1 (March 1991): 64–91.

Baskin, Jeremy. *Striking Back: A History of Cosatu.* London: Verso, 1991.

Beinart, William. "Worker Consciousness, Ethnic Particularism and Nationalism: The Experience of a South African Migrant, 1930–1960." In *The Politics of Race, Class and Nationalism in Twentieth Century South Africa.* Edited by Shula Marks and Stanley Trapido, 286–309. London: Longman Group, 1987.

Beinin, Joel. "The Palestine Communist Party 1919–1948." *MERIP Reports,* no. 55 (March 1977): 3–16.

———. *Was the Red Flag Flying There? Marxist Politics and the Arab-Israeli Conflict in Egypt and Israel, 1948–1965.* Berkeley: University of California Press, 1990.

Beit-Hallahmi, Benjamin. *The Israeli Connection: Who Israel Arms and Why.* New York: Pantheon, 1987.

Bekker, Simon, and Richard Humphries. *From Control to Confusion: The Changing Role of Administration Boards in South Africa, 1971–1983.* Pietermaritzburg, South Africa: Shuter and Shooter/ISER, 1985.

Ben-Gurion, David. *Memoirs.* New York: World Publishing, 1970.

Benson, Mary. *South Africa: The Struggle for a Birthright.* 2d ed. London: International Defence and Aid Fund for Southern Africa, 1985.

Benvenisti, Meron. *The West Bank Data Project: A Survey of Israel's Policies.* Washington, D.C.: The American Enterprise Institute, 1984.

———. *1986 Report: Demographic, Economic, Legal, Social and Political Developments in the West Bank.* Jerusalem: West Bank Data Base Project, 1986.

———. *1987 Report: Demographic, Economic, Legal, Social and Political Developments in the West Bank.* Jerusalem: West Bank Data Base Project, 1988.

Benvenisti, Meron, and Shlomo Khayat. *The West Bank and Gaza Atlas.* Jerusalem: West Bank Data Base Project, 1988.

Benvenisti, Meron, Ziad Abu-Zayed, and Dan Rubenstein. *The West Bank Handbook: A Political Lexicon.* Jerusalem: The Jerusalem Post, 1986.

Bishara, Azmy. "The Uprising's Impact on Israel." In *Intifada: The Palestinian Uprising Against Israeli Occupation.* Edited by Zachary Lockman and Joel Beinin, 217–29. Boston: South End Press, 1989.

Bloch, Graeme. "The United Democratic Front: Lessons of the 80's; Prospects for the 90's." Paper presented at the SAIS Conference, Johns Hopkins University, April 1992.

Bond, Patrick. "GEARing Up or Down?" *South African Labour Bulletin* 20, no. 4 (August 1996): 23–30.

Bonner, Philip. "Black Trade Unions in South Africa since World War II." In *The Apartheid Regime: Political Power and Racial Domination.* Edited by Robert M. Price and Carl G. Rosberg, 174–93. Berkeley: Institute of International Studies, 1980.

Brand, Laurie A. *Palestinians in the Arab World: Institution Building and the Search for State.* New York: Columbia University Press, 1988.

Brooks, Alan, and Jeremy Brickhill. *Whirlwind before the Storm: The Origins and Development of the Uprising in Soweto and the Rest of South Africa from June to December 1976.* London: International Defence and Aid Fund for Southern Africa, 1980.

al-Budeiri, Musa. *Tatawwur al-haraka al-'umaliyya al-'arabiyya fi filastin: Muqaddama ta'rikhiyya wa-majmu'at watha'iq, 1919–1948* (The development of the Arab workers' movement in Palestine: A historical preface and collection of documents, 1919–1948). Beirut: Dar Ibn Khaldun, 1981.

Budeiri, Musa K. *The Palestine Communist Party, 1919–1949: Arab and Jew in the Struggle for Internationalism.* London: Ithaca Press, 1979.

Bull, Vivian A. *The West Bank: Is It Viable?* Lexington, Mass.: Lexington Books, 1975.

Bundy, Colin. "Land and Liberation: Popular Rural Protest and the National Liberation Movements in South Africa, 1920–1960." In *The Politics of Race, Class and*

Nationalism in Twentieth Century South Africa. Edited by Shula Marks and Stanley Trapido, 254–85. London: Longman Group, 1987.

Burawoy, Michael. "The Capitalist State in South Africa: Marxist and Sociological Perspectives on Race and Class." In *Political Power and Social Theory 2.* Edited by Maurice Zeitlin, 279–335. Greenwich, Conn.: JAI Press, 1981.

———. "State and Social Revolution in South Africa: Reflections on the Comparative Perspective of Greenberg and Skocpol." *Kapitalistate* 9 (1981): 93–122.

Butler, Jeffrey, Robert I. Rotberg, and John Adams. *The Black Homelands of South Africa: The Political and Economic Development of Bophuthatswana and KwaZulu.* Berkeley: University of California Press, 1977.

Cainkar, Louise. "The Patterns of Institutionalized Exclusivity." In *Separate and Unequal.* Edited by Louise Cainkar. Chicago: The Palestine Human Rights Campaign, 1985.

Carmi, Shulamit, and Henry Rosenfeld. "The Origins of the Process of Proletarianization and Urbanization of Arab Peasants in Palestine." *Annals of the New York Academy of Sciences* 220, no. 6 (11 March 1974): 470–85.

Carter, Gwendolen M. "African Nationalist Movements in South Africa." *The Massachusetts Review* (autumn 1963): 147–64.

Central Bureau of Statistics [Israel]. *Census of Population, 1967.* Publication No. 1. Jerusalem: CBS, 1967.

———. *Statistical Abstract of Israel, 1983,* no. 34. Jerusalem: CBS, 1983.

———. *Statistical Abstract of Israel, 1985,* no. 36. Jerusalem: CBS, 1985.

———. *Statistical Abstract of Israel, 1988,* no. 39. Jerusalem: CBS, 1988.

Chazan, Naomi. "Israel and South Africa: Some Preliminary Reflections." *New Outlook* (Tel Aviv) (June 1988): 8–11.

Cobban, Helena. *The Palestinian Liberation Organisation: People, Power and Politics.* Cambridge: Cambridge University Press, 1984.

Cobbett, William, Daryl Glaser, Doug Hindson, and Mark Swilling. "A Critical Analysis of the South African State's Reform Strategies in the 1980s." In *State, Resistance and Change in South Africa.* Edited by Philip Frankel, Noam Pines, and Mark Swilling, 19–51. Johannesburg: Southern Book Publishers, 1988.

Cohen, Amnon. *Political Parties in the West Bank under the Jordanian Regime, 1949–1967.* Ithaca: Cornell University Press, 1980.

Cohen, Robin, and William Cobbett, eds. *Popular Struggles in South Africa.* Trenton, N.J.: Africa World Press, 1988.

Collinge, Jo-Anne. "The United Democratic Front." *South African Review III* (1986): 248–66.

———. "Waging War on the Bantustans." *Work in Progress,* nos. 62–63 (November–December 1989): 17–18.

———. "Tampering with Tradition." *Work In Progress,* no. 61 (September–October 1989): 24–29.

Connor, Walker. "Ethno-nationalism and Political Instability: An Overview." In *The*

Elusive Search for Peace: South Africa, Israel and Northern Ireland. Edited by Hermann Giliomee and Jannie Gagiano, 9–32. Oxford: Oxford University Press, 1990.

Cooper, Carole. "Bantustan Attitudes to Trade Unions." *South African Review II* (1984): 165–84.

Crankshaw, Owen, and Doug Hindson. "Class Differentiation under Apartheid." Paper presented at the annual conference of the Association for Sociology, University of Stellenbosch, July 1990.

Cronin, Jeremy. "Sell-Out, or the Culminating Moment? Trying to Make Sense of the Transition." Johannesburg, 1994. Mimeographed.

Curtis, Michael. "Africa, Israel and the Middle East." *Middle East Review* 17, no. 4 (summer 1985): 5–22.

Dakkak, Ibrahim. "Back to Square One: A Study in the Re-emergence of the Palestinian Identity in the West Bank 1967–1980." In *Palestinians over the Green Line: Studies on the Relations between Palestinians on Both Sides of the 1949 Armistice Line since 1967.* Edited by Alexander Scholch, 64–101. London: Ithaca Press, 1983.

Davies, Robert, and Dan O'Meara, "The Workers' Struggle in South Africa: A Comment." *Review of African Political Economy,* no. 30 (September 1984): 109–16.

Davies, Robert, Dan O'Meara, and Sipho Dlamini. *The Struggle for South Africa: A Reference Guide to Movements, Organizations, and Institutions.* 2d ed. 2 vols. London: Zed Press, 1984.

Davies, Robert, David Kaplan, Mike Morris, and Dan O'Meara. "Class Struggle and the Periodisation of the State in South Africa." *Review of African Political Economy* 7 (1976): 4–30.

Davis, Stephen M. *Apartheid's Rebels: Inside South Africa's Hidden War.* New Haven: Yale University Press, 1987.

Davis, Uri. *Israel: Apartheid State.* London: Zed Press, 1988.

Development Bank of Southern Africa. *SATBVC Countries: Statistical Abstracts, 1987.* Sandton, South Africa: 1987.

———. *Self-Governing Territories: Statistical Abstracts, 1990.* Republic of South Africa: Information Clearing House, 1992.

Ellis, Stephen, and Tsepo Sechaba. *Comrades against Apartheid: The ANC and the South African Communist Party in Exile.* London: James Currey, 1992.

Farsoun, Samih. "Settler Colonialism and *Herrenvolk* Democracy." In *Israel and South Africa: The Progression of a Relationship,* edited by Richard P. Stevens and Abdelwahab M. Elmessiri, 13–21. New York: New World Press, 1976.

Fine, Robert, and Dennis Davis. *Beyond Apartheid: Labour and Liberation in South Africa.* Concord, Mass.: Pluto Press, 1990.

Flapan, Simha. *The Birth of Israel: Myths and Realities.* New York: Pantheon, 1987.

Frangi, Abdallah. *The PLO and Palestine.* London: Zed Books 1983.

Frederikse, Julie. *The Unbreakable Thread: Non-Racialism in South Africa.* Bloomington: Indiana University Press, 1990.

Friedman, Steve. "Political Implications of Industrial Unrest in South Africa." In *Working Papers in Southern African Studies, Volume III.* Edited by D. C. Hindson, 123–48. Johannesburg: Ravan Press, 1983.

———. *Building Tomorrow Today: African Workers in Trade Unions.* Johannesburg: Ravan Press, 1987.

Gandhi, Mahatma K. "The Jews in Palestine 1938." In *From Haven to Conquest: Readings in Zionism and the Palestine Problem until 1948.* Edited by Walid Khalidi, 367–70. Washington, D.C.: Institute for Palestine Studies, 1987.

Gerhart, Gail M. *Black Power in South Africa: The Evolution of an Ideology.* Berkeley: University of California Press, 1978.

Gevisser, Mark. "Ending Economic Apartheid." *The Nation* (29 September 1997): 24–26.

Gharaibeh, Fawzi A. *The Economies of the West Bank and Gaza Strip.* Boulder: Westview Press, 1985.

Giliomee, Hermann. "The Changing Political Functions of the Homelands." In *Up against the Fences: Poverty, Passes, and Privilege in South Africa.* Edited by Hermann Giliomee and Lawrence Schlemmer, 39–56. New York: St. Martin's Press, 1985.

Giliomee, Hermann, and Jannie Gagiano, eds. *The Elusive Search for Peace: South Africa, Israel and Northern Ireland.* Oxford: Oxford University Press, 1990.

Graham-Brown, Sarah. "The Economic Consequences of Occupation." In *Occupation: Israel over Palestine.* Edited by Naseer H. Aruri, 167–222. Belmont, Mass.: AAUG, 1983.

———. "Impact on the Social Structure of Palestinian Society." In *Occupation: Israel over Palestine.* Edited by Naseer H. Aruri, 223–54. Belmont, Mass.: AAUG, 1983.

———. *Education, Repression and Liberation: Palestinians.* London: World University Service, 1984.

Granott, A. *The Land System in Palestine.* London: Eyre and Spottiswoode, 1952.

Greenberg, Stanley. *Race and State in Capitalist Development: Comparative Perspectives.* New Haven, Conn.: Yale University Press, 1980.

Greenstein, Ran. *Genealogies of Conflict: Class, Identity, and State in Palestine/Israel and South Africa.* Hanover, N.H.: Wesleyan University Press, 1995.

Gresh, Alain. *The PLO: The Struggle Within.* London: Zed Books, 1983.

Hallaj, Muhammad. "The Mission of Palestinian Higher Education." *Journal of Palestine Studies* 9, no. 4 (summer 1980): 75–95.

Halsell, Grace. "The Price of Occupation." *Middle East International,* no. 137 (7 November 1980): 11–12.

Hamza, Mohammad. *Abu-Jihad: Asrar bidayatihi wa-asbab ightiyalihi* (Abu-Jihad: Secrets of his beginning and reasons for his assassination). Saffaqas, Tunisia: Al-ʿArabiyya, 1989.

Hanegbi, Haim, Moshe Machover, and Akiva Orr. "The Class Nature of Israeli Society." *New Left Review* 65 (January–February 1971): 3–26.

Harkabi, Yehoshafat. *Israel's Fateful Hour.* New York: Harper and Row, 1988.

Heiberg, Marianne, and Geir Øvensen. *Palestinian Society in Gaza, West Bank, and Arab*

Jerusalem: A Survey of Living Conditions. FAFO report 151. Oslo: Fagbevegelsens senter for forskning utredning og dokumentasjon, 1993.

Herzl, Theodor. *Complete Diaries.* Edited by Raphael Patai. New York: Herzl Press, [1960].

Hillal, Jamil. *Al-Diffa al-gharbiyya: Al-Tarkib al-ijtima i wa l-iqtisadi, 1948–1974* (The West Bank: The social and economic structure, 1948–1974). Beirut: PLO Research Center, 1974.

———. "Class Transformation in the West Bank and Gaza." *MERIP Reports,* no. 53 (December 1976): 9–15.

———. "West Bank and Gaza Strip Social Formation under Jordanian and Egyptian Rule (1948–1967)." *Review of Middle East Studies* 5. London: Scorpion Publishing, 1992: 33–73.

———. "PLO Institutions: The Challenge Ahead." *Journal of Palestine Studies* 23, no. 1 (autum 1993): 46–60.

Hiltermann, Joost R. "Force for Change in the West Bank." *The Nation* (3 October 1987): 339–41.

———. *Behind the Intifada: Labor and Women's Movements in the Occupied Territories.* Princeton: Princeton University Press, 1991.

Hindson, Doug. "The Restructuring of Labour Markets in South Africa, 1970s and 1980s." In *South Africa's Economic Crisis.* Edited by Stephen Gelb, 228–43. Cape Town: David Philip, 1991.

Hirson, Baruch. *Year of Fire, Year of Ash: The Soweto Revolt, Roots of a Revolution?* London: Zed Press, 1979.

———. *Yours for the Union: Class and Community Struggles in South Africa.* Johannesburg: Witwatersrand University Press, 1989.

Hirst, David. *The Gun and the Olive Branch.* 2d ed. London: Faber and Faber, 1984.

Hitchens, Christopher. "Broadcasts." In *Blaming the Victims: Spurious Scholarship and the Palestinian Question.* Edited by Edward Said and Christopher Hitchens, 73–83. London: Verso, 1988.

Holland, Heidi. *The Struggle: A History of the African National Congress.* New York: George Braziller, 1989.

Horowitz, Dan. "Before the State: Communal Politics in Palestine under the Mandate." In *The Israeli State and Society: Boundaries and Frontiers.* Edited by Baruch Kimmerling, 28–65. Albany: State University of New York Press, 1989.

al-Hout, Bayan Nuwayhad. *Al-Qiyadat wa l-mu assasat al-siyasiya fi filastin, 1917–1948* (Political leaders and institutions in Palestine, 1917–1948). Beirut: Mu-assasat al-dirasat al-filastiniyah, 1986.

———. *Al-Sheikh al-mujahid izzidin al-qassam fi ta rikh filastin* (The Combatant Sheikh Izzidin al-Qassam in the History of Palestine). Beirut: Dar al-istiqlal, 1987.

Hudson, Peter, and Mike Sarakinsky. "Class Interests and Politics: The Case of the Urban African Bourgeoisie." *South African Review* 3 (1986): 169–85.

Hunter, Jane. *Israeli Foreign Policy: South Africa and Central America.* Boston: South End Press, 1987.

————. "South Africa: Israel's Friend in Need?" *Middle East International,* no. 348 (14 April 1989): 16–18.

Institute for Industrial Education. *The Durban Strikes, 1973: "Human Beings with Souls."* Durban: Ravan Press/IIE, 1976.

Institute for Palestine Studies. *United Nation Resolutions on Palestine and the Arab-Israeli Conflict.* 2 vols. Washington, D.C.: IPS, 1975–88.

International Defence and Aid Fund for Southern Africa. *Apartheid: The Facts.* London: IDAF Publications, 1991.

International Labour Organisation. *Report on the Conditions of Workers from the Occupied Arab Territories.* Geneva: ILO, 1980.

————. *Special Report of the Director-General on the Application of the Declaration Concerning the Policy of Apartheid in South Africa.* 72nd Session. Geneva: ILO, 1986.

Jabbour, George. *Settler Colonialism in Southern Africa and the Middle East.* Khartoum: University of Khartoum, 1970.

Jerbawi, Ali, and Ziad Abu-Amr. "Al-Sira' 'ala al-qiyada al-siyasiya fi'l-difa al-gharbiyya wa-qita' ghazza, 1967–1987" (The struggle over political leadership in the West Bank and Gaza, 1967–1987). Paper delivered at the Arab Thought Forum Centre, Jerusalem, 24 February 1987. Arab Thought Forum series (May 1987).

Jiryis, Sabri. *The Arabs in Israel.* New York: Monthly Review Press, 1976.

Joakimidis, C., and A. Sitas. "A Study of Strikes." *Work in Progress,* no. 6 (November 1978): 105.

Jordan, Z. Pallo. "Socialist Transformation and the Freedom Charter." In *Whither South Africa?* Edited by Bernard Magubane and Ibbo Mandaza, 89–110. Trenton, N.J.: Africa World Press, 1988.

————. "[The African Petty Bourgeoisie]." ANC Occasional Papers, Lusaka, February 1988: 1–19. Mimeographed.

————. [Z.P.J.] "Black Middle Class: Eleventh Hour Counter Insurgency or Acquiescence in Continued Domination." *Sechaba* (May 1983): 23–28.

Jordanian-Palestinian Joint Committee. Secretariat General. *Al-Lajna al-urduniyya al-filastiniyya al-mushtaraka li-da'am sumud al-sha'ab al-filastini fi'l-watan al-muhtal: Khilasat al-munjizat fi ashara sanawat (1979–1988)* (The Jordanian-Palestinian Joint Committee for steadfastness support of the Palestinian people in the occupied homeland: summary of accomplishments over ten years). Amman: April 1989.

Joseph, Benjamin Manashe. *Besieged Bedfellows: Israel and the Land of Apartheid.* New York: Greenwood Press, 1988.

Jureidini, Paul A., and William E. Hazen. *The Palestinian Movement in Politics.* Toronto: Lexington Books, 1976.

Kadi, Leila. "Origins of the Armed Resistance." In *Palestine: The Arab-Israeli Conflict.* Edited by Russell Stetler, 117–45. San Francisco: Ramparts Press, 1972.

Kanaana, Sharif. "Survival Strategies of Arabs in Israel." *MERIP Reports,* no. 41 (October 1975): 3–18.

Karis, Thomas, and Gwendolen M. Carter, eds. *From Protest to Challenge: A Docu-*

mentary History of African Politics in South Africa, 1882–1964. 4 vols. Stanford, Calif.: Hoover Institution Press, 1972–77.

Keenan, Jeremy. "Reform and Resistance in South Africa's Bantustans." *South African Review* 4 (1987): 117–36.

———. "Counter-revolution as Reform: Struggle in the Bantustans." In *Popular Struggles in South Africa.* Edited by William Cobbett and Robin Cohen, 136–54. Trenton, N.J.: Africa World Press, 1988.

Keller, Adam. *Terrible Days: Social Division and Political Paradoxes in Israel.* Amstelveen, Holland: Cypres, 1987.

Kenyon, Mike. "Dumped—And No Say, Either." *Work in Progress,* nos. 62–63 (November–December 1989): 19–21.

al-Khaas, Muhammad. "Municipal Legal Structure in Gaza." In *A Palestinian Agenda for the West Bank and Gaza.* Edited by Emile A. Nakhleh, 102–12. Washington, D.C.: American Enterprise Institute, 1980.

Khalidi, Rashid. "The Palestinians after Twenty Years." *Middle East Report,* no. 146 (May–June 1987): 6–14.

———. "Palestinian Peasant Resistance to Zionism before World War I." In *Blaming the Victims: Spurious Scholarship and the Palestinian Question.* Edited by Edward Said and Christopher Hitchens, 207–33. London: Verso, 1988.

Khalidi, Walid, ed. *From Haven to Conquest: Readings in Zionism and the Palestine Problem until 1948.* Washington, D.C.: Institute for Palestine Studies, 1987.

———. *At a Critical Juncture: The United States and the Palestinian People.* Center for Contemporary Arab Studies Reports. Washington, D.C.: Georgetown University, 1989.

Khalil, Saji, and Farouq Dawwas. "Al-Haraka al-jamahiriya fi'l-ard al-muhtala, 1967–1987" (The popular movement in the occupied territory, 1967–1987). *Al-Fikr al-Democrati,* no. 2 (spring 1988): 102–19.

Khouri, Fred J. *The Arab-Israeli Dilemma.* 2d ed. Syracuse: Syracuse University Press, 1976.

Kimmerling, Baruch. "Boundaries and Frontiers of the Israeli Control System: Analytical Conclusions." In *The Israeli State and Society: Boundaries and Frontiers.* Edited by Baruch Kimmerling, 265–82. Albany: State University of New York Press, 1989.

Kimmerling, Baruch, and Joel S. Migdal. *Palestinians: The Making of a People.* Cambridge: Harvard University Press, 1993.

Kuper, Leo. *An African Bourgeoisie: Race, Class, and Politics in South Africa.* New Haven: Yale University Press, 1965.

Lambert, Rob. "Trade Unions, Nationalism and the Socialist Project in South Africa." *South African Review* 4 (1987): 232–52.

Lambert, Rob, and Eddie Webster. "The Re-emergence of Political Unionism in Contemporary South Africa?" In *Popular Struggles in South Africa.* Edited by William Cobbett and Robin Cohen, 20–41. Trenton, N.J.: Africa World Press, 1988.

Lee, Richard. "Ethnicity, Militarism, and Human Rights: Israel and South Africa."
     Dialectical Anthropology 8, nos. 1 and 2 (October 1983): 121–28.

Legassick, M., and Harold Wolpe. "The Bantustans and Capital Accumulation in South
     Africa." *Review of African Political Economy* 7 (1976): 87–107.

Lesch, Ann Mosely. "The Palestine Arab Nationalist Movement under the Mandate." In
     The Politics of Palestinian Nationalism. Edited by William B. Quandt, Fuad Jabber,
     and Ann Mosely Lesch, 5–42. Berkeley: University of California Press, 1973.

———. *Arab Politics in Palestine, 1917–1939: The Frustration of a National Movement.*
     Ithaca, N.Y.: Cornell University Press, 1979.

———. "Palestine: Land and People." In *Occupation: Israel over Palestine.* Edited by
     Naseer H. Aruri, 29–54. Belmont, Mass.: AAUG, 1983.

———. "The Palestinian Uprising: Causes and Consequences." UFSI Field Staff
     Reports, Africa/Middle East, no. 1 (1988/1989): 1–11.

Locke, Richard, and Antony Stewart. *Bantustan Gaza,* London: Zed Books, 1985.

Lodge, Tom. *Black Politics in South Africa since 1945.* Johannesburg: Ravan Press, 1983.

———. "'Mayihlome! Let Us Go To War!': From Nkomati to Kabwe, the African
     National Congress, January 1984–June 1985," *South African Review III* (1986):
     226–47.

———. "State of Exile: The African National Congress of South Africa, 1976–86." In
     State, Resistance and Change in South Africa. Edited by Philip Frankel, Noam Pines,
     and Mark Swilling, 229–58. Johannesburg: Southern Book Publishers, 1988.

Luckhardt, Ken, and Brenda Wall. *Organize or Starve! The History of the South African
     Congress of Trade Unions.* London: Lawrence and Wishart, 1980.

Lustick, Ian. *Arabs in the Jewish State.* Austin: University of Texas Press, 1980.

———. *For the Land and the Lord: Jewish Fundamentalism in Israel.* New York: Council
     on Foreign Relations, 1988.

al-Madhoun, Rabae' K. *Al-Intifada al-filastiniyya: Al-Haykal al-tanthimi wa-assalib al-
     'amal* (The Palestinian uprising: Organizational structure and modes of operation.)
     Akka: Sharq Press, 1988.

Magubane, Bernard Makhosezwe. *The Political Economy of Race and Class in South
     Africa.* New York: Monthly Review Press, 1979.

Mandaza, Ibbo. "Southern Africa: U.S. Policy and the Struggle for National
     Independence." In *Whither South Africa?* Edited by Bernard Magubane and Ibbo
     Mandaza, 111–35. Trenton, N.J.: Africa World Press, 1988.

Mandel, Neville J. *The Arabs and Zionism: Before World War I.* Berkeley: University of
     California Press, 1976.

Mann, Michael. "The Giant Stirs: South African Business in the Age of Reform." In
     State, Resistance and Change in South Africa. Edited by Philip Frankel, Noam Pines,
     and Mark Swilling, 52–86. Johannesburg: Southern Book Publishers, 1988.

Marks, Shula, and Stanley Trapido. "The Politics of Race, Class and Nationalism." In
     The Politics of Race, Class and Nationalism in Twentieth Century South Africa. Edited
     by Shula Marks and Stanley Trapido, 1–70. London: Longman Group, 1987.

———. "South Africa since 1976: An Historical Perspective." In *South Africa: No*

Turning Back. Edited by Shaun Johnson, 1–51. Bloomington: Indiana University Press, 1989.

Marsh, Pearl Alice. "Labor Reform and Security Repression in South Africa: Botha's Strategy for Stabilizing Racial Domination in the 1980s." *Issue* 12, nos. 3–4 (fall–winter 1982): 49–55.

Marwell, Gerald, and Pamela Oliver. "Collective Action Theory and Social Movements Research." *Research in Social Movements, Conflict, and Change* 7 (1984): 1–27.

Marx, Anthony W. *Lessons of Struggle: South African Internal Opposition, 1960–1990.* Cape Town: Oxford University Press, 1992.

Mashinini, Alex. "Some Reflections on Botha's 'Reform' Policy—The Black Bourgeoisie." *Sechaba* (February 1984): 13–16.

Mazur, Michael. "Economic Development of Jordan." In *Economic Development and Population Growth in the Middle East.* Edited by Charles Cooper and Sidney Alexander, 210–79. New York: American Elsevir Publishing, 1972.

Mbeki, Govan. *South Africa: The Peasants' Revolt.* London: International Defence and Aid Fund for Southern Africa, 1984.

———. *The Struggle for Liberation in South Africa: A Short History.* Cape Town: David Philip, 1992.

McAdam, Doug. *Political Process and the Development of Black Insurgency, 1930–1970.* Chicago: The University of Chicago Press, 1982.

McCarthy, John D., and Mayer N. Zald. "Resource Mobilization and Social Movements: A Partial Theory." *American Journal of Sociology* 82, no. 6 (1977): 1212–40.

McDowall, David. *Palestine and Israel: The Uprising and Beyond.* Berkeley: University of California, 1989.

McIntosh, Alastair. "Rethinking Chieftaincy and the Future of Rural Local Government: A Preliminary Investigation." *Transformation* 13 (1990): 27–45.

McTague, John J., Jr. "Israel and South Africa: A Comparison of Policies." *Journal of Palestine Studies* 14, no. 3 (spring 1985): 101–9.

Meli, Francis. *South Africa Belongs to Us: A History of the ANC.* Harare: Zimbabwe Publishing House, 1988.

Metzger, Jan, Martin Orth, and Christian Sterzing. *This Land is Our Land: The West Bank under Israeli Occupation.* London: Zed Press, 1983.

Migdal, Joel S. "State and Society in a Society without a State." In *The Palestinians and the Middle East Conflict.* Edited by Gabriel Ben-Dor, 377–97. Tel Aviv: Turtledove Publishing, 1978.

———. *Palestinian Society and Politics.* Princeton: Princeton University Press, 1980.

———. *Strong Societies and Weak States: State-Society Relations and State Capabilities in the Third World.* Princeton: Princeton University Press, 1988.

———. "The Crystallization of the State and the Struggles over Rulemaking: Israel in Comparative Perspective." In *The Israeli State and Society: Boundaries and Frontiers.* Edited by Baruch Kimmerling, 1–27. Albany: State University of New York Press, 1989.

Mishal, Shaul. *West Bank/East Bank: The Palestinians in Jordan, 1949–67.* New Haven: Yale University Press, 1978.

Moleah, Alfred. "Israel and South Africa: The Unholy Alliance." *Palestine Focus* (August 1983): 1–2.

Moodie, T. Dunbar. "The Moral Economy of the Black Miners' Strike of 1946." *Journal of Southern African Studies* 13, no. 1 (October 1986): 1–35.

Moore, Barrington. *Social Origins of Dictatorship and Democracy.* Boston: Beacon Press, 1966.

Moore, Subithra Moodley. "The Politics of Beleaguered Ethnic States: 'Herrenvolk' Democracy in Israel and South Africa." Ph.D. dissertation, University of Washington, Seattle, 1989.

Morris, Benny. *Birth of the Palestinian Refugee Problem, 1947–1949.* Cambridge: Cambridge University Press, 1987.

Morris, Mike. "State, Capital, and Growth: The Political Economy of the National Question." In *South Africa's Economic Crisis.* Edited by Stephen Gelb, 33–58. Cape Town: David Philip, 1991.

Mu'assasat al-dirasat al-filastiniyya. *Al-Watha'iq al-filastiniyya al-'arabiyya li-'am 1967* (The Arab Palestinian documents for the year 1967). Edited and compiled by George Khouri Nassrallah. Beirut: Mu'assasat al-dirasat al-filastiniyya/Jami'at al-Khartoum, 1969.

Mufson, Steven. *Fighting Years: Black Resistance and the Struggle for a New South Africa.* Boston: Beacon Press, 1990.

Murray, Martin. *South Africa: Time of Agony, Time of Destiny.* London: Verso, 1987.

Mzala. "Umkhonto we Sizwe: Building People's Forces for Combat, War and Insurrection." Part 2. *Sechaba* (January 1987): 21–26.

Mzala, Comrade. "Revolutionary Theory on the National Question in South Africa." In *The National Question in South Africa.* Edited by Maria van Diepen, 30–55. London: Zed Books, 1988.

Naidoo, Kumi. "Internal Resistance in South Africa: The Political Movements." In *South Africa: No Turning Back.* Edited by Shaun Johnson, 172–205. Bloomington: Indiana University Press, 1989.

National Land Committee. *The Bantustans in Crisis.* Johannesburg: NLC, 1990.

Neuberger, Benyamin. "Nationalisms Compared: ANC, IRA and PLO." In *The Elusive Search for Peace: South Africa, Israel and Northern Ireland.* Edited by Hermann Giliomee and Jannie Gagiano, 54–77. Oxford: Oxford University Press, 1990.

Nolutshungu, Sam C. *Changing South Africa: Political Considerations.* Manchester: Manchester University Press, 1982.

———. "Strategy and Power: South Africa and Its Neighbours." In *South Africa: No Turning Back.* Edited by Shaun Johnson, 335–52. Bloomington: Indiana University Press, 1989.

Nzimande, Emmanuel Bonginkosi. "'The Corporate Guerillas': Class Formation and the African Corporate Petty Bourgeoisie in post–1973 South Africa." Ph.D. dissertation, University of Natal, Durban, 1991.

Oberschall, Anthony. *Social Conflict and Social Movements*. Englewood Cliffs, N.J.: Prentice-Hall, 1973.

O'Donnell, Guillermo, and Phillippe C. Schmitter. *Transitions from Authoritarian Rule*. Baltimore: The Johns Hopkins University Press, 1986.

O'Meara, Dan. "The 1946 African Mine Workers' Strike and the Political Economy of South Africa." *Journal of Commonwealth and Comparative Politics* 13 (1975): 146–73.

———. *Volkskapitalisme: Class, Capital, and Ideology in the Development of Afrikaner Nationalism, 1934–1948*. Cape Town: Cambridge University Press, 1983.

Pahad, Essop. "South African Indians as a National Minority in the National Question," In *The National Question in South Africa*. Edited by Maria van Diepen, 86–95. London: Zed Books, 1988.

Palestinian Liberation Organization. *Village Statistics 1945: A Classification of Land and Area Ownership in Palestine*. Beirut: PLO Research Center, 1970.

Peretz, Don. "Palestinian Social Stratification: Political Implications." In *The Palestinians and the Middle East Conflict*. Edited by Gabriel Ben-Dor. Ramat-Gan, Israel: Turtledove Publishing, 1978.

———. *Intifada: The Palestinian Uprising*. Boulder: Westview Press, 1990.

Pityana, Sipho. "The Black Middle Class at the Crossroads." *Sechaba* (January 1988): 7–10.

Pityana, Sipho Mila, and Mark Orkin. *Beyond the Factory Floor: A Survey of COSATU Shop-Stewards*. Johannesburg: Ravan Press, 1992.

Piven, Frances Fox, and Richard A. Cloward. *Poor People's Movements: Why They Succeed, How They Fail*. New York: Vintage Books, 1979.

Plascov, Avi. *The Palestinian Refugees of Jordan, 1948–1957*. London: Frank Cass, 1981.

Porath, Y. *The Palestinian Arab National Movement: From Riots to Rebellion*. Vol. 2. London: Frank Cass, 1977.

Pressberg, Gail. "The Uprising: Causes and Consequences." *Journal of Palestine Studies* 17, no. 3 (spring 1988): 38–50.

Price, Robert M. *The Apartheid State in Crisis: Political Transformation in South Africa, 1975–1990*. New York: Oxford University Press, 1991.

Qassmiya, Khayriya. "Al-Haraka al-wataniyya al-filastiniyya fi thulthay al-qarn al-hali" (The Palestinian national movement in the two-thirds of the current century). In *Encyclopaedia Palaestina, Vol. V: Studies in the Palestine Question*. Edited by Anis Sayegh, 41–163. Beirut: Encyclopaedia Palaestina, 1990.

Quandt, William B. "Political and Military Dimensions of Contemporary Palestinian Nationalism." In *The Politics of Palestinian Nationalism*. Edited by William B. Quandt, Fuad Jabber, and Ann Mosely Lesch, 43–153. Berkeley: University of California Press, 1973.

Republic of South Africa. Central Statistical Service. *South African Statistics, 1990*.

Rodinson, Maxime. *Israel and the Arabs*. 2d ed. Harmondsworth, England: Penguin Books, 1982.

Rogers, Barbara. *Divide and Rule: South Africa's Bantustans.* 2d ed., rev. London: International Defence and Aid Fund for Southern Africa, 1980.

Roux, Edward. *S. P. Bunting: A Political Biography.* Cape Town: Mayibuye Books, 1993.

Roy, Sara. *The Gaza Strip: A Demographic, Economic, Social and Legal Survey.* Jerusalem: The West Bank Data Base Project, 1986.

Ruedy, "Dynamics of Land Alienation." In *The Transformation of Palestine.* Edited by Ibrahim Abu-Lughod, 119–38. Evanston: Northwestern University Press, 1987.

Rueschemeyer, Dietrich, Evelyne Huber Stephens, and John D. Stephens. *Capitalist Development and Democracy.* Chicago: University of Chicago Press, 1992.

Ryan, Sheila. "The Colonial Exploitation of Occupied Palestine: A Study of the Transformation of the Economies of the West Bank and Gaza Strip." In *Zionism, Imperialism and Racism.* Edited by A.W. Kayyali, 169–95. London: Croom Helm, 1979.

Ryan, Sheila, and Donald Will. *Israel and South Africa: Legal Systems of Settler Dominance.* Trenton, N.J.: Africa World Press, 1990.

Sahliyeh, Emile. "West Bank Industrial and Agricultural Development: The Basic Problems." *Journal of Palestine Studies* 11, no. 2 (winter 1982): 55–69.

———. *In Search of Leadership: West Bank Politics since 1967.* Washington, D.C.: The Brookings Institution, 1988.

Said, Edward W. *The Question of Palestine.* New York: Vintage Books, 1979.

———. "The Mirage of Peace: Oslo I to Oslo II." *The Nation* (16 October 1995): 413–20.

Saleh, Abdel Jawad. "Genèse et évolution d'un mouvement de libération nationale: Le Fath" (The genesis and evolution of a liberation movement: Fatah). Ph.D. dissertation, University of Paris X, Nanterre, 1986.

Saleh, Samir Abdallah. "The Effects of Israeli Occupation on the Economy of the West Bank and Gaza Strip." In *Intifada: Palestine at the Crossroads.* Edited by Jamal R. Nassar and Roger Heacock, 37–51. New York: Praeger, 1990.

Saul, John. "Class, Race and the Future of Socialism." In *Popular Struggles in South Africa.* Edited by William Cobbett and Robin Cohen, 210–28. Trenton, N.J.: Africa World Press, 1988.

Sayigh, Rosemary. *Palestinians: From Peasants to Revolutionaries.* London: Zed Press, 1987.

———. *Too Many Enemies: The Palestinian Experience in Lebanon.* London: Zed Books, 1994.

Sayigh, Yezid. "The Palestinian Cause in World Politics." *Middle East International,* no. 324 (30 April 1988): 17–18.

Sayigh, Yusif A. *The Economies of the Arab World: Development since 1945.* London: Croom Helm, 1978.

Seckings, Jeremy. "The Origins of Political Mobilisation in the PWV Townships, 1980–84." In *Popular Struggles in South Africa.* Edited by William Cobbett and Robin Cohen, 59–76. Trenton, N.J.: Africa World Press, 1988.

———. "'Trailing Behind the Masses': The United Democratic Front and Township

Politics in the Pretoria-Witwatersrand-Vaal Region, 1983–84." *Journal of Southern African Studies* 18, no. 1 (March 1991): 93–114.

Seidman, Gay W. *Manufacturing Militance: Workers' Movements in Brazil and South Africa, 1970–1985.* Berkeley: University of California Press, 1994.

Semyonov, Moshe and Noah Lewin-Epstein. *Hewers of Wood and Drawers of Water: Non-Citizen Arabs in the Israeli Labor Market.* Ithaca, N.Y.: IRS Press, 1987.

Shafir, Gershon. *Land, Labor, and the Origins of the Israeli-Palestinian Conflict, 1882–1914.* Cambridge: Cambridge University Press, 1989.

Shahak, Israel. "Israeli Apartheid." *Race and Class* 30, no. 1 (1988): 1–12.

———. "A History of the Concept of 'Transfer' in Zionism." *Journal of Palestine Studies* 18, no. 3 (spring 1989): 22–37.

Sharabi, Hisham B. *Nationalism and Revolution in the Arab World.* Princeton: D. Van Nostrand, 1966.

Al-Shuaibi, Issa. "The Development of Palestinian Entity-Consciousness." Parts 2 and 3. *Journal of Palestine Studies* 9 (winter, spring 1980): 50–70, 99–124.

Simons, Jack, and Ray Simons. *Class and Colour in South Africa, 1850–1950.* 2d ed. London: Shadowdean, 1983.

Slovo, Joe. "South Africa—No Middle Road." In *Southern Africa: The New Politics of Revolution.* Edited by Basil Davidson, Joe Slovo, and Anthony R. Wilkinson, 106–210. Harmondsworth, England: Penguin Books, 1976.

———. "The Sabotage Campaign." *Dawn: Journal of Umkhonto we Sizwe,* Souvenir Issue [c.1986]: 24–28.

———. "The Second Stage: Attempts to Get Back," *Dawn: Journal of Umkhonto we Sizwe,* Souvenir Issue [c.1986]: 33–34.

———. "Negotiations: What Room for Compromise?" *The African Communist,* no. 130 (third quarter 1992): 36–40.

Smith, Charles D. *Palestine and the Arab-Israeli Conflict.* New York: St. Martin's Press, 1988.

Smith, David M. *Apartheid in South Africa.* Cambridge: Cambridge University Press, 1987.

Smith, Pamela Ann. "Aspects of Class Structure in Palestinian Society, 1948–67." In *Israel and the Palestinians.* Edited by Uri Davis, Andrew Mack, and Niva Yuval-Davis. London: Ithaca Press, 1975.

———. *Palestine and the Palestinians, 1876–1983.* London: Croom Helm, 1984.

Smooha, Sammy. "Israel's Options for Handling the Palestinians in the West Bank and Gaza Strip." In *State Violence and Ethnicity.* Edited by Pierre L. van den Berghe, 143–85. Niwot, Colorado: University Press of Colorado, 1990.

South Africa. *Report of the Commission of Inquiry into Legislation Affecting the Utilisation of Manpower (Excluding the Legislation Administered by the Departments of Labour and Mines).* Pretoria: Government Printer, 1978.

South African Communists Speak: Documents from the History of the South African Communist Party, 1915–1980. London: Inkululeko, 1981.

South African Institute of Race Relations. *Race Relations Survey, 1954–1955.* Johannesburg: SAIRR, 1956.

———. *A Survey of Race Relations in South Africa, 1973.* Johannesburg: SAIRR, 1974.

———. *Race Relations Survey, 1989–90.* Johannesburg: SAIRR, 1990.

South African Labour Bulletin. "Critique of the Wiehahn Commission." In *The Independent Trade Unions, 1974–1984: Ten Years of the South African Labour Bulletin.* Edited by Johann Maree, 138–57. Johannesburg: Ravan Press, 1987.

———. "The World Bank: Beggaring South Africa?" *South African Labour Bulletin* 20, no. 6 (December 1996): 23–26.

Stanbridge, Roland. "Contemporary African Political Organizations and Movements." In *The Apartheid Regime: Political Power and Racial Domination.* Edited by Robert M. Price and Carl G. Rosberg, 66–98. Berkeley: Institute of International Studies, 1980.

Stevens, Richard P. "Israel and Africa." In *Zionism & Racism: Proceedings of an International Symposium.* Publication of The International Organization for the Elimination of All Forms of Racial Discrimination, 163–73. New Brunswick: North American, 1979.

Stevens, Richard P., and Abdelwahab M. Elmessiri, eds. *Israel and South Africa: The Progression of a Relationship.* New York: New World Press, 1976.

Stork, Joe. "Israel as a Strategic Asset." *MERIP Reports,* no. 105 (May 1982): 3–13.

Streek, Barry. "Disunity through the Bantustans." *South Africa Review II* (1984): 259–70.

Surplus People Project. *Forced Removals in South Africa: The Surplus People Reports.* Vols. 1 and 2. Cape Town: SPP, 1983.

Swedenburg, Ted. "The Role of the Palestinian Peasantry in the Great Revolt (1936–1939)." In *Islam, Politics, and Social Movements.* Edited by Edmund Burke, III, and Ira M. Lapidus, 169–206. Berkeley: University of California, 1988.

Swilling, Mark. "The United Democratic Front and Township Revolt." In *Popular Struggles in South Africa.* Edited by William Cobbett and Robin Cohen, 90–113. Trenton, N.J.: Africa World Press, 1988.

Tamari, Salim. "The Palestinians in the West Bank and Gaza: The Sociology of Dependency." In *The Sociology of Palestinians.* Edited by Khalil Nakhleh and Elia Zureik, 84–111. London: Croom Helm, 1980.

———. "Building Other People's Homes: The Palestinian Peasant's Household and Work in Israel." In *Conference on Development in the Service of Steadfastness,* 3–40. Jerusalem: Arab Thought Forum, 1981.

———. "Factionalism and Class Formation in Recent Palestinian History." In *Studies in the Economic and Social History of Palestine in the Nineteenth and Twentieth Centuries.* Edited by Roger Owen, 177–202. Oxford: St. Antony's, 1982.

———. "Israel's Search for a Native Pillar: The Village Leagues." In *Occupation: Israel Over Palestine.* Edited by Naseer H. Aruri, 377–90. Belmont, Mass.: AAUG, 1983.

———. "What the Uprising Means." In *Intifada: The Palestinian Uprising against Israeli Occupation.* Edited by Zachary Lockman and Joel Beinin, 127–38. Boston: South End Press, 1989.

Taraki, Lisa. "The Development of Political Consciousness among Palestinians in the Occupied Territories, 1967–1987." In *Intifada: Palestine at the Crossroads.* Edited by Jamal R. Nassar and Roger Heacock, 53–72. New York: Praeger, 1990.

Tarrow, Sidney. *Power in Movement: Social Movements, Collective Action, and Politics.* Cambridge: Cambridge University Press, 1994.

Taylor, Alan R. "Vision and Intent in Zionist Thought." In *The Transformation of Palestine.* Edited by Ibrahim Abu-Lughod, 9–26. Evanston: Northwestern University Press, 1987.

TEAM International. *Health Services for Palestinians in Lebanon.* Beirut, Lebanon: TEAM, 1983.

Terreblanche, Sampie, and Nicoli Nattrass. "A Periodisation of the Political Economy from 1910." In *The Political Economy of South Africa.* Edited by Nicoli Nattrass and Elisabeth Ardington, 6–23. Cape Town: Oxford University Press, 1990.

Trabulsi, Fawwaz. "The Palestine Problem: Zionism and Imperialism in the Middle East." *The New Left Review* 57 (May 1969): 53–90.

United Arab Republic. Ministry of National Guidance. *Malaf watha'iq filastin: Majmu'at watha'iq wa-awraq khasa bi'l-qadiya al-filastiniyya* (File of Palestine documents: A collection of documents and papers specific to the Palestinian cause). Vol. 1: The years 637 to 1949. Cairo: 1969.

United Nations General Assembly. Thirty-eighth session. *Living Conditions of the Palestinian People in the Occupied Palestinian Territories: Report of the Secretary-General.* document A/38/278. 22 June 1983.

United Nations Conference on Trade and Development. *The Palestinian Financial Sector under Israeli Occupation.* Document UNCTAD/ST/SEU/3/Rev.1. New York: United Nations, 1989.

United Nations Relief and Works Agency. *Registration Statistical Bulletin for the Third Quarter.* UNRWA-HQ (October 1981).

———. *UNRWA—A Brief History, 1950–1982.* Vienna: UNRWA, 1986.

Unterhalter, Elaine. *Forced Removal: The Division, Segregation, and Control of the People of South Africa.* London: International Defence and Aid Fund for Southern Africa, 1987.

Usher, Graham. "Palestinian Authority, Israeli Rule." *The Nation* (5 February 1996): 15–18.

Van Arkadie, Brian. *Benefits and Burdens: A Report on the West Bank and the Gaza Strip Economies since 1967.* New York: Carnegie Endowment for International Peace, 1977.

Von Holdt, Karl. "Trade Unions, Community Organisation and Politics: A Local Case Study on the East Rand." *Labour Studies Research Report* 3. Sociology of Work Programme, Johannesburg: University of the Witwatersrand, 1987.

Waines, David. "The Failure of the Nationalist Resistance." In *The Transformation of Palestine.* Edited by Ibrahim Abu-Lughod, 207–36. Evanston: Northwestern University Press, 1987.

Walshe, Peter. *The Rise of African Nationalism in South Africa: The African National Congress, 1912–1952.* Berkeley: University of California Press, 1971.

Webster, Eddie. "The Rise of Social-Movement Unionism: The Two Faces of the Black Trade Union Movement in South Africa." In *State, Resistance and Change in South Africa.* Edited by Philip Frankel, Noam Pines, and Mark Swilling, 174–96. Johannesburg: Southern Book Publishers, 1988.

Weinstock, Nathan. *Zionism: False Messiah.* Translated and edited by Alan Adler. London: Ink Links, 1979.

Wiehahn Commission. *The Complete Wiehahn Report.* Johannesburg: Lex Patria Publishers, 1982.

Will, Donald Scott. "The Dynamics of the Settler State: A Comparative Study of Israel and South Africa." Ph.D. dissertation, University of Denver, 1990.

Wolpe, Harold. "Capitalism and Cheap Labour-Power in South Africa: From Segregation to Apartheid." *Economy and Society* 1, no. 4 (1972): 425–56.

———. "The Theory of Internal Colonialism: The South African Case Study." In *Beyond the Sociology of Development.* Edited by Ivar Oxaal, 229–52. London: Routledge and Kegan Paul, 1975.

———. "The Changing Class Structure of South Africa: The African Petit-Bourgeoisie." In *Research in Political Economy 1.* Edited by Paul Zarembka, 143–74. Greenwich, Conn.: JAI Press, 1977.

———. *Race, Class and the Apartheid State.* Paris: UNESCO Press, 1988.

———. "A Critique of the 'Internal Colonial' Thesis in its Application to South Africa." Department of Sociology and Law, Polytechnic of North London, n.d. Mimeographed.

Work in Progress. "Strikes in Southern Africa: Part 2." *Work in Progress,* no. 11 (February 1980): 54–59.

Wright, Erik Olin. *Interrogating Inequality: Essays on Class Analysis, Socialism and Marxism.* London: Verso, 1994.

Yasin, Abdel-Qadir. *Ta'rikh al-tabaka al-'amila al-filastiniyya, 1918–1948* (The history of the Palestinian working class, 1918–1948). Beirut: Markaz al-abhath, munathamat al-tahrir al-filastiniyya, 1980.

———. "Al-Haraka al-siyasiya fi qita' ghazza, 1948–1987" (The political movement in the Gaza Strip, 1948–1987). *Samed* 13, no. 84 (April–June 1991): 30–46.

Zille, Helen. "Restructuring the Industrial Decentralisation Strategy." *South African Review I* (1983): 58–71.

Zogby, James J. *Palestinians: The Invisible Victims.* Washington, D.C.: American Arab Anti-Discrimination Committee, 1981.

Zureik, Elia T. *The Palestinians in Israel: A Study in Internal Colonialism.* London: Routledge and Kegan Paul, 1979.

———. "Reflections on Twentieth-Century Palestinian Class Structure." In *The Sociology of Palestinians.* Edited by Khalil Nakhleh and Elia Zureik, 47–63. London: Croom Helm, 1980.

———. "Palestinians under Israeli Control." *Arab Studies Quarterly* 7, nos. 2 and 3 (spring–summer 1985): 104–19.

List of Interviews

South African Case

Graeme Bloch, Cape Town, 30 November 1992

Azhar Cachalia, Johannesburg, 27 January and 16 February 1993

Judy Chalmers, Port Elizabeth, 9 November 1992

Janet Cherry, Grahamstown, 10 November 1992

Neil Coleman, Johannesburg, 3 February 1993

Jeremy Cronin, Johannesburg, 19 February 1993, 18 July and
    23 August 1994

Chris Dlamini, Cape Town, 12 August 1994

Maynard Dyakal, Port Elizabeth, 5 August 1994

Buyiswa Fazzi, Port Elizabeth, 6 November 1992

Henry Fazzi, Cape Town, 18 August 1994

Tozamile Feni, East London, 4 August 1994

Archie Gumede, Pinetown, 28 October 1992

Willie Hofmeyer, Cape Town, 25 November 1992

Josiah Jelé, Cape Town, 18 August 1994

Palo Jordan, Johannesburg, 15 February 1993

Wolfram Kistner, Johannesburg, 22 January 1993

Tom Lodge, Johannesburg, 3 December 1992

Nonimzi Luzipo, Port Elizabeth, 6 November 1992

Vusi Madonsela, Durban, 29 October 1992

Sydney Mafumadi, Johannesburg, 22 February 1993

Yunus Mahomed, Durban, 30 October 1992

Henry Makoti, Cape Town, 18 August 1994

Jesse Maluleke, Johannesburg, 27 July 1994

Andrew Mapheto, Johannesburg, 27 December 1992

Moses Mayekiso, Johannesburg, 26 July 1994

Mzwanele Mayekiso, Johannesburg, 14 January 1993

Govan Mbeki, Port Elizabeth, 5 November 1992

Richard Mdakane, Johannesburg, 14 January 1993

Sizakele Mkhize, Durban, 30 October 1992

Rapu Molekane, Johannesburg, 15 January 1993

Eric Molobi, Johannesburg, 21 July 1994

Vali Mussa, Pretoria, 22 July 1994

Beyers Naudé, Johannesburg, 20 January 1993

Bulelani Ngcuka, Athlone, 27 November 1992

John Nkadimeng, Johannesburg, 2 February 1993

Stanley Nkosiyabo Peter, East London, 4 August 1994

Sanso Patekile, Cape Town, 18 August 1994

Leila Patel, Johannesburg, 22 August 1994

Sue Rabkin, Johannesburg, 13 January 1993

Rufus Rwexu, East London, 4 August 1994

Reg September, 18 August 1994

Walter Sisulu, Johannesburg, 15 February 1993

Ari Sitas, Durban, 28 October 1992

Jabu Sithole, Durban, 28 October 1992

Stone Sizani, Port Elizabeth, 4, 8 November 1992

Vesta Smith, Noordgesig, 17 January 1993

Raymond Suttner, Johannesburg, 2 February 1993

Karl von Holdt, Johannesburg, 19 January 1993

Mike Xego, Port Elizabeth, 6, 7 November 1992

Palestinian Case

Said Abdul-Hadi, Beirut, 28 March 1994

Assad Abdul-Rahman, Amman, 29 September 1994

Haidar Abdel-Shafi, Gaza, 15, 17 May 1994

Bahjat Abu-Gharbiya, Amman, 5, 12 February 1994

Nizar Abu-Ghazala, Amman, 26 June 1994

Ghazi Abu-Jiyab, Amman, 17 May 1994

Tawfiq Abu-Khousa, Gaza, 16 May 1994

Abu-Mujahid, Beirut, 24, 30 March 1994

Talal Ahmad, Damascus, 17 February 1994

Nabil Amr, Amman, 19 April 1994

Taysir Aruri, Amman, 1, 2, 6 February 1994

Abdul-Karim Ashour, Gaza, 17 May 1994

Ihab al-Ashqar, Gaza, 15 May 1994

Abdul-Hameed al-Baba, Amman, 8 February 1994

Mukhtar Ba'ba, Amman, 30 January 1994

Ibrahim Baker, Amman, 24 April 1994

Marwan Barghouthi, Ramallah, 8 May 1994

Rasem al-Bayari, Gaza, 15 May 1994

Fuad Besseiso, Amman, 23 June 1994

Ibrahim Dakkak, East Jerusalem, 5 May 1994

Khaled al-Fahoum, Damascus, 16, 22 February 1994

Adel Ghanem, Nablus, 19 June 1994

Rita Giacaman, Ramallah, 10 May 1994

Hassan al-Hanafi, Gaza, 13 May 1994

Hani al-Hassan, Amman, 27 June 1994

Naif Hawatma, Damascus, 23 February 1994

George Hazboun, Bethlehem, 11 May 1994

Bayan al-Hout, Beirut, 23, 28 March 1994

Shafiq al-Hout, Beirut, 22, 23 March 1994

Haidar Ibrahim, Irbid, Jordan, 1 July 1994

Marwan Kafarna, Gaza, 15 May 1994

Taysir Khalid, Amman, 7 February 1994

Ghassan al-Khatib, East Jerusalem, 12 May 1994

Mohammad al-Labadi, Amman, 16 April 1994

Khalil Mahshi, Ramallah, 10 May 1994

Abdulrahim Mallouh, Amman, 31 January 1994

Amal al-Masri, Beirut, 27 March 1994

Shahadeh Minawi, Nablus, 18 June 1994

Abu-Said Murad, Beirut, 29 March 1994

Hilmi Mussa, Damascus, 24 February 1994

Walid Mustafa, Amman, 29 January 1994

Abu-Ali Mustafa, Damascus, 24 February 1994

Suheil al-Natour, Beirut, 24 March 1994

Mamdouh Noufel, Amman, 11 April 1994

Mohammad Othman, Beirut, 28 March 1994

Mohammad al-Qudwa, Gaza, 15 May 1994

Mohammad Qunayta, Gaza, 16 May 1994

Salah Ra'fat, Amman, 18 April 1994

Amna Rimawi, Ramallah, 23 May 1994

Shaher Sa'ed, Nablus, 24 May 1994

Walid Salem, East Jerusalem, 7 April 1994

Bassam al-Salhi, Ramallah, 22 May 1994

Qais al-Samrai (Abu-Leila), Damascus, 21 February 1994

Yusif Sayigh, Beirut, 26 March 1994

Rosemary Sayigh, Beirut, 26 March 1994

Bassam al-Shak'a, Nablus, 19 June 1994

Maher al-Sharif, Damascus, 17 February 1994

Azmi Shuaibi, Ramallah, 4 May 1994

Salah Ta'mari, Amman, 12 May 1994

Salim Tamari, Ramallah, 22 May 1994

Lisa Taraki, Ramallah, 17 July 1989

Intissar al-Wazir, Amman, 2 February 1994

Index

AAC (All-African Convention), 44–45

Abdallah, King, 97, 197 n. 238, 202 n. 141

Abdel-Nasser, Gamal, 98, 101, 102, 108, 206 n. 223

Abna' al-Balad (Sons of the Land), 158

African Claims (1943), 45, 189 n. 44

African nationalism, 40, 49, 50, 79, 86–87, 89, 120 (*see also* PAC)

African states, 91, 120, 136, 140, 170

Afrikaners: "Afrikanerization," 82, 175; classes, 39, 78, 124, 181; nationalism, 40, 79, 120, 181; republics, 36, 39

AHC (Arab Higher Committee), 60, 61–62, 67, 68

Algeria, 106

All-Palestine Conference (1919), 55

All-Palestine Government, 100

al-nakba (the Catastrophe), 96

AMWU (African Mine Workers Union), 49, 190 n. 94

ANC (African National Congress) (*see also* armed struggle; MK; national movement, South African; YL): and African states, 91, 120, 136, 140, 170; and African unity, 37, 42, 50, 72, 118;

banning of, 90, 93, 95; and coloreds, 44, 45, 51, 80, 85, 86, 88, 142; and communists, 44, 80, 84, 85, 87 (*see also* CPSA; SACP); External Mission, 91–93, 135–38, 140; formation of, 40, 181, 187 n. 5; government, 3–5, 174–75; hegemony, 137, 140, 142, 171; and Indians, 44, 51, 80, 84, 85, 86, 142 (*see also* SAIC); and international support, 10–13, 135–36, 184 n. 24; and labor, 40, 44, 47, 51, 94, 134, 138, 139, 140, 142, 171, 174, 198 n. 37, 200 n. 81, 214 n. 125, 216 n. 168, 223 n. 1 (*see also* COSATU; SACTU); leaders, 16, 44, 45, 46, 49, 52–53, 71, 74, 79, 80, 83, 85, 87, 90, 91, 94, 117, 119, 137, 142, 143, 170, 171, 84, 198 n. 37, 200 n. 89, 201 n. 119; and mass base, 16, 19, 44, 45, 85, 94, 119, 171; membership, 84, 85, 86, 93, 140; and movement in South Africa, 168, 170, 171 (*see also* UDF); NEC, 41, 93, 140, 200 n. 89, 201 n. 119; nonviolence, 84, 90; and PAC, 90; passive resistance, 16, 17; radicalization of, 79, 80, 83, 84, 87; reformists,

45, 52; resources, 16, 88, 91, 95, 120, 136, 137, 143, 170, 171, 216 n. 166; and traditional leaders, 41, 45, 142–43; underground, 92–93, 94–95, 96, 136–37, 214 n. 120, 214 n. 123; and whites, 18, 43, 51, 88, 95 (*see also* SACOD)

ANC and PLO compared, 1, 5, 16, 17, 168–71 (*see also* national movements)

Anglo-Boer War (1899–1902), 36

Angola, 92, 127, 136, 140

ANM (Arab Nationalist Movement), 101, 107, 111

apartheid: and African middle class, 80, 82; and cheap labor, 75, 79, 81–82; and colored and Indians, 78, 79, 82, 88; constraints on economy, 121, 124–25, 131, 133; and international capital, 10, 90, 94, 201 n. 122; introduced, 50, 75, 79; legislation, 80, 82, 198 n. 43; and new social forces, 80, 145, 173–74; and traditional leaders, 81

APO (African People's Organisation), 44, 51, 88

Arab Congresses, 55, 56, 57, 192 n. 135

Arab Executive, 56, 59, 66, 192 n. 163

Arab League and PLO, 107, 112, 152, 160, 163

Arab nationalism (*qawmiya*), 56, 98, 106–7, 111, 116

Arab states: and colonial divisions, 54, 71, 98; and communist parties, 98, 101; development, 100, 118; funding for West Bank/Gaza Strip, 152, 160, 163, 218 n. 226, 222 n. 303 (*see also* JPJC); and Palestine, 68, 70; and Palestinian national movement, 106, 107, 111–12, 116; politics, 12, 71, 97–98; and Palestinians, 99, 111–12, 106, 116, 149, 160, 163, 182, 203 n. 162; and wars with Israel, 68, 97–98, 108, 111–12, 119, 196 n. 228

Arab unity, 37, 97–98, 100–102, 116, 118

Arab Workers' Conference (1930), 66

Arafat, Yasser, 16, 109, 112, 162, 163, 175–76, 178, 183 n. 2, 206 n. 230, 206 n. 232, 223 n. 14

al-Ard, 102, 157, 220 n. 263

armed struggle: and ANC, 16, 90, 91, 92, 95, 118, 119, 127, 135, 136–37, 140, 168 (*see also* MK); and leverage, 118, 119; and middle class leaders, 91–92, 168; and PLO, 18, 106, 107, 109, 111, 112, 119, 168

ashkenazim, 15, 97, 147

AZAPO (Azanian People's Organisation), 140

Baghdad Pact, 101

Balfour Declaration (1917), 54, 55, 57, 58, 191 n. 107

bantustans (*see also* exclusion, South Africa), 5; citizenship, 128, 142; creation of, 80–81, 128, 209 n. 31; decline of, 130, 134; elite, 128–29, 130, 132, 144; forced resettlement, 81–82, 128, 210 n. 36; income, 129, 210 n. 43, 210 n. 49, 211 n. 59; "independence," 2, 128, 129, 132; leaders, 81, 129, 130, 144, 211 n. 58; population, 128–30, 210 n. 38, 210 n. 42, 211 n. 54, 211 n. 65; and social control, 81, 128, 129, 130; and South Africa, 132, 142, 215 n. 163; and trade unions, 130, 144; and traditional social organization, 81, 129, 130, 141, 142, 143; and UDF, 139, 144; and women, 80, 130; and workers, 129, 130, 210 n. 43, 210 n. 44, 210 n. 51, 210 n. 53; and youth, 130, 139, 211 n. 55

Ba'th parties, 101, 207 n. 245, 219 n.240

BAWU (Black Allied Workers Union), 126, 209 n. 24

BC (Black Consciousness), 126, 135, 137, 140

BCM (Black Consciousness Movement), 126, 127, 130, 135

Bedouin, Palestinian, 194–95 n. 185, 219–20 n. 260

Begin, Menachem, 183 n. 3

Ben-Gurion, David, 202 n. 143

Botswana, 92, 140

bourgeoisie, Palestinian, 64, 146, 158, 166, 177–78, 180, 220 n. 274

boycotts: South Africa, 82–83, 134, 138, 139, 169; West Bank and Gaza Strip, 162, 169

Britain in Palestine: and Arabs, 57, 63, 192 n. 130; and Jewish colonization, 55, 58, 62, 181, 193 n. 146; and Jewish "national home," 37, 54, 62; and mandate, 36, 58, 63; and Palestinian elite, 70, 194 n. 171; and partition, 61, 68; repression, 61, 62, 63; and Zionists, 54, 55, 69, 71, 181, 191 n. 107

Britain in South Africa: and Africans, 36, 37, 40, 42, 43, 52; and Afrikaners, 36, 53, 71; and ANC, 43, 52; in Cape, 36, 37, 39, 40, 42, 43, 45, 71

British imperialism, 53, 71

Cairo Accords (1969), 110

Camp David Accords (1978), 148, 152, 153, 177

capital, international. See apartheid

capitalism. See settler colonialism

chieftancy/traditional leaders, African (see also bantustans): and ANC, 40–41, 45, 142–43; authority, 41, 50, 51, 73, 81; decline of, 134, 143, 179; in Natal, 216 n. 171; and land, 41, 43, 51; and state, 71, 81; and traditional social relations, 50, 51, 52, 72, 81, 134, 143, 178; and social control, 53, 81, 211 n. 57; tribal divisions, 41, 42

Christians, Palestinian: in Israel, 219–20 n. 260; in Lebanon, 110, 116, 206–7 n. 239; and national movement, 56, 69, 109, 159–60, 169, 221 n. 282; in Palestine, 8, 55–56, 59

citizenship: Africans, 14, 128, 134, 142, 143; Palestinians in Arab states, 160–61, 101, 103, 105, 203 n. 162, 206–7 n. 239; Palestinians in Israel, 14, 97, 118, 147–48, 156, 158, 219 n. 257

civics, South Africa, 134, 138, 144, 169, 171

"civil administration," Israeli, 147, 152, 153, 156

clan and kindship, Palestine: and national movements, 123–24; and Palestinian national movement, 69, 160, 161, 176, 177; politics, 56, 59, 69, 70, 104–5, 157, 193 n. 154

class (see also resources): agency, 29; alliances, 23–24, 25; autonomy, 24, 31–32, 34; formation, 24, 29–33; hegemony, 25–26, 29, 32; and national interests, 123; struggles, 26

Cloward, Richard A., 27, 187 n. 26

CNETU (Council of Non-European Trade Unions), 49

Cold War, 10, 98, 181

color bars, South Africa, 34, 43, 48, 78, 82, 187 n. 3, 188 n. 25

coloreds, 16, 185 n. 42; and Africans, 44, 86 (see also ANC); and apartheid, 79; and Congress Alliance, 86–88, 118; and franchise, 88; and government policies, 79, 80, 85, 88; radicalization, 45–46, 85; and segregation, 45; students, 126, 209 n. 16; and tricameral parliament (1982), 138, 214 n. 129; and UDF, 138, 139

Cominform (Communist Information Bureau), 87

Comintern (Communist International), 48, 49, 65, 66; and "Africanization,"

48, 74; and "Arabization," 65, 195
n. 202
communists. *See* CPI; CPSA; JCP; NLL;
PCP; SACP
Community Councils Act (1977), 131
Congress Alliance, 86–90, 95, 118
Congress of the People (1955), 89, 200
n. 84
Consultative Conferences (ANC): in 1969,
92, 93; in 1985, 140
CONTRALESA (Congress of Traditional
Leaders of South Africa), 143, 216
n. 171
convergence of struggles, 179; Palestine,
162, 167; South Africa, 127, 135,
140–41, 169
COSATU (Congress of South African
Trade Unions): and ANC, 139–40,
143, 215 n. 152; and negotiations,
143, 172, 223 n. 1; and political strug-
gles, 139, 141, 170; post-1994 election, 174; and UDF, 141
CPC (Coloured People's Congress), 85
CPI (Communist Party of Israel), 96–97,
157, 196 n. 208, 220 n. 265 (*see also*
Rakah)
CPSA (Communist Party of South Africa),
44, 51; "Africanization" of, 48, 74; and
ANC, 44, 48–49, 84, 85, 87; and black
workers, 48; and early trade unions,
47, 48; membership, 48; and Native
Republic, 48

Dayan, Moshe, 145–46
Declaration of Principles. *See* Oslo
Agreements
Defiance Campaigns, 85, 93–94, 118,
201 n. 118
democracy (*see also* democratization): and
capitalist development, 23, 24, 25;
and class, 23–26, 29; definitions of,
26, 186 n. 3, 186 n. 8, 186 n. 20; and
economic power, 26, 28–29, 33; and

national movements, 22, 23, 31, 39,
77; and Palestinian national movement, 35, 57, 59, 67, 109, 112, 153,
155, 160, 161, 166, 167, 175, 177,
178, 179; participatory, 34, 124, 161,
167, 173, 175; and PNA, 4, 6, 178;
representative, 34, 124, 173; and
South African national movement, 3,
35, 45, 93, 139, 141, 145, 174, 178;
transitions to, 24, 25
democratization (*see also* democracy): and
class, 23–26, 31, 33–34, 123, 124,
178–79, 180; defined, 33–34; of national movements, 2, 23, 33–34, 123,
124, 178–79, 180; of political orders,
23; as process, 25
demography: Israel, 14, 97, 183 n. 10;
Jews in Palestine, 8, 55, 58; Palestinian refugees, 9, 96, 97, 99–100, 113,
158, 207 n. 258; Palestinians in
Israel, 14, 97, 202 n. 138, 202 n. 139;
Palestinians in Palestine, 7, 8, 10, 183
n. 10, 55; Palestinians in West Bank
and Gaza, 7, 97, 184 n. 11, 184 n. 16,
185 n. 41; South Africa, 7, 16, 185
n. 42, 189 n. 57, 209–10 n. 34, 211
n. 65
DFLP (Democratic Front for the Liberation of Palestine), 111, 153, 154, 155,
161, 162, 163, 219 n. 242
diaspora, Palestinian, 96, 97, 100, 110,
116, 147, 156, 159, 178–79, 180
Druze, Palestinian, 219–20 n. 260
Durban: riots (1949), 87; strikes
(1972–73), 125, 168, 209 n. 7

Eastern Cape, 93, 201 n. 118
Eastern Europe. *See* socialist bloc
East Jerusalem, 4, 114, 145 (*see also*
Jerusalem)
economic oppression and exploitation. *See*
Wright, Erik Olin
economy, Israel: 145, 146, 148, 149, 150,

152, 165, 168, 217 n. 196, 222 n. 317, 222 n. 318

economy, Palestine: agriculture, 56, 63, 64; Arab commerce, 56, 59; Arab industry, 64, 65, 69–70, 73, 195 n. 195, 196–97 n. 234; Jewish capital, 55, 69, 191 n. 110, 195 n. 199; Jewish industry, 55, 64, 69–70, 195 n. 195, 196–97 n. 234; and Oslo Agreements, 4, 179–80; Second World War expansion, 67; West Bank/Gaza Strip, 97, 103, 105, 148, 149, 151, 166, 217 n. 202, 218 n. 222, 218 n. 226, 222 n. 318, 223 n. 320

economy, South Africa (*see also* bantustans): and African labor, 46, 47, 75, 78, 121, 125, 131; agriculture, 39, 46, 78, 124; commerce, 49; indigenous, 46–47, 51, 73, 81, 119; industry, 43, 46, 47, 49, 78, 124, 125, 189 n. 56; mining, 36, 46, 48, 49, 50, 51, 124; post-1994 elections, 3–4, 5, 173–75; recession, 47, 88

education: blacks, 82, 125–26, 198 n. 24, 209 n. 16; comparative statistics, 16, 185 n. 40, 209 n. 16; missionary (Palestine), 57; missionary (South Africa), 36–37, 41–42, 50, 52–53, 82; Palestinians, 100, 203 n. 158, 208 n. 285

Egypt, 98, 106, 113; and Camp David Accords, 148, 177; and Fatah, 206 n. 234; and Gaza Strip, 97, 102, 103–5, 146, 204 n. 183; and October War (1973), 111, 112; and PLO, 107–8

elite, African (*see also* chieftancy/traditional leaders, African; education): and African unity, 41, 42, 50, 72; and ANC, 40; aspirations to white society, 41, 42, 50, 53; and British, 36, 52, 53, 71 , 74; challenges to, 37; failure of, 74, 75; internal relations, 41, 45, 51, 52,

188 n. 10; and mass base, 37, 41–42, 44, 50, 52, 53, 72, 73; as movement leaders, 37, 52–53, 71–74, 178; and privileges, 41–42, 50, 71; and restraint, 44, 52, 53, 72; urban/educated, 40, 41, 42, 50, 52, 53, 190 n. 94; and workers and peasants, 44, 72

elites: and authority, 37, 38, 39, 71, 73, 77, 117; decline of, 38, 73, 75, 76, 117; and leverage, 38, 39; as movement leaders, 32, 37–39, 178; resources, 32, 37, 77, 117; and restraint, 32, 38, 39, 72, 76, 178; and ruling powers, 37, 38, 39, 71, 72, 119, 178; and traditional social relations, 38, 39, 76

elite/traditional leaders, Palestinian: and Arab patronage, 99, 146; and Arab unity, 37, 54, 72; authority, 73, 99; and British, 36, 55, 57, 58, 59, 60, 70, 71, 74, 194 n. 171; challenge to, 37, 59, 69, 146, 151; composition of, 56; decline of, 146, 150, 166, 177, 178; failure of, 74, 75, 146; of Gaza Strip, 105, 114, 153; internal relations, 56, 57, 68, 104–5; in Israel, 157; and Jews, 61, 70; and land sales to Jews, 61, 69, 194 n. 163; and mass base, 37, 54, 59, 60, 69, 70, 72, 73, 104; and middle class, 59–60, 69, 76, 99; as movement leaders, 37, 65, 67, 68–71, 71–74, 178; patronage, 56, 64, 68, 71, 150, 151, 153; and peasants, 58, 60, 68, 69, 70, 72; preservation of, 69, 72, 99, 104, 105, 151–52, 166; and restraint, 58, 59, 60, 72, 178; and traditional social relations, 69, 72, 74, 105; of West Bank, 104, 105, 146, 153; and workers, 66, 67, 68, 72, 196 n. 223

emigration, Palestinian (West Bank and Gaza Strip), 149, 150, 151, 166, 170, 182, 208 n. 281, 217 n. 198, 218 n. 216, 222 n. 303

Eretz Yisrael, 6, 9

exclusion, Palestine (*see also* settler colonialism): and Arab resources, 115; and bourgeoisie, 158; and diaspora, 96, 97, 156, 158, 179, 180; and indigenous social relations, 35, 69, 75; and Israeli objectives, 104, 145–46, 158; and leverage, 70, 97, 102, 113, 117, 156, 177, 180; and middle class, 100, 117, 118, 158, 177, 179–80; and movement objectives, 18–19, 37, 119–20, 179, 180; and peasants, 63–68, 73; political, 146, 156; and refugees, 97, 98–100, 158, 159, 179; and resistance, 100, 103, 104, 158; and settler project, 17–18, 34, 35, 55, 73, 75; and traditional social organization, 73, 75, 104, 120, 152, 160, 161, 166, 167, 180; in West Bank/Gaza Strip, 103–6; and workers, 35, 55; and Zionism, 55, 65, 69, 75, 96, 156

exclusion, South Africa (*see also* settler colonialism): and African middle class, 40, 53; and apartheid, 50, 75, 79; and bantustans, 80–81, 128–30, 141, 158; failure of, 141, 142, 144–45; of Indians and coloreds, 45–46; political, 37, 40, 43–44, 80–81, 126, 128, 138, 145; of rural population, 121, 127, 128–30, 132

Fatah: and Arab states, 106, 107, 108, 111, 160, 161–62; and bourgeoisie, 158, 220 n. 274; formation of, 102, 106; hegemony, 153; and *intifada,* 163, 164, 222 n. 310; and Jordan, 109–10, 206 n. 234; leaders, 106; and LNM, 112, 113; and mass-based organizations, 153, 154, 155, 160, 163, 164, 219 n. 242, 222 n. 310; and negotiations, 176; and occupied territories, 115, 153, 154, 164; and other factions, 111, 153, 154, 160, 161, 206 n. 230; and Palestinian national-ism, 106–7, 111; and PLO, 107, 108–9, 111, 153, 158, 160, 205 n. 216; and refugees, 109, 203 n. 154; and resources, 106, 111, 153, 154, 160, 161, 164, 222 n. 310; and trade unions, 154, 176; and traditional leaders, 151, 153

FATULS (Federation of Arab Trade Unions and Labor Societies), 67

Federation of Free Trade Unions of South Africa, 200 n. 79

fida'yin. See PLO

First World War, 37, 43, 54, 57, 63

forced removals, South Africa, 80, 82, 83, 128, 131, 134–35, 210 n. 36

FOSATU (Federation of South African Trade Unions), 133, 134, 138, 139, 170, 214 n. 125

France, 11–12, 54, 55, 61, 98, 106

Franchise Action Committee, 88

Freedom Charter, 89, 90, 93, 138, 140, 174

FRELIMO (Front for the Liberation of Mozambique), 136

Gaza Strip (*see also* economy, Palestine; land, Palestine; occupied territories, Palestine): administration, 216 n. 184; elite, 105, 114, 205 n. 194; Israeli occupation of, 113; labor force, 148–50; and Muslim Brotherhood, 102; and PLA, 108; population density, 217 n. 193; and refugees, 103–4, 204 n. 180; and resistance, 102, 113

GEAR (Growth, Employment, and Redistribution strategy), 174

general strike, Palestinian (1936), 60, 61, 63, 66–67, 68

General Union of Palestinian Workers, 176

Geneva Conventions, 152, 167

GFTU (General Federation of Trade Unions), 154–55

Greater Israel, 148, 183 n. 3

Greater Syria, 55, 191 n. 108
Great Revolt (1936–39), 61–63, 67, 68
Great Trek, 36
Gulf War, 12, 176
GUPS (General Union of Palestinian
    Students), 102, 106

Hagana, 62
Hamas, 185 n. 45
Hertzog Bills, 43, 45
Herzl, Theodor, 202–3 n. 147
Histadrut, 62, 65, 66, 67, 96, 150, 202
    n. 135
Holocaust, the, 11
homelands, black. *See* bantustans
Hope-Simpson Commission (1930), 59,
    193 n. 147
Hussein, King, 11, 101, 153, 162, 163
al-Husseini, Haj Amin, 57, 60–61, 62,
    67, 100, 104, 194 n. 163, 196 n. 223
al-Husseini, Musa Kazim, 56, 57
Husseini family, 56, 104, 193 n. 154

ICU (Industrial and Commercial Workers
    Union), 47, 51
IDF (Israeli Defense Forces), 162–63
IMF (International Monetary Fund),
    174–75
inclusion, Palestine (*see also* settler colo-
    nialism): in Arab states, 97, 101, 103,
    106, 110, 118, 158; and democratiza-
    tion, 168–69, 179, 180; economic,
    146, 150, 166; in Israel, 97, 156, 157;
    and leverage, 165, 167–68, 169, 177,
    179, 180; and new social forces, 168,
    177; and resistance, 165, 167–68; and
    traditional social organization, 150–51,
    166, 168, 177, 179; and West Bank/
    Gaza Strip, 103, 146, 148–50, 165,
    179; and workers, 34, 35, 148–50
inclusion, South Africa (*see also* settler
    colonialism): and apartheid, 79, 82,
    124–25, 173; and democratization,

179; failure of, 141, 142; and indige-
    nous elite, 37, 53, 179; and indige-
    nous social relations, 34, 73, 75; and
    leverage, 34, 94, 144, 169; and middle
    class, 8, 145, 117–18, 173–74, 180;
    and migrant labor, 73, 79, 81; and
    movement objectives, 18–19, 119,
    120, 179; and new social forces, 168,
    169, 179; political, 144–45; and resis-
    tance, 125, 127, 131, 144, 169, 180;
    and settler project, 17–18, 34, 73; and
    state objectives, 132–33; and tradition-
    al social organization, 73, 75, 129,
    144, 168–69, 179; and workers, 34,
    34–35, 40, 46–50, 75, 79, 80–82, 94,
    127, 130–31, 132, 141, 144, 169,
    179, 180
inclusion/exclusion (*see also* settler colo-
    nialism): and assets, 31, 78; and class
    and national interests, 123; and class
    resources, 31, 32, 122, 180; compared,
    73, 120; defined, 31; and democratiza-
    tion, 124, 168–69, 179; economic,
    156; and indigenous elites, 38, 179;
    and indigenous labor, 38, 77, 122–24,
    179; and indigenous social relations,
    122–23, 124, 179; and leverage, 31,
    78, 122, 123; and middle classes,
    77–78, 117; and movement objectives,
    17–19, 120, 179–80; and movement
    outcomes, 20–21, 182; and movement
    success, 2, 156, 182; and new social
    forces, 31, 179; political, 145, 156;
    and resistance, 2, 31, 77–78; and
    resources, 31, 32, 78; and settler
    colonialism, 31, 179; in South Africa/
    Palestine compared, 2, 73, 117,
    168–69, 179, 180; and traditional
    social organization, 37, 38, 123, 124
Independence Party (1932), 59, 70, 193
    n. 154
"independents," Palestinian, 107, 109,
    153, 205 n. 220

Indians, 16, 185 n. 42 (*see also* ANC;
SAIC): and Africans, 44, 45, 85, 88,
188 n. 33, 198 n. 42; and apartheid,
78, 79, 82; business, 78, 82; and
Congress Alliance, 86–88, 118; and
government policies, 39–40, 45, 85,
88, 187 n. 3; radicalization of, 44–45,
85; students, 126, 209 n. 16; and tricameral parliament (1982), 138, 214
n. 129; and UDF, 138, 139; young
militants, 188 n. 33
indigenous, 9, 23
influx controls, South Africa, 46, 78, 80,
128, 131, 134, 142
Inkatha, 142, 144
intifada, 11, 13, 14; casualties, 162; character, 162, 222 n. 308; and class, 162,
166; decline of, 165, 176; and democratization, 166; funding, 164; gains,
11, 177, 179; genesis, 162, 163; and
Islamic revivalists, 163; and Israeli repression, 14, 162, 163, 164, 168; leadership, 163–64, 176 (*see also* UNLU);
leaflets *(bayanat),* 163–64; and mass
organizations, 163, 164, 165, 166;
and negotiations, 176; and Palestinians in Israel, 162; and PLO, 163,
164, 176; as resource, 11, 176, 179,
185 n. 45
Iraq, 61, 97–98, 101, 107–8, 191 n. 105,
206 n. 237, 207 n. 245
Israel: "creating facts," 115, 146; deportation, 114–15, 147; economic benefits of occupation, 145, 148, 152, 217
n. 196, 222 n 317; establishment of,
68, 96; and *intifada,* 164, 165, 167,
222 n. 317; invasion of Lebanon
(1982), 156, 161, 164, 167; and the
occupied territories, 4, 113, 122,
145–46, 147, 149; Palestinian
citizens of, 14, 97, 118, 147–48,
156–58, 202 n. 138, 202 n. 139,
219–20 n. 260, 220 n. 261, 220

n. 262; and Palestinian exclusion, 104,
145–46, 158; and Palestinian labor,
150, 155; parastatal institutions, 14,
157, 220 n. 262; and PLO, 156, 163,
165, 178; and redeployment, 176–77,
178; and "refugee problem," 6, 98,
100, 112; repression, 14–15, 121,
147, 156, 164, 167, 168, 171, 185
n. 35; and resources, 15; settlements,
4, 114, 145, 148, 149, 208 n. 270,
217 n. 191 (*see also* Zionist movement); and state autonomy, 15, 185
n. 37 (*see also* economy, Israel);

JCP (Jordanian Communist Party) (*see
also* PCP), 147, 153, 154–55, 163
Jerusalem, 54, 60, 191 n. 108; Palestinian
civil disobedience, 114; Palestinian
elite of, 56, 60, 104, 193 n. 154; and
partition, 68
Jews in Palestine (*see also* Zionist movement): Arab views on, 56, 57, 194
n. 166; capital, 55, 64–65, 69, 191
n. 110, 195 n. 199; communists, 65,
96–97 (*see also* PCP); dependence on
Zionists, 62–63; immigration, 54, 55,
64–65
Jordan: collusion with Zionists, 197
n. 238, 202 n. 141; and Jordanian
intifada, 11; and Palestinians, 101,
109–10, 203 n. 162; and PLO, 107–8,
109, 110, 164; and West Bank, 97,
101, 103–5, 113–14, 151, 152, 153,
204 n. 175, 204 n. 176, 218 n. 222
(*see also* JPJC)
JPJC (Jordanian–Palestinian Joint
Committee), 152, 153, 163, 167,
170, 222 n. 303
Judea and Samaria, 147
June War (1967), 108, 119

Karameh, battle of, 109–10, 206 n. 234
kingdoms, African, 39, 53

labor movement, Palestine, 4, 67, 153, 154, 169–71; South Africa, 79, 89, 94, 95, 134, 139, 142, 143, 169–71

Labor Party (Israel), 14, 15, 96, 147, 157, 176, 185 n. 37, 217 n. 191, 221 n. 302

land, Palestine: British commissions, 59, 61, 62, 193 n. 146, 193 n. 147, 193 n. 148; Gaza Strip, 113, 205 n. 194; Israeli expropriation of, 102, 146, 148, 149, 156, 157, 166; and Israeli policies, 14, 148, 149, 157, 219 n. 257, 220 n. 262; and Jews/Zionists, 55, 58, 59, 63, 64, 69, 191 n. 109; Ottoman Land Code (1858), 63; Palestinian dispossession, 58, 64, 69–70, 96; and Palestinian migrant workers, 155, 217 n. 207; Palestinian ownership, 56, 58, 60, 64, 68, 73, 192 n. 122; and Palestinian peasants, 58, 59, 63, 64; and partition, 68; sales to Jews, 58, 61, 69, 192–93 n. 140, 194 n. 163; shortage, 59, 193 n. 148; West Bank, 217 n. 206

land, South Africa: and banstustans, 80, 81, 129; black ownership, 41, 42–43, 45, 82, 128; and elite authority, 51; legislation, 42, 43, 45; reform, 174; reserves, 42, 43, 47, 188 n. 27; and subsistence, 46, 47, 51, 81, 129

League of Nations, 36, 58

Lebanon, 105; civil war, 115, 112; and Haj Amin al-Husseini, 62, 67, 100; and Palestinian Christians, 110, 116, 206–7 n. 239; and Palestinian refugees, 97, 162, 203 n. 162; and PLO, 110, 159–62, 206 n. 237

Lesotho, 92, 140

leverage (see also exclusion, Palestine; exclusion, South Africa; inclusion, Palestine; inclusion, South Africa): and assets, 28, 30, 32, 77, 78, 123; class specificity of, 27, 28, 29, 39–33; and

elites, 38, 39; and middle classes, 77, 78, 123; and movements, 29, 30–33, 122, 123, 124; as power, 27, 28, 30, 31, 122, 124, 187 n. 26; and resistance, 39, 78, 122; as resource, 27, 122, 123; and settler colonialism, 30–33, 31, 77, 78, 122, 123–24; and traditional social relations, 123; and workers, 122–24

Likud, 14, 15, 147, 148, 168, 176, 217 n. 191

LNM (Lebanese National Movement), 112, 159

lobby: pro-Israel, 12

Luthuli, Chief Albert, 90, 200 n. 82

MacDonald, James Ramsey, 59

majority rule, 3, 48, 93, 173

Mandela, Nelson, 16, 84, 87, 90, 91, 93, 137, 143

Mapai, 157

Marxism-Leninism, 91, 111, 161

mass-based organizations, West Bank and Gaza Strip: and "blocs," 154, 155, 167; character of, 153–54, 156, 167; leadership, 156; and left, 153, 219 n. 242; and PLO, 163; proliferation of, 153, 163, 166–67

Mass Democratic Movement, South Africa, 141, 142, 174

MCA (Muslim-Christian Associations), 55–56, 59

McAdam, Doug, 27

Meir, Golda, 8

middle class, African (see also exclusion, South Africa; inclusion, South Africa): and apartheid, 82, 94, 117–18; and armed struggle, 118, 119; in bantustans, 128, 144; and black politics, 152, 167, 178; as buffer, 127, 145; and capitalism, 127, 131, 132, 145; and chiefs, 51; composition of, 132, 198 n. 23; expansion of, 127, 131, 132; and mass base, 41,

50, 71, 83, 84, 85, 178; as movement leaders, 83, 84, 90, 94, 96, 117–20, 145, 178; and national movement, 132, 145; petty bourgeoisie, 88, 131, 132, 212 n. 74 (*see also* NAFCOC); and property, 82; radicalization of, 76, 83, 84, 87, 94; and segregation, 40; and state, 127, 131; stunting of, 173–74, 180; and workers, 50

middle class, Palestinian (*see also* exclusion, Palestine; inclusion, Palestine): in Arab states, 100, 101, 116–17, 118; and armed struggle, 118, 119; class resources, 117, 118, 159; constraints to, 166; and elite, 59–60, 69, 74, 105, 117, 119; expansion of, 100, 116–17, 118, 166, 177, 180; fragmentation of, 116, 117, 118; and mass base, 152, 167, 178; as movement leaders, 97, 106, 116, 117–20, 159, 167, 178; and Palestinian nationalism, 100, 116, 159; radicalization of, 59, 69, 76, 101, 105–6; West Bank, 105, 152, 167

middle classes: and assets, 32, 77, 78, 123; and elites, 32, 76; hegemony, 32, 77, 119; and leverage, 77, 78, 123; and mass base, 76, 77, 119, 123; as movement leaders, 32, 76, 78, 117; resources, 32, 76–77, 78, 117, 123; and ruling powers, 77, 78, 119, 123; and working class, 32, 77, 123

migrant workers, African: and apartheid, 79; and bantustans, 81, 210 n. 43, 210 n. 51, 211 n. 53; decline of, 47; and migrant labor system, 40, 46–47, 51, 81, 127; and reserves, 40, 189 n. 57; and traditional social relations, 46–47, 50, 51, 52, 72–73

migrant workers, Palestinian, 146, 148, 149; and leverage, 169; and national movement, 154; organization of, 154, 155; and traditional social relations, 150–51, 166

mizrachim, 15, 97, 147

MK (Um Khonto we Sizwe) (*see also* armed struggle): actions, 91, 92, 94, 137, 213 n. 116; and ANC, 90, 91, 214 n. 120; "armed propaganda," 137; disaffection in ranks, 92; formation of, 90, 94; obstacles to, 92, 140; and political struggles, 137, 140; recruits, 91, 137, 214 n. 123; and workers, 94, 137, 140 (*see also* SACTU)

Moore, Barrington, 23, 24, 25, 186 n. 3

Mozambique, 92, 127, 136, 140

M-Plan, 93

municipal councils, West Bank: in 1972, 113–14; in 1976, 146–47, 152, 156, 166–67, 168, 216 n. 179

Muslim Brotherhood, 102

al-Nabulsi, Suleiman, 101

NAFCOC (National African Federated Chambers of Commerce), 132, 212 n. 76, 212 n. 77

Namibia, 92

al-Nashashibi, Raghib, 57

Nashashibi family, 56, 60, 61, 62, 104, 193 n. 154

Natal, 39, 45, 142, 216 n. 171

national democratic stage, 3, 87, 137–38, 173

National Land Day (1976), 157

national movement, Palestinian (*see also* armed struggle; national movements; PLO): and Arab resources, 97, 98, 111–12, 115–16, 120, 152, 160, 163, 167, 170, 176, 218 n. 226; and British repression, 63; and clan, 69; and class and national interests, 151, 154, 155, 166, 169, 170; and Cold War, 181; and communists, 65, 66, 74; competing organizations, 70, 73; and democracy, 160, 175, 177, 178, 179; and demography, 7–10; early demands, 55, 56, 57, 59, 61; early failures, 68, 75;

factionalization, 69, 105, 153, 154, 155, 160–61, 165, 167, 177, 193 n. 154; and Fatah, 154; formation of, 181; and "freezing of class struggles," 155, 166; and international support, 10–13; and Israeli state strength, 13–15; and Jews, 65, 66, 119–20, 179, 180; and *intifada,* 176; and labor movement, 169–71; leadership, 37, 59, 65, 67, 68, 69, 71, 72, 74, 100, 116, 119, 178; leadership shifts, 75, 76, 97, 119; in Lebanon, 110, 159–62; and leverage, 180; and negotiations, 176, 182; new directions, 108, 115–16, 118–19, 168–69; organizational weakness, 68, 69; and refugees, 6, 109, 161; and resources, 16, 176; as secular, 69, 102; and Soviet Union, 19–20, 182; and success, 6, 179; and traditional social relations, 69; and West Bank/Gaza Strip, 155–56, 162, 163; and workers, 66, 67, 169, 172, 176

national movement, South African (*see also* ANC; armed struggle; Congress Alliance; national movements): and Cold War, 181; and coloreds, 88; and communists, 48, 74, 86; and competing organizations, 73, 90; and democratization, 175, 178, 179; and demography, 7–10; early failures, 50, 75; economic goals, 132, 174; formation of, 181; and international support, 10–13; and labor movement, 169–71; leadership, 37, 71, 72, 74, 75, 90, 119, 178; and leverage, 172; moral appeals, 52; and negotiations, 182; new directions, 86, 94, 95–96, 118, 168–69; and petty bourgeoisie, 132; and South African state strength, 13–15; and Soviet Union, 19–20, 182 (*see also* Soviet Union); and traditional social relations, 50; and whites, 17, 18, 119,

179; and workers, 88, 95, 133, 140, 141, 169

national movements (*see also* national movement, Palestinian; national movement, South African): class resources, 31, 122; leaders and followers, 2, 19, 23, 32, 33, 76, 178; phases, 2, 17, 32, 33, 34, 178, 180–82; resources, 16; shifts in leadership, 32, 76; South African and Palestinian compared, 4–6, 7, 16–19, 117–20, 168–71, 172, 178; strategies and tactics, 17; success, 3

national movements, success/failure of: and demography, 2, 7–10, 20; and international support, 2, 7, 10–13, 20; and movement strength, 2, 7, 16–19, 20; and state strength, 2, 7, 13–15, 20

Nazis, 45, 64

negotiations: ANC and South Africa, 1, 20, 143, 171, 172, 175, 182, 223 n. 1; PLO and Israel, 1, 20, 165, 168, 171, 172, 175–77, 182, 223–24 n. 14

NEUM (Non-European Unity Movement), 44, 45

NGC (National Guidance Committee): in 1968, 208 n. 273; in 1978, 153, 156, 167, 170

1948 War, 68, 96, 181

Nkomati Accord (1984), 140

NLL (National Liberation League), 66, 67, 70, 196 n. 208

nonracialism, ANC, 1, 3, 5, 19, 86, 88, 89, 90, 95, 119, 120, 126, 140

NP (National Party), 15, 49–50, 78, 79, 85, 172, 174

NRC (Natives Representative Council), 43, 45, 84

NUSAS (National Union of South African Students), 126

OAU (Organisation of African Unity), 91, 136, 201 n. 99

occupied territories, Palestine: "bantus-tanization" of, 150, 177; as Israel's colonial periphery, 148; as market for Israel, 145, 148, 217 n. 196, 222 n. 317; population displacement, 113, 207 n. 258

October War (1973), 111, 116

O'Donnell, Guillermo, 24, 25, 186 n. 8

oil embargo, Arab (1973), 12, 111–12, 182, 207 n. 246

Orange Free State, 39

Oslo Agreements (Declaration of Principles), 2, 4, 175, 176

Ottoman Empire, 36, 37, 54, 55, 57, 63, 191 n. 108

PAC (Pan Africanist Congress), 89, 90, 95, 126, 127, 135, 136, 140, 200 n. 89

Pact government, 43, 188 n. 24

Palestine as Arab, 54, 57, 70–71

"Palestinianism" See Palestinian nationalism

Palestinian National Fund, 158, 160, 220 n. 274

Palestinian nationalism (wataniya), 108; and Arab nationalism, 98; of Fatah, 106–7, 111; and Jewish nationalism, 120; and Jews, 109; origins of, 100, 116, 119, 159; "Palestinianism," 99, 116; as self-reliance, 102, 106, 111, 116; in West Bank/Gaza Strip, 146

Palestinian state: and Jewish communists, 96-97; "national authority" (1974), 112, 117; and Oslo Agreements, 2; preparation for, 153, 166, 177, 180; "secular democratic state," 109, 112; sought, 153, 164, 176, 177, 180; and UN, 5

pan-Arabism, 61, 71, 98, 102, 104, 111, 116

pan-Islam, 98, 102, 116

partition of Palestine, 61, 68, 96, 101, 202 n. 134, 202 n. 135, 220 n. 263

pass laws, 42, 80, 82, 83, 85, 90, 142

PAWS (Palestinian Arab Workers' Society), 66, 67, 196 n. 223

PCP (Palestine Communist Party): pre-1948, 65–67, 74, 195 n. 202; 1980s, 16, 163, 171 (see also JCP)

peasants, African (see also bantustans; migrant workers), 43, 50, 51, 72–73

peasants, Palestinian, 56; and class interests, 62; "depeasantization," 69–70, 105; dispossession, 58, 60, 64, 69, 73, 116–17; indebtedness, 62–63, 195 n. 189; and land registration, 63, 195 n. 188; and leverage, 70; and national movement, 62, 68, 69, 70, 72; organization of, 60, 61, 70; proletarianization, 149, 151; and traditional leaders, 60, 68, 69, 70, 72, 73, 150–51; and traditional social relations, 69–70, 72–74, 104, 150–51; violence by, 58, 60, 61

Peel Commission (1937), 61

petty bourgeoisie, African. See middle class, African

PFLP (Popular Front for the Liberation of Palestine), 111, 112, 115, 153, 154, 161, 162, 163, 206 n. 230, 219 n. 242

Piven, Frances Fox, 27, 187 n. 26

PLA (Palestine Liberation Army), 107–8, 113

PLO (Palestinian Liberation Organization) (see also armed struggle; national movement, Palestinian): and Arab resources, 119, 120, 152, 160, 176; and Arab states, 9, 107–8, 112, 113, 115, 116, 160, 163, 176; bureaucracy, 160, 176; and class resources, 107, 159; consequences of 1982 invasion, 161, 164, 167; and democracy, 160, 175, 177, 178, 179; and diaspora, 110, 116, 159, 177–78, 180; Executive Committee, 108, 163, 175, 205 n. 220, 206 n. 231; and Fatah, 107, 108–9, 153, 158, 160, 161; and fida'yin, 108,

109–10, 111, 116, 158; formation of, 107; goals, 112, 117; hegemony, 164, 177; institutions, 159, 161, 162; international recognition of, 13; and *intifada,* 164, 168, 176; and Jews, 109, 120; in Jordan, 109–110, 152, 162, 164; leaders, 16, 107, 109, 205 n. 220, 206 n. 231; and leaders in West Bank/Gaza Strip, 164–65, 167, 170, 171, 176; in Lebanon, 110, 112, 113, 159–62; and leverage, 113, 117, 171; and mass base, 159, 160, 161, 167, 170, 171, 177; and mass organizations, 160, 164, 167, 171; member organizations, 111, 154–55, 160, 161, 162, 163, 168, 176, 207 n. 245; and occupied territories, 152, 153, 159, 161, 167, 168, 170, 171; and October War (1973), 111–12; and Palestinian bourgeoisie, 158, 220 n. 274; and PNF, 115, 147, 164, 170; and refugees, 109, 110, 113, 158, 159, 160, 161; and terrorism, 16–19; and trade unions, 168, 176; and traditional elite, 151, 166; transformation of, 108, 109, 112; in Tunis, 161–62; and UN, 112, 119; underground, 152, 163, 167; and West Bank, 114, 109, 146, 147, 159, 167; and working class, 160, 171, 176

PNA (Palestinian National Authority), 1, 177, 178, 179–80

PNC (Palestinian National Council), 109, 163, 175, 206 n. 230, 208 n. 274, 220 n. 274

PNF (Palestinian National Front), 114–15, 147, 164–65, 167, 170, 208 n. 274

Political Process approaches, 27, 28

"popular committees," West Bank and Gaza Strip, 162, 164, 169

Programme of Action (ANC), 83, 84

Progressive List for Peace, 157

proletarianization: in Israel, 156; in Palestine, 64, 69–70, 73; in South Africa, 46, 47, 169, 180, 190 n. 89; in West Bank/Gaza Strip, 105, 149, 150, 151, 154, 155, 166

al-Qassam, Sheikh Izzidin, 60, 61, 71

al-Qawuqji, Fawzi, 61, 71

Rabin, Yitzhak, 14

Rakah (Communist Party of Israel), 157, 220 n. 265

Rand Revolt (1922), 47, 48

RDP (Reconstruction and Development Programme), 174

refugees, Palestinian: and Arab hosts, 9, 99, 100, 103, 110; camps, 99–100, 103, 110, 112–13, 158, 159, 162, 221 n. 290; and class, 105, 149, 160; creation of, 76, 113, 207 n. 258; and dependence on PLO, 159, 160–61; and dependence on UN, 76, 105, 160 (*see also* UNRWA); and exclusion, 97, 100, 158, 159; and *intifada,* 162; and national movement, 6, 8, 9, 97, 98, 99, 102, 107, 109, 110, 113, 115, 116, 154, 158–59, 161; property in Palestine, 219 n. 257; repatriation, 5, 98; resettlement, 99, 104, 203 n. 150; and resistance, 99, 104, 110, 113; the Return (*al-'awda*), 97, 106, 110; Right of Return (*haq al-'awda*), 99; and traditional leaders, 99; and UN, 5–6

refugees, South African, 213 n. 104

Rejectionist Front, 112

resources (*see also* leverage): class specificity of, 29, 30; of elites, 37–39; of middle classes, 76–78; for national liberation, 32, 180; for state building, 32, 180; of workers, 122–24

Revolutionary Council (ANC), 93

Rhodesia. *See* Zimbabwe

Riekert Commission, 131, 141

RMT (Resource Mobilization Theory), 27–28, 186 n. 21

Robben Island, 137, 143
Rueschemeyer, Dietrich, 25, 26, 186 n. 20
Russia, 54 (*see also* Soviet Union)

SACOD (South African Congress of
    Democrats), 86, 88
SACP (South African Communist Party):
    and ANC, 85–86, 90, 91, 95, 134,
    136–40, 143, 173; formation of, 86;
    and MK, 90, 137; and negotiations,
    143, 172, 173; support for, 223 n. 1;
    and trade unions, 134, 138, 139; un-
    banning of, 143
SACTU (South African Congress of Trade
    Unions), 86, 215 n. 152; and ANC,
    89, 93–94, 95, 200 n. 82; decline of,
    93, 95, 133; membership, 200 n. 80;
    and MK, 94; and politics, 88–89, 200
    n. 79
SAIC (South African Indian Congress),
    44, 45, 51, 85, 87, 88
SANNC (South African Native National
    Congress), 187 n. 5
SASO (South African Students Organisa-
    tion), 126
Scandinavian countries, 91, 136
Schmitter, Phillippe C., 24, 25, 186 n. 8
Second World War, 45, 46, 67, 79, 125
segregation, policy of, 40, 42–43, 45, 49,
    50
"self-autonomy," West Bank and Gaza
    Strip, 148, 152, 156
self-rule, Palestinian, 1, 6, 176, 177
Seme, Pixley ka I., 40, 42
sephardim, 15 (*see also* mizrachim)
settler colonialism (*see also* inclusion/
    exclusion): capitalism, 31, 76, 77;
    economies, 17, 32, 34, 76, 77, 122;
    inclusionary/exclusionary compared,
    2, 21, 31–33, 34, 38, 78, 123–24, 179;
    and indigenous classes, 31, 34, 38,
    76–78, 117, 122, 123, 179; and in-
    digenous populations, 39, 187 n. 30;

and leverage, 30–33, 31, 77, 78, 122,
    123–24; and national movements, 17,
    21, 23, 30, 31, 34, 39, 77, 78, 122,
    123; in Palestine, 6, 8, 34–35, 37, 54,
    55, 62, 64, 69, 71–73, 75, 148 (*see also*
    Israel); in South Africa, 6, 17, 34–35,
    36, 37, 42, 50, 53, 71–73, 93, 187
    n. 1, 187 n. 2
Shamir, Yitzhak, 183 n. 3
Sharpeville, 90, 94
Shaw Commission (1930), 59, 193 n. 146
Shuqairi, Ahmad, 107, 108
Sisulu, Walter, 90
Slovo, Joe, 92, 173, 223 n. 323
Smuts, Jan, 45
socialism, 51, 67, 138, 142, 154, 173
socialist bloc, 91, 136, 182
social movements (*see also* Political Process
    approaches; RMT): and democratiza-
    tion, 2; and states, 29; theory, 22–23,
    26–29
South Africa: African citizenship, 14, 128,
    134, 142, 143; and free enterprise,
    127, 131, 132; government reforms,
    10, 121, 125, 127, 130, 131, 138, 139,
    141, 142; National Unity government,
    174; post-1994 elections, 3–6, 172–75;
    residency rights of Africans, 75–76, 80,
    117–18, 130, 131, 134–35, 142–43,
    212 n. 82; resources, 15; and sanctions,
    2, 10, 135, 141, 182; in Southern
    Africa, 15, 136; state autonomy, 15;
    states of emergency, 141, 215 n. 157;
    "Total Strategy" (1978), 127; tri-
    cameral parliament (1982), 138, 214
    n. 129
South Africa and Israel compared, 6–7, 15
Soviet Union (USSR), 6, 12, 19–20, 91,
    101, 112, 136, 181–82
Soweto uprising (1976), 127, 131, 135,
    136, 168
steadfastness *(sumud),* Palestinian, 148,
    152, 153, 166, 167, 182

Stephens, Evelyne Huber, 25, 26, 186 n. 20
Stephens, John D., 25, 26, 186 n. 20
structure and agency, 7, 20, 29
students: Palestine, 115, 159 (*see also* GUPS); South Africa, 125, 126
Suez Canal: tripartite invasion of, 98, 102
Suppression of Communism Act (1950), 85, 87, 198 n. 41
Supreme Muslim Council, 57
Swaziland, 92, 140
Sykes-Picot Agreement (1916), 54
Syria, 55, 61, 98, 101, 106, 107–8, 111, 113, 191 n. 105, 206 n. 237, 207 n. 245

Tambo, Oliver, 16, 84, 87, 91
Tanzania, 91, 136
Tarrow, Sidney, 28, 187 n. 27
terrorism, 11, 13, 16–19, 184 n. 26, 184 n. 28, 185 n. 45, 185 n. 46
townships, black, 5, 14, 17; business, 82, 88, 131, 132, 211 n. 69; community councilors, 131, 132, 134; community organizing, 134, 137, 139, 144; and "decentralization," 131, 134; and government policies, 80, 131, 132, 133, 134, 141, 145; and leverage, 144; living conditions, 134, 138, 139, 170 ; and resistance, 81–83, 90; and struggles, 125, 126, 127, 133, 134, 138, 139, 141, 143, 145, 169, 170 (*see also* Soweto uprising); and trade unions, 95, 138, 139, 141, 145, 169; and workers, 95, 125, 133, 134, 139, 140; and youth, 126, 127
trade unions: depoliticization of, 134, 145; politics of, 123
trade unions, Palestine (*see also* FATULS; GFTU; labor movement; PAWS; PCP): and class consciousness, 169; and class struggle, 155, 166; and colonial government, 66, 67; and communists, 66, 67, 74, 153–55; and factionalization,

154–55; and Fatah, 154–55; and Israeli policies, 150, 155; and the left, 153–55; membership, 66–67, 155; and migrant workers, 154; and national movement, 66, 67, 70, 153, 160, 168–71; and negotiations, 176; and PLO, 108, 160; and political organizations, 66; pre-1948, 66, 67, 70; and traditional leaders, 66, 67, 70; in West Bank/Gaza Strip, 150, 154–55, 168
trade unions, South Africa (*see also* COSATU; CPSA; FOSATU; ICU; labor movement; SACTU): and ANC, 40, 88, 89, 134, 137, 140, 171; and bantustans, 130, 144; and BC, 126; and communists, 47, 74; democratic unions, 82, 125, 133, 137, 139, 141, 169, 173; early African unions, 47, 49; and government legislation, 49, 82, 133, 141; leaders, 53, 133, 173, 174; and leverage, 169–70, 144; membership, 49, 200 n. 80; and national movement, 51, 53, 88, 89, 93–94, 95, 133, 138, 139, 140, 168–71, 200 n. 89; and negotiations, 172; political unionism, 88, 89, 139; and politics, 88–89, 94, 95, 125, 133–34, 138, 139, 141, 145, 169; "populism vs. workerism" debate, 88–89, 133–34, 140–41; and race, 126; recognition and registration, 49, 78, 133, 139, 145; resources, 95; and shop-steward councils, 134; strikes, 125, 197 n. 21, 209 n. 7; and UDF, 138, 139
Transjordan, 61, 97 (*see also* Jordan)
Transvaal, 39, 49, 84, 214 n. 120
Treason Trials (1956–61), 200 n. 85, 201 n. 119
Tunis, 161, 164

UAR (United Arab Republic), 98, 106
UDF (United Democratic Front) (*see also* Mass Democratic Movement):

affiliates, 138, 139, 171; and ANC, 138, 139, 140, 143, 170, 171; bantustans, 139, 144; campaigns, 138, 139; disbanding of, 173; formation of, 138; and government, 141, 143, 215 n. 157; leadership, 139; organization, 139, 171; traditional leaders, 142–43; and unions, 139, 140

Union of South Africa, 36, 39–40, 42, 50, 181

United Nations: Palestinian appeals to, 17, 119; partition plan (1947), 5, 68, 96 and PLO, 112; and refugees, 5–6, 76, 98, 118, 202 n. 134, 203 n. 150 (*see also* UNRWA); resolutions, 12–13, 112; Security Council, 11–12

United States: hegemony, 20, 181; and Israel, 10, 11, 12, 15, 181, 207 n. 246; and Middle East, 11, 12, 98, 101, 112, 181–82; and negotiations, 182; and Palestinian refugees, 99, 100, 104; and PLO, 11, 112, 115, 161; and regional surrogates, 10, 11, 181, 182; and South Africa, 11–12, 13, 181–82, 201 n. 122; and terrorism, 13

UNLU (Unified National Leadership of the Uprising), 173, 164, 221 n. 300

UNRWA (United Nations Relief and Works Agency): and reducing pressure on Israel, 152, 167; refugee dependence on, 76, 105, 160, 170; and refugees, 100, 158, 202 n. 136, 205 n. 203; and resettlement, 98–99, 104

UP (United Party), 78

uprisings (1980s), Palestinian and South African, 1, 11–12, 14, 19, 122, 168–69, 171, 172, 182 (*see also* intifada)

Urban Foundation (South Africa), 141–42

Village Leagues, 152

War of the Camps (Lebanon), 162

Wars of Dispossession, 37, 42, 53

al-Wazir, Khalil, 222 n. 310

Weizmann, Chaim, 59

West Bank (*see also* economy, Palestine; Jordan; land, Palestine; occupied territories, Palestine): elite, 104, 105, 146, 153; Israeli occupation of, 113; labor force, 148–51; land, 217 n. 206, 217 n. 207; municipal politics, 104, 113, 146–47, 152, 156, 166–67, 168, 216 n. 179; resistance, 113; and women, 150–51, 218 n. 216

whites, South Africa, 7; and Africans, 18, 40; business, 131, 142, 145, 171; classes, 5, 39, 40, 78–79, 142; colonization by, 17, 18, 73; communists (*see* CPSA; SACP); liberals, 43, 71, 72, 119; post-1994 elections, 5, 172–73; support for ANC, 18, 19, 86, 88, 90, 118, 139, 142; and Union of South Africa, 39–40, 50; workers, 46, 47–49

Wiehahn Commission, 131, 133, 141

workers, African (*see also* migrant workers, African; trade unions, South Africa; working class, African): and ANC, 40, 44, 47, 51, 89, 94, 140; and apartheid, 79, 80, 82, 121, 124–25; and bantustans, 129, 144; and "civilized labor" policy, 43; class consciousness, 169–70; and communists, 48, 74; and community struggles, 126, 133, 134, 169; divisions, 133; in industry, 46, 47, 49, 125, 189 n. 56; leverage, 53, 89, 94, 125, 141, 144, 169–70; militance of, 49, 50, 51, 78, 79, 82; and national movement, 86, 88–89, 133–34, 140, 141, 169–70, 171, 172; as political force, 51–52, 133; skilled, 124–25, 169; and state, 43, 132–33, 134; and traditional leaders, 41; and traditional social relations, 51, 81, 82, 119, 143–44, 145; unemployed, 80, 128, 129, 133, 175; unity, 133, 134; and urban economy, 82, 119; and urbanization, 46, 47, 49; and white workers, 34

workers, Palestinian (*see also* migrant workers, Palestinian; trade unions, Palestine; working class, Palestinian): and Arab industry (pre-1948), 195 n. 195, 196–97 n. 234; and "civilized labor" policy, 64, 195 n. 196; class consciousness, 62, 155, 169; class interests, 154; class struggles, 155; employed in Israel, 148, 149, 150, 155, 222 n. 318; and *intifada*, 162; and Jewish communists, 65, 74; and Jewish industry, 55, 64, 69–70; and Jewish workers, 34; leverage, 70, 169, 170; and national movement, 66, 70, 72, 111, 149–50, 153, 154, 160–61, 167, 170, 171, 176; and proletarianization, 149, 150, 151; and traditional leaders, 70; and traditional social relations, 150, 151, 155, 166; urban (pre-1948), 67; weakness of, 65, 68

working class: alliances, 25; autonomy, 25–26, 32, 34; and democratization, 25, 26, 34, 124; hegemony, 32, 124; and leverage, 122, 123, 124; and movement leadership, 32; and movement success, 34; and national interest, 34, 123; and national movement, 32, 34, 122, 124; and other classes, 32, 76, 77, 123; politics of, 25, 123; power, 24–25, 124; and settler capitalism, 76; and traditional social relations, 122, 123, 124

working class, African (*see also* exclusion; inclusion, South Africa; workers, African): and apartheid, 125, 145, 174; in bantustans, 129–30; class consciousness, 131–32, 169–70; and communists, 48; and democratization, 179; divisions, 133; expansion of, 49; leverage, 34–35, 53, 89, 125, 144, 169;

and national movement, 53, 141, 171, 172, 179; and national objectives, 133–34, 169–70; and negotiations, 171, 172; politics, 145; and post-1994 elections, 174, 175; as revolutionary, 131–32, 138, 174, 180; and state, 43, 131–32, 133; unity, 133; urban, 49, 144

working class, Palestinian (*see also* exclusion, Palestine; inclusion, Palestine; workers, Palestinian): bifurcation of, 155, 169, 180; class consciousness, 155, 169; and democratization, 35, 178, 179; and employment in Israel, 155, 169; and *intifada*, 162, 169; and Jewish communists, 65; leverage, 165, 169, 170; and national movement, 67, 171, 176, 177, 179; and negotiations, 174; stunting of, 65; and traditional elite, 67, 74; and traditional social relations, 35; weakness of, 35, 65, 66, 160, 176, 177, 178, 179, 180

World Bank, 174, 175

Wright, Erik Olin, 30–31, 187 n. 32

Xuma, Alfred, 45, 52

Xuma-Dadoo-Naicker Pact (1947), 45, 189 n. 49

YL (Youth League of the ANC): and communists, 84, 85; formation of, 46, 83; Manifesto, 86, 90; and other races, 84, 85, 86–87

Zambia, 136, 140, 142

ZAPU (Zimbabwe African People's Union), 92

Zimbabwe, 92, 127, 136, 213 n. 106

Zionism, 11, 12, 62–63

Zionist movement: claims to Palestine, 9; colonization of Palestine, 55, 62, 64–65, 191 n. 110, 195 n. 199; conquest of Palestine, 63, 68, 96, 181;

establishment of Israel, 17; formation of, 54–55; Jewish colonies, 55, 62, 63; Jewish exclusivity, 59, 64, 65, 70, 145, 193 n. 146, 193 n. 147; Labor Zionists, 55, 65, 66; and Ottoman Empire, 55; and Palestinian exclusion, 64, 98, 120, 148, 156, 202 n. 143, 202–3 n. 147

MONA N. YOUNIS is the program officer for the International Human Rights Program and the Peace and Security Program of the Joyce Mertz-Gilmore Foundation. She has worked on women's development projects in Palestinian refugee camps in Lebanon; conducted research in Jordan, Lebanon, Syria, and the Israeli-occupied West Bank and Gaza Strip; and contributed several studies to the United Nations Economic Commission for Western Asia.